THE USES AND ABUSES OF ARGUMENT

Critical Thinking and Fallacious Reasoning

Stephen S. Carey
Portland Community College

Mayfield Publishing Company

Mountain View, California
London · Toronto

Library of Congress Cataloging-in-Publication Data

Carey, Stephen S. (Stephen Sayers)
    The uses and abuses of argument / Stephen S. Carey.
      p. cm.
    Includes index.
    ISBN 0–7674–0517–X
    1. Critical thinking. I. Title.
BF441.C278   1999
168—dc21   99–23923
                                         CIP

Manufactured in the United States of America

10   9   8   7   6   5   4   3   2   1

Mayfield Publishing Company
1280 Villa Street
Mountain View, California 94041

Sponsoring editor, Kenneth King; *production,* Publishing Support Services; *manuscript editor,* Margaret Moore; *design manager,* Jean Mailander; *text and cover designer,* Linda M. Robertson; *manufacturing manager,* Randy Hurst. The text was set in 10/12 Times by Shepherd, Inc., and printed on 45# Highland Plus by Custom Printing Company.

Cover image: © Frank Collyer/SIS

Preface

I have taught critical thinking for over twenty years. Judging by student evaluations, my courses have been well received. But I do not think they have been altogether successful. Discussions with my students, past and present, reveal several problems. First, the majority of my students seem to retain and use very little from their training in critical thinking. In part, this is because much of what they learn is either difficult to apply or of little use in the analysis of real-world reasoning. Rare is the argument, other than contrived classroom examples, that can be profitably analyzed using the techniques of statement or predicate logic.

In addition, my students encounter great difficulty in mastering what is perhaps the most essential skill of the critical thinker—giving clear, sympathetic readings of actual arguments. This deficiency is compounded when students move on to the study of fallacious reasoning. Having digested the names and descriptions of a roster of fallacies, students often misread passages so that they appear to involve fallacious moves. For the most part, these problems are not the product of poor reading or writing skills (though both, on occasion, exacerbate the situation). Rather, the problems stem from two things. First, students are seldom provided with sufficient training in how to read, understand, and paraphrase arguments and in how to think about the strengths and weaknesses of anything other than easy textbook examples. Second, they are given little information about the kinds of nonfallacious argument that correspond to nearly every fallacy.

Ironically, almost all of my students report that the study of fallacies seemed the most interesting and significant part of their critical thinking courses. Why? I suspect that of all the topics covered in the typical critical thinking course, this is the one that strikes students as having relevance outside the classroom. In their daily lives, students are confronted by personal attacks, emotional appeals, appeals to authority, and the like, and so they see the value of studying the strategies involved in such appeals.

APPROACH

My goal in writing *The Uses and Abuses of Argument* has been to put together a text that both exploits the enthusiasm most students have for the study of fallacies and addresses the problems I have just mentioned. Six of the ten chapters are devoted to fallacies, though in a somewhat novel way. Corresponding to the thirty or so fallacies introduced is a sustained discussion of acceptable reasoning of the sort in question. My contention is that the well-known fallacies are effective precisely because they mimic acceptable reasoning. My hope is that students will take this material to heart and, as a result, become more adept at giving accurate and sympathetic readings of arguments.

ORGANIZATION

The first four chapters are a sort of necessary stage setting. They introduce essential skills needed for giving readings of arguments and then thinking critically about their worth. In writing these introductory chapters, I was guided by a single principle: I included only the techniques I, as a reader, writer, and thinker, find useful in dealing with arguments. Chapter 2 discusses what it is for a claim to be clear, various barriers to clarity, and ways of clarifying problematic claims. Chapter 3 introduces a set of analytic tools for thinking about argument strengths and weaknesses. Chapter 4 concentrates on problems students are likely to encounter in making sense of real-world arguments. The material in Chapters 2–4 plays an important role throughout the remaining chapters. Problems of interpretation are discussed and illustrated with reference to nearly every fallacy. The technique for dealing with inference introduced in Chapter 3 is used to explain the problems at the heart of many of the fallacies.

SPECIAL FEATURES

■ *"Media Watch" sections.* I have found that my students have great enthusiasm for information about the mass media. They seem particularly interested when they discover that there is a body of thoughtful, scholarly material on the topic of media criticism. Included in several chapters are sections devoted to the critical analysis of the mass media. Special attention is given to the problems media information sources pose for the critical thinker.

■ *Classification of fallacies.* A problem every "fallacy" text must solve is how to classify the fallacies it covers since there is no universal agreement about the basic categories into which fallacies fall. I discuss fallacious reasoning under six distinct headings, corresponding to the six chapters of Part II. Chapters 5, 6, and 7 deal with problems involving relevance, distortion, ambiguity, and redundancy. Chapters 8 and 9 concern fallacies associated with specific types of reasoning: analogical reasoning in Chapter 8 and reasoning involving generalizations and causes in Chapter 9. The persuasive techniques discussed in Chapter 10 are not, strictly speaking, fallacies for they do not occur in the process of giving arguments. For the most part, they are techniques used to manipulate an audience, usually as an adjunct to and occasionally as a substitute for argument.

■ *Exercises.* Every chapter contains at least 40 problems. Overall, there are more than 500, most taken from contemporary sources: advertisements, political tracts, editorials, letters to the editor, sales pitches, and the like. In addition, each fallacy chapter contains an exercise in which the student is asked to invent his or her own examples of fallacies. I have found that one of the most efficient ways to teach students about fallacies is to allow them to teach themselves, which they can do by making up their own examples.

■ *Conundrums.* Sprinkled throughout the text are twenty-three boxes containing what I call "conundrums." These are special problems designed to raise critical questions about the material in the text or to challenge students to apply what they have learned in unusual circumstances. The idea is to encourage students to think critically about everything, even the contentions of a textbook that attempts to teach them how to think critically! For teachers interested in getting students to write argumentative essays, the conundrums can serve another purpose: They can easily be made the subject of essays, with the added advantage that the student will not need to do excessive research to prepare.

■ *Instructor's Manual.* I have prepared an Instructor's Manual to accompany this text. The manual contains the answer to every exercise included in the text and additional exercises for each chapter that you can use for quizzes or exams. I have also made some comments on each of the "conundrum" boxes, describing responses that my students have had to these problems or pointing out directions that the discussion might take. The manual is available from the publisher and may be obtained either by contacting your local Mayfield sales representative or by phoning Mayfield's Customer Services Department.

ACKNOWLEDGMENTS

Thanks to my students over the years who have suffered through myriad drafts of the material that forms the basis of this book. Special thanks to Don Levi of the Philosophy Department of the University of Oregon. It is in large measure because of his efforts that I have come to see the importance of those aspects of logic and rhetoric that are the focus of this book.

My apologies to those authors whose examples I have inadvertently pirated. Fallacy examples are the proverbial fruitcakes of the critical thinking curriculum. The good ones tend to get passed around and reworked, and after a while their point of origin may get lost in the shuffle. I have acknowledged a few exercises I am sure I have borrowed from other texts. No doubt, there are more that should be acknowledged. Once again, my apologies to their authors.

I have also had the good fortune to receive the advice of several readers of earlier versions of my manuscript, including Joseph Keim Campbell, Washington

State University; Keith A. Coleman, Johnson County Community College; David Detmer, Purdue University Calumet; Jim Emineth; Frank K. Fair, Sam Houston State University; Peter Franta, East Los Angeles College; Richard C. Raines, De Anza College; and Justus Richards, Pasadena City College. There are few pages in this book that have not benefited greatly from the criticism and suggestions of these readers.

Finally, I am indebted to Ken King, philosophy editor at Mayfield, for his unwavering support, enthusiasm, and confidence as *The Uses and Abuses of Argument* has gone through the developmental process; to April Wells-Hayes and Vicki Moran for overseeing the production; and to Margaret Moore, whose copyediting has much improved the text.

Contents

CHAPTER ONE

Introduction to Critical Thinking

- A friend tells us she believes that an extraterrestrial spacecraft crashed on Earth in the 1940s and that the government is withholding information about it.
- A politician criticizes Affirmative Action programs for giving an unfair advantage to certain segments of the population.
- A television infomercial touts a foolproof way to make money with no initial investment, other than the modest purchase price of a course about the method.
- A front-page newspaper story reports that violent crime is decreasing nationwide.

We hear claims like these every day. Sometimes we let them slip by unchallenged. On other occasions we take the time to think about them, considering whether they are true or false, accurate or inaccurate, credible or incredible. It is on these occasions that we become critical thinkers. At one time or another, then, we all are critical thinkers.

WHAT DOES CRITICAL THINKING INVOLVE?

When we decide to think critically about such claims, we need to ask of them a series of questions:

- *What, precisely, is being claimed?* We cannot begin to think critically about the claim that violent crime is decreasing nationwide until we understand what the claim involves. Which crimes are classified as violent, and what are the details of the decrease?
- *Is there evidence supporting the truth of the claim?* Infomercials are filled with stories by people who say they have used the product and have had their lives immeasurably enriched by it. Are a few such cases the extent of the evidence that this product works?
- *Is the evidence sufficient to warrant acceptance of the claim?* Our friend tells us of many cases in which our government has withheld information from the public. But none of them involves alien spacecraft. Does the fact that the government has withheld information in other circumstances provide a good reason to believe the government has and is withholding information about crashed extraterrestrials?

> ### CONUNDRUM
>
> *Throughout the chapters to follow you will encounter boxes containing conundrums—problems that will challenge you to think critically about something claimed in the text or to apply the lesson of the text in a novel way. When you encounter a conundrum, pause for a few moments and try to solve the problem it poses. Here is the first conundrum.*
>
> Critical thinking involves the investigation of claims and their evidential underpinnings. But these underpinnings are themselves claims. Thus, we can think critically about the underpinnings of these claims and, in turn, about the underpinnings of those underpinnings. It seems the process of thinking about the evidence for a claim is a never-ending business. Is critical thinking, then, just an exercise in futility?

- *If the evidence is insufficient, what should we think and do?* In some cases we might be inclined to reject the claim; other times we might accept it on a tentative basis. Often we simply suspend judgment until further evidence emerges. Whatever we decide, we are involved in the process of critical thinking.

Our daily lives are filled with opportunities for critical thinking, primarily because we are constantly bombarded with appeals designed to get us to do or believe something. Advertisers, politicians, public relations companies, fashion experts, critics of all stripes, the media, even our friends want to influence our attitudes and actions. What we decide to do or believe very often makes an important difference to our lives. Informed decisions are possible only if we pause and ask, *What exactly does so-and-so want me to do or believe? What evidence is being offered, and how good is it?*

On other occasions we may need to persuade—to defend our position in the eyes of others or to overcome the resistance of others to doing what we think they should do. Nothing improves our chances of success more than a carefully prepared case, a clear and thoughtful enumeration of the evidence in favor of our position. If I am going to convince you of something, I must say precisely what I want you to believe or do and then back up my claim with a solid set of facts.

Critical thinking skills are called for in quarrels, disputes, arguments, and debates. They are needed in the classroom, the courtroom, the corporate office, the halls of government, and in every setting where allegations and proposals are set forth, debated, and resolved. They are indispensable to us in our responses to information and opinion flowing from a wide variety of sources—television, radio, newspapers, magazines, textbooks, and the Internet, to name a few. We must think critically to understand and evaluate newscasts, editorials, advertisements, political tracts, film and book reviews, and much more. The ability to think critically is required in every aspect of our lives.

The chapters that follow provide a set of conceptual tools for investigating claims and their underlying support. However, effective critical thinking also requires *knowledge* of the issues under investigation. As an example, consider the claim that Affirmative Action gives an unfair advantage to certain segments of the population. To make a decision about the accuracy of this claim, you would need to know a lot about the facts surrounding it. What is Affirmative Action? What are Affirmative Action programs designed to do? What historical problems led to their creation? What new problems did they seem to create? What segments of the population benefit from them, and what segments suffer? Without knowing something about these issues, you would not get far in your thinking about the original claim.

The critical thinking skills you are going to learn cannot substitute for careful investigation of the facts, nor will they teach you how to research the facts on any given issue. What they *can* do is help you figure out, first, what you need to know in order to think about the accuracy of a claim and, second, how to evaluate the information you unearth. The methods of critical thinking are a set of strategic guidelines that help us to think about and evaluate claims and evidence.

Of all the conceptual tools introduced in this book, two deserve special emphasis: argument and fallacy. We rely on one or both of them in nearly every situation in which we want to exercise our critical thinking skills.

ARGUMENT

When you think of an argument, you probably have in mind a verbal dispute or quarrel. For critical thinking purposes, however, an argument is not a dispute, though as we shall see, disputes involve arguments in the critical thinking sense.

An **argument**—in the critical thinking sense—is what *results* when someone advances a claim or series of claims as evidence for the truth of another claim. Thus, an argument is composed of the claims introduced as evidence along with the claim they are intended to support. The supported claim is called the **conclusion,** and the claims containing the evidence are called the **premises** of the argument. In the previous section, we said that critical thinking involves the investigation of claims and their underlying support. A central goal in studying arguments is to learn to decide when the evidence advanced in the premises of an argument is of sufficient quality to warrant our acceptance of the conclusion.

Here, for example, is a passage containing an argument:

Car manufacturers ought to be required—by law if necessary—to produce vehicles that are more fuel efficient. We are rapidly using up the world's supply of fossil fuels. Viable alternatives to the gasoline-powered engine are still a long way off. Unless we do everything we can to conserve fossil fuels, the remaining supplies will be depleted long before an alternative is in place.

The argument of this passage is straightforward. The conclusion is the view the argument's author is attempting to defend:

Car manufacturers ought to be required to produce vehicles that are more fuel efficient.

The passage also contains three claims intended to provide evidence for this conclusion:

1. We are rapidly using up the world's supply of fossil fuels.
2. Viable alternatives to the gasoline-powered engine are still a long way off.
3. Unless we do everything we can to conserve fossil fuels (including, presumably, driving vehicles that are more fuel efficient), we will run out long before an alternative is in place.

When people give arguments, they rarely bother to indicate explicitly which claim is the conclusion and which claims are premises. We can remedy this problem by writing arguments in **standard form**—premises followed by conclusion, separated by a line. In standard form, the argument we are discussing can be written like this:

Standard form
Premises

We are rapidly using up the world's supply of fossil fuels.

Viable alternatives to the gasoline-powered engine are still a long way off.

Unless we do everything we can to conserve fossil fuels (including, presumably, driving vehicles that are more fuel efficient), we will run out long before an alternative is in place.

Conclusion Car manufacturers ought to be required to produce vehicles that are more fuel efficient.

Once we have converted an argument into standard form, we can begin to think about the extent to which the premises provide or fail to provide support for the conclusion.

Can a claim be introduced as a premise without actually providing support for its conclusion? Consider the following argument:

> Anyone who believes in no higher power is an atheist. God believes in no higher power. So, God must be an atheist.

Do the premises of this argument actually support its conclusion? For more on this argument, look ahead to page 10.

Where Do Arguments Occur?

We give arguments when we set forth the rationales for positions we hold, as in the example we have just considered. But arguments occur in a wide variety of contexts where the aim of the arguer may not be simply to justify a claim. We often give arguments when we apologize, criticize, censure, approve, blame, praise, repent, excuse, predict, prophesy, forecast, endorse, recommend, question, assess, appraise, urge, propose, espouse, deduce, infer, distinguish, conjecture, and hypothesize.[1] So, for example, when someone offers an apology or excuse, makes a recommendation or attempts to criticize a view with which they disagree, he or she will do so by giving an argument.

---

[1]This list is drawn from the work of J. L. Austin. See particularly *How to Do Things with Words* (Cambridge: Harvard University Press, 1962).

Imagine, for example, that you and I have decided to go jogging together and have settled on a time and place to meet. I, however, fail to show up at the appointed time, and so you jog off by yourself, making a mental note to find a new jogging partner. Later that day you call me at work to find out what happened. "I was just about to call you," I say. "Would you believe I just got back to my office? On the way over to meet you, my car broke down. I had to have it towed, and by the time everything was taken care of, I knew you would have left without me. I was hoping you would call." Here, my aim seems in part to be to excuse my failure to meet you. And in so doing, I provide evidence for a claim, though the claim I am supporting is nothing I have said in so many words:

Unforeseen circumstances prevented me from keeping our appointment.

My evidence—the premises of my argument—is the sequence of events I outlined in our phone conversation.

Activities like predicting, hypothesizing, making "educated" guesses, troubleshooting, problem solving, deducing, and inferring may appear at first glance to have little in common with argumentation. In an argument, the point is to provide evidence for a claim. The point of inference, prediction, and the like, on the other hand, is to obtain new information based on what we already know. While driving, I hear a siren and instinctively slow down and pull over to the side of the road. I've drawn the obvious inference, based on past experience and the sounds I'm hearing now—some sort of emergency vehicle is in the vicinity. But activities in which we derive a new conclusion from what we know or believe all indirectly involve arguments. The thinking involved in such activities can usually be represented as a series of premises and a conclusion. Suppose, now, that you have just flipped the "on" switch on your reading lamp. The light does not come on. You glance down and assure yourself that the lamp is plugged in. So you unscrew the bulb and give it a gentle shake. It rattles a bit. From these facts you draw the obvious conclusion: The bulb must be burned out. Your intention here is not to give an argument in support of a position. You are simply trying to solve a problem. Nonetheless, your thinking can be represented via the following argument:

> The lamp won't work, although it is plugged in.
>
> The light bulb rattles in the way bulbs often do when they are burned out.
> _____
> The light bulb is burned out.

That this argument is implicit in the inference you have drawn is suggested by the following: If someone asked you *why* you believe the bulb is burned out, you would give as evidence the claims on which you based your inference.

The solutions to logic puzzles often require us to draw a number of inferences from a set of facts. Can you work out the solution to the following puzzle?

Before you on a table sit three bags of marbles, the contents of which you cannot see. You know that one bag contains all blue marbles, another,

continued

---

all red marbles, and the third, a mixture of red and blue. Each bag is mislabeled. Your job is to determine the content of each bag by taking samples. What is the smallest number of marbles you can sample in order to determine the content of each bag?

By the way, can you write out an argument for your solution? (If you are having problems with this puzzle, see the Solutions section at the end of the chapter.)

Earlier we noted that disputes, disagreements, quarrels, and the like also involve arguments, in the critical thinking sense. Imagine that you and I, both dyed-in-the-wool boxing fans, are having a tiff:

Me: For my money, Muhammad Ali is the greatest boxer who ever lived.

You: You've got to be kidding. Ali was great, I'll grant you that, but not the greatest. Look at the record. He lost to a number of mediocre fighters: Ken Norton, Larry Holmes, and Leon Spinks, to name a few.

Me: OK. He lost a few close fights, but that was when he was past his prime. You've got to keep in mind, Ali beat all the best heavyweights in the world, and beat them soundly, before he was forced to stop boxing because of his refusal to be drafted. And no boxer has ever matched Ali's combination of speed, size, and power.

You: Nevertheless, he was defeated several times. Many great fighters had better records, and many were just as quick and strong. Look at Sugar Ray Robinson and Roberto Duran. Pound for pound, they were superior fighters.

Me: I can't believe what I am hearing. Robinson or Duran wouldn't have lasted a round against Ali.

Now, although nothing of any great consequence is at stake in our dispute, it seems clear at least that both you and I are giving arguments, although arguments intended to support very different conclusions. The conclusion of my argument is that Muhammad Ali is the greatest boxer who ever lived. Yours, in turn, is precisely the reverse: Ali is *not* the greatest boxer. The premises of our respective arguments are the claims we have made in support of our conclusions.

Arguments and Explanations

One activity closely related to argument bears special mention—explanation. The point of an argument is to advance evidence that something is the case. By contrast, the point of an **explanation** is to make sense of *how* or *why* something is the case. Often the truth of what we are trying to explain will be assumed, so there will be no need to argue that it is the case. "Your bathroom sink has developed a leak," I tell you, pointing to the droplets of water slowly accumulating underneath. Looking under the sink, we discover a rusty spot on the trap from which water is dripping.

"Ah, here's the problem," you exclaim. "The trap has a hole in it." Your discovery does not establish that the sink is leaking. Indeed, we knew this before we began to look for the source of the problem. Your discovery constitutes an explanation of why the sink is leaking, not evidence that it is leaking.

Unfortunately, arguments and explanations can be difficult to distinguish. Both are often given in terms that bear a superficial similarity to one another.

> The reason your sink is leaking is that there is a hole in the trap

is similar in form to

> The reason I believe your sink is leaking is that there is a puddle of water underneath it.

Both of these remarks contain reasons, and both address questions we might have about why something is the case: *Why* do I think the sink is leaking, and *why* is it leaking? Moreover, an argument can be about an explanation, attempting to show that it is either correct or mistaken. A friend, we discover, has put her home up for sale. "Maybe she can't afford the payments. After all, it's a pretty expensive place," you speculate. "That can't be the problem," I reply. "She just got a big raise and recently inherited a big chunk of money." Here the point of my argument is to provide evidence that the explanation you have ventured must be wrong.

A final difficulty in distinguishing arguments from explanations stems from the fact that many remarks seem to involve both. Suppose, for example, you have asked me to have lunch with you this afternoon. "Sorry," I say, "I'd love to, but I've got a dental appointment at noon today. Maybe we could get together later in the week." Now, in part, I have explained why I can't have lunch with you today. But in giving my explanation I have also provided evidence for the truth of a claim, namely, that I can't have lunch with you today. Have I given an argument, an explanation, or both? The answer depends on the context in which my remark is made. If I have told you I can't make it, but you nonetheless doubt what I've said, my intent is to assure you that I can't make it. In these circumstances, my remark constitutes an argument. If, on the other hand, you accept that I cannot have lunch with you and wonder why, my remark constitutes an explanation. In general, the question of whether we are dealing with an argument or an explanation can be settled by reference to the context in which the remarks occur and the aims and interests of the parties.

Often the question of whether something is intended to explain or to provide evidence will need to be answered before we can think critically about the claims involved. Information that explains *why* a claim is so may not provide evidence that it is so. Similarly, information that may strongly suggest that a claim is true may not explain why it is true. Any subsequent criticism we may want to offer of an argument (or an explanation) will need to bear these facts in mind. An argument that fails to explain why its conclusion is the case is not thereby a poor one, and vice versa. Although our focus will be on the analysis of arguments in the chapters to follow, we will occasionally need to think about explanations of various sorts, and so it is important that we have a good working sense of both the similarities and differences between argument and explanation.

Why Bother to Put Arguments in Standard Form?

People give arguments in a wide variety of settings and for a wide variety of purposes. What is more, arguments are implicit in a large number of activities, many of which—like problem solving, predicting, and estimating—involve doing things other than setting forth claims along with their supporting evidence. Yet, with a little hard work, we can extract most arguments from their natural settings and write them in premises-conclusion form. This is the good news. The bad news is that in the exercises accompanying each chapter of this book you will be asked over and again to invest the time and effort required to cast arguments in standard form. What, you may wonder, is the point? Why should we bother rearranging arguments so that they display a particular form? There are three closely related reasons why we should become proficient putting arguments in standard form.

Deciding What the Argument Is   In their natural settings, arguments are rarely as simple and straightforward as the examples we have considered so far. Arguments are often expressed in terms that are unclear, incomplete, or both. Crucial pieces of arguments are sometimes hinted at rather than clearly stated. A premise or even the conclusion of an argument may be left out. The material from which we extract an argument may include claims that are not a part of the argument, or it may contain several related arguments. Here is an argument that involves several such difficulties. It is from the Letters to the Editor section of my local newspaper and seems typical of the level of complexity and clarity we are likely to encounter:

> To the editor: Here we go again. In a recent issue of your paper, still another letter writer says that if a unilateral ban on assault weapons were in effect, countless lives would be saved. Where does this writer get that idea?
> Prohibition didn't prevent people from obtaining liquor. Drug laws are not stopping people from getting drugs. Abortion bans did not stop women from getting abortions. And yet we are expected to believe that a gun ban will, somehow, magically, prevent lawbreakers from obtaining guns.
> Really, now. Just how stupid, or how blindly liberal, do the anti-gunners think we are?

The author of this passage clearly means to advance an argument, but its precise details are not easy to comprehend. What is the argument's conclusion? That a ban on assault weapons will not save lives? That such a ban will not prevent lawbreakers from obtaining guns? Both appear to be claims the author wants to defend. Is there more than one argument in the passage? In any event, the support for whatever is at issue comes in the form of a parallel drawn between prohibition, drug laws, abortion bans and the proposed ban on assault weapons. What similarity does the author see between these cases? Does he or she mean to be advancing the following claim? *Legal restrictions on just about anything are bound to fail.* Does the argument, in other words, depend on a claim that is not clearly stated in the passage? And if it does, is this the claim? For obvious reasons, the claim is false. Many legal restrictions are quite effective, for example, the restrictions we obey when we drive. Is it, then, that legal restrictions of a certain sort—like the ones mentioned in the body of the letter—are doomed to failure? In addition, parts of the letter seem irrelevant to whatever argument is being advanced. The accusations contained in the last paragraph contribute nothing to the content of the argument.

As this example suggests, the first thing we must do if we are to think critically about an argument is to decide what claim is being supported, what claims do the supporting, and what claims are irrelevant to the argument. There is no way to do this short of grappling with questions of the sort raised earlier and then carefully laying the argument out as a series of premises and a conclusion. Thus, the very act of trying to get at the premises and conclusion of an argument forces us to do everything we can to understand what is going on in the passage from which the argument is taken.

Contemplating Alternative Readings   The process of converting an argument into premises-conclusion form often requires us to make interpretive decisions—decisions about what the argument actually involves. In the preceding example, we have already discovered that there may be more than one way to set out its argument. When faced with choices about how to understand an argument, we should make the evidence contained in the premises as compelling as possible, given only the condition that we must try to reflect the thinking of the argument's author. The process of restating an argument gives us the breathing room required to contemplate alternative readings.

Uncovering Argument Strengths and Weaknesses   To think critically about an argument is to decide whether or not to accept it. This means deciding whether the premises do an adequate job of supporting the conclusion. Arguments are rarely given for claims that are obviously true or that are already accepted by their intended audience. The claims we argue about are open to debate; their truth is unsettled. And this means the arguments given in their defense will rarely succeed in making an open-and-shut case. Not surprisingly, most arguments have both strengths and weaknesses.

Getting at the strengths of an argument is accomplished by giving a strong, sympathetic reading, one that captures the thinking that must have motivated its author. Getting at the weaknesses inherent in an argument involves thinking about several things. First, *one or more of the premises may be questionable.* A claim we have every reason to believe false provides little evidence for anything. Second, *the support provided by the premises, even if they are highly plausible, may be questionable.* We may find, that is, that a set of premises actually provides much less support than it initially appeared to provide. In thinking about potential weaknesses in an argument, we may unearth issues that require further exploration before we can make up our mind about the argument. We may find, for example, that a crucial premise may itself require some support or that other issues need to be explored before we can decide whether the premises support the conclusion.

The long and the short of it, then, is that just about every aspect of thinking critically hinges on our ability to take arguments apart and put them back together again in standard form. Before we can offer insightful criticism of an argument, we must have before us a reading that is clear, accurate, and sympathetic. Only then can we systematically address the two evaluative issues mentioned earlier, issues discussed in depth in Chapter 3. Are there reasons to believe any of the premises implausible or false? Is there a problem with the evidence purportedly provided by the premises? If the answer to the latter question is no, chances are good the argument involves a *fallacy*.

FALLACIES

At the most basic level, a **fallacy** is an error in reasoning. A fallacious argument, then, is one in which the premises fail to support the conclusion. But a fallacy is more than a mere mistake. A fallacy is a mistake in reasoning that has the power to persuade precisely because the reason it is an error may be difficult to see. The following argument does not involve a fallacy even though it plainly involves an error.

> Portland, Oregon, has a population of 800,000.
> _____
> Portland, Oregon, is west of the Mississippi.

But the mistake involved in this argument is so transparent that no one is likely to be taken in by it. A fallacy, by contrast, is a mistake that is likely to go unnoticed and that, as a result, has the potential to convince when it should not. In the chapters to follow, we will investigate roughly thirty different fallacies. All involve common mistakes people make when they reason *and* fail to discern in the reasoning of others. Two examples follow.

An article in *Discover* magazine urged readers who fly to "know where the exits are and rehearse in your mind exactly how to get to them." Why? Because interviews with almost 200 survivors of fatal airline accidents found that "more than 90 percent had their escape routes mentally mapped out beforehand."[2] The problem with this argument is that we have no way of knowing what percentage of those who did *not* survive rehearsed their escape routes. What if roughly the same proportion of nonsurvivors knew the escape routes? Lacking this comparative data, we cannot determine whether the fact that survivors knew their escape routes is evidence that this knowledge increases one's chances of surviving a crash. This is an example of a type of fallacy that occurs when an argument provides an incomplete and misleading picture of the relevant evidence by failing to include an important piece of information. By leaving something out, the argument's author makes the argument appear much more decisive than it really is. This fallacy is called, appropriately, **omitting information.**

Here is another example, but one that involves a very different sort of mistake:

> Anyone who believes in no higher power is an atheist. God believes in no higher power. So, God must be an atheist.

Set out in standard form this argument is

---

[2]This example is cited by Thomas Gilovich in *How We Know What Isn't So: The Fallibility of Human Reason in Everyday Life* (New York: Free Press, 1991).

CONUNDRUM

Often the point of an argument will be to get someone to *do* something. Other ways to persuade are by coercion (the use of force or threats) or by manipulation as in the following remark, made by a mother to her teenage son:

> Of course, it's up to you to decide whether or not to go to college. But I'm sure you know how much it would have meant to your father, were he still alive, if you were to get your degree.

How should we characterize this sort of persuasion? Does it involve an argument? If so, do you think it involves a fallacy?

Anyone who believes in no higher power is an atheist.

God believes in no higher power.

God is an atheist.

Does this argument make a convincing case that God must be an atheist? Both of the premises look to be true. (The second premise is tricky. *On the assumption* there is a God, it would seem to be true that God must not believe in any higher power.) Moreover, the premises seem to support the conclusion. If God believes in nothing higher and if one who believes in nothing higher is an atheist, it would seem to follow that God is an atheist. Nonetheless, the argument is fallacious. The fallacy it commits involves a subtle change in the meaning of certain key terms. What does it mean to say that anyone who believes in *no higher power* is an atheist? It means that any such person believes there is no God, no supernatural being with powers vastly greater than ours. But what could it mean to say that *God* believes in *no higher power?* That God does not believe in God? No. The most sensible reading of this claim is that God does not believe in and is not beholden to anything higher that God. This argument, then, is guilty of concealing the fact that it uses "X believes in a higher power" in two distinct ways. From the fact that, say, I believe in no higher power, it follows that I do not believe in God. From the fact that God believes in no higher power, properly understood, it does not follow that God does not believe in God. All that follows is that God does not believe in anything higher than God. This argument involves the fallacy of **equivocation,** one of several fallacies that operate by subtly switching the meaning of a key word or phrase in the course of stating the claims composing an argument.

WHY STUDY FALLACIES?

Part II of this book—six of the ten chapters—is devoted to the analysis of fallacies. Why spend so much time and effort on what is essentially *bad* reasoning? One obvious reason is that people do, with some frequency, give fallacious arguments. To make matters worse, fallacious appeals can be sophisticated and effective, as the examples we have examined reveal. Simply put, they work. Many of the fallacies we will consider were identified by the Greek philosopher and scientist Aristotle around 350 B.C. This fact alone is testimony to their effectiveness. Obvious or transparent mistakes are unlikely to be perpetuated once they have been detected and understood. Thus, fallacies are worth studying in order to learn to resist them when they are directed at us and to avoid committing them ourselves. But there are other, perhaps less obvious, reasons for a sustained study of fallacious reasoning.

Understanding Good Reasoning

Earlier we noted that an argument can go wrong in two basic ways. The information contained in the premises may be questionable, or the premises may fail to provide adequate evidence for the conclusion. An acceptable argument, then, is one whose premises are highly plausible and whose conclusion is well supported by the information in the premises. Unfortunately, there is no quick and easy way to determine whether a given argument meets these requirements. In many cases, the evaluation of an argument requires common sense, the hard investigative work required to get at the facts surrounding an argument, and an understanding of the various fallacies we will study. To a large extent, an acceptable argument is one that simply makes sense, given what we know about the topic at issue, and, moreover, *that does not involve a fallacy.* Thus, one important reason to devote so much time and space to the study of *bad* reasoning is that it indirectly adds to our sense of what *good* reasoning involves.

Detecting Fallacies that Mimic Good Reasoning

Many fallacious appeals are effective because they resemble good reasoning. For example, in Chapter 5 we will consider the ways in which various *illicit* appeals to authority can be exploited in mounting arguments. In many cases, the fact that a person says something is so is not a reason to believe it so, even if that person is an expert. ("Physician-assisted suicide is morally wrong. I recently spoke to my doctor and she is opposed to it, so it must be wrong.") Yet this kind of fallacious appeal can be effective precisely because it resembles a *legitimate* appeal to authority. ("Without surgery, my knee is probably not going to get any better. I've had it examined by three specialists, and they all agree in this diagnosis.") Proper analysis of nearly every fallacy we will discuss requires a parallel discussion of acceptable reasoning of the type in question. To understand why certain appeals are fallacious, we need to appreciate how they differ from legitimate appeals. So, as we learn to recognize many types of fallacious reasoning, we will also be learning about acceptable reasoning of the type at issue.

Avoiding Attractive but Unwarranted Inferences

Many fallacies are effective in that they encourage us to draw conclusions that seem right even though they are not warranted by the facts. Such fallacies often trade on our failure to understand what is required to support a particular claim. Suppose you hear a news report about a medical study showing that heavy caffeine consumption doubles the risk of bladder cancer. Careful reading of the data suggests that the study was competently carried out. Should you watch your consumption of coffee, soft drinks, and other sources of caffeine? At first glance, the evidence provided in the study seems to suggest this. But you must be careful here. Before making up your mind, you need more information. You know that heavy caffeine consumption doubles the risk of bladder cancer, but you don't know what *rate* is being doubled. If the incidence of bladder cancer is low, then a doubling of the risk may be low as well. Suppose the rate of bladder cancer is just a few cases per 100,000 people. Even a doubling of this rate is relatively low, still just a few cases per 100,000. Thus, lacking the right comparative data, we may draw a seemingly reasonable conclusion that is not warranted by the facts. Our discussion of fallacies that encourage us to make such errors in judgment will provide a correction for the all-too-human tendency to arrive at conclusions too quickly.

THE MASS MEDIA

Much of what we believe is derived from the mass media: television, radio, newspapers, magazines, books, journals, and the Internet. Television sets are in over 98 percent of all U.S. households; radios are in 99 percent. As of 1998, 62 million American adults have access to the Internet, up from 46 million in 1997. Areas of the media devoted to the dissemination of news play a particularly important role in the formation of our beliefs. In 1995, 61.5 percent of U.S. adults said they read a newspaper daily. (In 1970 this number was 77 percent.) Nearly half of Americans admit to getting all of their news from television. But the media shape our beliefs in another, more subtle way.

The impact of the mass media on our lives can be seen from the following facts. In the United States there are currently

260,000 billboards
11,500 newspapers
11,600 periodicals
27,000 video stores
362,000,000 television sets
400,000,000 radios
40,000 books published every year
60,000,000,000 pieces of junk mail every year

How the Mass Media Shape Our World View

Each of us has a **world view**—a set of beliefs, attitudes, and biases in terms of which we think about events in the world around us. Our world view is multifaceted, malleable, and rarely well articulated. It is our basic outlook on society, economics, politics, religion, morality, and science. Your responses to questions like the following depend on certain aspects of your world view. Do you believe that free-market economies are the most efficient means of creating and distributing wealth? The most equitable? Should governments have the right to punish political dissidents? Should church and state be separate? Are professional athletes overcompensated? Are women and minorities treated fairly in the marketplace? In society in general?

It is worth noting the extent to which our world views come into play when we think critically about things. Our world view functions as a filter through which our experiences pass and in light of which we determine their significance. So, for example, your willingness to take seriously the views of a politician may hinge on your sense of how closely his or her political commitments correspond to your own. Similarly, your feeling about what our government should (or should not) be doing to deal with the problems of the inner cities depends on your general view of the proper role of government in dealing with social issues as well as on your overall impression of how serious these problems are.

Our world views are shaped in part by the views and attitudes of family, friends, teachers, and others around us, but no single factor does more to shape our world views than the mass media. Think, for example, of your view of what it is like to live in a developing nation, a country in which poverty is ubiquitous and a middle class nearly nonexistent. If you are like me, you have probably spent little or no time in such places. Your view, like mine, comes from the picture of such countries painted by media news sources.

The delivery of news is one relatively modest aspect of the mass media. Most television and radio programming is given over to lighter fare: sitcoms, dramas, and talk shows. A large chunk is advertising. The same is true of print media, in particular, magazines and newspapers. Most of the space in a typical daily newspaper (normally 80 to 85 percent) is devoted to advertising and feature items. Much of what passes as entertainment in the media plays a role in shaping our world view. For example, what many of us believe about people from ethnic backgrounds other than our own owes a lot to the kinds of characters and situations we encounter in dramatic programming. I do not live in New York City, yet I have a clear image of what life there is like. It is fast-paced and hectic. Crime and violence are a constant threat. New Yorkers are excitable and abrupt. If this picture seems familiar, it is because it is founded largely on stories spun out in a few TV sitcoms, dramatic series, and movies.

Mass Media and the News

Local and national television and radio news programs, newspapers, and national newsmagazines like *Time* and *Newsweek* are the main sources of most people's information about the world. Much of what the news media do, they do well. Today's news is collected and disseminated with a rapidity that would have been unimaginable even twenty years ago. There is a high level of accuracy in the material produced by journalists, reporters, editors, and the other players in the news industry. Although factual errors do occur in the reporting of news, most news sources readily acknowledge their mistakes.[3]

---

[3] Unfortunately, retractions are rarely given the same emphasis as the original story. On February 20, 1998, the lead story in my local newspaper carried the following headline and subhead: "FBI says 2 planned to use anthrax: The suspects, arrested in Nevada, allegedly were trying to arrange a lab test of the deadly germ warfare agent." Four days later, on February 24, another story carried the following headline: "Two men cleared of all charges in anthrax scare." The latter story, however, took up about one-quarter of the space given the first story and was placed on page 8, under a considerably smaller headline, with no subhead.

Nonetheless, the picture of reality presented in the news media leaves much to be desired. The problem is not so much with what is covered in the news media as it is with what is omitted. *Most media news coverage is both oversimplified and incomplete.* A typical television news story will last anywhere from fifteen to seventy-five seconds. Not much can be fully and accurately covered in this amount of time. Most of the background information necessary to understand an event is omitted; complex issues and events are oversimplified to fit the time allotted the story. A half-hour newscast has the time and space to cover no more than two dozen or so items in about twenty minutes. (The remaining ten or eleven minutes per half hour are devoted to ads, promotional material, public service announcements, and lead-ins.) Thus, what becomes the "news" on any given telecast is a tiny fraction of the information available. The print media are subject to the same pressures. The length of your daily paper, for example, is determined by the amount of nonclassified advertising scheduled for that day. Only after the length is set and space made for all feature items are news stories added. There is a predetermined amount of space left for the news. From the hundreds of pages of copy available to the average daily paper, only a small fraction make it into print. And the stories that do survive the selection process are often severely edited to make space for other stories.

Not all the news about the news is bad. The media often do a competent job of covering important events. Stories of overriding importance are often given sufficient time or space to go beyond superficial investigation of the facts and issues. Television news specials and expanded editions of newsmagazines and newspapers may be prompted by such events. But as a general rule, depth of coverage is not the main concern of the media.

Several factors are responsible for the tendency in the mass media toward oversimplification and omission, factors we will discuss in depth in the chapters to follow. None contributes more than this simple fact: The mass media are commercial enterprises. With the exception of publicly owned electronic media, like public television and radio, the overriding concern of the media is to turn a profit. A small share of newspaper and magazine revenue comes from circulation. *All* of the income for electronic media and most of that for print media, however, come from the sale of advertising. Consider the cost of a thirty-second commercial on the final episode of the television series *Seinfeld,* broadcast in May 1998: two million dollars! Not surprisingly, that particular episode of *Seinfeld* was one of the most highly watched programs of the decade. As this example suggests, the amount that can be charged for advertising is in direct proportion to the size of the audience and, to a lesser extent, the nature of the audience. (A magazine that appeals to people who have a lot of discretionary income can charge more per reader than, say, a magazine that attracts a less affluent readership.)

The first concern of the mass media, then, must be to gather in as many readers, listeners, or viewers as they can. The bigger the audience, the more revenue to be realized from advertising. A newspaper, magazine, television show, or radio program acquires a healthy circulation or audience share by ensuring that stories are high in entertainment value. The average television viewer is but a flick of the finger away from something that may be more entertaining; more and more people are turning from print to electronic media for their news. So, papers and magazines must continually strive to produce coverage that will keep their audience's attention. Thus, news stories are selected largely on the basis of their perceived interest to the viewing audience. Televised news stories typically involve events that can be covered briefly and have a strong visual appeal. A remarkably large portion of the typical television newscast is devoted to "human interest" stories—stories about tragedies, like natural disasters, plane and train crashes, and scandals, particularly those involving celebrities. We, the audience, tend to be the most interested in stories that are close to home. Thus, little time is devoted to international issues unless they have a direct impact on our lives. The local takes precedence over the national story and the national over the global. Little time and space is devoted to complex and abstract issues, to events that do not lend themselves to brief encapsulation, or to events largely of significance in other parts of the world.

A nonprofit organization, Project Censored,[4] puts together a yearly list of the ten most important stories that received little or no attention in the mass media. Typically, these stories involve complicated issues that could not be covered in the brief time span allotted a television news item or the few column inches taken up by most newspaper stories. In 1996, for example, the top three underreported stories were about

- the proliferation of nuclear materials in Earth orbit,
- the role of Shell Oil in fomenting civil unrest in Nigeria, and
- the provisions of a national minimum-wage bill intended to benefit corporations and the wealthy.

Now, whether these were the most important or least covered stories of 1996 is perhaps debatable. But what is not debatable is the fact that they received little attention in the major media owing largely to the fact that they are too complex or too far removed to be of interest to the majority of viewers or readers. On a similar note, consider the fact that in its 75-year history, the two best-selling editions of *Time* magazine were those published the week of and the week following the death of Princess Diana.

Advertising

The mass media, we have noted, are commercial enterprises—nothing more than vehicles for the presentation of commercial messages. And the amount of money spent on advertising is immense. In 1996, according to *Advertising Age,* U.S. businesses spent 66.7 billion dollars on advertising in the mass media. The average person is exposed to 3,000 commercial messages a day, thanks to the mass media. Commercials have the highest per-minute production costs of anything in the media. They are designed to persuade, and they generally do a very effective job of accomplishing their goal. Commercials influence our decisions about what to eat, drink, wear, drive, who to vote for, and who and what is "in" and "out." They play a central role in shaping our sense of the kind of person we think we ought to be. Not surprisingly, many of the fallacies we will investigate in Part II occur with stunning frequency in the commercial messages that permeate the media.

---

[4]Project Censored is associated with the Journalism Department at Sonoma State University in Rohnert Park, California.

Thinking Critically About the Mass Media

To become competent critical thinkers about the mass media, we need to have a good deal of information on two basic topics. First, we must be aware of the constraints under which the media operate—the pressures that determine the content of informational and entertainment programming. Second, we need to understand the techniques the media use to gain and keep our interest, including the techniques advertisers employ to gain our allegiance to whatever they are trying to sell us. Several chapters contain Media Watch sections devoted to the ways in which the lessons of the chapter apply to the mass media. Many chapters (including this one) include exercises that involve analysis of the media.

ADOPTING A CRITICAL POINT OF VIEW

If this chapter has left one indelible impression, it must be that thinking critically demands a lot of us. To become effective critical thinkers, we must endeavor to be

- **fair**—willing to take a balanced look at all sides of an issue, even those with which we disagree;
- **sympathetic**—willing to entertain and give credence to points of view other than our own on an issue;
- **skeptical**—unwilling to accept at face value claims for which there is little rational basis; and
- **open-minded**—willing to revise our beliefs in light of new information.

Needed to think critically

To be successful at understanding and evaluating the thinking of others, we must give them a fair and sympathetic hearing. Skepticism should temper any tendency we have to accept claims too quickly and uncritically. Open-mindedness underscores our commitment to the value of thinking critically. The frame of mind we must maintain in order to be effective critical thinkers is called the **critical point of view.** Taking the critical point of view, however, requires one additional trait, a trait perhaps less obvious than the others.

In addition to being fair, sympathetic, skeptical, and open-minded, we must be **self-reflective**—willing to think critically about the ways in which our expectations, beliefs, and preconceptions can influence our evaluation of other people's thinking. The influence of these factors on the ways we assess information is well understood and documented. For example, a classic study done in 1960 surveyed voters who had watched the Kennedy-Nixon debates, the first presidential debates to be televised. The study revealed that those who were pro-Kennedy thought Kennedy had won the debate, whereas those who were pro-Nixon thought Nixon had won. In another, more recent experiment, trained football referees were shown one of two videotapes of the same aggressive play in a football scrimmage. In one tape, the aggressive team wore white uniforms; in the other, the same team ran the same play, but while wearing black uniforms. Surveys conducted in a wide range of cultures have shown that the color black is often associated with death and evil. Not surprisingly, the referees who had seen the black-uniformed version rated the play as much more aggressive and deserving of a penalty than those who had seen the white-uniformed version. Just think about the implications of this study for the perpetuation of racial **stereotypes.**[5]

In still another experiment, subjects were asked to identify their view on capital punishment. Both groups—advocates and opponents—were given two studies, one arguing for the deterrent value of capital punishment, the other purporting to show that capital punishment does not deter. The material presented to the subjects compared homicide rates in various states, before and after capital punishment. The subjects were then asked to evaluate the material. The results were striking. Participants rated the study consistent with their beliefs to be well-conducted, reliable research but uncovered numerous flaws in the research at odds with their beliefs about capital punishment.[6]

Given the extent to which elements of our own point of view can color our responses, we need to understand when this is happening and to correct for potential distortions. Suppose your political sympathies lie with the left (or the right) and you encounter an argument from a different political perspective. Can you take the critical point of view in thinking about the argument? Can you, that is, be objective, sympathetic, and open-minded in thinking about the argument? Can you give a reading of the argument that captures its strengths as well as its weaknesses? The proof of this particular pudding is, as they say, in the eating. Find an argument for a sensitive position with which you disagree and make every attempt to be convinced by it, to "see" the argument in the way it must seem to its author. Reflect carefully on your relationship to the argument and its author. Where, precisely, do your points of view differ? Can you correct for any distortions in your reading due to an unfriendly point of view? You will find this a daunting challenge. To make matters worse, you may never know if you have fully succeeded, for you may continue to have serious misgivings about this argument. Lest you disagree, try the following warm-up exercise. First, recall our discussion earlier of the issues surrounding one of today's most controversial topics—Affirmative Action. If you are a member of one of the groups likely to benefit from Affirmative Action, build a strong, reasonable case for the dismantlement of Affirmative Action programs. If you are not among these groups, do just the opposite: Make a case for the continuation of such programs.

From this exercise, you are likely to gain a clearer understanding of what might motivate someone to hold a view different from your own and of where your real differences lie. This is not a mere academic exercise. The solution to any real conflict depends on the extent to which the disputants have taken the time to understand one another and carefully think through their differences.

Adopting the critical point of view amounts to making a commitment to an open, honest, fair hearing of the issues surrounding any controversial issue. Of the components of the critical point of view—fairness, sympathy, skepticism, open-

---

[5]A *stereotype* is a simplified, inaccurate conception of a large group of people. Stereotypes can be used either to idealize or to demean. We will discuss issues surrounding the use of stereotypes in argument in Chapter 9.

[6]These examples are borrowed from Gilovich, *How We Know What Isn't So: The Fallibility of Human Reason in Everyday Life.* For more examples and a more detailed treatment of the studies we have just discussed, see, particularly, Chapters 4 and 5.

mindedness, and self-reflection—the last is perhaps the most essential. Unless tempered by a willingness to reflect on the influence of our own point of view, none of the other components is likely to be realized.

CHAPTER SUMMARY

1. At the most basic level, to think critically is to investigate the basis for the claims we believe to be the case.

2. An **argument,** for critical thinking purposes, is a series of claims related in a special way. The claims making up the argument's **premises** are intended to provide support for another claim, the argument's **conclusion.** An argument is in **standard form** when it is written out as a series of premises separated from the conclusion by a line. To think critically about an argument is to try to decide whether the evidence advanced in its premises warrants our acceptance of its conclusion.

3. Arguments and explanations differ in that the point of an argument is to provide evidence for the truth of a claim, the argument's conclusion. The point of an **explanation** is to make sense of how or why something is the case; the point of an argument is to provide evidence that something is the case.

4. The evaluation of most arguments requires information from the background of facts and issues surrounding the argument. To evaluate an argument involves thinking about
   a. the plausibility of the premises,
   b. the extent to which the premises support the conclusion, and
   c. background issues that must be resolved if the argument is to be evaluated.

5. A **fallacy** is a mistake in reasoning that is likely to go undetected and, thus, have considerable persuasive power.

6. The mass media have an enormous impact on our **world view**—our outlook on basic issues in politics, society in general, economics, religion, morality, and science. The most influential and pervasive of the mass media are television, radio, newspapers, magazines, and movies. Much of the information we obtain from the mass media is oversimplified and incomplete, owing mainly to the media's need to attract and keep a large audience. As we consume the information the media have to offer, we must always remind ourselves that the goal of the media is to keep our attention by keeping us entertained. The primary goal of the mass media, even the news media, is, thus, *not* to inform.

7. Effective critical thinking demands that we take the **critical point of view;** that is, we must endeavor to be
   a. **fair**—willing to take a balanced look at all sides of an issue, even those with which we disagree;
   b. **sympathetic**—willing to entertain and give credence to points of view other than our own on an issue;
   c. **skeptical**—unwilling to accept at face value claims for which there is little rational basis;

  d. **open-minded**—willing to revise our beliefs in light of new information; and
  e. **self-reflective**—willing to think critically about the ways in which our expectations, beliefs, and preconceptions can influence our evaluation of other people's thinking.

EXERCISES

A. The following passages all involve arguments. For each, decide first what the author of the argument is trying to do. Is the author, for example, defending a position, making an excuse, giving advice, or drawing an inference? Then give a clear statement of the argument's conclusion and premises, set out in standard form.

(A solution to Exercise 6 is provided on page 24.)

1. People are addicted to a substance if they cannot voluntarily stop using it. Many smokers cannot quit. Thus, smoking is an addiction.
2. Ted Kennedy could never be elected President, now that he's divorced.
3. *(In response to Exercise 2)* You don't know what you're talking about. Look at Ronald Reagan.
4. There must be something to Chinese herbal medicine. After all, it's been practiced in Asia for thousands of years.
5. In his most recent public appearance, Boris Yeltsin looked thin and pale. He must have suffered another heart attack.
6. In announcing his withdrawal from the 1992 presidential race, Ross Perot said the following: "I'm not going to run if I can't win, and it looks like my candidacy will only serve to send the race to the House of Representatives."
7. *Titanic* is just another bit of mindless Hollywood fluff. The characters lack depth and interest, and the plot is so transparent it is hard to see it as anything other than a lame excuse of three hours of razzle-dazzle special effects.
8. Politics and morality are inseparable. And as morality's foundation is religion, religion and politics are necessarily related. —*Ronald Reagan*
9. To the editor: I read the birth and wedding announcements almost every day. I like to see if I know anyone or what people name their babies. I also read the obituaries. I used to read them with a morbid curiosity—to see who died of what at what age. Now I've had to face reading my own father's obituary. He died recently of a brain tumor at age fifty-seven. I will never again read the obituaries with such a detached attitude. I will know that each was someone's loved one and that one little paragraph does not do justice to a person's life.
10. That new blockbuster movie must be doing very well at the box office. I went to see it the night it opened, and the theater was jam-packed.
11. I've got to get a new roof put on my house, and, unfortunately, it's going to cost a lot of money. I've gotten a number of bids. The cheapest was about $2,800; the most expensive, about $3,400. My guess is that I'm going to have to fork out somewhere in the neighborhood of $3,000 to get the job done.
12. *(In response to 11)* Don't bet on it. Contractors always bid low. Somehow things always have a way of costing half again as much as you think they are going to cost.
13. *The following is from a commentary by the authors of a scientific study in which cell phones were claimed to be a cause of many car accidents.*

The study received a lot of attention. Most media reports were accurate. One occasional inaccuracy, however, has been the claim that using a cellular telephone is the same as driving drunk. Not true. Driving with an alcohol level of 80 mg per deciliter is associated with a relative risk of collision of 4, which is about what we found for cellular telephones. However, a level of 120 mg per deciliter is associated with multiplication of risk by a factor of 10 (and higher levels have higher risks). Furthermore, alcohol circulates in the blood for hours, whereas a telephone call lasts only minutes. The cumulative risks associated with intoxication are greater than those associated with cellular telephones.[7]

14. *A:* Are you ready to leave?
    B: Yeah. Let's go.
    A: OK. But first, give me your car keys. I'm going to drive.
    B: No way. I'm fine. I haven't had that mush to drink.
    A: Yeah, right. Did you hear what you just said?

15. Can I borrow your lawn mower one last time? I know I said that the last time I borrowed it, but mine's still in the shop and won't be ready for another week or two. The guy said he had to special-order some part.

16. Animals have moral rights despite the fact that they are not human beings. The short and long of it is that animals are every bit as capable of suffering as are we humans. And because of this, they have the same rights as we do not to be subjected to unnecessary pain and misery at the hands of another.

17. *A:* If my study of critical thinking has taught me one thing, it is that there is no such thing as absolute truth.
    B: Well, think again.
    A: What do you mean?
    B: What you have just said can't be true.
    A: I don't follow you.
    B: You've said there is no such thing as an absolutely true statement. Right?
    A: Yes.
    B: And you believe this?
    A: I said I did, didn't I?
    B: In other words, you are absolutely convinced of the truth of at least one thing: the claim that there is no such thing as absolute truth!

18. I can't believe I forgot all about your birthday. What can I say? The bar exam was the next day, and I was so nervous and wound up, I couldn't even remember what day it was. I'm really sorry.

19. The smile, which appears in infants from the ages of two to four months, invariably evokes affection from adults and reinforces bonding between caregiver and infant. In all cultures and throughout life, smiling is used to signal friendliness, approval, and a sense of pleasure. Each culture molds its meaning into nuances determined by form and the context in which it is

---

[7]*New England Journal of Medicine,* 337, no. 2 (1997): 128.

displayed. There is no doubt that smiling is hereditary. It appears on schedule in deaf-blind children and even in thalidomide-deformed children who are not only deaf and blind but crippled so badly they cannot touch their own faces.[8]

20. *Question:*

It was a warm Sunday and the sermon was long. A man was dozing beside his wife in their pew and dreaming that he lived at the time of the French Revolution and had been sentenced to death by guillotine. As the blade was falling, his wife noticed he was asleep and touched him on the back of the neck, right at the spot where the blade would have struck. The man died instantly. *Why can't this story be true?*

Answer:

If the man had died instantly this way, we could not have known he was dreaming.

B. Which of the following passages involve arguments, and which involve explanations? If you are having problems deciding about a passage, try the following strategy. First, determine what claim appears to be at issue—that is, what claim the passage is about. Then ask yourself: Is the passage trying to provide evidence that the claim is true, or is it trying to make sense of how or why what is claimed is so? To answer this question, you may need to imagine a context in which the claims made in the passage might occur.

(A solution to Exercise 1 is provided on page 24.)

1. My basement must be leaking again. After last night's storm, there was at least an inch of water all over the basement floor.

2. Tiger Woods is the best young golfer in the game today. Though he has not yet chalked up the results of a Palmer or a Nicklaus, he has made more money and won more tournaments than any other player under age thirty now on the pro tour.

3. Tiger Woods is the best young golfer in the game today. He's got nerves of steel, great ability to concentrate, and nearly perfect form.

4. In the past ten years, college tuition has increased by more than 200 percent nationwide. During the same period, the median annual income of all newly hired college graduates has declined from $44,000, in 1998 dollars, to about $42,500. A college degree is simply not worth as much as it was ten years ago.

5. Smith must have lost her job. I saw her standing in line down at the unemployment office.

6. Newt Gingrich is constantly being pilloried in the newspapers and on television. But then what do you expect from news media with such an obvious left-wing bias?

7. Julius Rosenberg was undoubtedly a Soviet spy. Although he denied he was a Soviet agent, new evidence to the contrary has recently emerged. The for-

[8]Edward O. Wilson, "Resuming the Enlightenment Quest," *The Wilson Quarterly* (Winter 1998): 21.

mer head of KGB (the Soviet equivalent of the CIA) now admits that Julius Rosenberg was one of his agents, though Rosenberg's wife, Ethel, was not.

8. *(In response to 7)* OK. Maybe Rosenberg was a Soviet agent. But he didn't spy because he was a communist or even anti-American in his political leanings. Rosenberg was convinced that the only way to keep the world safe from nuclear weapons was for both sides in the international arena to have nuclear weapons. This would be the only way to ensure that they were not used.

9. The chances that there is intelligent life elsewhere in the universe are much slimmer than we might like to imagine. Out of the millions and millions of species that have evolved on planet Earth, only one has had the capacity to think at a level sufficiently high to even contemplate the possibility of life elsewhere, let alone create the technology necessary for interstellar communication. Great intelligence may very well be an evolutionary quirk—a highly improbable accident—and not something we would expect to see arising with any frequency elsewhere in the cosmos.

10. The following note was printed on the back cover of a textbook sent by a publisher to teachers whom they hoped would order the book for their classes.

FREE PROFESSIONAL COPY—NOT INTENDED FOR SALE
The sale of free professional copies deprives authors of royalties and publishers of revenues and contributes to the higher prices of textbooks to students.

C. Do the mass media really devote as little space and time to the news as we have claimed? First, pick up a copy of your local newspaper. Go through the entire paper with a felt-tip pen, crossing out everything not devoted to news. Cross out ads, features, comics, sports, contests, and anything else primarily intended to entertain rather than to present the news. Then figure out the ratio of column inches devoted to news *to* inches devoted to other things. We said that no more than 15 to 20 percent of the space in a typical daily paper is devoted to news. Is this true of your paper? Next, view a half-hour television news program, watch in hand. Note the amount of time devoted to commercials, promos, lead-ins, and between-story chitchat and the length of each news story. How many minutes are devoted to news? How long was the average story? How many stories took more than forty-five seconds? In total, how many stories were covered?

D. A number of facts about the mass media were cited in this chapter. Among them were the following:

■ Television sets are in over 98 percent of all U.S. households.
■ 61.5 percent of U.S. adults say they read a newspaper daily.
■ Only 46 percent of Americans say they trust what they see on television.
■ In 1996, U.S. businesses spent 66.7 billion dollars on advertising in the media.
■ The average U.S. citizen is exposed to about 3,000 commercial messages every day.

None of these claims, however, was documented. Here is a good spot to exercise your critical acumen. Can you do the research necessary to determine whether these claims are true? (Nearly all of these facts were obtained from the Internet.)

SOLUTIONS

Exercise A

6. In this passage, Perot is justifying his decision to pull out of the 1992 presidential race. He gives two reasons. He came to realize that he was not going to win but that he might pick up enough electoral votes so that the outcome would be decided by a vote of the House of Representatives. In standard form, Perot's argument is as follows:

> I'm not going to get enough votes to win the election.
> I may, however, get enough votes to ensure that the House of Representatives will decide the race.
> I don't want the election decided in the House of Representatives.
> _____
> I'm going to withdraw from the race.

Note that the last premise is unstated in Perot's remarks, probably because of its obviousness.

Exercise B

1. An argument. At issue in this passage is the claim that my basement must be leaking. The remaining claim provides evidence that my basement is leaking. And the fact that there is an inch of water on the floor does not explain why it is leaking.

Solution to the Puzzle on pages 5–6

This problem can be solved by taking one marble from the bag labeled "mixed." Since all the bags are mismarked, this bag contains either all red or all blue marbles. If the marble we select is red, the bag is filled with red marbles. We know the bag labeled "red" is mismarked as well, so it must contain all blue marbles or blue and red ones. But it cannot be the mixed bag, for this would mean that the bag marked "blue" is accurately labeled. And this is inconsistent with one of the facts—that each bag is mismarked. Therefore, the bag labeled "red" must contain all blue marbles and the bag labeled "blue" must be mixed. (The same reasoning, of course, could be used in the event that the marble selected was blue, the only other possibility.)

CHAPTER TWO

Claims

At the most basic level, critical thinking is about the investigation of claims and their underlying support. But before we can begin to think about the support for a claim, we must make sure we understand it. Now tell me, can you make sense of the following?

Leptons are fermions that lack strong interactions.

The problem with this claim is that it involves notions with which most of us are unfamiliar. But claims involving only the most familiar terms can be difficult to understand as well. Suppose that I've agreed to drive you to school this morning. "How long will it take me to get to your place?" I ask. "At this time of day, quite a while," you reply. Although I have a sense of what you mean, I am unclear on exactly what you are telling me. I certainly don't have enough information to decide how much extra driving time I need to plan for.

In this chapter we will look at the major impediments to clarity—the reasons why claims often are hard to decipher. Once we have a sense of the various problems that can contribute to a lack of clarity, we will consider ways to avoid them. What can we do to make sure the things we say and write are clear? You have no doubt been in situations where you are asked to reply to a question like "So just what do you mean by . . . ?" In the conversation about driving time, the next thing I will say is, "What do you mean, *quite a while*?" When asked to explain what we mean, we are, in effect, being asked to provide a definition, although not a dictionary definition. Rather, we are being asked to clarify how we are using the word or phrase at issue. Providing clarification is not always easy to do. So, in the second half of this chapter, we will discuss various ways of defining our terms and then introduce criteria by which to determine whether a definition does its job. But first, a pair of notions needs to be clarified. Perhaps you have already wondered, "Just what does he mean by a *claim* and by the notion of *clarity*?"

CLAIM MAKING

A **claim** is a stretch of discourse in which the aim of the speaker or writer is to assert that something is or is not the case. At first glance it may seem that just about every remark we make involves a claim. But we use language to do a lot of things other than making claims. We use words to raise questions; give commands; make requests, promises, and threats; take vows and oaths; express our feelings

(*Ouch!*); and much more. In none of these activities is our aim to assert or deny anything. Claim making differs from these activities in another important way. Of all the things we say and do, making a claim is the only activity that results in something that is true or false. Consider some of the things we might *do* with words other than making claims:

How far is it from Boston to Atlanta?

I swear to tell the truth, the whole truth, and nothing but the truth.

Please leave.

Sign on the dotted line, if you will.

I give up.

None of these remarks is true or false nor is any the kind of remark that *could be* true or false. So, for example, someone who says, "Please leave," is making a request, not claiming that something is the case. Here are a few remarks that do involve claims:

WWII ended in 1945.

WWII ended in 1954.

It will take you quite a while to get to my place.

I wish I were a bit taller.

Each of these remarks makes an assertion about what is or is not the case. Claims are usually expressed as statements in the declarative mood, like the preceding ones. But remember, to make a claim is to *do* something—to assert that something is or is not the case. On occasion, other grammatical forms are used to make claims. Consider

Surely you don't think Bill is as dishonest as Rush claims he is, do you?

This is a claim though, grammatically, it is in the form of a question. What is asserted is that Bill is not as dishonest as Rush says. To make matters worse, declarative statements can be used to do things other than make claims. Imagine that you and I are trying to decide which movie to see tonight. "Anything's fine," I say, "but I don't particularly like foreign films." My aim in saying this is not simply to claim that I don't like foreign films. My aim is to make a polite suggestion, namely, that we go see anything but a foreign film. In a different context, the same remark might be intended to function just as a claim. You might ask me if I enjoy foreign films, and I might simply reply, "No, I don't like foreign films. Why do you ask?"

Claims are the only type of remark that can be true or false. Although every claim must be one or the other, it is not always easy to decide whether a given claim is true or false. Consider the following claim:

There is no intelligent life in the universe other, that is, than on planet Earth.

This claim is no doubt true or false, but like many claims, we are in no position to say which. In Chapter 3 we will consider some of the telltale signs that a claim may be false and will find that questions about the veracity of a claim often have no clear-cut answer. Even after carefully examining the evidence, we may find that a claim is

CONUNDRUM

Claims, we have said, are true or false. But what about the following?

Mr. Spock is from planet Vulcan.

First of all, there is no Mr. Spock and there is no planet named Vulcan. What are we to make of this claim? Is it true or false? Or is it a claim at all?

difficult to classify. A controversial claim may turn out to be highly likely, quite dubious, or somewhere in between.

DESCRIPTIVE AND VALUE-LADEN CLAIMS

The claims we have examined so far have one thing in common: Each provides a *description* of something the claim's author believes to be the case. **Descriptive claims** can be either about the world around us or about the world inside of us or others.

Mars is the fourth planet from the sun

and

He promised to repay the money he borrowed

are examples of the former.

I really love mashed potatoes and gravy

and

She wants to become a doctor

are examples of the latter.

Not all claims, however, are intended to describe how things are. Claims can be about values—aesthetic, ethical, political, or whatever—and about how we think things should be or ought to be. Here are some typical claims involving values:

Abortion is wrong.

You shouldn't invest in companies that use child labor.

You should try to keep your weight down.

Woody Allen hasn't made a decent movie in years.

Scott Joplin was the greatest American composer.

At first glance it may seem odd to call these remarks *claims,* so little do they seem to have in common with descriptive claims. This is largely because it is difficult to imagine any simple or clear-cut procedure for deciding whether a claim involving values is true or false. Many claims seem to be mired in controversy. But they are claims nonetheless. Deciding whether to accept or reject a **value-laden claim** may

> **CONUNDRUM**
>
> Two terms are often used to comment on claims: *fact* and *opinion*. What exactly is a fact? Are all true claims facts? Are all facts true claims? Can value-laden claims be facts? And what about opinions? What are we being told when someone tells us something we have claimed is "just an opinion"? What are we saying when we preface a remark with "Well, in my opinion . . ."? Can someone's opinion be true? Can an opinion be a fact?

be difficult, and there are no doubt some claims that are unresolvable. But this can be true of descriptive claims as well.

There are 2,563,742,218 pennies now in circulation in the United States

and

O.J. murdered his wife

are descriptive claims though claims as difficult to decide about as the most perplexing and intractable value-laden claims. Moreover, it is possible to give a strong argument in defense of a claim involving values, an argument suggesting the claim is true. Presumably, there are some very good reasons why we *shouldn't* invest in companies that exploit children or why we *should* try to keep our weight to a reasonable level. Indeed, if someone can tell us more about what he or she means by *a decent movie,* we may be able to decide whether Woody Allen has made any lately.

CLARITY

So far we have said what it is for a remark to be a claim, and we have noted that claims can be descriptive or value-laden. But what does it mean for a claim to be *clear?* Although it is hard to say much in general about what **clarity** involves, at least this much can be said: A remark is clear if it is understood by its author and intended audience. This is true of remarks of all sorts, not just claims.

I swear to tell the truth, the whole truth, and nothing but the truth

is clear despite the fact that it is an oath, not a claim. Remember, claims assert that something is or is not so. So a claim will be clear if what it asserts is understood by all parties.

Our definition of clarity is a bit too restrictive. There are claims that will not be fully understood by everyone who hears or reads them but that are nonetheless clear. Recall a claim introduced earlier. I have it on good authority that

Leptons are fermions that lack strong interactions

is about as clear as possible, although you and I may not fully understand what it asserts. This example suggests the need for a modification to our definition. The preceding claim may be clear to those who know what fermions, leptons, and strong interactions are. (In fact, fermions and leptons are families of fundamental particles, and strong interactions are those involving the force that binds the nucleus of the atom.) But there are many circumstances in which this claim would baffle its intended audience. We need, then, to add this caveat to our definition: A *remark* is clear, in a given context, if it is understood by all parties; a *claim* is clear if, in a given context, what it asserts can be understood by all parties. By contrast, a claim lacks clarity if, *in a given context,* there is some question, not about its truth or falsity, but about what it means to be asserting. The question of whether a claim is true or false can be raised only after we understand it. One sign that a claim is clear, then, is this: The commitments made by a claim are sufficiently spelled out to enable us to figure out how to think about its truth or falsity.

IMPEDIMENTS TO CLARITY

The clarity of a claim can be compromised by two basic sorts of difficulty. First, a claim can be unclear because, in its context, it can be understood in more than one way. Such claims are said to suffer from **ambiguity.** Suppose that you encountered a sign at the supermarket, in the produce section, that said

> All varieties of apples—49 cents.

Just how much do the apples cost? Are apples 49 cents each or 49 cents per pound? Second, a question about what is being asserted may be caused by a failure to specify how a key word or phrase is being used, in a given context. Such claims are **vague.** Imagine that you have been waiting for me at a restaurant and I'm already half an hour late. So you call me at home to find out what the problem is. I tell you that a friend I haven't seen for years stopped by and we are catching up. I go on to assure you:

> Don't worry, I'll be there pretty soon.

In part, what I have said is clear. I intend to meet you. But another part of what I have said is vague. What does *pretty soon* mean? Fifteen minutes? An hour? Sometime before the restaurant closes? The problem with my remark is that I have not been specific in saying what I mean by *pretty soon.*

The distinction between ambiguity and vagueness may itself seem fuzzy. The difference between the two can be further clarified by examining our response to a problematic claim. If our response is, "Do you mean this or that?" where we can be fairly specific in describing the alternatives, the claim is ambiguous. If, on the other hand, our question is "So, just what do you mean?" the claim is vague. Unfortunately, the distinction between ambiguity and vagueness is not exclusive. A claim may be both ambiguous and vague when it admits of a small set of interpretations, one or more of which is vague, or when it is vague in one part, ambiguous in another. The supermarket sign discussed earlier would have been both vague and ambiguous had it said instead

> Some fruits and vegetables—49 cents.

Before we take a closer look at problems that can contribute to the ambiguity or vagueness of a claim, two points need to be emphasized. The first, a note of warning, the second, an important reason why we should value clarity in writing and speech.

The note of warning is very simple: *Don't be picky!* It is possible to find fault with just about any remark by singling out a word or phrase that seems ambiguous or vague. This is because words usually have more than one meaning and many of the standard dictionary definitions are themselves broad and general. This does not mean that words are intrinsically sloppy and imprecise. Rather, it means that words are versatile and economical tools. But it also means that it is easy to criticize a remark on the ground that there may be a question about how a speaker or writer is using some word or phrase. We must make a point of engaging in such criticism only when something turns on the question of how a key word or phrase is being used. If I write or say something that you cannot understand, criticize away. If, on the other hand, you have a good sense of what I mean, there is little point in the kind of pedantic criticism that often motivates questions like "So, just what did you mean by . . . ?"

Clarity is an indispensable persuasive tool. Our arguments are not going to be convincing if our audience must struggle to understand them. But a good deal more is at stake in taking the time to express ourselves clearly. When we think about something, we generally think in words; thinking of this sort is like talking to ourselves. Indeed, the reverse is true as well. We often "think" out loud. This does not mean that all mental activity is necessarily linguistic. Feeling, forming mental "pictures," and remembering, for example, do not take the form of an internal dialogue. Nonetheless, when we discover that something expressed in words is unclear, we have a good sign that the underlying thinking is muddled as well. Why? Because the underlying thinking is itself a kind of linguistic activity. It is tempting to believe that when we fail to express ourselves clearly there lurks inside us a pristine thought, unencumbered by vagueness or ambiguity. The thought, we think, is clear though we have not yet found the right words to express it. But this belief is often illusory. Thinking of the sort that stands behind the claims we make is itself a linguistic activity though one we carry out in our own minds. But when we express our thoughts, problems we encounter in saying what we mean usually indicate a problem in the thought thereby expressed. So, in learning to avoid the linguistic pitfalls we will discuss, and in learning to be clear in saying and writing what we mean, we are also learning how to clarify our thinking and how to spot fuzziness in the thinking of others. If something can be thought clearly, it can be expressed clearly.

Ambiguity

We have said that a remark is ambiguous if it can be taken in more than one way and if it occurs in a context where there is no clear indication of how it is to be taken. Without the latter requirement, we would have to regard just about any claim as ambiguous.

Your glasses need to be cleaned

appearing here in a contextual vacuum, admits of two plausible interpretations. Is it your eyeglasses or drinking glasses that need cleaning? But claims do not generally

Cartoons and jokes often depend on semantic ambiguity. (*Source:* © 1998 CREATORS SYNDICATE, INC.)

occur in a contextual vacuum. Thus, the preceding claim is ambiguous in neither of the following:

> Your glasses need to be cleaned. They've got spots all over them, and you know the people who are coming to dinner are fastidious.

> I can't believe you didn't see that car behind us. Your glasses need to be cleaned.

Only when a remark's context fails to provide grounds for a single plausible interpretation is it ambiguous. Ambiguity can result from a failure to specify the semantic or referential meaning of a key word or phrase or from the grammatical structure of a claim.

Semantic Ambiguity   Earlier we noted that most words have multiple meanings. A remark is semantically ambiguous when it's not clear which meaning of a key word or phrase is intended. Lacking a context,

> Your glasses need to be cleaned

is semantically ambiguous because the word *glasses* can be taken in more than one way. Or consider

> He is closer to his father than to his mother.

Is he physically closer or emotionally closer? Of course, had the remark gone on

> He is closer to his father than to his mother, which is why he talks with him and not her about his problems

the meaning of this claim would be clear.

Referential Ambiguity   Nouns, pronouns, and descriptive phrases are often used to identify things. Consider

> I am not feeling too well today.

Here, *I* obviously refers to the author of the remark. Don't confuse the sense, or semantic meaning, of a word or phrase with its referent. Of course, a single word, like *I,* can be used to refer to many things. Moreover, words and phrases having different meanings can be used to *refer* to a single thing. The two phrases that follow have different meanings yet identify the same individual:

The first President of the United States

The husband of Martha Washington

A claim is referentially ambiguous when it fails to make clear what a key word or phrase refers to. If someone were to say

Smith is in big trouble with the boss

in a context where there are several employees named Smith, the claim would be referentially ambiguous. Often, the imprecise use of pronouns results in referential ambiguity.

You are in big trouble

said while pointing in the direction of more than one person would be referentially ambiguous. Of course, the way to eliminate such ambiguity is by more accurately describing the referent.

You—the guy with the pink sweatshirt on—are in big trouble

eliminates the ambiguity of the previous remark. Unfortunately, descriptions can perpetuate ambiguity, sometimes intentionally, as in the following:

I have it on good authority that a member of our congressional delegation has paid no income tax for the past five years.

Just which congressional delegate is being charged with tax evasion? Come to think of it, is he or she being charged with tax evasion or simply being good at finding legal loopholes? This claim looks to be both referentially and semantically ambiguous!

Grammatical Ambiguity   Ambiguity can also result from poor sentence structure. (Grammatical ambiguity is sometimes called **amphiboly.**) Suppose you found this instruction on an essay test:

Write a 3–4-page response to two of the questions that follow.

Are you to write a total of 3–4 pages or 6–8 pages? Both interpretations are consistent with the instruction. The ambiguity here cannot be resolved by asking how a key word or phrase is being used or what its referent is. To clarify this instruction, we would need to rewrite it. Depending on what the instruction actually means, we could add a word here and there to clear things up:

Write a 3–4-page response to each of two of the questions that follow.

Write a total of 3–4 pages in response to two of the questions that follow.

If a claim must be rewritten to eliminate the ambiguity, it is grammatically ambiguous.

Any attorney will tell you it is crucial to frame questions for witnesses in terms that are clear and unambiguous. A poorly phrased question can have unexpected results. The following exchanges and questions were taken from a book, *Disorder in the Court.* They're things people actually said in court, word for word.

Attorney: What is your date of birth?
Witness: July fifteenth.
Attorney: What year?
Witness: Every year.

Attorney: What gear were you in at the moment of impact?
Witness: Gucci sweats and Reeboks.

Attorney: This myasthenia gravis—does it affect your memory at all?
Witness: Yes.
Attorney: And in what ways does it affect your memory?
Witness: I forget.
Attorney: You forget? Can you give us an example of something that you've forgotten?

Attorney: And where was the location of the accident?
Witness: Approximately milepost 499.
Attorney: And where is milepost 499?
Witness: Between milepost 498 and 500.

Attorney: Did you blow your horn or anything?
Witness: After the accident?
Attorney: Before the accident.
Witness: Sure, I played for ten years. I even went to school for it.

Attorney: Now, doctor, isn't it true that when a person dies in his sleep, he doesn't know about it until the next morning?

Attorney: You say the stairs went down to the basement?
Witness: Yes.
Attorney: And these stairs, did they go up also?

Attorney: Is your appearance here this morning pursuant to a deposition notice which I sent to your attorney?
Witness: No, this is how I dress when I go to work.

Attorney: All your responses must be oral, OK?
Witness: OK.
Attorney: What school did you go to?
Witness: Oral.

Attorney: You were not shot in the fracas?
Witness: No, I was shot midway between the fracas and the navel.

What do you suppose the witness in the last example thinks a fracas is?

Vagueness

We have said that a claim is vague when it is not clear what is being asserted. So, for example, the claim

> Many Americans do not have health insurance

is vague despite the fact that we do have some initial sense of what it means. We often accept such claims—or, rather, entertain them for the sake of argument—without first trying to clarify them. "Many Americans," I say, "have no health insurance at all, and so we need to overhaul our health-care delivery system." "Hogwash," you reply. "If we try to change it wholesale, we will just make it worse." We could debate this point for hours, yet we might never pause and ask ourselves just what the claim that got us started really means. The problem, of course, is due to the phrase *many Americans.* Until we have some sense of the number or percentage of people who lack health insurance, we learn very little in being told that many Americans do not have health insurance. In this example, vagueness is an impediment to understanding. How we take this claim depends greatly on the numbers.

> One percent of all Americans do not have health insurance

and

> Nearly a third of all Americans do not have health insurance

tell us very different things. So, in this example our understanding of a claim turns on the meaning of a key phrase. If something like the former is what is meant by *many Americans* in the original claim, the dispute in which we are engaged has little point.

Vagueness does not always impede understanding. On occasion, a carefully worded though vague claim will be as clear as circumstances allow. We should not automatically criticize a claim that is somewhat vague. For example, look at the following description of what the Americans with Disabilities Act of 1990 (the ADA) requires of employers:

> The ADA prohibits employment discrimination against qualified individuals with a disability who, with or without reasonable accommodation, can perform the essential functions of the job. Specifically, the act prohibits not making reasonable accommodations to the known physical or mental limitations of an otherwise qualified individual, unless such accommodations would impose undue hardship on the operation of the business.

Simply put, this passage informs us that if you are an employer, you must make reasonable accommodations for individuals with disabilities unless making such accommodations would impose an undue hardship on your business. Suppose you were running a business and you wanted to know what the ADA requires of you. "Reasonable accommodations," I say, "unless that involves an undue hardship on your business." Your response is understandable: "But what are *reasonable* accommodations? And how much hardship is *undue?*" This is a good example of vague language but language that is nonetheless about as clear as possible, given the job the passage has to do. The ADA has the potential to affect every American business and millions of disabled citizens. Any brief description of how the ADA applies to them will have to be vague. What constitutes *reasonable accommodations* and *undue hardships* will vary with the size and nature of the business and the kind of disability for which accommodation must be made. These phrases will be gradually clarified as the ADA touches businesses large and small.

Several kinds of claims run a high risk of being unnecessarily vague. Among the more prominent are claims that rely on

overused words and phrases

jargon and technical terms

terms used to make comparisons

qualifying phrases

Claims that compare, qualify, and employ overused expressions or jargon can be clear. But too often, these devices mask the meaning of a claim.

Overused Words and Phrases   Most words have a relatively short list of standard meanings. A chair is a familiar piece of furniture; the chair may be the person who runs a meeting; such a person may be said to chair the meeting. On occasion, however, a term gets severed from its familiar meaning because it is overused. Imagine what would happen if we began to expand, indiscriminately, our use of a simple word, like *chair,* so that many other sorts of objects, people, and actions came to be known as chairs. The broader and looser we got in our use of the word, the less precise we would be when we used it. After a certain point, the word would become worn and dull, like a knife that through constant use has lost its edge. Statements that rely on overused terms say very little. Slang expressions wear out rapidly, through overuse. Consider:

A: I just attended the first lecture in my critical thinking class.
B: What did you think of it?
A: It was totally outrageous!

Did A like the lecture? Get something from the lecture? Hate the lecture? *Totally outrageous,* like its contemporaries and predecessors (*groovy, wicked, awesome, cool,* etc.), is used so often to say so many things that it has come to say very little. About all that seems clear here is that A hasn't said much about the class.

Like slang, political labels often wear thin through overuse. All of the following are used so often to refer to so many different things that they no longer have well-defined standard meanings:

liberal

conservative

right wing

leftist

democratic

fundamentalist

environmentalist

feminist

family values

Who would not own up to being in some sense an environmentalist or in favor of family values? What government would not characterize itself as furthering democratic ideals? All of this is not to say that we should refrain from using such terms. Rather, if we choose to use them, we need to make our usage clear. If someone remarked,

> The environmentalists are going to be the death of American business,

we would need to pin him down on what he means by *environmentalists* before letting him go any further. Lacking clarification, we must regard this claim as saying very little.

Jargon and Technical Terms   Every field of endeavor has its technical language or jargon. (*Jargon* is, thus, one of our technical terms!) Car mechanics, plumbers, doctors, lawyers, teachers, chemists, biologists, tennis and bridge players all generate their own specialized vocabularies, and with good reason. Recall a claim discussed earlier:

> Leptons are fermions that lack strong interactions.

These technical notions are indispensable to particle physicists much as *torts, writs of habeas corpus,* and *injunctions* are terms needed by lawyers and *book, no-trump,* and *finesse* by bridge enthusiasts. In its place, then, a technical language serves a legitimate function. Used properly, jargon can be effective and can be used to say things that resist clear or straightforward statement in ordinary language. But people often use jargon when it is unnecessary, and the result is discourse that is unnecessarily difficult to follow. Why do people do this? For a lot of reasons. A sprinkling of technical language can lend the impression that one is an expert or at least knows what one is talking about. (Would you think to question the expertise of someone who made the claim about leptons?) Technical language can be used to intimidate. If I don't understand your jargon, I may simply decide to accept what you have said as gospel rather than reveal my ignorance. Jargon can also be used to mask the fact that one really has little to say or to suggest that something commonplace is profound or novel. Consider, for example, the following remark by two educational researchers in which they tell us about something they call *the educational sciences:*

> The educational sciences serve as a common structure within which enquiry of significance for the fundamental aspects of the applied field of education can be conducted.[1]

To their credit, the authors of this passage have been very inventive; they have started their own technical language featuring such phrases as

> the educational sciences
>
> enquiry of significance
>
> fundamental aspects
>
> applied field of education

---

[1]From a pamphlet, *Personalizing Educational Programs—Utilizing Cognitive Style Mapping,* by Joseph E. Hill and Dereck N. Nunney (Bloomfield Hills, Mich.: Oakland Community College, 1971).

The impression they leave us with is that a group of scientists, educational scientists, conduct research or, as they like to say, an "enquiry of significance for the fundamental aspects" of "the applied field of education." My guess is that all they are saying is that they make a living studying teaching.

The convoluted structure of this last example contributes to its vagueness. But complicated structure is not, by itself, a sin. Some ideas are complicated and need to be expressed in complicated ways even when entirely clear. Recall our description earlier of the ADA:

> The ADA prohibits employment discrimination against qualified individuals with a disability who, with or without reasonable accommodation, can perform the essential functions of the job. Specifically, the act prohibits not making reasonable accommodations to the known physical or mental limitations of an otherwise qualified individual, unless such accommodations would impose undue hardship on the operation of the business.

Both sentences in this passage are long and complex. But here, by contrast with our previous example, the complex structure does not render the passage unclear nor is meaning impeded by the creation of a jargon out of strings of words.

Terms Used to Make Comparisons   Many claims turn on some sort of comparison. The claims below are clear because the things being compared are all explicitly mentioned.

Mt. Everest is taller than the Matterhorn.

The average American worker makes more than the average Canadian.

A claim that involves a comparison but fails to mention one of the terms or fails to give us sufficient information to know what to make of the comparison is **comparatively vague.** I recently bought a package of cheese, the label of which proclaimed

Now with 20 percent less cholesterol.

Less than what? Some other brand? Earlier versions of this brand? Note that this claim is comparatively vague in two ways. Suppose we were to call the manufacturer and find out that what it meant is that it has reduced the amount of cholesterol in its own cheese. The claim is still not clear. It suggests that this is a low-cholesterol product, but is it? Just how much cholesterol are we talking about? Until we find out the amount of cholesterol in the new, improved product, we have no clear sense of what exactly it is the manufacturer is claiming about its cheese.

Claims involving averages are often comparatively vague. During a strike in 1996 by major league baseball players, critics of the player's union often cited the fact that the average major league player makes in excess of $1.2 million a year. The strike, it seems, was fueled more by greed than need. Yet critics always seemed to omit the information necessary to make sense of this statistic. This average is the **mean,** arrived at by dividing the total of all salaries by the number of players. Yet, at the time of the strike, there were a handful of players making much more than the average salary. Each of the highest-paid players made more than $8 million per year. If, say, 5 percent of the players made $5 million or more per year, then the vast majority of players made considerably less than the average cited. A much simplified version of this case can be used to illustrate. Suppose there are just 50 major league players and that the mean salary is, as our critics suggest, $1.2 million per year. Total salary is $60 million per year. But suppose also that five "superstars" are paid $8 million each per year. This accounts for $40 million of the $60 million. So, the total salary of the remaining 45 players is $20 million, or an average of about $440,000 per year, less than half the average originally cited. Does the average player make $1.2 million or about $440,000? Take your pick. Averages signify very little unless accompanied by the important facts and figures necessary to decipher how they were calculated. Averages that conceal such information are comparatively vague.

Claims about averages can be ambiguous as well, since there are three distinct ways of arriving at an average figure. We have considered an example of a mean average. But an average can also be a median or a mode. The **median** is the figure in the middle of a series of figures while the **mode** is the figure that occurs most frequently. Thus, from a single set of numbers, we may be able to derive three different averages. So, when a claim is about an average, we need to know which of these three types is at issue. If this is not specified, the claim is semantically ambiguous.

Qualifying Phrases   Sometimes it is necessary to qualify a claim in order to make it as plausible as possible. For example, if I am not sure whether I will be able to meet you at a particular time, I might say, "I'll try to be there on time, but I *may* be a few minutes late." And this may be as accurate as I can be, given the circumstances. However, the use of qualifiers can render a claim vague. The result is often a claim that is much less clear than it initially appears. Shortly before the Gulf War, for example, my local newspaper carried a front-page story about the possible buildup of U.S. troops in the Persian Gulf. Its headline read

U.S. DEPLOYMENT IN GULF MAY GROW

Note that this headline does not claim what we might be tempted to think it claims. It does not claim that more U.S. troops will be deployed to the Persian Gulf or even that this is a strong possibility. In fact, it is not clear exactly what it says, thanks to the insertion of *may*. The problem here is not simply that the headline is qualified; qualifiers have their legitimate uses and can result in claims that are not vague. Contrast that headline with these alternatives, both involving qualifiers, and each a good deal more informative:

U.S DEPLOYMENT IN GULF A STRONG POSSIBILITY

U.S. UNLIKELY TO DEPLOY MORE TROOPS

By contrast with these alternatives, the original headline is so broadly qualified that it comes close to telling us nothing.

In advertising, such claims are often called **weasels** in acknowledgment of the fact that through the subtle insertion of modest qualifying phrases, they "weasel out" of much of what they appear to be asserting. Consider, for example, this claim:

Our exterior paint will protect your house for up to five years longer than any other brand on the market today.

There is more than one way to weasel out of a claim. (*Source:* © 1998 CREATORS SYNDICATE, INC.)

This claim is not comparatively vague. We are explicitly told what brands the brand in question is being compared to. What makes this claim vague is the phrase *up to*. The claim does not say the brand of paint in question *will* last five years longer; it says that it *could* last five years longer. What exactly does this mean? Be wary of advertising pitches that are too good to believe for somewhere therein lurks a weasel. Not long ago I was the lucky recipient of a piece of mail that said in very large print on the envelope:

> STEPHEN S. CAREY
> HERE'S THE FIRST PAYMENT ON
> YOUR $1,666,675.00 PRIZE!!!

Unfortunately, in tiny print just above the big news was the following:

> if you have returned the Grand Prize winning number, we'll say:

Included in the envelope was my first payment, a check in the amount of $66,667. In the bottom left corner of the check, in print of what must be the smallest size decipherable without a magnifying glass, came the bad news in the form of another weasel:

> non-negotiable

MEDIA WATCH: THE LANGUAGE OF ADVERTISING

One way to convince us to buy something is by rational persuasion. Why should we purchase product X or service Y? Product X may be better than its competitors. Service Y may cost less than similar services provided by other companies. The problem, however, is that there may be no good reason to prefer one product over its competitors. In 1990 alone, over 13,000 new products were introduced in the United States, three-quarters of which were food items. Whatever differences there are between various brands of, say, potato chips, cookies, or soap powders are probably superficial. And this presents advertisers with a challenge. How can we be persuaded to choose one product or service over others that are essentially the same? How, that is, can advertisers give us reasons to buy their products and services *if* there really are no good reasons? The problem is exacerbated by Federal Trade Commission regulations prohibiting deceptive or unfair advertising.[2] Two techniques are used over and over by advertisers to get around this problem. Both depend on types of vagueness. And both, as it turns out, result in claims that do not run afoul of FTC regulations!

Pseudo-claims

A **pseudo-claim** is a claim about a product that, in the final analysis, tells us little or nothing, appearances to the contrary. For example, a recent magazine ad for a number of Kellogg's cereals (Special K, Crispix, Corn Flakes, and Raisin Bran are pictured), begins with a question: "Can cereal reduce the risk of heart disease?" It goes on to provide the following answer: "Experts agree that eating low-fat foods like these cereals along with cutting down on saturated fat and cholesterol may help reduce the risk of heart disease. So keep it up, and eat your cereal. Cereal. Eat it for life. Kellogg's." At first glance, this ad seems to claim that eating Kellogg's cereals will help us to reduce our risk of heart disease. But look carefully at what it actually says. The first thing to notice about this claim is the way in which it is qualified. According to "the experts" (who are they, anyway?), a diet low in saturated fat and cholesterol *may* help reduce the risk of heart disease. It doesn't tell us a low-fat, low-cholesterol diet *will help* nor does it attempt to clarify precisely what it means by *may help*. Whom might it help, and what are the chances it will help? As you can see, the content of this crucial claim comes to very little. It is a classic example of a pseudo-claim that operates by the careful use of what we have termed *weasels*.

An ad for Nivea Visage Anti-Wrinkle and Firming Creme makes the following claim: "Clinically proven to dramatically reduce the appearance of wrinkles in weeks." No doubt, the clinic in which the tests were run is owned by Nivea . . . or is it? We don't know because the ad does not tell us. Note also the marvelous weasel in the claim. Will Nivea reduce wrinkles? No, even though it is advertised as an anti-wrinkle claim. But it will reduce the *appearance* of wrinkles. Does this mean that it will cover them up? Make them more attractive somehow? Your guess is as good as mine. The only thing we can say for sure is that the ad does not promise that Nivea will do what it at first glance appears to be promising, namely, remove wrinkles.

Often, key advertising claims make use of words whose meaning, in the context of the claim, is overly vague. Consider the claims made in the following ad for a product called GinkgoIQ. The ad appeared in a nationally distributed newspaper supplement, *Parade Magazine:*

> GinkgoIQ is a carefully formulated nutriceutical that promotes mental clarity and helps you get your edge back. It's made with Guaranteed Potency Herbs (GPH) so you know it contains the optimal amount of Ginkgo Biloba, which

---

[2]The Federal Trade Commission defines a deceptive ad as "any representation, omission, or other practice that is likely to mislead the consumer acting reasonably under the circumstances to the consumer's detriment." Unfair advertising is defined as "acts or practices that cause or are likely to cause substantial injury to consumers, which is not reasonably avoidable by consumers themselves and not outweighed by countervailing benefits to consumers or competition." As you can see, these definitions are vague and fuzzy around the edges. The result is that it is very hard to make a compelling case that an ad is unfair or deceptive. Couple this with the fact that the FTC has a long appeals procedure for advertisers who disagree with its decisions and you can see why very few ads are pulled for violation of FTC regulations.

increases the supply of blood and oxygen to the brain and has been clinically proven to increase alertness and short-term memory. It also contains ginseng for energy, plus L-Glutamine and B vitamins, essential to healthy brain function.

Setting aside the jargon—*nutriceuticals, Guaranteed Potency Herbs,* and the like—note the verbs used in the key claim. GinkgoIQ is formulated (carefully, thank goodness) to *promote* mental clarity and to *help* you *get* your edge back. In some way, then, GinkgoIQ will assist you to achieve greater mental clarity and sharpness (presumably this is what is meant by getting your edge back). But note what this claim does not say. It does not say GinkgoIQ will make you think more clearly and sharply. Rather, it will assist you, encourage you, to accomplish this. (What, precisely, do you suppose this means?) Later on, the ad claims GinkgoIQ contains many things *essential to heathy brain function.* It does not claim, however, that you or your brain will function in a healthier way if you use the product. Despite the fact that the ad is carefully composed to claim very little, it goes on to make one very clear claim in the small print near the bottom:

> These statements have not been evaluated by the Food and Drug Administration. This product is not intended to diagnose, treat, cure, or prevent any disease but rather as a dietary supplement intended for nutritional support.

Another great example of backing out in the fine print of what is claimed in boldface.

In *Doublespeak,* a book with the tantalizing subtitle *How Government, Business, Advertisers, and Others Use Language to Deceive You,* William Lutz writes at length about what he terms "the biggest weasel word used in advertising doublespeak." The word is *helps.*

> It does not mean to conquer, stop, eliminate, end, solve, heal, cure or anything else. But once the ad says "help," it can say just about anything after that because "help" qualifies everything coming after it. The trick is that the claim that comes after the weasel word is usually so strong and so dramatic that you forget the word "help" and concentrate only on the dramatic claim. You read into the ad a message that the ad does not contain. More importantly, the advertiser is not responsible for the claim that you read into the ad, even though the advertiser wrote the ad so you would read that claim into it.[3]

Think for a moment of some of the many advertising claims that rely on this overused word. A product, it may be claimed, will

> help fight tooth decay
>
> help reduce stress
>
> help control dandruff
>
> help you look younger
>
> help you achieve financial security

---

[3]William Lutz, *Doublespeak: From "Revenue Enhancement" to "Terminal Living." How Government, Business, Advertisers, and Others Use Language to Deceive You* (New York: Harper and Row, 1981), p. 86.

You've used the toothpaste for months now. Unfortunately, your dentist informs you that you've got a few new cavities. Don't blame the toothpaste. The ad said only that it would help you in your fight against decay, not that it would prevent cavities.

Pseudo-differentiation

We have good reason to buy a product or service if it is demonstratively better or cheaper than the competition. Often advertisers make use of comparatively vague claims to imply that their product is superior to others. Though the differences they extoll are trivial at best, nonexistent at worst, the claims they make are constructed in such a way that it would be hard to prove them false. Here are a few claims taken from a single advertising supplement to my Sunday newspaper. The supplement contained about twenty-five ads.

> *Wisk HE* and front-loading machines create a high performance system that gives you:*
>> Brighter and whiter clothes after just one wash
>> Better overall cleaning
>> Better stain removal
> *Versus using a conventional detergent in a front-loading machine
>
> A better carpet cleaner—*Formula 401*
>
> Nothing cures better! *Mycelex-3*
>
> A better way to clean wood & glass furniture . . . *New Pledge*
>
> *X-14* is *better!** Removes soap scum *better** Removes mildew stains *fastest**
> *Compared to the leading brand
>
> Superior whitening* + fresh scent = great value! *Gain Bleach*
> *Versus leading value brands
>
> More choices. More solutions. More answers. *RadioShack*

As you can see, several of these ads do make an attempt to provide the basis for the comparison they make. *Wisk* works better than conventional detergents. *X-14* is better than the leading brand at removing scum and mildew stains. The ads don't, however, tell us what these other products are, and so their comparisons remain virtually empty. By the way, did you spot the weasel word, *virtually*, in the preceding sentence? It does a lot of work in the advertising world. *For virtually spotless dishes, nothing beats Cascade.* Just how clean do you suppose *Cascade* will get your dishes, according to this claim?

CLEARING THINGS UP: DEFINING TERMS

When we encounter a word or phrase used in a way we do not fully understand, we can ask for clarification, if the speaker or writer is available. Lacking an author whose brains to pick, we can attempt to clarify the word or phrase by using contextual clues. A request for clarification can involve either of two things. We may simply want to know the standard meaning of a term, if it is unfamiliar to us. The best way to find the standard meaning is, of course, to look up the word in a dictionary. Here, for example, is a term with which you may not be familiar: *epistemology*. My dictionary defines *epistemology* as "the study or theory of the origin, nature, methods, and limits of knowledge." To clarify the meaning of a term in this way is to give a **dictionary** or **lexical** definition.

Often, however, a request for clarification may not be satisfied by a dictionary definition of the problematic word or phrase. The standard definitions of the words themselves may be clear, but there may remain some question about how the words are being used in their current context. Suppose someone were to give the following argument:

> You can discount everything she says about men. After all, she's a radical feminist.

To understand this argument, we need to know what the author means by *radical feminist*. Looking up *radical* and *feminist* in our dictionary is not going to help much here. At best we may be able to patch together an account of what the phrase could mean. What we require is a **precising,** not a dictionary, definition. To give a precising definition is to clarify how a word or phrase is being used in a specific context. If the author of the preceding argument is unavailable, all we can do is try to define the phrase in a manner consistent with the remainder of the passage and other contextual clues.

Don't assume that a precising definition of a word or phrase is wrong if it seems at odds with what the dictionary suggests. Dictionaries give us more or less standard usage, but usage is not always more or less standard. If I use a word in a way that differs from what the dictionary says about its proper use, my usage is proper, as long as I have made myself clear to my intended audience. You no doubt have encountered arguments that seem to turn on the definition of some term. Someone might argue, for example: "Well, Smith says that abortion is murder. He can't be right. My dictionary defines *murder* as . . . ." The implication here is that, among other things, Smith's argument goes wrong in seriously misconstruing the meaning of *murder*. In fact, in the context of Smith's argument, *murder* can mean whatever Smith wants it to mean, as long as Smith clearly specifies how he is using the term.

New words are entering our vocabulary all the time, many as a result of new technologies and scientific discoveries. *Quasar* and *pulsar* were invented by astronomers to describe newly discovered types of stars. *Byte, gigabyte, megabyte, Web browser,* and *Internet* have emerged from the proliferation of high-speed computers. New phrases are

---

Many new words enter our vocabulary as acronyms—words formed by combining the first (or first few) letters of the words in a phrase. So, for example, the acronym *radar* is derived from the phrase "<u>ra</u>dio <u>d</u>etecting <u>a</u>nd <u>r</u>anging." Can you supply the phrases that are the basis for the following acronyms?

PAC	*AIDS*
WASP	*RAM*
sonar	*ROM*
laser	*FOIA*
scuba	*IRA*
FIGMO	*Y2K*

Can you think of others?

often introduced to describe novel situations from daily life. One of my favorites is a phrase used to describe a now familiar fact of life in office cubicles. When people pop up to see what is going on in adjoining cubicles, they are said to be *prairie-dogging.*

The definition of a new term or phrase is called a **stipulative** definition. Given the rate at which new terms and phrases crop up, the ability to apply familiar terms to new situations becomes all the more imperative if we are to keep our stock of words at a manageable level. The only alternative is to constantly add new terms via the process of stipulative definition—another reason it is important that we learn to give workable precising definitions. Better to say precisely what we mean by *prairie-dogging* than to invent a new term—*progging,* perhaps—to describe the behavior in question.

Methods of Definition

There are several methods we can use to clarify the meaning of words and phrases when the standard dictionary meaning is not relevant.

The Use of Examples   We can define by giving examples of what we mean or by citing other words that have roughly the same meaning as the word or phrase at issue. Both of these methods of definition can be risky. Here is a definition that relies on examples of what the phrase at issue is being used to refer to:

> By a *Christian conservative,* I mean somebody like Jerry Falwell or Pat Robertson.

Though this definition gives a rough sense of the meaning of *Christian conservative,* the phrase is still not clear. An obvious question remains: What is it about Falwell and Robertson that makes them Christian conservatives? Moreover, examples can easily be taken in the wrong way. Is part of the preceding definition that one must be a male to be a Christian conservative? As you can see, examples often confound as much as they clarify.

This is not to say that examples have no place in the process of definition. Thinking in terms of examples is often a good way to begin the process of defining and also a good way to test proposed definitions. Just what is it about Falwell and Robertson that makes them good examples of Christian conservatives? Can we arrive at a definition that includes these two but excludes people like Jesse Jackson or Billy Graham? Moreover, examples are often an effective supplement to the defining process. I would not want to introduce someone to the concept of a *weasel* or the notion of *jargon* without a few examples to help me out. But examples alone rarely suffice to give a complete or clear definition.

Synonymous Definition   To define by giving other words and phrases having roughly the same meaning is to give a **synonymous** definition. We might, for example, explain the meaning of *remorse* as "guilt" or "regret." In fact, precisely these synonyms are used in the definition of *remorse* my dictionary provides. But it is rare to find two words that are identical in meaning. Thus, an effective synonymous definition needs to include several words that are close in meaning. You've undoubtedly heard people describe a book, movie, or TV show as a "cross between." For example, I might describe the film *Jurassic Park* as a "cross between" *Treasure Island* and *Godzilla.*

This is similar to the strategy employed in giving effective synonymous definitions. We give a sense of what one word means by giving a series of other words with the implicit assumption that the meaning of the word at issue lies somewhere between the meanings of the others.

Analytic Definition   Definition by example or by synonym can be instrumental in providing some initial sense of how a word or phrase is being used in a particular context. But if we desire real precision, we must turn to a third method of definition: **definition by genus and difference,** or, for short, **analytic** definition.

To give an analytic definition is to specify conditions for the use of a word or phrase. These conditions will set forth characteristics for membership in the group referred to by the word or phrase being defined. For example, we might define the phrase *Christian conservative* as follows:

> By a *Christian conservative,* I mean someone who subscribes to the tenets of fundamentalist Christian theology and who believes that his or her basic moral values should be embedded in our laws.

Two things go on in this definition. First, we have specified a broad category into which all such people fall: They are all people who subscribe to basic fundamentalist Christian tenets. But this category is too broad, for there may be people who would fit this description yet who we would not classify as Christian conservatives. So then in our definition we exclude people who do not believe that a particular set of religious values should be embedded in civil law. This is essentially the process of analytic definition. We first give the broad *genus* under which subjects covered by the phrase in question fall and then give the *difference,* the feature or features that distinguish the subjects in question from other members of the genus.

By the way, is our proposed definition correct? It depends on what we mean by *correct.* Is this roughly how most people would define *Christian conservative?* Our definition does seem to capture much of what people mean when they speak of conservative Christians. So as a dictionary definition it is not too bad. But as a precising definition the answer to our question is yes, it is correct. It seems clear who the author of the definition means to both include and exclude by the phrase *Christian conservative.*

The key to giving a serviceable analytic definition is to be as precise as circumstances allow in setting forth features of the genus and difference. Here is an ideal analytic definition:

> A triangle is a plane, closed figure, having exactly three sides.

Among the members of the *genus* plane (two-dimensional), closed figures, triangles are those that have exactly three sides. Unfortunately, we cannot always achieve this level of precision in an analytic definition. Many of the words and phrases we will want to clarify allude to groups or classes of things that are fuzzy around the edges. Recall a phrase discussed earlier: *radical feminists.* It is unrealistic to think that we can specify exactly the features that all and only radical feminists have in common, at least in any way that does justice to a realistic reading of what the phrase may mean. Just about any definition we arrive at will leave out something or include too much.

Even the most commonplace terms cannot be defined with the kind of rigor provided in our definition of *triangle.* Consider, for example, a definition of a familiar word:

Chair—a seat for one person having four legs and a rigid back.

On one hand, this definition is not too bad. It provides us with a fairly precise genus. But if it is intended to reflect standard usage, the definition is not too good. What of three-legged chairs, beanbag chairs, and basket chairs that hang from the ceiling? We could, perhaps, try to save our definition by arguing that such "chairs" really are not chairs at all. But any definition that excludes these odd bits of furniture is out of step with common usage. Thus, the difference in the preceding definition of *chair* looks too restrictive.

The way to accommodate our problem cases is not by trying to build a better mousetrap—by trying to refine the difference so that it incorporates the features common to all types of chairs. Rather, the solution lies in recognizing that analytic definitions need not provide us with differences that are airtight. For many words and phrases, a workable analytic definition need only set forth differences that are typical of the class of things in question. With one small addition, the earlier definition, then, seems perfectly correct:

Chair—a seat for one person, *typically* having four legs and a rigid back.

Are beanbag and hanging basket chairs consistent with this definition? Yes, for the definition now claims only that having four legs and a rigid back are features *typical* of the majority of chairs. Beanbag chairs and hanging basket chairs are called chairs because, although they do not display all the features typically associated with chairs, they do display some. What is more, they seem to fit under the genus. Thus, hanging basket chairs have a rigid back and are designed for one person but they lack legs. Beanbag chairs take a shape resembling a chair when they are sat on although in other respects they are unlike other sorts of chairs.

Given our ever-changing and expanding world, the level of precision of the last example is about the best we can generally hope for. We need to find ways of describing things without constantly expanding our vocabulary. And one effective way to do this is to apply familiar words in new situations that bear some resemblance to the standard situations and things we use our words to describe. If our current stock of words is to enable us to cope with new situations, we must be prepared to expand their applicability. Thus, oversized bags of beans are best regarded as chairs, atypical features and all. Our only other option would be to invent a new term.

Constructing Acceptable Definitions

A definition is a good one if it provides a clear account of how a word or phrase is being used. There are several rules of thumb to follow in constructing definitions. First, in defining a term we should avoid using words that are derivative of the term being defined. If I am trying to clarify the meaning of *fecund,* I need to do more than point out that *fecund* means "having the property of fecundity." Second, a definition should avoid terms that are obscure, relative to the term being defined. Consider this definition:

Felicific—hedonistically optimific.

CONUNDRUM

Consider the following definition:

Northwestern states—Oregon, Washington, Montana, and Idaho.

This seems a perfectly accurate way of defining *Northwestern states*. What method of definition is involved here? Is it one of the methods we have discussed or something else?

It is doubtful that one who did not understand *felicific* would be helped by this definition. Remarkably enough, this definition is nearly accurate. However, a less obscure and much clearer definition would be

> *Felicific*—the action, out of all alternatives, that promotes the greatest amount of happiness or pleasure for all concerned.

Third, a definition should avoid atypical characteristics. Suppose I defined *chair* in the following way:

> *Chair*—a seat for one person typically having four legs and a rigid back and made out of metal.

The features given in the difference do describe one sort of chair. However, the final feature—being made out of metal—renders the definition much too restrictive and narrow if it is intended to cover the sorts of things we normally think of as chairs. The problem in the following definition is an atypical and, thus, much too restrictive genus:

> *Professional athlete*—a man who is paid to play a sport.

Fourth, the difference must be sufficiently precise to distinguish the things being defined from other things falling under the genus.

> *Chair*—an article of furniture designed to be sat on

includes many things under the difference that are not chairs; as a definition it is too broad.

Fifth, a definition should not specify what is excluded under the difference when it can specify what is included. Consider

> *Chair*—a piece of furniture that is not a table or a couch.

Although what it says is true, this definition is much too inclusive. Obviously, a lot of articles of furniture are neither tables nor couches but are not thereby chairs.

As you can see, the trick to giving a good analytic definition is to do two things. First, give a genus that includes all the features common to the things in question despite their being common to other related things as well. Second, give the features that both typify the things in question and distinguish them from other things falling under the genus. In general, the more precise we are in giving both genus and difference, the clearer our definition.

Bias and Persuasive Definition

There is one additional requirement an acceptable definition must meet: A definition should be expressed in terms that are not biased. Just about any state of affairs can be described in a lot of ways. Compare the two claims that follow, both of which might be used to describe the same event:

> The noisy protesters shouted down the speaker.
>
> Some members of the audience expressed their objections in a lively and dramatic fashion to the view of the speaker.

The image of the people making all the noise is very different in these two descriptions. If different observers of the event gave these descriptions, we would probably assume that the truth about what took place lies somewhere between the two. Why? Because each description looks to involve the observer's biases. The author of the first description is probably in sympathy with the view of the speaker, whereas the author of the second description sides with the audience against the speaker.

A claim involves **bias** if it conveys its author's biases, prejudices, values, and so on under the guise of simply offering a description. Now, there is nothing wrong with making claims that involve our values, biases, and so forth. The American journalist H. L. Mencken once said, "Religion is fundamentally opposed to everything I hold in veneration—courage, clear thinking, honesty, fairness, and, above all, love of the truth. In brief, it is a fraud." Although we may disagree with the sentiments expressed by Mencken, we cannot fault him for failing to make his bias clear and explicit. The following remarks, however, do involve biased descriptions. Think first of someone who disagrees with your view on something important, someone who refuses to be swayed by your arguments. You might describe such a person as "narrow-minded, rigid, and highly inflexible." I, on the other hand, who agree with your opponent, might describe her as "consistent, thoughtful, and highly insightful." Both remarks are biased and are deceptive in that they are intended to express our attitudes toward the person, while appearing to be just a description. In general, a good test for whether a description involves bias is this: If in hearing or reading a descriptive passage, you learn more about the speaker's or writer's attitudes than about whatever is being described, the claim is probably biased.

Euphemism can be used to insert bias in a remark. A euphemistic description avoids potentially objectionable features of whatever is being described. In attempting to avoid objectionable language, euphemisms are often inaccurate descriptors. To describe a person who is dangerously overweight as "plump" or "rotund" is to speak euphemistically. Descriptions that convey a negative bias are often called **dysphemisms.** To speak of a conservative politician as a "right-wing extremist" is to engage in dysphemism.

A good example of the way euphemism can lead to bias is the following. Recently a chain of supermarkets in my area was struck by its employees as the result of a protracted labor dispute. The day after the strike began, "help wanted" ads appeared in all the local media. In their ads, the grocers explained that a "temporary work stoppage" had left a number of positions vacant. At first glance, this may seem nothing more than an accurate description and, in one sense, it is. But it is biased in that it conspicuously and intentionally leaves out a fact about the work stoppage that could be important to many potential new employees: The company is seeking new workers because its regular employees are on strike, not because they have stopped working.

At the beginning of this section, we said that a definition should avoid the use of biased language. A definition that employs bias is called a **persuasive** definition. Persuasive definitions are, in a sense, not definitions at all. Rather, they are designed to convey a value or prejudice while appearing to do something else—clarifying the meaning of a word or phrase. The following is a subtle and deceptive instance of a persuasive definition:

Abortion—the act of taking the life of a pre-born human being.

The key notion in this definition—the notion of a pre-born human being—reflects a certain attitude toward abortion. Someone who gave this as a definition would be more interested in advancing a certain view about the morality of abortion than in simply clarifying what the word means. To see the bias in this definition, compare it to the definition given in my dictionary:

Abortion—the expulsion of the fetus from the womb before it is viable.

Bias is perhaps more insidious when it occurs in definitions than anywhere else. The point of giving a definition is to clarify the use of a key word or phrase, often because the word or phrase plays a key role in a premise of the argument. If we accept a persuasive definition, we risk tacitly agreeing with the claim the argument is trying to establish. It would, for example, be difficult to take issue with an argument for the immorality of abortion if we accept as a premise of the argument the persuasive definition given earlier.

CHAPTER SUMMARY

1. A **claim** is a stretch of discourse in which the aim of the speaker or writer is to assert that something is or is not the case. Claims are the only remarks that can be true or false. Broadly speaking, claims can be divided into those intended to describe and those intended to express our values.

2. A remark is clear, in a given context, if it is understood by both its author and its intended audience. A remark can lack clarity because it is vague or ambiguous.

3. Nearly every remark can be found lacking in some respect, and criticism should be reserved for those cases where something turns on the question of how a key word or phrase is being used. Don't be picky and pedantic in your criticism of a remark.

4. A remark is **ambiguous** if, in context, it can plausibly be understood in more than one way, though in a relatively limited number of ways. Semantic ambiguity occurs when a key word or phrase has more than one interpretation. Referential ambiguity occurs when the referent of a word or phrase is unclear. Grammatical ambiguity is the result of poor sentence structure.

5. A remark is **vague** when precisely what is being asserted or denied is unclear. Whereas an ambiguous remark has more than one interpretation, even in context, a vague remark has no single, plausible interpretation. Overused words, jargon, terms used to make comparisons, and qualifying phrases frequently contribute to vagueness.

6. To define a word or phrase is either to clarify its standard, dictionary meaning or to specify a nonstandard use in a given context. Definition can be accomplished by giving examples or synonyms or by giving the genus and difference for things of the type being defined. The difference in most definitions includes typical features while the genus includes common features.

7. A definition lacks clarity if it
   a. uses terms having the same root as the term being defined,
   b. uses terms that are obscure, relative to the term being defined,
   c. gives atypical features in the genus or difference,
   d. gives overly inclusive features in the difference,
   e. specifies by excluding when it can specify by including, or
   f. expresses an underlying bias rather than clarifying the term.

   A definition involving an atypical genus or difference is too narrow. A definition involving an overly inclusive difference is too broad.

8. A **biased** remark serves to convey an attitude, prejudice, opinion, and so on while appearing to be intended to describe.

9. A **persuasive** definition is a counterfeit definition. Persuasive definitions are constructed to convey a bias while appearing to clarify the meaning of a word or phrase.

10. Advertisements often traffic in vague language. Pseudo-claims are so vague as to say virtually nothing. Claims involving pseudo-differentiation are comparatively vague.

EXERCISES

A. Which of the following remarks might typically be used to make claims? Which are descriptive and which involve values?

   (Solutions to Exercises 1 and 7 are given on page 55.)

   1. Excessive exposure to the sun causes skin cancer.
   2. Smoking is not allowed in this restaurant.
   3. Did you remember that we have a lunch date next Friday?
   4. You can't look at a sleeping cat and be tense.
   5. If the Superbowl is the greatest game ever played, how come they keep playing it every year?
   6. I have a hunch George Washington didn't really have wooden teeth.
   7. Please leave your coat and hat at the door.
   8. Beauty is in the eye of the beholder.
   9. I can't remember whether dolphins are fish or mammals.
   10. It is absolutely essential that all college students be required to take at least one course in critical thinking.
   11. You must be at least eighteen years old to vote in this state.
   12. I hope to be a millionaire by the time I'm thirty.
   13. You've got to study at least four hours per day to succeed in college.
   14. I now pronounce you husband and wife.

15. Do that one more time and I'm leaving.
16. Didn't you promise to meet me at noon yesterday?
17. *(In response to 16)* Yes.
18. *(In response to 17)* Well, then, you should be ashamed of yourself.
19. There is a tenth planet in our solar system, beyond the orbit of Pluto.
20. *Portland Trail Blazers coach Mike Dunleavy speaking of Michael Jordan:* The guy is the greatest player to ever play this game, from the standpoint of intelligence, competitiveness, and athleticism.

B. Comment on problems that affect the clarity of the remarks below. Determine whether each is vague or ambiguous, and isolate the source of the problem. If a remark strikes you as vague, for example, be specific in diagnosing the problem. Does it involve overly broad qualifiers, inappropriate jargon, an incomplete comparison, and so on? Remember, don't be picky. If a claim seems clear enough, say so.

(Solutions to Exercises 1 and 14 are given on pages 55–56.)

1. Hurry! These sale prices are good for a limited time only.
2. Excessive exposure to the sun can cause skin cancer.
3. Beta Computers is the computer store with more. When you purchase your computer at Beta, you get more than a great system. You get more selection, more training, and more service.
4. What do I think about Smith's views on animal rights? Well, there just may be something in what she says.
5. By the year 2000, two out of three Americans could be illiterate. —*from an ad by an organization called* Coalition for Literacy
6. Abraham Lincoln wrote the Gettysburg Address while traveling from Washington to Gettysburg on the back of an envelope. —*from a student essay*
7. How was my weekend? Well, it was different.
8. One of the doctors who performed the surgery is guilty of malpractice.
9. Of the doctors we've surveyed, 60 percent of those who expressed a preference said they would recommend Bayer over Anacin.
10. I devote a sizable fraction of my income to charitable causes.
11. My father is sore because I ran over his foot.
12. Over the past ten years, the median income of American workers has increased substantially.
13. The President sent her congratulations.
14. All my life I wanted to run for President in the worst possible way—and I did. —*former Presidential candidate Walter Mondale*
15. Only those students will be admitted to this college who have achieved high scores on the Scholastic Aptitude Test.
16. Coke tastes better.
17. When a young man, my father and I played tennis together.
18. Warning: The Surgeon General has determined that cigarette smoking is dangerous to your health.
19. Happy Homes sells more real estate than nearly anybody else in the area.
20. Kents—for lower tar and nicotine.
21. All male students are required to have their hair cut in an appropriately manly way.

22. I prefer an abbreviated phraseology, distinguished principally by its tendency to foster lucidity in interpersonal communication.

23. Our bank has assets steadily growing toward the 100-million-dollar mark.

24. Religious holidays may be recognized or noted, but they may not be observed or celebrated. —*from a public school principal in a memorandum to the staff*

25. JESUS IS COMING—LOOK BUSY —*from a bumper sticker*

26. When clauses on confirming forms sent by both parties conflict, each party must be assumed to object to a clause of the other conflicting with one on the confirmation sent by himself. —*from the U.S. Uniform Commercial Code*

27. This society at this time is riddled with toxic substances. According to studies, some of the things that are put in a can of peas or a can of soup are, let's face it, toxic. They are preservatives and the action of preservatives is to impede decay. In other words, those things might be great for the manufacturer as they preserve his product, but they could be very bad for the consumer. —*from* The Purification Rundown, *a pamphlet published by the Hubbard Dianetics Foundation*

28. Approximately 1.4 million people will be diagnosed with cancer this year. Yet the majority of adults are still unaware that as many as one-third of all cancer deaths in the U.S. are related to diet. The American Cancer Society recognizes that low-fat, high-fiber diets rich in fruits and vegetables containing nutrients like vitamin C may reduce the risk of some types of cancer. 100% pure Florida orange juice is an excellent source of vitamin C and can play an important role in this type of cancer-fighting diet. 100% pure Florida orange juice. Are you drinking enough? —*from an ad by the* Florida Orange Juice Association

29. Holistic healing focuses not on getting rid of symptoms but on empowering the individual to establish a state of mental, emotional, physical, and spiritual harmony and wellness in which health is a constant in life.

30. The mission of hospice is to make the lives of the terminally ill fulfilling and comfortable. Measure 16 could offer the terminally ill a lingering, agonizing death that could drag on for days. We can do so much better than that. People should die with dignity, comfort, and peace. I'm voting no on 16.

C. Advertisements often involve claims that are carefully tailored to say much less than they may appear to say. Carefully read several ads in a national magazine—the slicker the format the better—and see if you can spot a few claims that exploit various kinds of vagueness and ambiguity. Be on the lookout for pseudo-claims and claims that involve pseudo-differentiation.

D. State the genus and difference implicit in each definition below.

(A solution to Exercise 6 is given on page 56.)

1. A full house is a poker hand consisting of three of a kind and a pair.

2. A dog is a small furry animal that barks.

3. A juvenile is a person between the ages of 11 and 17.

4. A barrister is a British lawyer who is legally empowered to argue a case in the courtroom.

5. A shirt is a garment for the upper part of the body, typically with sleeves, collar, and a front opening, and sometimes worn under a coat or another, heavier shirt.

6. Insanity is an unsoundness of mental condition that modifies or removes individual legal responsibility.
7. Pickle ball is a game played on a small court divided by a net and utilizes a small wooden racket and a whiffle ball.
8. Socialistic governments control the means of production.
9. A compromise is the sacrifice of a basic principle for a personal gain.
10. The Ojibwa are a tribe of Algonquian Indians of the Lake Superior region.

E. On the assumption that the following are intended to capture standard usage, comment on any problem you see in the following definitions. To review, a good definition will

- avoid terms having the same root as the term being defined;
- avoid terms that are obscure, relative to the term being defined;
- provide typical features in the difference and common features in the genus;
- avoid overly inclusive features in the difference;
- specify by including rather than excluding when possible; and
- clarify without expressing a bias.

Note: Once again, don't be picky. If a definition seems acceptable, say so.

(Solutions to Exercises 1 and 5 are given on page 56.)

1. A drug is a medicinal substance that can have an effect on the mind or the body.
2. A true conservative is one who seeks realistic and practical ideals.
3. Faith may be defined briefly as an illogical belief in the occurrence of the improbable. *—H. L. Mencken*
4. Behavior modification is a method of dealing with problems that are emotional, psychological, psychiatric, or physical in origin.
5. Mysticism is just tomorrow's science dreamed today.
6. A dog is a small furry animal that barks.
7. Language is any systematized combination of sounds that have a meaning for all members of a social organization.
8. *Algorithm*—any formally definable recursive function.
9. *Net*—an open fabric with the threads woven, knotted, or twisted together at regular intervals, forming meshes of varying sizes.
10. *Capital punishment*—legalized murder.
11. A cloud is a semitransparent mass with a fleecy texture suspended in the atmosphere whose shape is subject to continual and kaleidoscopic change.
12. A star is any stellar object.
13. A clock is an instrument for keeping time.
14. A normal person is one who does not act abnormally.
15. Socialism is that form of government in which the wealth of the creative and energetic is divided up among the rest of the populace.
16. Philosophically speaking, an immaterialist is a person who does not believe in the existence of a world outside the mind.
17. Rock journalism is people who can't write interviewing people who can't talk for people who can't read. *—Frank Zappa*
18. *Squarks and Sleptons*—bosonic counterparts of quarks and leptons, which must exist according to supersymmetry theory. *—from* Interactions, *by Sheldon L. Glashow*

19. Undue hardship means that an accommodation would be unduly costly, extensive, substantial, or disruptive, or would fundamentally alter the nature or operation of the business. *—from a pamphlet explaining the Americans with Disability Act of 1990*

20. As for despair, the term has a simple meaning. It means that we shall confine ourselves to reckoning only with what depends upon our will, or on the ensemble of probabilities which make our action possible. *—from* Existentialism and Human Emotions, *by Jean-Paul Sartre*

F. Clarify the word or phrase in italics in each of the statements below. In other words, define each word or phrase in a manner that is clear and consistent with the remainder of the passage. Try this strategy in arriving at your answer. First, give a list of conditions for the application of the word or phrase—a genus and a difference. Next, think of some examples referred to by the word or phrase that your proposed definition excludes or examples your definition includes that ought to be excluded. Then modify your definition and hunt for more examples. Continue until you are satisfied you have a clear definition.

(A solution to Exercise 4 is given on page 56.)

1. People often play *mind games* with one another, without even realizing they are doing so.
2. It drives me nuts when people who are essentially nothing more than skilled at their craft refer to their job as a *profession.*
3. We've all had those moments when we feel we know what is going to happen to us next, almost as though we have already been through the experience. There's nothing strange or spooky about this. It's just *déjà vu.*
4. I don't believe in the Loch Ness monster, but I'm not entirely convinced there isn't one either. You might say I'm kind of an *agnostic.*
5. The poor guy thinks of nothing but work. He doesn't even have a *hobby.*
6. Let's face it. There is no *justice* in this life. I spent most of the morning working with a student. Now I find out he has withdrawn from the class.
7. How can you tell me we live in a *democracy* when less that 40 percent of those eligible to vote ever show up at the polls?
8. Since prayer has been taken out of the public schools, we have witnessed a steady decline in *family values.*
9. Good old-fashioned American *entrepreneurship* is what has made this country great.
10. In the past two decades we have seen a steadily shrinking *middle class,* as more and more wealth is concentrated in the hands of the elite.

G. All of the passages in this exercise involve bias. Identify the words and phrases that do the most to lend the particular bias each expresses. Comment on the attitude, opinion, prejudice, and so on that seem to motivate the author of the passage.

(A solution to Exercise 7 is given on page 56.)

1. The animal-rights crowd, which is largely sympathetic toward much of the environmental fringe movement, believes there is a continuum from a mos-

quito to a rat to a boy. They seem to think that all life forms on the planet, other than human beings, peacefully coexist. —*from* The Way Things Ought To Be*, by Rush Limbaugh*

2. We need to clean up our election laws so that politicians can no longer throw millions of dollars of special-interest money at the people in an attempt to buy votes.

3. I just got off the phone with some bureaucrat from the governor's office who gave me the complete runaround when I tried to set up a private meeting with the governor.

4. I doubt that Jones will get the promotion. Sure, her department is the most productive in the company, largely because she demands so much of her people. Anybody who is that pushy doesn't have the interpersonal skills to make it in upper-level management.

5. I really get a kick out of the neat little arguments theologians give to make it look as though their belief in the supernatural is not so intellectually embarrassing after all.

6. Are you in favor of allowing construction union czars the power to shut down an entire construction site because of a dispute with a single contractor . . . thus forcing even more workers to knuckle under to union agents? —*from a questionnaire circulated by U.S. Senator Orrin Hatch, R-Utah*

7. Every time you eat a can of tuna, you implicitly endorse the slaughter of innocent dolphins that are trapped in the nets of tuna fishermen.

8. Many Republicans seem to harbor the quaint notion that running a government is just like running a business.

9. Although I oppose new taxes, I see no reason not to impose a reasonable user's fee on automobile drivers in the form of a modest increase in the price of a gallon of gasoline.

10. After a U.S. bombing raid in Cambodia in 1974, a U.S. Air Force colonel told reporters: "You always write it's bombing, bombing, bombing. It's not bombing! It's air support!" (This remark was the winner of the yearly "Doublespeak" award in 1974, given by the journal *Quarterly Review of Doublespeak.*)

SOLUTIONS

Exercise A

1. A descriptive claim
7. A request, not a claim

Exercise B

1. Vague. The problem is the phrase "limited time only." This could mean just about any period of time. About all we know for sure is that the sale is bound to end sometime.

14. Ambiguous. Humor often operates by exploiting an unintended ambiguity. (Remember that old chestnut "Take my wife . . . please"?) In this exercise, Mondale means by the phrase "in the worst way possible" something like

"something I really wanted to do." But the second statement, "and I did," is consistent with another apparently unintended reading of the first phrase. Mondale now seems to be saying he ran a poor campaign!

Exercise D

6. The genus is unsound mental conditions, and the difference is conditions that remove individual legal responsibility. Falling under the genus but not the difference might be mental conditions, such as paranoia and mood swing, that are not so serious that they require involuntary institutionalization or other legal measures.

Exercise E

1. This definition seems to include too much. First, under the genus, "medicinal substances," we will need to include anything one might take to deal with an ailment. Chicken soup, for example, will be included here. But the problem is with the difference: "having an effect on the mind or the body." Placebos and ice packs seem to meet this condition, but neither are generally considered to be drugs.

5. This is a persuasive definition. We learn nothing about what mysticism might be, but we do learn that the definition's author believes that mystics—whatever they might be—have the remarkable ability to understand things long before scientists do.

Exercise F

4. An agnostic is generally said to be a person who neither believes nor disbelieves in the existence of God, generally on the ground that there can be no evidence one way or the other. But this passage is about the Loch Ness monster, not God, and it does not suggest that there is no evidence for Nessy. It seems, rather, to suggest that agnosticism is an attitude one can hold toward anything whose existence is controversial. The definition implicit in the passage seems to be something like this:

> An agnostic is one who suspends belief in the controversial when there is insufficient evidence to warrant belief.

We might further clarify this use of *agnostic* by considering what it rules out— by thinking about what it might be to be an atheist or a theist, and not an agnostic, with respect to the Loch Ness monster.

Exercise G

7. The bias here stems from the use of two key terms: *slaughter* and *innocent.* The first brings to mind the picture of a slaughterhouse in which animals are routinely and intentionally killed and dismembered. Although some methods of fishing for tuna do result in the killing of dolphins, it hardly follows that dolphins are slaughtered. (Of course, from the fact that they are not slaughtered, it does not follow that their killing is unintentional. That dolphins will be trapped in tuna nets is predictable.) And just what is the point of describing dolphins as innocent? Could they be guilty of something for which their entrapment in tuna nets is punishment? The term is used here to get us to think of dolphins as being very much like human beings, whose lives we would never think to risk in this way. After all, the notions of innocence and guilt seem to apply in the main to human actions.

CHAPTER THREE

Assessing Arguments

The premises of an argument are meant to provide support for its conclusion by introducing evidence for its truth. To assess an argument is to decide whether or not it provides support. Two basic steps are involved in assessing an argument. First, we need to lay out the argument in terms that make clear what claims are intended to provide support and what claim is supported. We want to give a reading that avoids vagueness and ambiguity, and we want crucial terms to be properly defined. The second step is to evaluate the evidence advanced in the premises. In this chapter we concentrate on the second step but will return to the first in Chapter 4. To begin, we need to understand what it means for a set of premises to succeed in supporting a conclusion, the main topic of this chapter.

WHEN IS AN ARGUMENT ACCEPTABLE?

The point of an argument is to provide evidence that the argument's conclusion is true. To succeed, an argument must satisfy two basic requirements. First, the premises of an acceptable argument must be acceptable. An argument that depends on premises we have good reason to believe false provides little evidence for its conclusion. I doubt anyone would be impressed by this argument: "O.J. couldn't have done it. He was in London, England, on the day his wife, Nicole, was murdered in Los Angeles." In fact, there is indisputable evidence that O.J. Simpson was in the Los Angeles area that day. Second, the premises must provide us with a good reason to accept the conclusion. So, for example, we would reject this argument even though its premise is true: "Lincoln was not a great president. Though elected twice, his victories were by the narrowest of margins." The problem with this argument is that its premise does not seem to provide any reason to suppose the conclusion true. The size of Lincoln's electoral margins has little to do with the question of whether, by any definition, he was a great president.

Consider now what is involved in trying to decide whether an argument satisfies these two requirements. Imagine I have just told you I think a close friend of ours, Smith, is going to put her house up for sale. You are surprised to hear this because you know she purchased it only a year or so ago. So you ask me why I believe this. "Well," I say, "I drive by her place every day on the way to work, and twice this week I've noticed a car in the driveway with the name of a local real estate agency on it. And not just one. The second time it was a car from a different real estate agency."

Is my argument acceptable? Are you ready to accept my conclusion now that you have heard my evidence? Before answering these questions, let's set out my argument in standard form:

> On two occasions this week, the cars of real estate agencies have been parked in Smith's driveway.
>
> ---
>
> Smith is going to put her house up for sale.

To assess this argument we must think about two things: the believability of its premise and the extent to which the premise provides us with a reason to accept the conclusion.

■ *Is the premise true?* I've told you what I've seen. But is what I've reported accurate? A couple of possibilities come to mind. I may have misidentified the cars. Maybe I misread what was on the sides of the cars. So, is the premise of my argument true? Your response here depends precisely on the reasons you may have to think any of these possibilities to be likely. The stronger your suspicions, the more reason you have to think the claim I've made to be false. If you have no such suspicions, then you have every reason to accept what I've said as true. Under what conditions, then, is my premise acceptable? When we can uncover no good reason to believe it false.

■ *Does the premise provide us with a good reason to accept the conclusion?* This question is trickier. To decide whether one claim constitutes a reason for another, we must think about the relationship between the two. Our concern here is not with whether the premise or even the conclusion is, in fact, true. Rather, we are concerned with determining the likelihood the conclusion will be true, *on the assumption* that the premise is true. The inclusion of "on the assumption" here is crucial. We can think about the relationship between a premise or premises and a conclusion, even when we have good reason to believe the premises false. Think once again of an example given earlier: "O.J. couldn't have done it. He was in London, England, on the day the murder took place." Though false, the premise of this argument does, in a sense, provide a reason to accept its conclusion. For if the premise were true, it would provide a good reason to suppose the conclusion true as well!

To decide whether the premise of my argument is a *good* reason for my conclusion, we need to find a way to think about the relative likelihood of the two claims, the likelihood, that is, that the conclusion will be true *if* the premise is. The way to do this is to think of possible circumstances under which the premise would be true yet the conclusion false. The less likely such circumstances, the stronger the reason provided by the premise. Conversely, the more likely such circumstances seem to us, the weaker the reason we have to accept the conclusion. So, assuming that what I've said in the premise of my argument is true, what is the likelihood that the conclusion will be true as well? Must my conclusion be true on this assumption? Is it highly likely to be true? At all likely?

To answer these questions, we must think about possible reasons why real estate agents might be parked in Smith's driveway even though she is not contemplating selling her house. A number of possibilities come to mind. Maybe she's thinking about going into the real estate business and so is talking with representatives of various companies. Perhaps she has friends who work for the companies in question and they both just happened to visit in the same week. Or it may be that the real estate agents' visits were unsolicited. Maybe the agents were canvassing the area, trying to find new properties to put on the market.

What, then, are we to say about the "evidence" provided by my argument? Do we accept it or reject it? Is the support I have provided acceptable or unacceptable, weak or strong, or in between? These are not easy questions to answer. But this much at least seems clear: The support I have provided is acceptable only to the extent we can rule out the possibilities just described. The stronger, the more likely, any of them are, the less compelling my evidence.

This example illustrates two important points about argument criticism. The first is that an acceptable argument is, in large measure, one we have no good reason to believe unacceptable. To decide whether the premises of an argument are true, we must consider the circumstances under which they would be false. The less likely such circumstances are, the more likely the premises are to be true. Similarly, to decide whether premises provide a good reason to accept the conclusion, we must think about circumstances under which the conclusion would be false even if the premises were true. Once again, the less probable those circumstances, the stronger the evidence provided by the premises.

The second point is that argument criticism is often not a matter of characterizing the argument as correct or mistaken. (There are bound to be exceptions to this rule—arguments in which one or more of the premises is false or in which the premises conspicuously fail to provide a reason to adopt the conclusion.) Argument criticism often involves gauging the *strength* of the evidence offered in the premises. This we do by thinking carefully about the likelihood of circumstances that would undermine the support—circumstances in which the premises would be false and circumstances in which the conclusion would be false even though the premises were true. The material that follows in this chapter is a series of suggestions that should help you decide about the strengths and weaknesses of an argument.

ASSESSING PREMISES → exception directives

Claims are either true or false. Ideally, we would like the claims that constitute the premises of an argument to be true. Indeed, we would not accept as evidence a claim we have good reason to believe false. But the truth of a claim can be difficult to determine with certainty. Restricted to those claims about which we are absolutely certain, we would neither accept nor be able to mount many acceptable arguments. A more workable requirement is that the claims constituting the premises of an acceptable argument must be plausible. A **plausible** claim is one we have good reason to believe true or, at any rate, no good reason to believe false.

How, then, do we decide whether a claim is sufficiently plausible to be accepted as evidence? Imagine, for example, that I want to convince you the government needs to make interest-free loans available to college students. Among the "facts" I cite to make my case lurks the following:

> In real dollars, adjusted for inflation, the average cost of a college education has nearly tripled in the past fifteen years.

Just how do we set about determining whether this claim is true? It is not obviously true nor would it be easy to verify. Suppose you were sent to the library to check out this claim. After deciding on source material—say, an almanac, encyclopedia, or statistical database—how would you isolate the facts and figures you need from the mass of information at your disposal? And if your search came up empty, where would you turn? Of course, these are difficulties we rarely have the luxury of pondering, for we seldom have the time, inclination, or interest to check the "facts" with which we are confronted.

A good rule of thumb to follow in assessing the accuracy of purported statements of fact is to accept a claim only as long as there is no good reason to believe it suspect. This rule tells us that the plausibility of a claim is in inverse proportion to the reasons we may have to believe it false; the greater our doubts about a claim, the less its overall plausibility. Thus, the claim about the cost of a college education should be treated as being somewhat suspect because common sense suggests that something is amiss. Very few costs increase this dramatically in such a short period of time, particularly when adjusted for inflation. Does this mean the claim is false? Of course not. It does mean that its plausibility is questionable and that we probably should not accept it at face value.

Don't underestimate the value of common sense in thinking about the plausibility of a claim. If a claim seems at odds with our overall understanding of things or with our experiences and observations, we have reason to question its plausibility. Recently, I heard of a new weight-loss program that offers a "money-back guarantee." It claims I will be able to lose twenty pounds in two weeks with no reduction in calorie intake and no need to exercise. Now, I must confess, I have tried to lose weight on more than one occasion. My experience strongly suggests that, short of surgery, there are two ways to do this: eat less or exercise more. Thus, given what I have learned and experienced in the past when trying to lose weight, I have a good reason to be suspicious about the claims made in behalf of this amazing new weight-loss program. As this example suggests, we need to be wary of claims that seem too good to be true.

Other than using common sense, how do we decide when a claim is suspect? There are several telltale signs. Claims that exceed a reasonable level of precision should be questioned. Suppose I tell you that 43.5 percent of all Americans falsify information on their income tax returns. No doubt some people do falsify information, and it may be possible to come up with some reasonable estimate of the percentage who do, but my estimate seems much more precise than anything we might reasonably hope for. We should also be suspicious of claims that make heavy use of the kinds of qualifying devices discussed in Chapter 2. Claims that are comparatively vague and claims that involve weasels may be designed to mask the fact that their authors are unsure about the truth of what they are saying.

We can often gain some sense of the plausibility of a claim by considering its source, its author. Sometimes, information about the author will suggest that a claim is true, particularly when the author is an expert on the topic at issue in a claim. By contrast we may be justified in questioning a claim when its author has some vested interest in its truth. Suppose I want to convince you that every college student should take a course in critical thinking. Coincidentally, I make my living

> ### CONUNDRUM
>
> The best we can do by way of verifying most claims is to determine that they are highly plausible. Are there claims we can properly say we *are certain* are true? Can you think of any examples? Before you begin to hunt for possible candidates, think about what it might be about a claim that would prompt us to conclude that it is certain as opposed to being highly plausible.

teaching and writing textbooks for such courses. I cite the fact that "reliable studies have shown" nearly all college freshmen cannot read and comprehend arguments of the sort found in sources like letters to the editor. Am I to be believed? Perhaps. But given the argument I am trying to advance and its close connection to my financial interests, it seems possible I am exaggerating in order to dramatically make my point. The issues surrounding the question of when to accept expertise and what sorts of personal information may be relevant in assessing claims are complex. We will return to these issues in our discussion of fallacies of relevance in Chapter 5.

Keep in mind, in thinking about the plausibility of a claim, that we are not restricted to two possible outcomes: true or false. A claim may strike us as being highly plausible, remotely possible, or somewhere in between. How, for example, would you rate the plausibility of the claim that there is intelligent life elsewhere in the universe? On one hand, we have the fact that no such intelligence has been detected and that, as far as we can tell, only one of the five million or so species that have developed on Earth has this capacity. On the other, we have the fact that the universe is such an immense place that it could contain a huge number of planets with similar conditions to our own. Is it that unlikely intelligence would develop elsewhere? No matter where we come down on this question, the claim that there is other intelligent life in the universe seems neither preposterous nor a near certainty.

Don't fall prey to the assumption that a claim should be rejected if it is *conceivable* that it is false. I suppose it is at least conceivable, for example, that George Washington was not really President of the United States. It is possible this is a bit of propaganda cooked up by a group of powerful conspirators. But although this is barely conceivable, it does not make the preceding claim implausible. There is just too much confirming evidence that Washington was indeed President. To establish the implausibility of this claim, we would need to mount a case of greater strength than that provided by all the evidence that the claim is accurate. Remember, our rule of thumb is that there must be good reason to believe a claim suspect before it can be regarded as lacking plausibility.

In the end, our rule may lead us to accept a claim that is false or even to reject a claim that is true. But these are risks we always run given that we lack the time and resources to investigate every claim we are asked to accept. At the very least, our rule of thumb should prevent us from rejecting claims unless we have good reason to do so.

ASSESSING INFERENTIAL STRENGTH: THE MAIN METHOD

In thinking about the possible weaknesses of an argument, we must consider not only the plausibility of its premises, but also whether or not the premises provide us with a good reason to accept the conclusion. When we contemplate the relationship between a set of premises and a conclusion, we are thinking about the **inference** from premises to conclusion. The question of whether an inference is acceptable can be raised apart from the question of whether the premises on which it is based are true or false; it can be framed in a way that sets aside the question of whether or not the premises are true. *Would the premises, assuming they were true, entitle us to accept the conclusion as well?* It is one thing for a set of premises to be highly plausible and quite another for the inference from premises to conclusion to be reasonable.

Inferential Strength

Thinking about the inference implicit in an argument is complicated by the fact that inferential **strength** is often a matter of degree. The inferential link between a set of premises and a conclusion can be so strong that the conclusion is a certainty, provided the premises are true. Consider, for example, this argument:

> The value of the stock I've just purchased in company X will increase by at least 25 percent in each of the next four years.
>
> ---
>
> The money I've invested in X will more than double in value within four years.

If the premise of this argument is true, the conclusion must be true as well. Now, the chances that the premise is indeed true seem quite low. Despite this, the inference from premise to conclusion is ironclad. It would be impossible for the premises to be true—for the value of the stock to increase by 25 percent in each of the next four years—and the conclusion false—for my investment in that stock to fail to double in the same period of time.

A set of premises need not provide an airtight reason in order to provide a reasonably strong level of support for a conclusion. Consider another argument:

> Smith and I have been meeting for lunch once a week for months now.
>
> Smith is almost always late.
>
> ---
>
> Smith will be late for our lunch date today.

Even if the premises of this argument are true, it is possible that its conclusion will be false. Despite Smith's track record, she may show up on time today. But from the fact that my conclusion may turn out to be false, it does not follow that the inference implicit in the argument is incorrect or unreasonable. If the premises are true, it seems at least highly likely that the conclusion will be true as well, all things being equal. (All things would not be equal, for example, if we had some reason to believe that Smith will make an extra effort to be on time today.) Thus, an inference can be acceptable even when it does not entitle us to rule out the possibility that the conclusion of the argument is false.

It may seem that the inference implicit in the preceding argument is fairly weak. From the fact that Smith is *almost always* late it does not follow that Smith *will* be late today. What does follow, instead, is that Smith is *likely* to be late. But these two versions of the conclusion involve the same claim:

Smith will be late.

Where the versions of the claim differ is in the qualification with which each is issued. **Qualifiers** are words and phrases used to express an arguer's level of confidence in the truth of his or her conclusion, given the evidence provided by the premises. These are frequently used qualifiers:

It is probable that

It is possible that

It is almost certainly the case that

It is likely that

It is highly likely that

It is unlikely that

There is a good chance that

There is a(n) ___ percent chance that

It must be the case that

Don't confuse qualifiers with a notion discussed in Chapter 2, weasels. The point of a qualifier is not to weasel out of anything. The point is to make clear how likely an arguer thinks his or her conclusion is, given the evidence in the premises. Note also that a properly qualified conclusion strengthens the inference, often, however, at the expense of a much less sensational conclusion. So, in the preceding argument, the evidence is much stronger when offered in defense of

It is highly likely that Smith will be late

than of the more dramatic

No doubt about it. Smith is going to be late.

When we are thinking about the strength of an inference, it is crucial to keep in mind the qualification with which a conclusion issues. It will take a much stronger case to reject a carefully qualified conclusion. The same factors that may show a conclusion to be *somewhat unlikely,* given the truth of the premises, may not show it to be *highly unlikely.*

One fact about qualified conclusions may at first seem paradoxical. Imagine that I have observed several unusual facts about my next-door neighbors: Their newspaper has not been collected for several days, their lawn has not been mowed, and their car has not been driven. From this I conclude that the neighbors must not be at home. Suppose, however, it turns out that they were at home; several days later I talked with them and discovered they were preoccupied with a personal matter and didn't bother with their normal routine. We must not be too quick to reject my inference as incorrect. From the facts with which I began, it may follow that it was highly likely the neighbors were not at home. That my conclusion turned out to be wrong does not mean my inference itself was incorrect. Given the facts at my disposal, it was reasonable for me to conclude that the neighbors were not at home. Thus, if it turns out that the neighbors were home after all, I can reasonably reply, "Well, given the facts, I was at least right in thinking the evidence pointed in the direction of their not being home."

To take another example, a weather forecast can make a great deal of sense yet be wrong. "There is an 80 percent chance of rain tomorrow," the meteorologist predicts, pointing to a satellite photo in which a storm front is moving our way. The inference here seems right. But the next day it does not rain. Nonetheless, there is a sense in which the forecast was the right one to make. Curiously, in the circumstances we have imagined, a forecast that turned out to be correct would have been inferentially incorrect! If the evidence strongly suggests rain, a prediction to the contrary would be unwarranted.

Of course, a failed inference cannot always be saved by claiming it was intended to establish only the likelihood of its conclusion. Returning to the example about the neighbors, suppose I had based my inference about them on nothing more than, say, the fact that yesterday's paper had not been picked up. In this circumstance my inference would be unwarranted, despite any protestations I might make that I only intended it to establish the probability of my conclusion.

How to Test an Inference

Every argument is advanced with the tacit assumption that its inference is reasonable— that its premises, if true, constitute a reason to accept its conclusion. To assess an inference we must arrive at some estimate of its strength. Just how confident can we be that the conclusion will be true, provided the premises are true? A simple, general method that will enable us to decide about the strength of most inferences is to ask if there are circumstances under which the premises of the argument would be true but the conclusion false. After isolating any such circumstances, we must estimate their likelihood. As a general rule, the credibility of the case we build against a particular inference will be in proportion to the likelihood of the circumstances we come up with. The more realistic the circumstances, the weaker the inference. Conversely, the less likely such circumstances are, the stronger the inference.

Note that our test involves two distinct steps. For any argument

$$\frac{P_1 \dots P_n}{C}$$

we must think about two things to estimate the strength of its inference:

1. circumstances under which $P_1 \dots P_n$ would be true but C would be false,
2. the likelihood of these circumstances.

In thinking about the likelihood of any circumstances we come up with, keep in mind that all possibilities are not equally likely. A set of circumstances that are only remotely likely to occur provide little reason to reject an inference.

Now, let's consider the results our test yields when applied to a few arguments. The following passage is taken from a book, *See, I Told You So,* by Rush Limbaugh, a popular radio personality. In this passage, Limbaugh is trying to determine the approximate number of people who attended a fund-raiser called Dan's Bake Sale:

> We can argue about how many people were there. No one will ever know for sure because the event was unprecedented in the annals of Old Town Square in Fort Collins. The local authorities estimated that at least 35,000 showed up. The media reports generally guessed at between 25,000 and 45,000. Let me tell you a few reasons why I know there were considerably more—probably at least 65,000. First of all, my staff took 25,000 copies of *The Limbaugh Letter* and gave them away. Many people didn't get one, so you know there had to be considerably more than 25,000 in attendance.[1]

The passage presents three estimates of the number of people who showed up at the bake sale. Sticking with the most conservative estimate, we can set out the argument of the passage as follows:

> Limbaugh's staff gave away 25,000 copies of *The Limbaugh Letter.*
>
> Many people in attendance did not get a copy of *The Limbaugh Letter.*
> ___
> Considerably more than 25,000 people were at Dan's Bake Sale.

At first glance, the inference implicit in this argument may seem unproblematic. Limbaugh is only venturing an estimate, and a modest one at that, given other estimates available.

But are there realistic circumstances under which we can accept the information in the premises and yet deny the conclusion? In other words, is it feasible to suppose that 25,000 copies of *The Limbaugh Letter* were distributed, that many people did not get a copy, but that considerably *fewer* than 25,000 were at the bake sale? A moment's reflection turns up an interesting possibility. Whenever I pick up free literature—particularly literature that is controversial and, even better, that normally costs something—I tend to pick up several copies, some for friends and some, I must admit, just because they are free. I suspect many people do the same thing. In light of this new information, the inference in Limbaugh's argument looks questionable. Even if the premises are true, it seems likely that the conclusion is false.

Is the inference in Limbaugh's argument, then, unreasonable? This is not an easy question to answer. The answer depends on the number of people who took multiple copies of *The Limbaugh Letter.* If, say, we had reason to believe that people were limited to a single copy (suppose Limbaugh supporters were handing them out, one to a customer), then the conclusion might follow. All things considered, it seems unlikely that pains were taken at the bake sale to make sure nobody received more than one copy of *The Limbaugh Letter.* Had such pains been taken, Limbaugh probably would have mentioned this fact as a way of strengthening his argument. But all of this is, of course, speculation. Perhaps the argument involves nothing more than an honest oversight, a failure to include a fact crucial to the inference.

___

[1]Rush Limbaugh, *See, I Told You So* (New York: Simon and Schuster, 1993), p. 104.

Completeness

The example we have just considered underscores the importance of providing *all* the information on which an inference is based. If a crucial piece of information is missing—as in the case of Limbaugh's argument—the audience for the argument will be left to wonder whether the author is intentionally suppressing something or is simply unaware of a potential weakness in the argument.

An argument is **complete** when its premises contain all the information on which the inference from premises to conclusion is based. A good rule of thumb to follow in thinking about the completeness of an argument is this: An argument is probably incomplete if it is unclear why the argument's author thinks the inference a reasonable one. (Whether its author thinks the argument complete is another matter. As we have seen, an arguer may simply fail to consider something necessary for the inference.) Suppose, for example, a sportscaster were to predict that the Yankees will win the league championship since they are five games ahead of the second-place team, the Red Sox. As you may know, each team plays 162 games during the regular baseball season. If both teams have only a few games left to play—say, fewer than ten each—the inference is relatively strong. But if the teams have played only a few games—if it is near the beginning of the season—the inference is much weaker. Whether the inference is weak or strong, the argument is incomplete as originally stated. It does not provide us with all the information necessary to understand what its inference involves.

Keep in mind here that a complete version of an argument need not include every piece of information that suggests its conclusion is true. Returning to the previous example, there may be other reasons to think the Yankees will win the pennant. Perhaps several key players on the Red Sox have been injured of late and there is no other team close to the Yankees in the standings. But these facts are not relevant to the inference implicit in the argument under consideration. They may, however, form the basis of other arguments for the claim that the Yankees will win the championship.

Thinking About Broad, Underlying Assumptions

It may be necessary, in assessing the strength of an inference, to think about issues and circumstances of a more general sort than those mentioned in the argument. Consider the following letter to the editor:

> To the editor: Our government has no business funding abortions. A recent poll reveals that nearly 80 percent of all Americans oppose abortion outright or believe that the federal government should not help to pay for abortions.

The argument of this letter is, at first glance, quite simple:

> Nearly 80 percent of all Americans oppose abortion or believe that the federal government should not fund abortions.
> _____
> Government should not provide funding for abortions.

The first thing to note is that the premise seems too good to be true. It is doubtful that 80 percent of Americans would agree to anything on a topic this controversial. But for purposes of investigating the premise's underlying inference, let's ignore this problem. How reliable is this inference? Applying our test, we begin by thinking about whether we can imagine circumstances in which the premise would be true yet the conclusion false. Can we, that is, come up with circumstances under which we could grant that most Americans oppose abortion or abortion funding yet deny that the government should continue to fund abortions?

If we confine our thinking to the topic at issue in the argument—abortion—we will make little headway in assessing its inference. I suppose we could simply grant the premise yet deny the conclusion: "I'll admit that most Americans oppose abortion, but I still think the government should provide abortion funding." But what would our rationale be? What reason might there be to take this position other than sheer pigheadedness? If we are to show the inference behind this argument to be questionable, we must show that one can *reasonably* embrace the premise yet deny the conclusion. The way to do this is to think about the broad principle on which the inference is based. According to the argument, the government should not fund abortions because the majority of Americans are opposed to abortion. Why does the argument's author believe this? Presumably, because he or she believes that, in general, government policy should reflect the beliefs of the majority of the people.

Having framed the issue in this way, it should be apparent what kind of evidence we would need to show the inference problematic: cases in which a government-mandated policy would be justified even though the majority of people opposed it, but cases other than the one mentioned in the argument. What if the majority of the people opposed laws prohibiting discrimination on account of race, religion, or gender? Or what if the majority favored imposing restrictions on free speech? Would the government be wrong to enact laws protecting free speech or prohibiting discrimination? Now, the cases we have imagined are not that realistic. Doubtless, most Americans favor laws prohibiting discrimination and guaranteeing free speech. Nevertheless, these cases do suggest a problem for the inference implicit in the argument. We can grant its premise yet deny its conclusion on the ground that there are circumstances in which governmental laws and policies need not reflect the will of the people.

But from this consideration, we cannot conclude that the inference implicit in the argument is weak. At best, we have shown that the argument is incomplete and that other issues need to be considered to gauge the strength of its inference. Before we can decide about the inference, we need additional information. We need to know why the argument's author believes the case he or she is interested in—government funding of abortion—is unlike the cases we have imagined. In what kinds of cases should governmental policy reflect the will of the people, and in what kinds of cases should policy supersede majority opinion? And what is it about abortion that makes the argument's author think it is a case of the former sort?

Note, by the way, that the conclusion of the argument is not qualified. The argument's author does not argue that it is *probable, likely,* or whatever that the government should not fund abortions. Rather, the author's intent seems to be to introduce a consideration that he or she thinks counts strongly against the appropriateness of government funding for abortions. (Does he or she think the conclusion a certainty? Perhaps, though a reading of the conclusion that contains some qualifier to this effect seems strained. "*I'm certain that* the government should not fund abortions" or "*It must be the case that* the government should not fund abortions" seem artificial and

CONUNDRUM

To think about the inference of an argument, we need to consider the likelihood of circumstances in which the premises would be true and the conclusion false. But what if the premises of an argument are highly implausible? Consider the following argument:

World population will soon stabilize and then gradually begin to shrink.

New technological breakthroughs will enable us to provide adequate food, clothing, and shelter to all the people of the world without depleting natural resources or polluting the environment.

In the near future, we will no longer be doing the sort of damage to the environment of our planet we are now doing.

Is there a way to assess the inference of this argument, given that both of its premises seem highly unlikely?

forced.) Nevertheless, the issue before us remains the likelihood that the conclusion will be true when the premise is false.

Our test for inferential strength is not going to enable us to give a precise estimate of the strength of every inference. Often, as our last example suggests, it will enable us only to arrive at a sense of other issues that must be explored if an inference is to be assessed. Moreover, just because we cannot find a problem with the inference implicit in an argument, it does not follow that there is no problem. We may simply not know enough about the topic at issue to have spotted the problem, or we may have overlooked something. However, our test will, in many cases, prompt us to ask the right questions, questions that stand a good chance of unearthing substantial difficulties that may surround an inference.

ASSESSING INFERENTIAL STRENGTH: AN ALTERNATIVE METHOD

The method we have introduced for assessing inferential strength has focused on the search for circumstances under which the premises of an argument might be true and the conclusion false. The more likely such circumstances, the more questionable the inference. There is, however, an alternative technique we can use in assessing the strength of an inference. Earlier, we noted that every argument is advanced with the tacit assumption that its inference is reasonable—that its premises, if true, constitute a reason to accept its conclusion. Another way to investigate the inference is to make the assumption explicit and then to estimate its plausibility. How do we make the assumption explicit? Consider again the generalized schemata for argument:

$$\frac{P_1 \dots P_n}{C}$$

Under what conditions would $P_1 \dots P_n$ constitute evidence for *C?* When it is hard to imagine circumstances under which $P_1 \dots P_n$ would be true yet *C* false? When we have reason to suppose the following claim to be true:

If $P_1 \dots P_n$ are the case, **then** *C* also will be the case.

Claims having the form

If (   )$_1$, then (   )$_2$

are called **hypothetical,** or **conditional,** claims. They assert neither that what is in (   )$_1$ is the case nor that what is in (   )$_2$ is the case. But they are claims nonetheless—claims about the conditions or circumstances under which (   )$_2$ will be the case. So, for example,

If it is 6 P.M., then the news is on

claims neither that it is 6 P.M. nor that the news is on. What it does claim is that if it is 6 P.M., then the news is on. Like any claim, a hypothetical claim can be assessed for plausibility. Under what conditions would

If (   )$_1$, then (   )$_2$

be false? Conditions under which (   )$_1$ would be true yet (   )$_2$ false. Under what conditions would

If it is 6 P.M., then the news is on

be false? If it is 6 P.M. but the news is *not* on.

Under what conditions, then, would the inference implicit in

$$\frac{P_1 \dots P_n}{C}$$

be suspect? Precisely the conditions under which the hypothetical claim

if $P_1 \dots P_n$, then *C*

would be false. So, to investigate the inference behind an argument, we can formulate a hypothetical claim to the effect that the conclusion will be true when the premises are true and then think about its plausibility. The less likely the hypothetical claim is to be true, the more suspect the inference implicit in the argument.

This simple example utilizes our second method for testing inferences:

Charlie is a member of the U.S. Marine Corps.

Charlie is at least eighteen years old.

The conclusion of this argument will follow from its premise if it is true that

> If Charlie is a member of the U.S. Marine Corps, then he is at least eighteen years old.

If this claim is true, the inference in the argument seems quite strong. By the way, is it true? The claim is true only if there are no exceptions to this age requirement—only, that is, if everyone who is a member of the U.S. Marine Corps is at least eighteen years old. We could, then, have just as easily given one of these more generalized claims as the basis of the inference:

> If *one* is to be a U.S. marine, one must be at least eighteen years old

or

> *Anyone* who is a U.S. marine must be at least eighteen years old.

In using this second method, we must consider any qualification that occurs in conjunction with the conclusion. Consider, for example, this argument:

> Charlie is in the U.S. Marine Corps and has a college degree.
> _____
> Charlie is *probably* an officer.

How strong is the inference in this argument? Suppose we gave the following as the hypothetical claim corresponding to the premise and conclusion:

> If Charlie is a marine and has a college degree, he is an officer.

On this reading the inference is faulty, for this claim is undoubtedly false. A more accurate reading, in light of the qualifier in the conclusion, would be

> *It is probable* that if Charlie is a marine and has a college degree, he is an officer.

This qualified version seems much more plausible than the earlier version. Can we conclude, then, that the inference is strong? Not yet. To get a sense of how strong this inference is we would need more information. How probable is it that a marine with a college degree will be an officer? What percentage of such marines are officers? If the percentage is high enough, it may be reasonable to conclude that Charlie is an officer, given that we have no other information about Charlie on which to base our conclusion. (Many non-officers in all branches of the military go to college as preparation for careers outside the military. Is there any reason to think this of Charlie? If so, we may need to reassess the inference in the preceding argument.)

Our second method of thinking about inferential strength will yield the same result as the main method, when both are applied to the same argument. To see this, consider again an argument used to illustrate the main method:

> Nearly 80 percent of all Americans oppose abortion or believe that the federal government should not fund abortions.
> _____
> Government should not provide funding for abortions.

The corresponding hypothetical claim is lengthy.

If nearly 80 percent of all Americans oppose abortion or believe that the federal government should not fund abortions, then the government should not provide funding for abortions.

The plausibility of this claim seems to depend on whether we can find a general principle of which it is an instance, something like

If a clear majority oppose something, the government should not fund that thing.

Under what conditions would this more general hypothetical claim be false? It would be at least suspect if it turns out there are cases in which a government policy or program might reasonably be at odds with the attitude of the majority. If we can unearth such cases, we might then try to redefine the general principle above so that it can accommodate those cases.

If a clear majority oppose something, the government should not fund that thing, unless, that is, the thing involves . . . .

At the least, we should be able to arrive at a sense of the issues that must be resolved before we can determine the strength of the inferential assumption made by this argument. Note that the sorts of cases and issues we will want to think about are precisely those cases and issues we were led to consider by applications of the main method to this argument.

DEDUCTION AND INDUCTION

Many discussions of inference begin by distinguishing between two types of argument to which correspond distinct standards for inferential correctness. These are *deductive* and *inductive* argument.

A correct **deductive argument** is one in which the inference from premises to conclusion is **valid;** if the premises are true, the conclusion must be true as well. Here is an example of a valid argument:

(1) All critical thinking teachers are independently wealthy.

I am a critical thinking teacher.

I am independently wealthy.

One of the premises of this argument is, alas, false. But the argument is nonetheless valid. If both premises were true, the conclusion would have to be true as well. In addition to involving a valid inference, a correct deductive argument has premises that are themselves true. An argument that is valid and has all true premises is called a **sound** argument.

(2) All the planets in our solar system trace out roughly elliptical orbits around the sun.

The Earth is a planet in our solar system.

The Earth traces out a roughly elliptical orbit around the sun.

Since both of the premises of (2) are true, we can rest assured that the conclusion is true as well. Thus, whereas (2) is sound, (1) is **unsound.** Despite the fact that (1) is valid, it does not establish its conclusion because one of its premises is false.

Validity is the product of certain purely *formal* features of an argument's structure. An argument's **form** is made up of those aspects of the argument that can be represented in abstract from its **content,** that is, from what it is about. Argument (2) is *about* the Earth and the other planets and the shape of their orbits around the sun. The form (2) exemplifies is

(3) All A's are B's.

x is an A.
_____

x is a B.

Note first that (3) is a general form, a form shared with other arguments. Argument (1) is also an instance of (3). What makes (3) valid are the meanings of certain key terms—all and is—and the positions of the letters that stand for the substantive notions that are the argument's content—A, B, and x. You can convince yourself of the validity of (3) by thinking of it in terms of our first test for inferential strength. Can you imagine circumstances in which every A is a B and in which x is an A but not a B? The fact that such circumstances are unimaginable shows that (3) is indeed a valid form. The importance of the positions of A and B can be seen by examining what happens when they are reversed in the first premise. The result

(4) All B's are A's.

x is an A.
_____

x is a B.

is not a valid form. We can easily imagine circumstances in which although all B's are A's, x need not be a B even if it is an A. To do so, substitute just about anything for A and B and consider the result. Here is one possibility:

(5) All lawyers have graduated from college.

x has graduated from college.
_____

x is a lawyer.

Obviously, many people who have graduated from college become something other than lawyers.

A good **inductive argument,** in contrast to a deductive argument, is one in which the premises provide grounds for thinking the conclusion probable. Unfortunately, it is hard to say much in general about what makes an inductive argument strong. This is because inductive strength, unlike deductive validity, is a matter of degree. Some inductive arguments are stronger than others. To make matters worse, the reasons a given inductive inference is strong cannot be captured in a representation of its form. Consider, for example, the following inductive argument:

The proofs of mathematics are instances of deductive reasoning. Here is an example that illustrates the power and elegance of mathematical proof. Think of a standard chess or checkerboard. On the board there will be 32 white and 32 black squares. Imagine now that we have removed two opposite corner squares—one from the top left and one from the bottom right side. Since the opposite corners of a 64-square playing board are the same color, both of the squares we have removed will be black or white, depending on how we set up the board originally. Next, imagine you are given 31 dominoes, each shaped to cover two squares. Is it possible to arrange the 31 dominoes so that they cover the remaining 62 squares on the board? Here is a proof that this cannot be done. Let's assume we have removed the two white corner squares, although the proof would be the same had we begun by removing the two opposite black corner squares.

- The corners that were removed from the board were both white. Therefore, there are now 32 black squares and only 30 white squares.
- Each domino covers two neighboring squares, and neighboring squares are always of different colors.
- Therefore, no matter how they are arranged, the first 30 dominoes laid on the board must cover 30 white squares and 30 black squares.
- Consequently, you will always be left with one domino and two black squares.
- But all dominoes cover two neighboring squares, and neighboring squares are opposite in color. However, the two squares remaining are the same color, and so they cannot both be covered by the one remaining domino.
- Therefore, covering the board with 31 dominoes is impossible.*

With a bit of work, each step in this proof could be rewritten so that it displays a valid form involving true premises. The conclusion of each step then becomes one of the premises of the following step.

*Many thanks to Simon Singh for this version of the proof in *Fermat's Enigma* (New York: Anchor Books, 1997).

(6) Eighty percent of the students at this college had a high school GPA of 3.5 or higher.

Smith is a student at this college.

Smith has a high school GPA of 3.5 or higher.

By deductive standards, (6) is invalid. It is not difficult to imagine circumstances in which both of its premises might be true yet its conclusion false. How strong, then, is the inference implicit in (6)?

Although many (but by no means all) inductive arguments have recognizable forms, their strengths and weaknesses do not derive from their formal structure.[2] We might, for example, give the following as the form of (6):

(7) N percent of all A's are B's.

x is an A.
————————————

x is a B.

Knowing only this about (6), we cannot gauge its inferential strength. To determine its strength we would need to know, first of all, what percentage N represents.[3] Fortunately we do know this: Eighty percent of all A's are B's. But even this information is not enough to allow us to decide about the strength of the inference. We need to know what A, B, and x represent, and we may also need other information from the background against which the argument is given. Suppose, for example, that students whose parents are alumni and students with very high SAT scores are often admitted to the college in question despite having a GPA below 3.5. Suppose also that there are a few other minor exceptions to the 3.5 GPA requirement. To determine the strength of (6) in these circumstances, we would need to know whether there is any reason to think that Smith is among any of the groups for whom exceptions are made. If we can find no such reason, the inference looks strong. Conversely, the more reason we have to suspect Smith may be an exceptional case, the weaker the inference.

The circumstances we have imagined for (6) are just that—imagined. But every inductive argument is given against a particular factual background, and to this we must turn if we are to think about the inferential strength of an inductive argument. This, then, is a crucial difference between deductive validity and inductive strength. Validity can be determined by reference to an argument's form alone. Knowing that an argument is of the form

(5) All A's are B's.

x is an A.
—————————

x is a B.

we have everything we need to determine the correctness of its inference. To decide about the strength of an inductive argument, we must look beyond its form to the content of the claims it involves and to the backdrop of facts against which it is given. Thus, knowing that an argument is of the form

(7) N percent of all A's are B's.

x is an A.
————————————

x is a B.

we are not yet in a position to decide about the strength of the inference it involves.

---

[2]In Chapters 8 and 9, we will discuss several common forms inductive arguments take as well as the nonformal considerations that are relevant in thinking about the strengths and weaknesses of such argments.

[3]That inductive strength is a matter of degree can be seen by plugging in different percentages, higher than 50, for N. "Ninety percent of all A's are B's and x is an A" provides stronger support for "x is a B" than does "Fifty-one percent of all A's are B's and x is an A."

It may seem that the deduction/induction distinction has little cash value, beyond its usefulness in illustrating some important points about inferential strength. After all, most of the arguments people give are inductive. Generally, arguments are given in circumstances where there is some question about the truth of the claim at issue. It is hard to imagine that in such a context an argument can do more than provide a measure of evidence for its conclusion. But although most of the arguments we are likely to give and encounter are not going to be deductively valid, the notion of deductive validity can help us to think about their strengths and weaknesses.

Often, in working with an argument, it's useful to reconstruct it so that it is deductively valid. Indeed, this is the strategy we adopted in the previous section. To think about the hypothetical claim corresponding to a set of premises and a conclusion is to think about what would make the argument deductively valid. The addition of

If $P_1 \ldots P_n$, then C

to

$$\frac{P_1 \ldots P_n}{C}$$

yields a deductively valid argument of the form

(8) If $P_1 \ldots P_n$, then C

$$\frac{P_1 \ldots P_n}{C}$$

(8) is a valid form since there are no conceivable circumstances under which claims for the form

If $P_1 \ldots P_n$, then C

and

$P_1 \ldots P_n$

could be true while C is false.

Once we have provisionally rewritten an argument so that it displays a deductively valid form, we can begin to think of how the premises and conclusion of the valid first draft will need to be modified. What changes do we need to make our reading of the argument reflect the author's thinking and whatever information we have from the argument's factual background? Having arrived at an accurate reading, we will be able to think about the merits of the argument's underlying inference. Thus, the notion of deductive validity can be of considerable practical value. No doubt most of the arguments people give are not going to be deductively valid. Nonetheless, it will often be worthwhile to anchor our initial thinking about the inference of an argument in a consideration of what would make the argument deductively valid.

STRONG AND WEAK REFUTATION

To assess an argument we must think about two things: Are there reasons to think any of its premises implausible? Are there reasons to think its inference problematic? On occasion we may encounter arguments that are so poorly thought out, we must reject them on the ground that their premises are clearly false or provide little or no support for the conclusion. Or we may reject an argument on the ground that it involves one of the fallacies we will discuss in Chapters 5 through 10. Frequently, however, this type of **strong refutation** is not going to be possible.[4]

Keep in mind, arguments are usually given for controversial claims. This means that there will probably be interesting and plausible arguments available both for and against the claim at issue. Thus, many of the arguments we assess are not going to be altogether unreasonable or implausible. Our goal in assessing such an argument is to offer **weak refutation.** This involves bringing to light any grounds there might be for reasonable doubt about the argument, rather than grounds for wholesale rejection. It may also involve thinking about the argument against the background of its rivals. You've probably had the unsettling experience of holding a view, only to discover that a stronger case can be made for an opposed view. It is possible that an argument may strike us as credible in part because we are unfamiliar with the opposed view. Thus, one way to think about problems an argument may face is to review arguments that may be directed against the conclusion at issue.

As we have seen, argument criticism can take a number of approaches. It may involve giving reasons to believe the inference or one or more of the premises suspect. It may simply involve raising issues that demand further exploration before we can decide about the inference or the acceptability of the argument's premises. Or it can take a more indirect course: We may be able to uncover plausible arguments for views contrary to what is at issue. An effective way of arguing, for example, against voting for a particular candidate would be to show that there are better reasons to vote for an opponent. Our goal in this indirect approach is to show that, on balance, a stronger case can be made against the conclusion of the argument at issue than for it.

But no matter what strategy we pursue in assessing an argument, our work will require that we give our own arguments. To question the plausibility of a claim or the reasonableness of an inference is to *argue* against that claim or inference. And so the very standards we apply in criticizing the work of others we must also heed in giving our criticisms.

Our goal should not be to pick holes in a view with which we disagree, although if real holes we find, so be it. Rather, our goal should be to utilize our critical thinking skills to come to better understand the view under criticism *and* the basis of our response to that view.

---

[4]I am indebted to Douglas N. Walton for pointing out how very unlike strong refutations are interesting and insightful critiques of arguments. See Chapter 1 of his *Informal Logic: A Handbook for Critical Argumentation* (Cambridge: Cambridge University Press, 1989).

Though lighthearted, the criticism contained in the following letter is thoughtful and compelling. It seems that a Mr. Williams regularly contributes archaeological "finds" from his backyard to the Smithsonian Institute, along with arguments for their proper place in the fossil record.

Smithsonian Institute
207 Pennsylvania Avenue
Washington, DC 20078

Dr. Mr. Williams:

Thank you for your latest submission to the Institute, labeled "93211-D, layer seven, next to the clothesline post . . . hominid skull."

We have given this specimen a careful and detailed examination, and regret to inform you that we disagree with your theory that it represents conclusive proof of the presence of Early Man in Charleston County two million years ago.

Rather, it appears that what you have found is the head of a Barbie doll, of the variety that one of our staff, who has small children, believes to be "Malibu Barbie."

It is evident that you have given a great deal of thought to the analysis of this specimen, and you may be quite certain that those of us who are familiar with your prior work in the field were loathe to come to contradiction with your findings. However, we do feel that there are a number of physical attributes of the specimen which might have tipped you off to its modern origin:

1. The material is molded plastic. Ancient hominid remains are typically fossilized bone.
2. The cranial capacity of the specimen is approximately 9 cubic centimeters, well below the threshold of even the earliest identified proto-hominids.
3. The dentition pattern evident on the skull is more consistent with the common domesticated dog than it is with the ravenous man-eating Pliocene clams you speculate roamed the wetlands during that time.

This latter finding is certainly one of the most intriguing hypotheses you have submitted in your history with this institution, but the evidence seems to weigh rather heavily against it. Without going into too much detail, let us say that:

A. The specimen looks like the head of a Barbie doll that a dog has chewed on.
B. Clams don't have teeth.

Harvey Rowe
Chief Curator, Antiquities

CHAPTER SUMMARY

1. To assess an argument, we must determine (1) whether the premises are plausible and (2) whether the premises support the conclusion.

2. The assessment of most arguments requires that we make some estimate of the argument's strength, rather that simply classifying it as correct or mistaken.

3. As a general rule, the **plausibility** of a claim is in inverse proportion to the reason we have to suspect it false.

4. The **inferential strength** of an argument can be tested in two ways:
   a. by thinking about circumstances in which the conclusion would be false and the premises true and then estimating their likelihood, and
   b. by formulating a hypothetical claim out of the premises and conclusion, adding any necessary qualifiers, and then thinking about its plausibility.

5. An argument is **complete** if its premises contain all the information on which its inference is based.

6. An argument is **deductively valid** if its conclusion cannot be false when its premises are true. An argument is **inductively strong** when its premises render its conclusion highly probable.

7. **Strong refutation** involves showing that an argument is incorrect: that one or more of its premises is false or that its inference involves a mistake. **Weak refutation** involves getting at weaknesses in arguments that are not altogether unreasonable. Since most arguments on controversial topics have both strengths and weaknesses, argument assessment is more often a matter of weak rather than strong refutation.

EXERCISES

A. For each pair of claims below, try to decide which is the more plausible, given everything you know on the subject at issue. If you are unable to do so, comment on the information you would need to have to decide about the claims and how you might get that information. If both claims seem equally implausible, write an alternative that seems plausible.

(A solution to Exercise 7 is given on page 81.)

1a. Our government is withholding information from the public about a crashed alien spacecraft and may have possession of both the remains of the craft and its occupants.
1b. Our government has made public all the information it has about purported alien spacecraft and their occupants.
2a. This book is printed on recycled paper.
2b. This book is not printed on recycled paper.
3a. *Titanic* has grossed more money than any other film in history.
3b. *Gone With the Wind* (released in 1939) is the biggest grossing film of all time.
4a. Some people are able to pick up the thoughts of others by ESP.
4b. There is no such thing as ESP.
5a. What goes around comes around.
5b. Good things happen to bad people and vice versa.

6a. Financially speaking, the average American is better off today than was the average American of fifty years ago.

6b. Americans today have a lower standard of living than did Americans fifty years ago.

7a. We use only 10 to 20 percent of our innate brain capacity.

7b. We use every bit of our brain capacity.

8a. Within the next few years we can expect to see the development of computers that can think and feel, that is, computers that are conscious.

8b. Computers, by their very nature, will never be conscious.

9a. The mass media regularly suppress stories that are potentially offensive to their advertisers.

9b. The media do not suppress stories if they deem them newsworthy.

10a. The price of oil is dictated by marketplace demand.

10b. The price of oil is determined by an informal monopoly of oil-producing countries and global energy corporations.

11a. The author of this book is politically conservative.

11b. The author of this book is a liberal.

12a. Most eastern Europeans would emigrate to the United States if given the opportunity.

12b. Most eastern Europeans are content to live where they are.

13a. Alcoholism is primarily a genetically based problem.

13b. The genetic predisposition to alcoholism is exceedingly weak, perhaps non-existent.

14a. Racism and sexism are on the decrease in the United States.

14b. Racism and sexism are on the increase in the United States.

15a. Most of what you learn in a college algebra class will never be used.

15b. Much of what you learn in a college algebra class you will apply at some point in your life.

B. Determine the strength of the inference implicit in each of the following arguments. When you have spotted a problem, give your reasons.

(A solution to Exercise 5 is given on page 81.)

1. The bulb on that lamp is probably burned out. I flipped the switch and it didn't come on.

2. She must not have a telephone. She isn't listed in the phone book.

3. There can be little doubt that extraterrestrials have visited Earth. To this day, the government has refused to declassify much of the information it has about UFO sightings.

4. How do we know that subliminal advertising works? Well, advertisers spend a considerable amount of money inserting subliminal messages into their ads. Why would they do this if subliminal persuasion were ineffective?

5. Mr. Stewart is genuinely fond of children. He would undoubtedly make a good teacher in a kindergarten or a day-care center.

6. She probably makes at least $200,000 a year. After all, she's an M.D.

7. People can be drafted when they are eighteen. So, they ought to be allowed to drink when they are eighteen as well.

8. There must be something to astrology. Everything my astrologer said about me, based on the chart he drew up, turned out to be absolutely true.

9. Territorial aggressiveness is not instinctive among human beings because it is not universal. Many cultures are not territorially aggressive.

10. He must have been up all night. His eyes are swollen and red, and his clothes are all wrinkled.

11. Racial discrimination conflicts with established public policy. Therefore, an institution that practices racial discrimination is not entitled to a tax exemption.

12. Life must have been created in roughly the way outlined in the Old Testament. After all, there is considerable evidence today that the theory of evolution is wrong.

13. Can you possibly deny that women are more intelligent than men? On average, women score much higher than men on intelligence tests.

14. It would seem that the moon can have an effect on our behavior. Look at all the strange and bizarre things police officers, paramedics, and emergency-room personnel report when the moon is full. Crimes, accidents, and even births seem to occur with more frequency! Ask any police officer or paramedic and they will confirm that when the moon is full, their clients all seem to go a bit crazy.

15. A recent poll reveals that nearly 60 percent of all Americans think the government is withholding information about UFOs. We must demand that the government make this information public.

16. Animals have moral rights despite the fact that they are not human beings. The short and long of it is that animals are every bit as capable of suffering as are we humans. And because of this, they have the same rights as we do not to be subjected to unnecessary pain and misery at the hands of another.

17. A person is addicted to a substance if he or she cannot voluntarily stop using it. Many smokers cannot quit. Thus, smoking is an addiction.

18. In his most recent public appearance, Boris Yeltsin looked thin and pale. He must have suffered another heart attack.

19. The other day, I met a guy who claims to be a priest in the Church of Satan. As it turns out, satanists are pretty nice people. We had a nice chat. He told me about the things he and other satanists believe and invited me to attend one of their services. And he wasn't at all pushy or opinionated.

20. I'm in favor of limiting the amount of time a person can serve in a public office. By doing this, we automatically increase participation in government, and anything that increases participation is ultimately going to make the system more democratic.

SOLUTIONS

Exercise A

7. 7b. looks to be the more plausible. People who claim we use a very small proportion of our brains seem to base it on the fact that what we know today about how the brain operates is a small fraction of what there is to know. However, most biological systems have few if any redundant or unnecessary parts. Thus, it seems likely that all the neurocircuitry in our brains plays some role in the brain's overall functioning. 7a. may be more plausible than it seems if interpreted to mean that most of what we consciously *do* involves a small fraction of total brain capacity or functioning.

Exercise B

5. Suppose we admit that Stewart is genuinely fond of children. Can we nonetheless reasonably deny that he will make a good kindergarten teacher or day-care worker? It seems possible that one could like children but not be very good at working with them for a variety of reasons. Perhaps Stewart has little patience with children or a difficult time communicating with them. It would seem, then, that the inference is questionable. Given we know only that Stewart is fond of children, it does not follow that he will work well with them.

CHAPTER FOUR

Welcome to the Real World:

Arguments in Context

The arguments we have analyzed so far have been straightforward. In most cases, their premises and conclusions have been easy to discern, and the passages from which they were taken were selected precisely because they involved arguments. But in their natural settings—in context—arguments typically present a wealth of interpretive problems. As noted in Chapter 3, before we can assess an argument we must make sure we understand it. To this end, we want to give a reading that at once captures the thinking of its author and makes the argument as strong as possible. The material in this chapter addresses some of the major problems we will encounter in giving sympathetic yet accurate readings of arguments. The first problem is deciding whether a passage actually involves an argument.

RECOGNIZING ARGUMENTS—TELLTALE SIGNS

Many of the things people say and write do not contain arguments. Consider, for example, this letter to the editor:

> In a recent article, you quote a family-law specialist saying divorced women don't need the courts for a name change, but give no details. Here's how: (1) take your birth certificate and divorce decree to the Social Security office and request a new card in your birth name; (2) use these documents to get a driver's license in your birth name; (3) notify credit card companies and magazines of your new name, and send them copies of your new license and your Social Security card.

Although this passage makes a number of claims about what one must do to make a legal name change, it does not involve an argument. The author's intent is to set out the steps involved in making a legal name change, not to argue that anything is the case. If we attempted to rewrite the passage as a series of premises and a conclusion, we would be reading something into it that is not there.

So, our first problem is to decide whether a passage involves an argument or arguments. There are several clues we can look for in reading a passage.

Premise and Conclusion Indicators

These are words and phrases typically inserted to indicate when a claim is intended to function as a premise or conclusion.

Since the market has made record gains in the past few months and, moreover, *since* large gains are normally followed by short-term losses, *it follows that* you shouldn't invest in the market now.

In this passage, the italicized words and phrases are examples of a stylistic device used to let the audience for an argument know which claims are premises and which are conclusions. Common **conclusion indicators** are

thus

hence

therefore

so

consequently

it follows that

it can be concluded that

Common **premise indicators** are

because

since

for

as shown by

in view of the fact that

Thus, if we find indicator words and phrases inserted between important claims in a passage, we are likely to find an argument involving these claims.

One premise indicator—*because*—deserves special mention, for it is often used to give an explanation rather than an argument. Suppose I tell you a friend of ours, Smith, is selling her house. You find this hard to believe; she bought the house recently and has told us both how much she likes it. "What makes you think this?" you ask me. "Well," I reply, "because I drove by her place this morning and there was a 'for sale' sign on the front lawn." In this context, the claim following *because* constitutes my evidence that Smith is selling; it is a premise of my argument. But suppose now you ask me why she is selling. I might reply, "Because she lost her job and can no longer afford the payments." Here the claims following *because* are intended to explain why Smith is selling, not to argue that she is indeed going to sell. Thus, when we encounter a passage in which claims are connected via *because,* we need to pause and ask ourselves, is the point of the passage to establish the claim following *because* or to explain why the claim is the case?

Qualifiers

As we discovered in Chapter 3, a set of premises may provide less than perfect support for a conclusion. We should not be surprised, then, to find an arguer taking pains to inform the audience about his or her level of confidence that the conclusion is the case. One way to do this is by including words or phrases used to qualify the conclusion. If one or more claims is said to be *probable, possible, nearly a certainty, a good bet, highly likely,* and so on, chances are very good the author will go on to argue for the claim she or he has qualified.

Context

The context, or setting, in which an argument occurs can provide an important clue. Some contexts are more likely than others to contain arguments. Letters to the editor, editorials, sales pitches, political speeches, debates, and quarrels, for example, are the sort of context in which we expect to find arguments. News reports, the chitchat of everyday conversation, poems, novels, and short stories are examples of contexts in which we rarely encounter arguments.

Controversy

Look for some acknowledgment that a claim mentioned in the passage is controversial. Remember, the point of an argument will probably be to resolve some question about a claim. Often, before mounting an argument, an arguer will provide motivation for the argument by suggesting that the claim he or she wants to defend is not without its detractors. Be on the lookout for **counterconsiderations,** claims that acknowledge problems for something the author is interested in. A passage that begins with

> Despite the fact that it is regressive and seems to discriminate against the poor, I intend to vote for the proposed new sales tax since . . .

is probably going to offer an argument for the new tax. Look also for evidence that the author is dissatisfied with a particular view. This is a strong indication the author will argue against that view. The following is the opening paragraph of a lengthy letter to the editor:

> Recent articles about so-called subsidization by the federal government of logging road construction on federal timber sales are entirely misleading. In actuality, these purchaser road credits are allowances for the costs of required construction separate from the competitively bid timber auction prices.

Here, the author's reference to the "so-called" subsidization as well as the claim that recent articles "are entirely misleading" suggest the author is unconvinced by a particular view and will make a case against it.

Tone of Voice

The **tone** of voice of a passage may provide another clue. **Irony** or **sarcasm** may be used to belittle a view, and this is often a sign of an impending argument against that view. Beware that a sarcastic remark may be intended to assert precisely the opposite of what it says. Here is the complete text of another letter to the editor:

> The state Lottery Commission has made life a lot easier for video-poker machine players. No longer is it necessary to convert ten- and twenty-dollar bills into ones and fives in order to play. Now the machines will accept ten- and

twenty-dollar bills directly. No more unseemly, boring waiting for smaller bills; no gambling downtime!

Probably the Lottery Commission, in this time of almost instant electronic financial communication, can find a way for these poker machines to process a whole paycheck for immediate use by a video-poker player. Now that will be real progress!

Taken at face value, this passage seems to argue that anything the Lottery Commission can do to speed up the rate at which people play video poker is for the good. However, the sarcastic tone of the passage suggests the author means the opposite. The author's point seems to be that making video poker easier and quicker to play is an underhanded way for the state to extract more money from gamblers.

A critical tone does not always mean a passage contains an argument. People can express strong sentiments about something without mounting an argument. If a passage is sufficiently ironic, pithy, or venomous, it is tempting to assume that it must involve an argument, even if the argument is not immediately discernible.

Let me get this straight. Our legislators gave state employees a 3 percent raise and gave themselves 10 percent. They gave $4.8 million to the horse- and dog-racing industries but didn't fund the libraries. They finished without finding a way to improve our highways. Not to worry. The residuals from the latest legislative session gave us enough manure to fill every pothole in every road in the state.

The author's tone suggests he or she has a bone to pick with some of the spending decisions made by the state legislators. But this is all that is said in the passage. By the author's standards, at any rate, the legislators made some disastrous decisions. But what evidence is there these decisions were wrongheaded? The passage gives no clue as to what the author's answer might be. Thus, it seems best regarded as an expression of the author's view, but not an argument for it. No doubt we could cobble together an argument for the claim that these decisions were wrongheaded. It is not difficult to figure out what might have motivated the author to express these sentiments. But we have no reason to believe that such an argument is present, lurking in the author's prose.

PARAPHRASING ARGUMENTS

Having decided that a passage contains an argument, we can begin thinking about what the argument involves. What are its premises? What is its conclusion? This is where the going gets tough. Arguments, in their natural setting, can be difficult to understand. They are often poorly organized. Parts of the argument may be left unstated or so badly stated as to require substantial revision to make clear exactly what is being claimed. Sometimes, it may not be clear what is at issue. Moreover, argumentative discourse often contains a good deal of information that is either redundant or irrelevant to the argument it involves. As you can see, giving an *accurate* reading can be tricky.

The need to give accurate readings of arguments is perhaps nowhere more essential than in the practice of law. The following remarks are from an article, written for attorneys, that appeared in many state bar association periodicals. The title of the article is "Back to Basics: Simple Tips for Dissecting Arguments." It was written by Jason Vail, an attorney with the Florida attorney general's office.

> One of the keys to effective advocacy is understanding what your opponent is trying to say. Without a clear understanding of your opponent's legal position and reasoning, you can't attack effectively.
>
> Understanding is not always easy. The arguments of some lawyers peal like fine crystal. Some lawyers just don't want to be understood; they'd rather hide the poverty of their position behind a fog of words. Others simply can't write well, and their arguments are like spaghetti, on which the reader must conduct a careful autopsy to identify the parts and see how they fit together.
>
> Even with the finest of argument, however, it is worthwhile to spend the time "unpacking" it, stripping it to its bare premises so that you can run your mental fingers around its structure, searching for flaws.
>
> So when your opponent's next brief hits your desk, take a deep breath, let that knot in your stomach unfurl, fetch your pencil and notepad, and take the argument apart. It will be worth the time and effort, for then you'll see all its warts and blemishes fully exposed. And you'll know what to attack.

Here, for example, is a passage written at the level of difficulty we are likely to encounter:

> Ideally, anyone charged with a crime in the United States is entitled to his or her day in court. The litany of rights is familiar: The accused is presumed innocent until found guilty beyond a reasonable doubt and has the right to be tried by a jury of his or her peers before an impartial judge.
>
> The reality, as anyone involved with the criminal justice system can attest to, is far different. In the vast majority of cases, the "accused" has no trial. His or her "day" in court is the few minutes it takes to plead guilty. In fact, only about 10 percent of the people charged with crimes actually go to court. Most just strike a deal—a guilty plea in exchange for a promise of reduced charges or a lighter sentence. Bargains are generally struck with the prosecutor; the judge usually rubber-stamps them. So much for justice in this country!

Where do we begin in sorting out the argument of this passage? Well, first, are there any telltale signs that the passage actually involves an argument?

There does seem to be one strong clue. In the second paragraph, the author comments that "the reality" is far different from the "ideal" described in the first paragraph. And this is a pretty controversial claim; something isn't working as it is

> **CONUNDRUM**
>
> Most passages containing arguments present interpretive problems in part because they provide a wealth of information not germane to the argument. The following argument, however, goes to the opposite extreme.
>
> Logicians, being human, err.
>
> The argument is given in just four words! (Logicians are human beings and so are prone to commit errors.) Can you top this by constructing a coherent argument containing only three words?

supposed to be working. What? The part of our criminal justice system that guarantees people the right to stand trial when accused of a crime. So, the passage does seem to contain an argument, an argument whose conclusion might be stated as follows:

Our criminal justice system is not working as it is designed to work.

Of course, several slight variations on this version of the conclusion would be equally accurate. But this reading does seem to reflect the concerns of the passage's author.

Thinking About Support

After we have figured this much out, the next step is to arrive at a statement of the argument's premises. Before we begin to worry about the premises—the evidence—provided in the passage, let's think about the strategy that should guide us when extracting arguments from the passages in which they originate. Our goal should always be to come up with a reading of the argument that is as strong and plausible as we can make it given that it reflects the author's thinking. To this end we should give a reading that is consistent with our requirements for an acceptable argument—a reading in which the inference is as strong as possible, in which the premises are stated in plausible terms, and in which the conclusion is qualified, when appropriate, to reflect the quality and extent of the evidence. In addition, we want every claim in our reading to be as clear as possible and to eliminate any irrelevant parts of the passage: padding, redundancies, and background material. Giving a sympathetic reading increases the chances that any subsequent criticisms we may make will be directed at something important in the argument. So give the arguer the benefit of the doubt. When facing an interpretive choice, opt for the one that contributes the most to the argument, unless, of course, something the arguer says suggests otherwise.

Understanding Point of View

Usually, the most effective way to begin thinking about the details of an argument is to set aside the passage in which it occurs and ask yourself, What would be required to support this conclusion, from the point of view of its author? **Point of view** is a nebulous notion that refers in general to a person's beliefs and attitudes on the topic at issue. Point of view is not always possible to discern, but it is worth spending a few moments speculating about an author's overall perspective on the issues. For one thing, an appreciation of an author's point of view may help us confirm that we understand the argument as it was intended. For another, it may help us get "inside the mind" of the author in a way that will enable us to think from his or her perspective and thus anticipate the argument he or she is trying to make. In the case of the preceding passage, the author's general dissatisfaction with the way the criminal justice system operates seems clear. Now we can begin to think about the general direction the author might take in arguing that something is wrong with the system.

A moment's reflection suggests that to show the system is not working, we would need two things: first, some claim about how it ought to work and, second, a claim to the effect that it is not working in this way. With this in mind, we can return to the passage with some sense of what its argument might involve. And, indeed, the passage seems to make the requisite claims. *Ideally,* people are entitled to certain things when accused of a crime. *In reality,* most people do not receive these things. Thus, the argument of the passage might be paraphrased to make its conclusion and premises clear and explicit as follows:

> Under our criminal justice system, people accused of a crime ought to be presumed innocent until tried and found guilty by a jury of their peers before an impartial judge.
>
> The vast majority of people accused of crimes are neither tried nor found guilty.
> _____
>
> Our criminal justice system is not working as it is designed to work.

This reading seems very close to what the author of the passage must have had in mind.

Note also that by first thinking about what it would take to effectively defend the conclusion of this argument, we have been able to eliminate from our reading much of what is said in the passage. This way of thinking about arguments is often an effective way of deciding not only what arguments involve but also what is irrelevant. Speakers and writers often add a good deal of material that is not needed for their arguments. By focusing on what is required to support a claim, we may be able to arrive at a reading that not only is complete and sympathetic but also clears away those parts of the passage that are not relevant to its argument. It is not always easy to decide whether a claim is relevant to an argument. Many fallacies introduce irrelevancies in the process of mounting arguments—our main topic in Chapter 5.

The strategy we have just employed needs to be exercised with caution. Having anticipated the argument we would expect to find in a passage, we must pay careful attention to what the passage actually says. Otherwise, we run the risk of "reading in" an argument that the passage does not involve. After arriving at a reading of an argument, always ask yourself: Does my reading depend largely on information provided in the original? Does the original passage make more sense when reread in light of my paraphrase?

Understanding Anecdotes

One interpretive issue that comes up in giving readings of many arguments has to do with the use of **anecdotal evidence.** People often introduce general claims by way of an illustration or two, frequently leaving the general claim unstated. Why? Because specific instances—anecdotes—can bring to an argument a kind of immediacy and persuasive power that generalizations lack. Moreover, the use of anecdotes can mask the fact that the author has not given careful thought to the precise details of the general claim being illustrated. Look, for example, at this argument:

> I think car phones should be banned. Well, perhaps not banned altogether, but people should not be allowed to use them when they are driving. Only this morning I read a story in the newspaper about a guy who caused a three-car pile-up when he swerved into another car on the freeway while he was trying to punch in a number on his cellular phone.

One way to understand this argument is to leave it pretty much as it is. But on this reading, the argument seems weak, even silly. I doubt anyone would favor restricting car-phone use on the basis of a single incident. But then this is undoubtedly not what the author of the passage means to be arguing. The anecdote is introduced to illustrate a more general claim: *Many accidents are caused, in part, by drivers who are busy talking on car phones,* or something similar. It is difficult to say much more about the general claim the author means to be making. Does he or she believe that more accidents are caused by the use of car phones than by other factors that contribute to auto accidents, factors we are nonetheless willing to tolerate? Do car phones cause more accidents than, say, playing with the radio or cassette player? But although we would be hard-pressed to say just what the arguer is claiming, it seems clear that we need to replace the anecdote with a general claim in our paraphrase of the argument. In this case, the best we can do is to come up with a version that seems plausible and does the work the argument demands of it.

Don't be surprised if the most plausible reading of a claim based on an anecdote remains problematic. Perhaps the general claim was introduced via anecdotal evidence to mask a problem with the more generalized version of the claim.

Coping with Poorly Constructed Arguments

On occasion a passage may resist any clear interpretation, and we may need simply to conclude that, although it appears to involve argumentation, it is not clear what the argument is. At most we will be able to speculate about what the passage's author may be trying to argue. The following letter to the editor appeared days after a doctor who performed abortions was murdered:

> No good has come from the shootings of abortionists, but we must remember the gruesome violence perpetrated daily upon tiny humans who are dismembered and killed in the womb. Some people in this country are attempting to awaken this nation's conscience to this violence. The vast majority of these people are peaceful, and they are involved in helping distressed pregnant women find positive, nonviolent solutions. Because these

people are not acting for themselves, but for others who cannot march in the streets or speak for themselves, many others do not understand them and they have become the targets of hatred and abuse. However, they consider the lives they've saved to be worth what they've endured.

Now, the author's point of view seems clear: The author is opposed to abortion and seems to be in sympathy with abortion protesters but plainly is disturbed by the shooting of the doctor. If nothing else, the language used in many descriptive phrases makes this clear: "gruesome violence perpetrated daily on tiny humans" (as if the violence would be less troublesome if perpetrated against slightly larger humans), "distressed pregnant women," and "positive, nonviolent solutions." Most of the claims in the letter are clear enough. One claim is somewhat ambiguous: "Some people in this country are attempting to awaken this nation's conscience to this violence." Are the people alluded to here the people who oppose abortion or the people who actively participate in anti-abortion activities, like protesting in front of abortion clinics? In addition the passage contains an indicator word—*because*—in the next to last sentence and a counterconsideration in the opening clause. Taken together, all of these clues suggest the author is giving an argument.

The problem with the letter is that it is not clear what its author is interested in arguing. At least three possibilities seem consistent with the language of the passage and the author's point of view. Does he or she mean to be arguing that the shooting was justified? A couple of things said in the passage suggest this: the need to awaken people to the violence of abortion as well as the fact that the doctor "dismembered" and "killed" "tiny humans" in performing abortions. Or is the point to argue that most abortion protesters would not condone murder and so should not be condemned by the actions of a single person? Or is the author's real interest to explain why abortion protesters are misunderstood? The last two sentences of the passage seem to offer an explanation for the last possibility.

One reason this passage is so hard to understand is that it is not clear what its author is responding to. Anyone familiar with the tragic events described in the passage would probably wonder what would motivate a person to go to this extreme in defense of his or her moral convictions. It is one thing to believe abortion morally reprehensible but another to take a life in order to defend this belief. Yet the passage doesn't really address this concern. Thus, it is hard to understand what its point really is. There is a lesson to be learned from this. Most arguments are given in response to something. Thus, in trying to figure an argument out, always ask yourself who the audience for the argument is. What view, what position, on the topic at issue is the author responding to? If we can figure this out, we can usually make some headway in understanding the argument. And if we still cannot make sense of the argument, we at least stand a good chance of understanding why this is so.

It is difficult to know how to answer any of the interpretive questions we have just raised. If we were to paraphrase the argument of this passage, we would have to do a lot of speculating, for the letter's author has not made clear how various things claimed in the letter square with one another or even what his or her main concern is. No doubt, someone with a point of view similar to the author's would sympathize with the sentiments expressed in the letter and might even claim to understand its argument. The lesson to be learned from this is that a point of view shared by arguer and audience can impede understanding. If we tend to sympathize with an arguer's sentiments, we risk ignoring any difficulties in an argument that we have every intention of accepting. So, although we must consider the author's point of view, we must also recognize the influence our own point of view may have as we attempt to give a reading of the passage. Of course, we must recognize when our point of view is at odds with that of an arguer as well. If we are unsympathetic to the point of view from which an argument emanates, we must resist the temptation to give a paraphrase that does not do justice to the author's thinking.

COMPLICATING FACTORS

Two additional facts about argument prove useful in working on complicated passages. The first is that arguments are often intended to raise objections to other arguments. Such arguments are called **counterarguments.** Understanding when a passage is intended to mount a counterargument can aid us in sorting out its details. Second, many passages involving arguments are much more complicated than the ones we have examined so far. Each of the passages with which we have been working (with the possible exception of the last one!) has contained a single argument. But argumentative passages frequently contain several interrelated arguments. We may find a complex of interrelated arguments, arguments for more than one conclusion, or several distinct strains of argument for a single conclusion. Let's consider each of these points in detail.

Counterarguments

Don't be surprised to find that the point of an argument is to criticize another argument. Arguments, we have noted time and again, involve controversy and so there will likely be interesting arguments for contrary positions. Thus, to support a particular position a person may want to comment on weaknesses in the support offered for a contrary view. The thinking here is that if one of two rival views is wrong, we have reason to take the other view seriously. Here is a fairly straightforward example of a counterargument:

> Many authorities claim the only way to make our students competitive with those of other industrial nations is to increase the length of the school year. But I don't think this is going to solve the problem. If our students are receiving poor instruction, simply extending the amount of time they are in the classroom won't change this. What we need is a no-nonsense, stripped-down curriculum and better teachers.

Two things go on in this passage. The author first identifies a position with which she or he disagrees and then mounts an argument against that position. Now, a counterargument is really just an argument, but one whose conclusion is that some claim is not the case or that an argument is problematic. Nevertheless, the discovery that a passage involves a counterargument can provide a crucial clue as to the conclusion of the author's argument. It may also help us to make sense of a passage that involves statements seemingly at odds with one another; some of the statements may be part of the position the author is countering. Moreover, the discovery that a passage involves a counterargument reminds us that we need to get clear on two things: the argument mounted in the passage *and* the view to which it is opposed. In deciding how to structure the argument, we need to decide what parts of the passage directly address the view under attack and so must do everything we can to understand what that view is.

Under attack in the preceding passage is the claim that lengthening the school year will make our students more competitive. So, the conclusion of the argument is the denial of this claim, and the premises are the claims that suggest the view at issue is wrong. We can write out the argument of the passage as follows:

> Our students are not competitive with those of other industrial nations because they are receiving poor instruction.
>
> The only way to improve instruction is via curriculum changes and hiring better teachers.
> _____
> Lengthening the school year will not make our students more competitive.

This reading seems strong and plausible and seems to capture the thinking of its author. (Note also that the argument makes use of an explanation in its first premise.)

Complex Argument

Suppose I gave this argument:

> A fetus is a human being.
>
> Every human being has the right not to be deprived of its life.
> _____
> Abortion is morally wrong.

Doubtless there are a lot of people who would not accept this argument. For many, the problem would not be the argument itself, but rather one of the premises, probably the first. Knowing this, I would want to supplement my argument with another argument designed to support the first premise. I might then give a second argument to this effect:

> In the normal course of events, a human fetus will become a fully developed human being.
> _____
> A fetus is a human being.

The result of my efforts would be a **complex argument.** I have given one argument and then added another in support of one of the premises of my first argument. The two arguments are linked in sharing a common claim:

> A fetus is a human being.

The entire argument can be written out in standard form as

> In the normal course of events, a human fetus will become a fully developed human being.
> _____
> A fetus is a human being.

Every human being has the right not to be deprived of its life.

Abortion is morally wrong.

As you can see, the claim that the fetus is a human being serves as the premise of the main argument and the conclusion of a supporting argument.

Argumentative discourse often involves this sort of complexity. Often the point of an argument is to bring new information to the attention of its audience that both supports the conclusion and is noncontroversial. But just as often, arguments involve a premise that is questionable; here, the author may provide additional support for the questionable premise of the main argument. In such an argument, the real point may be to focus on supporting the questionable premise, and the main argument may be given just to show the importance of that premise. Of course, a complicated passage may involve even more complexity: More than one premise may be supported, and, on occasion, additional support may be introduced for the supporting premises.

In any event, it is important to recognize when a passage involves a complex argument, for if we fail to do this we are likely to misunderstand the component arguments. If, for example, we failed to recognize the complex structure of the abortion argument given earlier, we might paraphrase it as a single argument:

In the normal course of events, a human fetus will become a fully developed human being.

A fetus is a human being.

Every human being has the right not to be deprived of its life.

Abortion is morally wrong.

This reading is problematic. Why would someone maintain the first premise if the second premise is true? The first premise seems redundant. However, if we understand that the first premise is intended to support the second premise, not the conclusion of the main argument, the overall argument makes more sense.

Independent Arguments and Arguments with Independent Premises

A single passage may contain arguments for more than one conclusion and may even contain more than one argument for a single conclusion. Look at the following passage:

On average, a college graduate earns several thousand dollars more per year than the average high school graduate. Moreover, if you put off going to college now, it is just going to cost more if you decide to go later on. Thus, you should plan on starting college in the fall.

Despite its brevity, this passage involves arguments for two distinct claims. The passage first argues that you should go to college. Why? Because a college education increases your chances of making a good income. But the passage also argues that you should go to college *as soon as possible*. Why? Because costs are going to increase. So, in this passage we have two independent arguments, intended to support two distinct conclusions. The first argument is

> A college graduate earns several thousand dollars more per year than the average high school graduate.
> _____
> You should plan to attend college.

The second argument is

> The cost of a college education is always increasing.
> _____
> You should go to college as soon as possible.

Now consider a slight variation on the preceding passage:

> On average, a college graduate earns several thousand dollars more per year than the average high school graduate. In addition, a college education exposes people to a whole new world of things they might otherwise never discover: art, literature, philosophy, and more. Thus, you really ought to think seriously about going to college.

This passage seems to involve a single argument. At any rate, only one conclusion is ventured and supported:

> On average, a college graduate earns more than the average high school graduate.
>
> A college education exposes people to a whole new world of things, like art, literature, and philosophy.
> _____
> You ought to think seriously about going to college.

Suppose, now, that we could show that the first premise does not provide much support for the conclusion. (Perhaps the income differences are due to socioeconomic differences between the two groups. People who go to college are more likely to come from a background that gives them an advantage in the search for high-paying jobs: social connections and interests that make them more attractive to employers with whom they share these connections and interests.) Even if we had succeeded in undermining the support provided by the first premise, we would have left the second premise untouched. The second premise might very well provide support for the conclusion. This is because the two premises of this argument are independent of one another. Neither requires the other in order to support the conclusion.

Putting this argument in standard form presents a minor problem: Do we represent it as a single argument or as a pair of independent arguments for the same conclusion? Either way will do, although if we opt for the former, we must constantly remind ourselves that the two premises support the conclusion independently of one another. Weaknesses we find with one premise do not affect the evidence provided by the other. Compare the argument we have just considered with one in which multiple premises jointly support the conclusion:

> There is a three-hour time difference between the east and west coasts.
>
> It is currently 11 A.M. in New York City.
> _____
> It must be 8 A.M. in Los Angeles.

CONUNDRUM

Imagine you are a juror in a murder trial. The prosecutor introduces several pieces of evidence, all suggesting the accused is guilty. Several witnesses have testified that the accused was in the immediate vicinity of the murder around the time the crime was committed. DNA evidence suggests there is a strong likelihood that blood found at the scene of the crime could be that of the accused. The accused has no alibi for his whereabouts at the time of the crime. Taken together, do these pieces of evidence constitute a single argument or three separate arguments?

The conclusion of this argument depends on both premises. If the first premise is rejected, the second premise ceases to provide support for the conclusion and vice versa.

It is generally worth taking the time to determine whether premises are jointly required in order to support a conclusion. Many complicated arguments offer several considerations, all bearing on a single conclusion. If we find that one or perhaps more strains of evidence are problematic, we need to decide how this effects the remaining evidence. To do this, we must know which of the premises must be linked to support the conclusion and which can provide support independently.

CHAPTER SUMMARY

1. Much written and spoken discourse does not involve argumentation. Clues are often provided by premise and conclusion indicator words, qualifiers, context, signs of a controversy, counterconsiderations, and tone of voice.

2. A consideration of the author's overall **point of view** may help you decide which claims are and are not premises. Before setting out the premises of an argument, always ask yourself what it would take to make a strong case for the conclusion. Then give the strongest and most plausible reading consistent with the language of the original. Add any necessary qualification in stating the conclusion.

3. A consideration of what the author of an argument is responding to often gives an initial sense of what the argument is.

4. A **counterargument** offers criticism of another argument.

5. A **complex argument** is a series of related arguments in which some claims function as both premises and conclusions.

6. The premises of an argument are independent when they involve strains of evidence that can be evaluated separately. Premises are dependent when they are jointly required to support a claim.

EXERCISES

A. Many of the passages below involve arguments. Several involve complex arguments, some may involve more than a single argument. Be on the lookout as well for counterarguments. For each passage, give a sympathetic reading of the argument or arguments or give your reasons for thinking the passage does not involve an argument. (Remember, an explanation is not an argument!) Make your readings as strong as possible, given the language of the passage. Your final result should be in premises-conclusion form. Then comment on any weaknesses you see in the argument. Think specifically about the following:

- Are there any reasons to question the inference?
- Are there any reasons to question the plausibility of any of the premises?
- Can you think of a good argument for a claim contrary to the conclusion of the argument under consideration?

A simple yes in response to any of these questions is not enough. Give your reasons. Don't become frustrated if you find some of these exercises difficult to complete. Many of the problems you encounter will be discussed in detail in future chapters. Several exercises will be revisited at the appropriate time. For now, do the best you can and keep in mind that these exercises approximate the level of complexity of the arguments we encounter in our daily lives. Finally, don't be surprised if you find that some of the arguments do not seem to involve any obvious mistakes. There are, after all, good arguments!

(A solution to Exercise 6 is given on page 102.)

1. One of the chief dangers of advertising is that it acts on us without our being aware of its influence. Easily 90 percent of us believe we are personally immune from advertising—that commercials have little or no effect on our buying habits. Yet the facts show otherwise. Sales figures for products prior to and after a large-scale advertising campaign almost always reveal a substantial increase in sales after the product is advertised.

2. I'm not going to vote for the Republican candidate for the Senate because she is opposed to government-backed grants for college students. In a speech she delivered just the other day, she said that students and their parents, not the government, should underwrite the cost of the students' own education. And to make matters worse, she wants stricter laws governing the availability of abortion.

3. It really ticks me off the way the traffic cops in some states pick on out-of-state drivers. Last year on my vacation I was pulled over for speeding in three different states, and in each case I was just driving along with the flow of traffic. It seems clear to me the police want to ticket out-of-staters, knowing full well they are unlikely to come back, a month or so later, to protest in court.

4. Religious holidays—like Christmas and Hanukkah—should not be celebrated in public schools. To do so would be to violate the constitutionally mandated separation of church and state. Moreover, celebrating such holidays discriminates against religions whose holidays are not celebrated. By celebrating Christmas in the schools we indirectly discriminate against Jews, Buddhists, Muslims, and Hindus.

5. In general, we look for a new law by the following process. First, we guess it. Then we compute the consequences of the guess to see what would be implied if this law that we guessed is right. Then we compare the results of the computation to nature, with experiment or experience, compare it directly to observation, to see if it works. If it disagrees with experiment it is wrong. In that simple statement is the key to science. *—from "Seeking New Laws of Nature," by Richard Feynman*

6. To the editor: The tenets of Marxism say that any means will be justified if the end is achieved as desired. In a democracy or republic, the will of the people must be adhered to as expressed through their representatives in Congress. In sidestepping Congress, Ollie North and his band used the Marxist doctrine to pursue democracy. It doesn't make sense to me either.

7. To the editor: The other day as I read the newspaper, I was relieved and assured to find that our earnest representatives in Washington D.C. have again turned their solemn attention to the agonizing problem of controlling flag burning. The season is again upon us when the skies are fouled, the sunlight dimmed, and the nostrils seared with the stench of smoldering, backyard flag fires.

   It is right that our elected representatives should put aside those contentious arguments about campaign-finance reform, tobacco, term limits, health care, and so on, and speak about an issue to which we can all subscribe. The American flag is our nation's proud symbol and does not deserve to be used as bonfire fodder.

   Perhaps as they speak, they will also realize that our proud flag should not be wrapped as a shield to protect the cheap and sleazy vote-getter.

8. To the editor: In response to your editorial "Baseball's Foul Ball," regarding Cincinnati Reds owner Marge Schott's ouster from the game due to her offensive remarks about Adolph Hitler, I'd like to point out an error in your citation of the First Amendment. Although I wholeheartedly agree with the premise that Schott should be allowed to speak her mind without fear of repercussion, it is not in the power of the First Amendment to protect her. The First Amendment only guards against government intrusions. Major league baseball, being a private entity, can censor and censure her to its pleasing.

9. She won't be running the Boston marathon this year. She's out of shape and doesn't have the money to spend on a plane ticket and hotel reservations. Remember, she had to borrow a lot of money just last month to pay for a new roof for her house. And she told me the other day that she hasn't had the time to train, what with the second job she's taken to pay off the home-improvement loan.

10. Whatever President Truman's reasons for dropping atomic bombs on Japan, Truman's decision cannot have been based on concern with ending the war expeditiously. The Japanese were already defeated and ready to surrender, because of the Allies' effective sea blockade and the already successful bombing of Japan with conventional weapons. Truman knew the Japanese were close to surrender and that the much-feared invasion of Japan was not going to be necessary. Why, then, did he order the bomb to be dropped on Hiroshima and Nagasaki? Shortly after the first atomic bomb test, Truman remarked to an advisor that the bomb "would keep the Russians straight."

11. To the editor: I would like to take a moment to express my gratitude to our state legislators for their efforts to recriminalize the possession of less than one ounce of marijuana. As a former college instructor who left academia to practice criminal law, I am fully aware of what this legislation will mean to my checkbook. I laud all efforts to construct jails, treat a medical problem (addiction) as a criminal matter, and generally increase my caseload.

    Funding education does nothing but engender a sense of self-worth and a broadened awareness of the richness of life and enhances one's chances of financial success. It does nothing for my criminal law practice. In fact, funding education cannot help but endanger my income, since education exposes students to the richness of life found in art, music, theater, math, and science.

    Education does nothing but dissuade students from vandalism, theft, drug use, and violence—all activities on which my practice is dependent. By diverting public funding from education to the criminalization of possessing less than an ounce of marijuana (a substance that has been demonstrated to have some positive medicinal uses), my criminal law practice is enhanced and my financial security ensured.

12. If individuals live only seventy years, then a state or a nation or a civilization which may last for a thousand years is more important than an individual. But if Christianity is true, then the individual . . . is more important for he is everlasting and the life of a state or a civilization, compared with his, is only a moment. —*from* Mere Christianity, *by C. S. Lewis*

13. A large nationwide study done in 1991 on church affiliation uncovered some interesting facts. One was that church affiliation in the far western states— California, Washington, and Oregon—is much lower than anywhere else in the country. More people in the western states than in any other part of the country claim affiliation with no organized religion. No doubt, this is due to the fact that, for some reason, most new age movements originate on the west coast and many such movements require that one set aside conventional beliefs in God and the hereafter in favor of something much more akin to the non-Judeo-Christian notion that we are all part of an amorphous something and that this is all there is to the idea of God. This notion, of course, flies in the face of the basic religious ideas of those who founded our country—the ideas at the core of the Judeo-Christian religions.

14. To the editor: In narrowly defining seatbelt usage as driver "self-protection," Marie E. Birnbaum overlooks the restraint's safety role in keeping a driver in place: at the vehicle controls during multiple-event collisions and severe maneuverings in accident avoidance. In these cases, a vehicle with an unbelted driver flung from its controls has the potential of becoming an unguided missile, bound, perhaps, for the pedestrians Ms. Birnbaum seeks to protect. Moreover, any unbelted occupant of a vehicle is a potential battering ram in a collision that can injure others in car or truck compartments. Viewed in this light, seatbelt usage is not a matter of libertarian choice but of civic responsibility.

15. What if I told you I know of a bank that would multiply your deposits by ten and pay you interest at the current rate on the full amount? If you deposit, say, $1,000, you will be paid interest on $10,000. Would you invest? This is why the purchase of a home is the best investment you can make in today's

market. Most people who buy homes make a down payment of about 10 percent of the purchase price. Yet the total value of the property tends to increase at roughly the rate of inflation, the approximate rate most banks pay on savings deposits. What this means is that for an initial investment of 10 percent of the purchase price of your home, you receive interest—in the form of increased property value—on a sum ten times the amount of your investment.

16. User's fees are an entirely appropriate and fair method of paying for government services not used by all. If you want to use public transportation, you are required to pay a fee to do so. Public parks and campgrounds generally charge for admission and for overnight campsites. We don't complain about these fees, for we see the logic in requiring users to pay for services not utilized by all. Similarly, people who choose to use public libraries should be charged for the services they receive. A modest checkout fee seems entirely fair and equitable. Why should those who choose not to use the public libraries be forced to help pay the way of those who do?

17. To the editor: In a recent editorial you said that our state should take the lead in using school vouchers to improve education. On the surface, this argument sounds reasonable. Providing tax money for private-school attendance could improve education.

    However, there are a number of important reasons our state should not even consider school vouchers.

    The First Amendment of our Constitution declares that "Congress shall make no law respecting an establishment of religion, or prohibiting the free exercise thereof." Since 85 percent of all private schools are religiously affiliated, diverting funds from the public treasury would require all Americans to contribute to the churches and other houses of worship that operate private schools.

    Because taxpayers have no say in the operation of these schools, the result would be taxation without representation.

    Ninety percent of our nation's children attend public schools. To ask these schools to accept inadequate funding so that tax dollars can be diverted to private religious schools is obscene. Forcing people to support religious institutions through school vouchers is a clear violation of the separation of church and state and should be thoroughly rejected.

18. To the editor: I've had it! Another instance in which innocent citizens were killed while a police officer chased the driver of a stolen car. The police bureau later determined that the officer used "proper procedures" in making the decision to pursue the stolen vehicle. I beg to differ. If a procedure that has reportedly put citizens in harm's way is proper, then it needs some serious revision. Any of us who have had a car stolen know that the police bureau has little, if any, interest in even investigating such a theft, much less sending an officer to take a written report. They'll invite you to come down to the station and fill out the paperwork, but that's about the extent of their involvement.

    But, by God, let some idiot go by a patrol car in one of those stolen cars and it's "Katy, bar the door." Chases of 60 mph to 70 mph through crowded neighborhood streets are becoming all too common as are the death and

---

CONUNDRUM

Now that you have struggled through the problems in Exercise A, you are aware that people typically are not as clear as they could be in setting forth their arguments. This is particularly vexing because the point of giving an argument is to convince the audience of something, and it is hard to succeed when the audience must struggle to follow the argument. Why, then, do people speak and write in ways that require considerable paraphrase to make their views clear? A number of factors contribute to this problem. What do you suppose they are?

---

dismemberment of innocent people caught in the middle. Is it really worth it to nail someone for a crime such as this when the same crime elicits almost no reaction from the same people when the perpetrator isn't fixed squarely in their crosshairs?

19. To the editor: A January 13 news analysis on the shift toward self-reliance in the welfare system quotes a Harvard economist as saying that America is "growing up and we are getting out of the European mode, which is more the welfare state." But this ignores an essential aspect of the Western and Northern European welfare states, as is often the case in American analysis.

   The European welfare state is not only and not even in the first place about giving away money to people who have fallen behind. It is about creating a public space shared by high-income and low-income people: amenities like schools, universities, hospitals, parks, low-cost transportation, and swimming pools. That is why France, for instance, spends four times as much per capita on its infrastructure as our federal and state governments combined.

   In Europe, the well-to-do get more out of this than the poor, for they live longer, take better care of themselves, send their children to universities, use the libraries more, and so forth. Admittedly, this lessens the enterprising spirit such as we find it in the United States, and as a result there is more unemployment and less wealth in absolute terms. However, I do not doubt that it creates more human happiness. The resulting social climate in European welfare states is less aggressive and more pleasant, and the quality of life for everyone is improved.

20. To the editor: I don't usually agree with the President, but I would like to applaud his plan to seek a big cut in the National Endowment for the Arts budget. Something is really wrong with our national values when a war hero freezes to death on the streets of Washington D.C. while a poet gets a $25,000 grant to write poetry. As a libertarian, I would like to see the National Endowment for the Arts eliminated. As a filmmaker, I would like to see some responsibility in the art community.

B. In this exercise you will write an argument, but in reverse. Your argument should be for or against *one* of the following claims, although you may want to qualify the claim you select. Structure your argument by setting out its premises and conclusion. Don't shy away from complex arguments and arguments that provide independent strains of support. Finally, rewrite your argument in prose. Be sure to help your reader by making your argument interesting, readable, provocative, and clear.

1. The death penalty should be abolished.
2. Animals have moral rights.
3. We have a moral obligation to be vegetarians.
4. Private citizens should not be allowed to own handguns.
5. All forms of gambling should be illegal.
6. Condoms should be distributed in public schools.
7. Students who sit in the front of the classroom will get the best grades.
8. Personality is reflected in handwriting.
9. We should stop building freeways and build mass transit instead.
10. Professional boxing should be abolished.

C. Write a dialogue between two people who hold opposed views on some topic. Try to build in at least three related arguments—an argument, a counterargument, and a reply to the counterargument. When you have completed your dialogue, write out the arguments involved in the dialogue and comment on their relationships. Here is an example:

A DIALOGUE

Willy: As I see it, the big problem with our educational system is the lack of talented teachers. And, let's face it, the way to solve this is by paying teachers a lot more money. You get what you pay for. And unless we're willing to increase teachers' salaries, we're going to continue to have a lot of mediocre teachers in our schools.

Nilly: I agree, we have a problem. But I don't buy your solution.

Willy: You've got a better idea?

Nilly: That's not what I'm saying. I just don't see how throwing money at the problem is going to help. Great teachers aren't motivated by money; they go into teaching knowing full well they aren't going to get rich. If you increase teacher pay, you are just going to attract people interested in making money, not people committed to teaching our youth.

Willy: That's just idiotic! Teachers, like everybody else, have got to make a decent living. Motivation can go only so far. A lot of people with the potential to be great teachers and a real desire to make teaching their profession end up choosing to put their talents to work in a job that promises a decent income.

Nilly: Well, so much for their great motivation . . .

THE ARGUMENTS AND THEIR RELATIONSHIPS

1. Willy's opening argument:
   Better pay will attract better teachers to our educational system.
   We need better teachers.

   We should increase pay for teachers.
2. Nilly's counterargument, intended to attach Willy's first premise:
   Good teachers are not motivated by money.

   Increases in salary will not attract better teachers.

3. Willy's reply, intended to show that Nilly's conclusion does not follow:
   If people with the potential to be good teachers cannot make a decent living
   at teaching, they will opt for other professions.

   Even though good teachers are not motivated by money, increased salary will
   nonetheless be necessary to attract good teachers.

SOLUTIONS

Exercise A

6. This passage is not easy to understand. The author's point of view does seem
   clear, though. He or she is opposed to the way Ollie North behaved in front of
   Congress. (North "sidestepped" Congress by lying when asked about the Reagan administration's involvement in the affairs of Iran and Nicaragua.) So the
   point of the passage seems to be to argue that what North did was wrong. More
   specifically, it was wrong because it involved a tactic used by Marxists. Hence,
   we might represent this part of the argument as follows:
   North's actions were based on the belief that the end justified the means.
   The tenets of Marxism say that any means will be justified if the end is
   achieved as desired.

   North acted on Marxist, not democratic, principles when he lied to Congress.
   But the passage also attempts to justify one of the premises of this argument:
   North claimed that he was right to lie to Congress, essentially because he
   believed his lies were justified in the name of national security.
   This argument assumes that the end justifies the means.

   North's actions were based on the belief that the end justified the means.
   This reading of the passage seems to make sense and seems sympathetic to the
   author's point of view. The second argument seems unproblematic. But the
   inference in the main argument seems to involve a subtle mistake. Assume that
   Marxist doctrine claims the end can justify the means. It would seem we can
   nonetheless deny that North acted on the basis of Marxist principles. Many people who are not Marxists believe that, on occasion, an end can justify means,
   even an otherwise questionable means. Normally, it is wrong to lie, but it may
   be possible to justify a lie to avoid greater harm. Suppose, for example, that I
   could save a life by lying. Here, the means—telling a lie—would justify the
   end—saving a human life. Simply because Marxists believe the end can justify
   the means, it does not follow that anyone who acts on this basis is a Marxist or
   is acting on principles inconsistent with a democratic form of government.
       All of this is not to say that what North did was not wrong or inconsistent
   with the demands of a democratic form of government. We can conclude only
   that, even on a sympathetic reading, the passage does not establish this.

CHAPTER FIVE

Relevance

A NOTE OF CAUTION

The remaining chapters of this book are about fallacies. It might be a good idea to print the following warning in the margin of each page:

Caution: The material contained herein has been known to induce intellectual double vision. When applying this information, you may see fallacies where none exists!

This warning should be taken seriously. As we learn more and more about fallacies, it will be easy to read arguments in ways that make them appear to be fallacious, even when they are not. Remember, when we extract an argument from its original setting, we are giving a reading of the argument—that is, implicitly making a decision to represent the argument in a particular way. And we must constantly remind ourselves to resist committing what we might call the **fallacy fallacy**—giving a distorted reading of a passage designed to make its argument appear fallacious.

Most of the examples and exercises we will work with will involve fallacies, and at times it will seem as though most reasoning is fallacious. Laboring under this assumption, we are likely to begin analyzing a passage by trying to spot a fallacy. But keep in mind, the examples and exercises in the remaining chapters do not represent a cross section of the arguments people give, for many arguments are not fallacious. Moreover, many of our examples and exercises involve controversial topics, topics on which you already have a point of view. When we encounter an argument for a position at odds with our own, it can be tempting to belittle the argument. What better way to do this than to read a mistake or two into it?

Here is a good way to test your suspicion that a passage involves a fallacy. After reading the passage carefully, identify its conclusion. Next, construct an argument for the conclusion, based on information from the passage, but which is a clear instance of the fallacy you suspect the passage involves. Finally, compare your reconstruction to the passage on which it is based. If you are "seeing" a fallacy where none exists, chances are good your reconstruction will bear little resemblance to the original passage. Your reading will probably seem (even to you, its author) artificial and contrived. If, instead, your reading seems to fit—if it seems to capture the thinking of the original passage—you are probably right to suspect the argument involves a fallacy. In this manner, you can use your increasing knowledge of fallacies to arrive at sympathetic readings of both fallacious and nonfallacious arguments. Think of fallacies, first, as something to avoid in extracting arguments from their original contexts. If you cannot give an accurate reading of a passage that does not involve a fallacy, you can be confident you have not inadvertently misrepresented the thinking of the argument's author.

CLASSIFYING FALLACIES

In this and the remaining chapters, we will deal with fallacies under a number of distinct headings: fallacies of relevance, distortion, and manipulation; fallacies involving the misuse of key terms; fallacies in analogical and causal reasoning; and fallacies involving generalizations. These headings are somewhat tentative and provisional. Unfortunately, there is no universally accepted scheme for classifying fallacies. No doubt this is because the ways in which people can go wrong when they argue are so many and varied that any fixed scheme for classifying them is bound to be a bit contrived. Some of the fallacies we encounter will fit under more than one heading, and a few will seem out of place no matter how we classify them. For the most part, however, our categories can provide us with some initial sense of the basic strategy involved in a particular kind of mistake. In the end, understanding a particular fallacious argument involves understanding how and why that argument goes wrong. When classification of an argument seems somewhat forced, we can look past our general headings and concentrate on the problems peculiar to the argument.

TYPES OF RELEVANCE

Relevance is a relative notion. To comment on the *relevance* of something is to remark on its connectedness to something else.

> The research she is engaged in is likely to be of great relevance.

The point of this claim is that her research will have an impact on the larger questions she is investigating. By contrast, to remark that something is *irrelevant* is to comment on its lack of connection to whatever is at issue. An argument is guilty of a **fallacy of relevance** when it introduces evidence that has no direct bearing on the claim at issue. Indeed, fallacies of relevance might more accurately be described as fallacies of *irrelevance.*

In deciding whether one claim is relevant to another, we must first distinguish between two levels of relevance. A claim may be relevant to the topic at issue in an argument without being relevant to the argument—without, that is, being a premise of the argument. This distinction between **topic relevance** and **evidential relevance** is important, for many fallacies of relevance introduce information that is relevant in the first way only. Consider the following argument for an increase in the minimum wage:

> In the past decade, the minimum wage has not kept pace with inflation. The number of people who work minimum-wage jobs has increased during the same period of time.
>
> ---
>
> The minimum wage should be increased.

The first premise seems clearly relevant to the conclusion, for it suggests the minimum wage has actually decreased over the past decade. In other words, if this premise is true, we have some reason to take the conclusion seriously. The relevance of the second premise, however, is another matter. In one sense, the second premise is relevant—it is about the topic at issue in the argument. But it does not seem to provide evidence for the argument's conclusion. Would a decrease in the number of people earning the minimum wage be a reason to decrease the minimum wage? Of course not. Thus, the fact that the number of people earning the minimum wage has increased is similarly irrelevant to the claim at issue. The second premise seems topic relevant but not evidentially relevant to the argument's conclusion.

A TEST FOR RELEVANCE

It is not always easy to decide whether a claim is evidentially relevant or merely topic relevant. A good test for evidential relevance follows. Suppose someone argued

$$\frac{P}{C}$$

in circumstances where we are not certain of the evidential relevance of P to C. We might ask the arguer, "So, if P were not the case, you would grant that C is not so?" If the reply is negative, we have reason to suspect that P is irrelevant to C, for what the reply tells us is that the arguer believes that C is the case whether P is true or false, plausible or implausible. This suggests that P is evidentially irrelevant to C.

To take a simple example, consider an argument given by someone, X:

> Smith has already served two terms in the Senate, and it's time to give somebody else a chance. So, I'm going to vote for his opponent.

Now, in one sense, X's reason is surely relevant; unless X is lying, we can assume X believes the reason offered to be relevant. But X may be mistaken in thinking this. If we suspect X's reason for voting against Smith is irrelevant, we might ask, "So, if Smith had served only one term, you would vote for him?" If X wouldn't vote for Smith even under this condition, we have a reason to think that X's stated reason is irrelevant. Whether or not Smith has served two terms, X would vote against him. So, the fact that Smith has served two terms cannot be X's reason for opposing Smith. X may have another reason or no reason at all, and, once we reveal that X's stated reason is irrelevant, the burden is X's to provide us with a more convincing argument. At most we have shown that a particular claim does not support X's position, not that X's position is unsupportable. X may have other, better reasons for supporting Smith. Of course, if X assures us that, indeed, if Smith had served only one term, X would consider voting for Smith, we would have evidence that the reason X has given is entirely relevant, at least in X's view.

But there remains a larger issue concerning relevance, an issue on which our test can provide additional insight. Convinced that X believes his or her reason to be evidentially relevant, we may nonetheless disagree with X. We may feel that X's reason is not a good reason to oppose a candidate; generally, length of service is not a good yardstick by which to measure the fitness of a person for public office. In other words, we may disagree with X's belief about the relevance of length of service. To resolve this disagreement, we can once again use our test for evidential relevance. If we could show that, in a variety of cases where candidates have served more than a single term, there may be overriding reasons to reelect them, we could argue that length of service is irrelevant to the question of who should be elected. Our argument here would embrace our general standard for relevance. On the question of whether or not a candidate should be reelected, we might argue, length of prior service has no bearing. Whether one has served no terms or a number of terms, the question of fitness for office remains open.

FALLACIES OF RELEVANCE

Our test for relevance can provide some initial sense of whether one claim is evidentially relevant to another. But often, pointing out that a claim is irrelevant is not enough, particularly when the claim makes an interesting observation about the topic at issue. The fallacies we discuss in this chapter all involve ways of introducing claims that have a measure of persuasive power, even when they are evidentially irrelevant. Our goal is to come to understand why each type of appeal is fallacious and how this fact can so easily go unnoticed.

The Genetic Fallacy

Many fallacies occur principally in counterargument, and this is true of the genetic fallacy. The **genetic fallacy** is committed when information about the source, or genesis, of an argument is advanced as a way of criticizing the argument. Conspicuously lacking in such a move is any consideration of the real issues involved in the argument. Consider this argument:

> The U.S. Constitution provides for the unrestricted ownership of private property, so there should be no laws limiting the uses an individual makes of his or her property.

Someone opposed to this argument might reply:

> Well, what do you expect of a document conceived and written by a handful of wealthy, upper-class landowners?

Although this rejoinder is true, it is irrelevant to the argument at issue. At issue in the argument is the question of whether laws can limit the use an individual makes of his or her property. Does the Constitution prohibit such restrictions? The fact that the Constitution may have been written by a group of people with a particular set of interests does not address the connection between the premise and the conclusion nor does it provide a reason to think the premise false.

   The genetic fallacy can be difficult to detect. It is easy to confuse information pertinent to the source of a claim with information relevant to its justification. For example, the question "Why do you believe it is wrong to steal?" can be taken in two ways. It can be taken as asking for an explanation of how one has come to hold this belief. Here, an appropriate answer might be "Because I have been taught this." But the question may be about the reasons why one accepts this belief as correct. In response to the latter reading of the question, the fact that one has been taught that stealing is wrong is irrelevant. What is at issue is not the origin of this belief but, rather, its justification: What reasons are there to think stealing is wrong? Relevant responses might be "In a world where stealing is condoned, no one could be secure in their property," or "Because it says so in the Bible and the Bible is the source of moral law." Since all three responses we have examined work as answers to the question "Why do you believe it is wrong to steal?" it is easy to mistakenly assume that all three responses address the same issue. Yet, to advance a fact about how one has come to believe stealing is wrong as a justification for that belief is to commit the genetic fallacy.

   One common variation on the genetic fallacy criticizes a claim on the ground that some of its more unsavory advocates constitute its source. We might call this

FIGURE 5.1   A classic example of the genetic fallacy. Who do you suppose the fellow on the left is? (*Source:* Tribune Media Services, Inc. All rights reserved. Reprinted with permission.)

variation **guilt by association** since it involves the implicit assumption that anyone who favors the claim under fire is somehow in sympathy with the group identified as its source. Imagine someone advancing this argument:

> The U.S. tax code should be made more progressive; the wealthy must be made to pay at a higher tax rate than the middle class. The reason is that the wealthy can exploit loopholes and deductions not available to the rest of us. So, if we allow the wealthy to be taxed at the same rate as the nonwealthy, the wealthy end up paying at a much lower rate.

In response to this argument, a critic might reply: "This is all well and good. But did you know this argument is a central plank in the platform of the American Labor Party, a political party that embraces socialist/communist principles?" Now, this may be true, but it is irrelevant to the argument at issue. This criticism goes wrong in two ways. First, it conflates the source of a belief with its justification and so is a clear instance of the genetic fallacy. Second, it invites us to assume that the sympathies of anyone who favors this view are identical to those of the group said to be the source of the argument. No doubt, people of many political persuasions would give similar arguments for progressivity in the tax code. The preceding response thus operates effectively only if we can be convinced to ignore this fact and to associate the argument with a group whose basic ideas many people today would find objectionable.

Personal Attacks

Another effective though fallacious way of countering an argument is the **personal attack**—ignore the argument and criticize its author. The fallacy of personal attack is nothing more than a personalized version of the genetic fallacy. The source that is made the subject of criticism is the argument's author. Why personal attacks can be so effective should be clear: If I can convince you that the person giving an argument is unreliable, lacks expertise, and so on, then I can perhaps convince you that his or her argument is without merit because of its source. Although personal attacks can involve just about any factor critical of an argument's author, several types of attack are particularly effective and commonly used. These are attacks that concentrate on a person's lack of expertise or experience, point of view, vested interests, and lack of consistency.

Lack of Expertise or Experience   If I can convince you that the person giving an argument doesn't know what he or she is talking about, I can probably get you to reject the argument. One way to do this is to question the arguer's expertise:

> Smith wants our school system to go "back to basics," to concentrate on teaching reading, writing, and arithmetic. No doubt, Smith's proposal is well intentioned. But I ask you, should we take seriously the views of a plumber on matters of important educational methodology and policy? Ladies and gentlemen, if you have a leaky faucet, I suggest you ask Smith for advice. But we are not talking about a simple plumbing problem here. We are talking about the future of our children.

The criticism mounted in this passage can be simply stated:

Smith is not an expert on school reform.

Smith's proposal for school reform should be rejected.

Perhaps Smith's proposal should be rejected. But by focusing on the author of the proposal, critics fail to give legitimate reasons why the proposal is a poor one. The fact that Smith is not an expert on educational matters is no reason to think that his proposal is wrongheaded.

Experience is often thought to confer a kind of expertise, and an arguer's lack of experience can be made the focus of a personal attack:

Politician A: If elected, I will balance the state budget. Frankly, I can't promise this will not require a temporary income tax surcharge, but we've got to get our fiscal house in order.

Politician B: Unlike my opponent, I have spent twenty-five years running a business. When you have to meet a payroll, you know how to balance the books. And you don't do it by asking your customers to pay more. You cut expenses. Maybe if A had a little experience trying to keep a business in the black, he would be able to figure this out.

Politician B has given no argument against A's claim that a tax surcharge may be necessary to balance the budget. He has, instead, only insinuated that A's analysis of the situation must be wrong because A lacks the experience required to deal with budgetary crises.

Point of View   Knowing a person's point of view on an issue often provides some initial sense of the arguments he or she is likely to countenance and oppose. This fact can be used to suggest that an arguer is the victim of *groupthink*—that he or she has advanced an argument because it is accepted by people of the same point of view, and not necessarily because the argument has any merit. Someone gives an argument against abortion. Someone else replies:

Well, what do you expect from a Catholic?

A politician defends her vote for a measure calling for more vocational training for prison inmates. A critic laments:

Just what you would expect from a "tax and spend" liberal.

Both of these replies are carefully designed to suggest that the person under attack is merely regurgitating the "party line," not thinking and arguing carefully about the particular case at issue. And both replies provide no evidence that the arguments under attack are defective.

Vested Interests   One way to undercut the credibility of an arguer is to question his or her impartiality, particularly by suggesting that the arguer has a vested interest in the conclusion of the argument being advanced. Suppose someone argues that public school teachers deserve a substantial raise in pay. Ignoring the details of the argument, someone else points out that the arguer's spouse is a teacher and so the arguer stands to profit if a pay raise is granted. This fact is irrelevant to any argument that might be advanced but is an effective way of questioning the arguer's objectivity.

Organizations and groups, as well as individual arguers, can form the basis for a personal attack based on vested interests. Recently, the American Medical Association (the AMA) took the position that there is currently little scientific evidence that acupuncture can alleviate pain. It is not difficult to imagine how a supporter of acupuncture might reply:

> Well, what do you expect? Every person who is helped by an acupuncturist is one less paying client for the mainstream medical community represented by the AMA. So, of course, the AMA is going to deny that acupuncture works.

By questioning the motives of the AMA (more precisely, the motives of the AMA members in favor of the AMA position on acupuncture), this rejoinder manages to deflect interest from whatever argument the AMA position may be based on. Attacks on the impartiality of groups, like the AMA, can be particularly insidious. Suppose that a few AMA members respond by denying that self-interest has influenced their view. Even if we accept their protestations, we may easily remain convinced they do not represent the dominant view of the group.

In one way, information about the interests of an arguer in his or her argument is not irrelevant. Knowing that a person stands to profit if his or her argument succeeds, we have good reason to look carefully at the facts on which the argument is based. We have, that is, some reason to suspect the arguer's impartiality. But this suspicion alone is not a reason to reject his or her argument though it should prompt a certain amount of skepticism; such a person may be too quick to advance and accept as evidence claims that need careful scrutiny.

Inconsistency   If we spot an inconsistency in an argument, we have found a real flaw. Two claims are inconsistent if both cannot be true.

The Bengals won the Super Bowl in 1990

and

The Rams won the Super Bowl in 1990

are inconsistent. Although both claims could be false, both cannot be true. If two premises are inconsistent, they cannot jointly support a conclusion, for at least one of them must be false; if a premise is inconsistent with a conclusion, it provides no support. The criticism in the following passage, for example, turns on an apparent inconsistency in the argument under attack:

> To the editor: Associate Editor X is right on target in his opposition to school prayer. But he misses the mark in his support of a school voucher system. In his arguments opposing organized prayer in the public schools, X advocates a clear separation of church and state. But he doesn't consider how his plan would use tax money, in the form of school vouchers, for sectarian religious purposes.
>
>   Does X believe that parents should be able to use government vouchers to send their children to schools that discriminate against children on the basis of their religion? Christian schools, for example, that do not permit Jewish,

Hindu, or Buddhist children to attend would be financed with tax money in the form of school vouchers. Is this separation of church and state?

Church-affiliated schools are free to discriminate on any basis they choose: religion, race, creed, color, or gender. And they are under no obligation to accept students who suffer from learning or physical disabilities or who are limited-English speakers. These students are far more expensive to educate than average students.

It doesn't take a genius to predict that a tax-supported voucher system would promote segregation in our schools. I urge X to reconsider his advocacy of school vouchers.

The object of this passage is to point out that X is inconsistent in advocating both a separation of church and state and public funding for private schools. This charge of inconsistency seems entirely relevant and suggests some weaknesses in X's position that need to be overcome if his view is to be consistent. Can, for example, X refine his view on vouchers so that religious discrimination will not be permitted by schools eligible for vouchers? Lacking clarification of this crucial issue, X's position does seem to involve a serious inconsistency.

By contrast, a **fallacious charge of inconsistency** cites some apparent inconsistency in the beliefs or behavior of the author of an argument that, as it turns out, is irrelevant to the argument. For example, parents might urge their teenage son or daughter not to smoke, rehearsing the usual reasons. The teen might then reply:

But you smoke. So, why is it wrong for me?

Though the parents are indeed guilty of inconsistency in failing to follow their own advice, this fact is irrelevant to their argument against smoking. The reasons they may have given for not smoking may be entirely good and sufficient ones; the fact that the parents smoke is beside the point. Charging an opponent with an inconsistency can be an effective, though fallacious, way of countering criticism. Suppose the teenager promises not to smoke but breaks his or her promise. The parents decide corrective action is in order: no allowance for the next three months. "One cannot," they point out, "break one's promises without paying the consequences." The teen replies: "And what of your promise to quit smoking? I don't see any penalty you are paying just because you still haven't stopped." This sort of response is likely to stop us in our tracks, but, strictly speaking, it is irrelevant. The fact that one promise has been broken does not justify breaking another.

A fallacious charge of inconsistency can be leveled on the basis of a set of seemingly inconsistent beliefs on the part of an arguer. This sort of charge is commonplace in political rhetoric:

My opponent says she is against any tax increases, but two years ago she voted for more than two billion dollars in new taxes.

What renders this attack irrelevant is the fact that circumstances change. There may be good reasons to oppose new taxes today but equally compelling reasons to support a tax increase at another time. The arguer may be perfectly consistent in favoring one and opposing the other.

Does the title of this book commit a fallacious personal attack? No. Though it does involve name-calling, it does not attack Rush Limbaugh as a means of countering any argument he might have given. Name-calling may not be nice, but it is not fallacious. As unflattering as it is, the title of this book is not a fallacious personal attack. To think otherwise is to commit the fallacy fallacy!

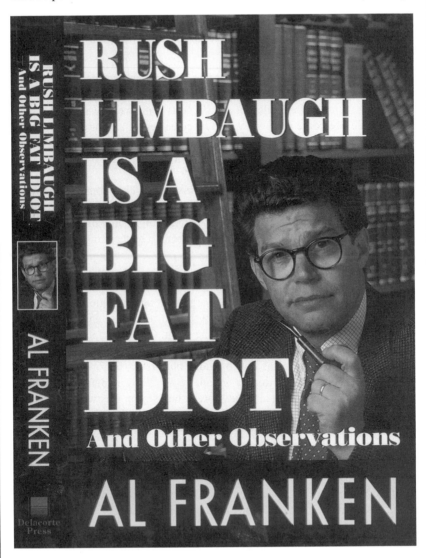

From *Rush Limbaugh Is a Big Fat Idiot* (jacket cover) by Al Franken. Copyright. Used by permission of Delacorte Press, a division of Random House, Inc.

Nonfallacious Uses of Personal Information   All this said, there are circumstances in which information about the author of an argument is *not* irrelevant to the argument. Consider this slight variation on the previous argument:

> My opponent says that throughout her political career she has opposed any increase in taxes. Yet only two years ago she voted for a bill that increased taxes in this state by two billion dollars annually.

Despite the fact that it makes allegations about a person, this appeal does not seem to be fallacious. The person in question claims to be opposed to new taxes, yet the evidence suggests this claim is false. (No doubt the candidate being criticized would argue that this apparent inconsistency has some explanation and, thus, is irrelevant.) Similarly, it seems appropriate and relevant to give, as a reason for not lending money to someone, the person's past record of failing to repay debts. But the occasions where personal information will be relevant are limited. If the claim at issue is about the character or behavior of a person, information about that person will play an important and relevant role.

Similar considerations justify the admissibility of certain sorts of information about the character or behavior of witnesses in legal proceedings. Imagine a witness in a civil or criminal case who testifies that the defendant has said certain incriminating things. On cross-examination, the defense attorney may try to "impeach" the witness, that is, attack the character of the witness as a way of countering his or her testimony. Fortunately, this sort of move does not involve the fallacy of personal attack. Under the law, it is often said, relevance is *probative worth.* What is relevant in legal testimony is any information that, in the judge's estimation, may "advance the enquiry" by enabling judge or jury to get to the truth of what is at issue. On this standard for relevance, evidence is generally disallowed as *irrelevant* if it does not bear on the question of what happened or if it could create a prejudice in the mind of the jury either for or against the defendant. Within these guidelines, information about the character of a witness is generally allowed as a means of raising questions about the veracity of a witness's testimony. The credibility of a witness may be attacked in a number of ways, all relevant and permissible. Information may be introduced about prior statements by the witness inconsistent with current testimony, bias against or partiality toward parties to the case, defects of sensory or mental capacity, conviction of crimes involving dishonesty or false statement, and self-interest of the witness in the outcome of the case.

Now, as a way of criticizing an argument, such information would be irrelevant. To cite the mental incapacity of an arguer or the fact that he or she has been convicted of a crime—outside the courtroom—would be to commit the fallacy of personal attack. But this is not the role such information generally plays in the courtroom. A witness testifies that something happened. The issue before judge and jury is not the quality of an argument given by the witness. Rather, the question is: Is the testimony of the witness to be believed? As it bears on the answer to this question, information about the character and behavior of the witness may be entirely relevant.

Beyond the special instances we have just considered, it is not always easy to decide when information about a person's conduct or character forms the basis for relevant criticism. In recent years, for example, many political campaigns have focused on issues involving the "character" of various candidates for public office.

Is the fact that a candidate dodged the draft years ago, may have engaged in extramarital affairs, or may have profited from investments because of the candidate's political influence relevant in a discussion of his or her qualification to hold office? The answer will vary depending on what the facts are, but perhaps this much is clear: To the extent that a candidate's actions are a reliable indicator of how he or she will behave in the future in the conduct of official duties, information about those actions may be relevant. However, when such information is exploited simply to belittle a candidate or to attack the credibility of his or her views, its use is fallacious. We must, then, be wary of political rhetoric designed to deflect attention from the real issues by focusing our attention on the character of a candidate. Information about the character of a candidate, no matter how lurid and sensational, is no substitute for reasoned criticism of the issues. It does not seem unreasonable to suggest that those critics who make character the focus of political debate have little to offer by way of substantial criticism.

Appeals to Authority

We must often rely on information provided by experts. If we were to accept only those claims we have personally investigated and found to be satisfactory, we would accept very little. My car won't start and I haven't the vaguest notion why, so I have it towed to a garage. That afternoon, I get a phone call from the mechanic who is working on my car: "You need a new fuel injector. I might be able to repair the old one for a lot less money, but I can't guarantee how much longer it would last. My advice is to put in a new one." Should I rely on the advice of my mechanic? And am I thinking and acting rationally if I do so? The only evidence I have that a new fuel injector is needed is the word of a mechanic that this is so. I haven't examined the fuel injector nor would I know what to look for if I did examine it. The evidence I have is, thus, secondhand.

If I decide to act on my mechanic's advice, I will be acting on the basis of the following argument, called an **appeal to authority:**

> My mechanic recommends that I have a new fuel injector installed.
> _____
> I ought to have a new fuel injector installed rather than having the old one repaired.

This argument looks suspiciously similar to many of the personal attacks we have examined. In a *personal attack,* a claim is *criticized* on the basis of those who believe it. In an *appeal to authority,* a claim is *defended* on the basis of those who believe it. Yet, as this example suggests, appeals to authority are not always irrelevant. I don't know anything about fuel-injection systems nor do I have the time, interest, or inclination to investigate the necessary technical information. In these circumstances, it seems reasonable to rely on an expert's advice. However, many appeals to authority are fallacious. Suppose I have doubts about my mechanic's advice. I might ask another mechanic to look at my car. But what if, instead, I consult my friend, a well-known psychic. I ask him what he "feels" will happen if I have the old fuel injector repaired. He tells me he senses something amiss, something dangerous in my future if I don't heed my mechanic's advice. Here we have another appeal to authority:

A well-known psychic believes I need to replace my fuel injector.

I ought to replace the fuel injector.

This new argument does seem to be fallacious; the premise seems irrelevant to the conclusion. Setting aside the question of whether psychics can actually see or "feel" the future, my friend the psychic is not a mechanic. Hence, his judgment on the state of my fuel injector is questionable.

These two examples suggest that appeals to authority are neither exclusively fallacious nor exclusively nonfallacious. In general, an appeal to authority will be nonfallacious when two conditions are met. First, *there must be a clear need to rely on expert advice.* An appeal to authority is no substitute for a careful look at the facts when this is possible. But when this is not possible, an appeal to authority may be warranted, for example, when a judgment requires the experience that comes with expertise. A person is considering buying a house, but the roof looks to be in questionable shape. The person knows he or she will not be able to afford a new roof for several years. Will the current roof last that long? Here it makes sense to consult someone who has replaced a lot of roofs and who may be able to come up with an accurate estimate of how long the old roof will last.

This first condition governs the admissibility of expert testimony in the courtroom. Such testimony is generally allowed when the subject of the testimony is "so distinctively related to some science, profession, business, or occupation as to be beyond the ken of the average layman."[1] A specialist in forensic medicine, for example, might testify that in his or her expert opinion a set of blood stains at the scene of a murder indicates a particular sequence of events at the time of the murder, a sequence consistent with the theory of the crime advanced by the prosecutor. Here, the question of whether the evidence of the blood stains confirms the prosecutor's theory seems "beyond the ken" of the average juror. Thus, it is reasonable that the jury rely on the testimony of experts in the relevant specialties.

Second, *the advice of an expert must fall within his or her area of expertise.* If I am to accept the recommendation of P on X, P should be an expert on the general area in which X falls. It is this fact about nonfallacious appeals to authority that saves them from a charge of irrelevance. If the claim at issue is one on which a person is an expert, the person's expertise may be relevant, particularly when the first condition is met. Lacking the time, ability, or knowledge to reach a decision on a difficult matter, I must defer to someone whose expert judgment is reliable and verifiable.

The second condition for a nonfallacious appeal to authority is also reflected in the legal requirements for the admissibility of expert testimony. An expert witness must "have sufficient skill, knowledge, or experience in that field or calling as to make it appear that his opinion or inference will probably aid the trier in his search for truth."[2] This second requirement for expert testimony is not as straightforward as the first. As a general rule, expert evidence is inadmissible if "the court believes that the state of the pertinent art or scientific knowledge does not permit a reasonable

---

[1]Edward W. Cleary, *McCormick's Handbook of the Law of Evidence,* 2nd ed. (St. Paul, Minn.: West, 1972), p. 29.
[2]Ibid., p. 30.

Imagine we are at a baseball game. The pitcher winds up and throws the ball to the plate, but the batter refuses to swing. The umpire raises her fist and calls out, "Strike one." "Baloney," you say, "she got that one wrong. The pitch was clearly not a strike." "Of course it was a strike," I reply. "The umpire calls them as she sees them. If she said it was a strike, it *was* a strike." Am I making an appeal to authority, fallacious or otherwise? Or is there a better way to characterize my argument?

opinion to be asserted even by an expert."[3] A case decided in 1923 (*Frye v. United States*) set the standard for the reasonableness of an expert opinion. A "reasonable" opinion was said to be one based on a technique or theory that has gained general acceptance among experts in the field in question. But recent court decisions have permitted expert testimony based on newly emerging theories or techniques on which experts in the relevant fields may not concur.

An appeal to authority is fallacious when one or both of the two conditions just discussed are not met. In a nonfallacious appeal, the opinion of an expert is required to get at the truth of things and the opinion must be the result of genuine expertise. This is true even, as in the courtroom, where the opinions and the theoretical perspectives of expert witnesses may differ. In a fallacious appeal, some source of authority is introduced, not because it is necessary or even relevant but, rather, because of the persuasive force that attaches to the very idea of expertise. Such appeals often work by exploiting our intellectual insecurities: If the "experts" believe X, who am I to disagree and why should I need to see arguments for X? These appeals often make use of the following questionable sources of authority.

Misplaced Expertise   A nonfallacious appeal to authority makes use of expert opinion on matters that fall within the area of the authority's expertise. But the opinions of an expert in one area should carry little weight outside his or her field of expertise. Yet the aura of authority with which we invest experts makes it tempting to cite them indiscriminately. Consider the following argument:

To the editor: Concerning David Suzuki's article "God, Evolution One," it is absurd to claim, as Dr. Suzuki and other evolutionists do, that one cannot be a true scientist if he or she believes in a literal interpretation of the Bible. Kepler, Newton, Faraday, Pascal, Pasteur, and a host of other great scientists firmly believed in special creation and the personal omnipotent God of creation, as well as believing in the Bible as the word of God. They certainly entertained no thoughts of conflict between science and the Bible.

---

[3]Ibid., p. 31.

The experts, the scientists, cited here have impeccable credentials in their respective fields. Newton, for example, was both a gifted mathematician and one of the most important figures in the history of physics. But Newton and the others cited in this passage were unfamiliar with the modern theory of evolution, and so their support for the biblical story of creation can hardly be said to be the informed opinion of experts in the field of evolutionary biology or related areas. Thus, the fact that each is a great scientific figure in his own field of endeavor has little bearing on the theory at issue in the passage. As to the existence of God, it is hard to imagine who might qualify as an expert. Thus, the appeals to authority contained in this passage seem intended to impress us with the good company "special creationists" keep, but they provide no argument for that theory.

Celebrity   Advertisements often feature well-known figures from the world of entertainment, sports, and, occasionally, politics. For years, the spokesperson for a well-known brand of coffeemaker was the famous baseball player Joe DiMaggio. The implied authority of such people stems not from their expertise but simply from the fact that they are well known. Advertisers obviously hope we will be so impressed by the fact that certain celebrities endorse their products that we will purchase them ourselves.

Sheer Numbers   If the majority of experts attest to the correctness of a claim on which their expertise is relevant, this may constitute evidence the claim is correct. But many appeals rely on the seeming authority provided by the fact that a large number of people endorse a claim. Although no real expertise is involved, the sheer number of people who favor a claim can lend an air of authority. Advertising often exploits this device by suggesting that the popularity of a product is a reason to buy it. In political campaigning, appeals for candidates and ballot measures often consist in nothing more than long lists of names of individuals, organizations, and businesses that support the person or measure.

Reference to Unspecified Expertise   In this common device employed in fallacious appeals, the arguer suggests that "the experts" or "scientific studies" or "recent statistical analyses" reveal something, but doesn't bother to say who these "experts" are or give the details of the "studies" or "analyses." The following appeal sounds remarkably well informed:

> Several recent empirical studies have provided compelling evidence that there is a genetic factor for obesity.

The actual evidence for a genetic factor for obesity is, of course, to be found in the studies mentioned. Perhaps there are such studies, and perhaps they do provide evidence for a genetic factor. But in the preceding appeal, the point seems to be to impress us with the fact that the source of the evidence is science while not providing any evidence, "scientific" or otherwise. The real problem with this sort of appeal, then, lies not so much with its lack of relevance as with its failure to provide any evidence at all, relevant or irrelevant.

Tradition   The fact that something has been believed true for a long time may appear to provide evidence that it is true. Such appeals suggest both that a lot of people have

An impressive but nonetheless questionable appeal to authority. Is the fact that Albert Einstein was a member of the American Federation of Teachers a good reason for others to join?

AMERICAN FEDERATION OF TEACHERS / AFL-CIO

"I consider it important, indeed urgently necessary, for intellectual workers to get together, both to protect their own economic status and, also, generally speaking, to secure their influence in the political field."

—ALBERT EINSTEIN
commenting on why he joined the AFT

Used by permission of American Federation of Teachers and Corbis/Bettman.

believed the claim and that the claim has stood the test of time; if the claim were mistaken, it would not have persisted for so long. That many of the things we currently believe have been believed for a long time, though true, seems largely incidental. Many claims we now recognize as false were believed throughout much of recorded history and by huge numbers of people. As recently as the eighteenth century, bloodletting was considered the most effective and humane cure for many physical ailments. Nearly everyone, including the experts, believed this. Moreover, bloodletting had been standard practice for centuries, at least in the medical tradition of the Western world.

Appeals to tradition exploit the fact that a claim has a historical legacy—it has been around for a long time. This is another method used frequently in advertising, often very subtly. Why should you invest with the brokerage firm I represent? We've been doing business for over fifty years. A TV ad for my brokerage firm will probably feature an elderly character actor whose face is kindly and wise. Our typical broker, it seems, has many years of experience. Who better to invest with?

No doubt, experience is one measure of expertise. If, for example, I suffer from severe, prolonged lower back pain, I may finally decide to heed my doctor's advice and have surgery. Experience will of course be one factor I will consider in choosing a surgeon, but it is one among many. How up-to-date is his or her training? What is his or her success rate? How wedded is this surgeon to surgery as opposed to other options? What do other doctors think of him or her? In and of itself, the fact that this surgeon has a lot of experience is of little relevance. Fallacious appeals to the authority conferred by tradition or experience tend to ignore the very factors that may render the experience of an expert relevant.

Appeals to Ignorance

When we are not sure about a claim, our uncertainty may stem from the fact that there is no convincing evidence, one way or the other, or because equally plausible arguments can be given both for and against the claim. The fallacy **appeal to ignorance** occurs when the lack of compelling evidence against (or for) a claim is given as a reason to believe the claim true (or false). In general, the fact that there is no evidence a controversial claim is false is irrelevant to the question of whether the claim is true. Similarly, the fact that there is no evidence a controversial claim is true is no reason to believe it false. In the absence of evidence one way or the other, we are entitled to conclude only that we just have no firm idea whether the claim is true or not.

As mentioned earlier, appeals to ignorance can occur in arguments both for and against claims. As an argument in defense of a claim, an appeal to ignorance will take the form

> There is no evidence C is not the case.
> _____
> C is the case.

The following argument is an example of this form:

> The Bible tells us that the world and everything in it was created in six days. After hundreds of years of attempting to account for the origins of life, science has yet to disprove the Bible. Thus, the biblical account of creation must be fundamentally correct.

Ernie By Bud Grace

FIGURE 5.2   If the victim of this appeal had read a book on fallacies, she would have known to ask "What evidence do you have that it does?" before handing over her donation. (*Source:* Copyright 1997 by King Features, Inc. World rights reserved. Reprinted with special permission of Kings Features Syndicate.)

That there is no scientific evidence the biblical story of creation is wrong does not constitute evidence that it is right. An appeal to the failure of science to falsify the Bible is, thus, irrelevant as a means of establishing the biblical account of creation. As a means of disproving a claim, an appeal to ignorance will take the form

> There is no evidence that C is the case.
> ───────────────────────────────
> C is *not* the case.

A number of scientific studies suggest that secondhand cigarette smoke can cause lung cancer. Against this charge, a spokesperson for the tobacco industry might argue:

> All of the studies done to date are inconclusive. A few suggest a weak link between secondhand cigarette smoke and lung cancer, but they have generally been unable to control for other factors that might cause lung cancer. Several of the studies suggest that the evidence for a connection is so minimal that no conclusion can be drawn, one way or the other.

This argument suggests that there is no link between secondhand cigarette smoke and lung cancer. All that it succeeds in showing, however, is that the studies in question have not established such a link. That there is no unequivocal evidence for a connection between secondhand smoke and lung cancer is not evidence there is no causal link. If the preceding passage is intended to argue that there is no link, it involves an appeal to ignorance.

You have probably heard the adage "It is impossible to prove a negative." Doubtless, this notion derives its plausibility from what we have said about appeals to ignorance. Often, to attempt to "prove a negative" is to attempt to prove that something is not so. And what could prove that a claim is not so other than the fact that there is no evidence it is so? Such an argument seems a clear instance of our second type of appeal to ignorance:

> There is no evidence that C is the case.
> ───────────────────────────────
> C is not the case.

However, there are circumstances in which a "negative" claim—a claim that something is not so—can be well supported and, moreover, in which the primary evidence is the lack of evidence in favor of the claim. Consider the following argument:

> Under carefully controlled scientific conditions, no psychic has been able to perform an act of telekinesis, that is, moving a physical object by sheer mind power alone. When pains are taken to set up experimental conditions that completely rule out the possibility of trickery, even the most accomplished psychic loses his or her ability to perform. It would seem, therefore, that there is no such thing as telekinesis.

A believer in telekinesis might reply: "This shows nothing more than the experimenters' inability to discern the effect in question. Just because they can't find it in the laboratory, doesn't mean it doesn't exist. Remember, you can't prove a negative."

But our critic has ignored a crucial fact about the argument in question. An appeal to ignorance occurs in arguments involving conclusions that are genuinely open to debate—claims we have no clear reason to believe, one way or the other. However, if a claim initially appears exceedingly improbable, the burden of proof lies with its advocates. In such circumstances, a failure to provide strong positive evidence for a claim is itself evidence that the claim is not so. A claim is improbable if it stands little chance of being true. For example, the claim that I will win the lottery if I purchase a single ticket is highly unlikely to be true, given that millions of tickets are sold. This example suggests that we can often make an antecedent estimate of the likelihood a claim is true, independent of any arguments that might be given for its truth. To do this, we must consider the likelihood of the claim being true against the background of everything we know relevant to the claim.

Now, think again about the earlier example objecting to the argument against telekinesis. The argument our critic has attacked claims that telekinesis does not occur precisely because there is no compelling evidence that it does occur. To decide whether or not this argument constitutes an appeal to ignorance, we must consider the probability that telekinesis does occur against the backdrop of everything we know or believe relevant to this claim. In fact, everything we have learned, from both scientific investigation and ordinary experience, about how people realize their intentions suggests that something more than a mere act of willing a thing to happen is required to make that thing actually happen. Suppose that a pencil on a table several feet away from you is balanced precariously on end. Without walking over and touching the pencil, can you figure out a way of knocking it over? Undoubtedly, you can think of many ways. Throw something at the pencil. Stomp up and down. Ask someone else to knock it down. Just wait and hope it falls over.

In general, then, we have an enormous body of evidence that intending something to happen is not sufficient to make it happen. Some sort of intervening process is required. This suggests that telekinesis is at least inconsistent with everything we now believe about the way we humans realize our intentions. Thus, the very idea of telekinesis seems exceedingly improbable. Does this mean telekinesis is impossible? No, of course not. But it does mean that, without clear and unambiguous evidence that telekinesis is real, we have every reason to remain skeptical about its existence.

CONUNDRUM

In our discussion of appeals to ignorance, we have noted that when a claim is extraordinary, the burden of proof falls on those who advocate the claim. Suppose somebody claims to have witnessed a miracle. Are there conditions under which you would accept the evidence of his or her testimony? In answer to this question, the seventeenth-century Scottish philosopher David Hume said:

> No testimony is sufficient to establish a miracle unless the testimony be of such a kind that its falsehood would be more miraculous than the fact which it endeavors to establish.

What do you suppose Hume means by this? Is the standard for acceptable testimony Hume labors to set forth in this passage consistent with what we have said about the burden of proof for extraordinary claims? Is Hume's standard a reasonable one?

The argument

There is no clear and unambiguous evidence for telekinesis.

It is highly unlikely that there is such a thing as telekinesis.

is not an appeal to ignorance. The argument would perhaps be fallacious if it claimed, categorically, that telekinesis is impossible. But this it does not claim. All that is claimed is that, lacking clear and unequivocal evidence for telekinesis, it seems highly unlikely that telekinesis exists.

Our critic might go one step further by claiming that our rejection of telekinesis is, if not an appeal to ignorance, at least evidence of a kind of narrow-mindedness. We are, the critic might suggest, "incapable of opening our minds to new paradigms, new ideas." We might reply that this is a nice example of another fallacy of relevance, a personal attack. But we might also point out that being open-minded does not mean accepting uncritically any claim on the ground that it is at least conceivable that it might be true. Obviously, many things are conceivable yet highly improbable. We do not lack an open mind if we refuse to countenance the highly improbable in the absence of compelling evidence.

What, then, are we finally to make of the adage "You can never prove a negative"? One adage deserves another: We must take it with a "grain of salt." If a claim is genuinely open—if we have no way of estimating whether it is probable or improbable—the adage is of course correct. The absence of evidence for such a claim is not evidence the claim is false, and, in such circumstances, to judge a claim false is to reason fallaciously. However, to the extent that a claim is improbable, a failure to produce positive evidence can reasonably be taken to suggest the claim may be false.

The same can be said for negative claims about the highly probable. Suppose someone tried to convince us that no human being has yet walked on the moon—that the moon landings were staged on an elaborate set somewhere in the bowels of the Pentagon by operatives of the Central Intelligence Agency. This seems an extraordi-

> **CONUNDRUM**
>
> You are undoubtedly familiar with the book *Where's Waldo?* This chapter might be subtitled *Where Are the Fallacies?* Somewhere, in the body of this chapter, two fallacies of relevance are committed. Can you find them?

nary claim, completely at odds with an enormous body of evidence for the moon landings. Yet, if pressed, we might find it difficult to cite anything other than circumstantial evidence for the moon landings: news clippings and videos and the testimony of people who claimed to have watched the landings on TV or to have witnessed the launching from Cape Canaveral. Our skeptic will be quick to point out our embarrassing lack of direct evidence. In reply, we need to respond that the burden of proof lies with him, not us. Without some spectacular evidence that no moon landings took place, we have every reason to believe that they did. In rejecting our skeptic's claim for lack of evidence, we do not engage in an appeal to ignorance.

CHAPTER SUMMARY

1. A fallacy of relevance occurs when information is introduced in the premises of an argument that has no bearing on the truth or falsity of the conclusion.

2. If a claim, P, is relevant as a means of establishing another claim, C, the answer to the following question should be affirmative: If P were not the case, would it follow that C is not the case? A negative answer to this question suggests that C follows whether or not P is the case and, so, that P is irrelevant to C. Establishing that one claim is irrelevant to another does not thereby establish that the latter claim is false.

   FALLACIES OF RELEVANCE

   Genetic fallacy   Occurs when information about the source, or genesis, of a claim is advanced as evidence the claim is false.

   Example: We can discount the views of the animal-liberation movement. The movement was begun by a bunch of dissatisfied radicals from the sixties bent on finding a fresh audience for their "oppressed masses" mumbo jumbo.

   Personal attacks   The person who holds a view or gives an argument is attacked as a means of criticizing his or her argument or view. Effective personal attacks often focus on the following:

   i. the arguer's lack of experience or expertise

      Example: We must reject Councilman Smith's proposal for additions to the city light-rail system. Only a transportation engineer could fully absorb the technical data on which a realistic proposal would need to be based. Though Smith is no doubt a competent attorney, a traffic engineer he is not.

   ii. the fact that an arguer is rehearsing arguments merely because they are consistent with a general point of view

      Example: Of course the senator is in favor of a tax hike. What do you expect from a "tax and spend" liberal?

    iii. the fact that the arguer has a vested interest in whatever he or she is arguing for

        Example: Sure, supporters of self-service gas stations claim that gas is cheaper in states that allow self-service. But look who those supporters are: the big oil companies who stand to profit from self-service.

    iv. the fact that the arguer's behavior or beliefs appear to be inconsistent with the claim he or she is now making

        Example: How can you believe what the President says about the need for prayer in the public schools? He doesn't even go to church.

Appeals to authority   Not all appeals to authority are fallacious. Fallacious appeals to authority result when some source of authority is introduced, not because it makes any necessary contribution to the argument, but because of the persuasive force that attaches to the very idea of expertise. Fallacious appeal will often cite factors other than expert opinion. They may rely on the following:

    i. misplaced expertise

        Example: The fact that 70 percent of all practicing scientists do not believe in God is good enough evidence for me to be an atheist.

    ii. celebrity

        Example: Bo knows.

    iii. the sheer number of people who support a view

        Example: Join the Pepsi generation.

    iv. the fact that the view has been accepted for a long time

        Example: There must be a God. Every culture in the history of the world has advanced some sort of belief about the existence of a transcendent being.

    v. unsubstantiated references to "the experts," "scientists," "studies," and so on

        Example: Now is not the time to invest in the stock market. A solid body of economic experts advise putting your money in an interest-bearing account instead.

Unsubstantiated references to sources of expertise lack relevance because they contain no real information relevant to the claim at issue.

Appeals to ignorance   To argue that a claim is true because no one has shown it false or that a claim is false because no one has proven it true.

    Example: Environmental alarmists have not been able to prove that fluorocarbons are depleting the ozone layer. Hence, it seems clear these chemicals are not damaging the environment in the way the alarmists suppose.

When a claim is highly improbable, the burden of proof lies with its advocates. To reject such a claim in the absence of positive evidence is not to commit an appeal to ignorance.

EXERCISES

A. Comment on fallacies you spot in the following passages. Some passages may involve more than one fallacy, others may involve none, and in some it may be difficult to decide whether there is a fallacy. In each passage, justify your answer by explaining why something contained in the passage is irrelevant or why the passage only appears to involve a fallacy. In some of the passages, it will be helpful to determine first whether the passage gives an argument or a counterargument. It may also be helpful to apply our general standard for relevance in thinking about problematic cases—cases in which you are unsure of the relevance of a claim. (See Point 2 on page 123 in the Chapter Summary.) Always try to be as sympathetic as possible. Remember:

> *The material contained herein has been known to induce intellectual double vision. When applying this material, you may see fallacies where none exists.*

(Solutions to Exercises 1 and 21 are given on page 130.)

1. 40 PERCENT OF UNIVERSITY PROFS BELIEVE PLANTS AND ANIMALS HAVE ESP —*headline from* The National Enquirer
2. If Alger Hiss pleaded the Fifth Amendment when questioned about his possible involvement in the Communist Party, he must have been a communist.
3. I admit I may have stretched the truth a bit in reporting income tax deductions. But where's the harm? Everybody fudges here and there on their taxes.
4. Even some scientists and engineers reject the theory of evolution. So, why should I accept it?
5. 26 million Americans can't be wrong. Reelect Senator Jones. —*bumper sticker*
6. Goldbach's conjecture (every even number is the sum of two prime numbers) must be true, for no one has yet come up with a counterexample or a proof that it is false.
7. You're telling me I drink too much? I don't think I've ever seen you without a drink in your hand.
8. It makes me sick every time I hear the Republicans argue for a capital gains tax reduction. I know the argument: allow people to make more profit and they will stimulate the economy with their investments. Of course, who do you suppose is going to gain the most from capital gains reduction? Wealthy Republicans, of course.
9. To the editor: State prisons are now poised to ban "pornographic material" on the startling ground that "reading these materials causes urges that can be taken out on individuals" and the justification that "if we've prevented rape, we've done our job."

   I am unaware of any proof that reading so-called pornographic materials causes antisocial behavior. Indeed, one could more cogently argue that these materials relieve those "urges" that might be taken out on individuals. Rather than a reasoned policy to prevent prison rape, this seems merely a mean-spirited move to deprive an already sexually deprived group of one of the few, harmless sexual outlets they have. This is a cynical, hypocritical, and stupid policy that shall do far more harm than good.
10. The U.S. Supreme Court has declared tuition tax credits to be constitutional. A Gallup Poll indicates 51 percent of Americans are in favor of some form of tuition tax credits. Clearly, the government ought to adopt a system under which people are given credits for the money they spend to send their children to private schools.

11. You say you are opposed to gun control? Did you know that, in the name of fighting crime, Adolph Hitler argued for a disarmed citizenry in Germany?

12. It is ironic that the same legislative body—the state senate—that allows smoking in its chamber appears likely to defeat a House-passed, 10-cent-a-pack tax on cigarettes. —*from a newspaper editorial in favor of an increase in the tax on cigarettes*

13. We're the biggest and most prestigious employee organization of any kind (26,000 members statewide). We got that way the same way you did—by being the best. So, naturally, we're very interested in you and what interests you. —*from a union membership drive flier*

14. You can be assured of expert work at Smash and Crash Body Shop. Our staff has a hundred years of combined experience.

15. No one who drives a car to work when public transportation is available has the right to tell me that my cigarette smoke is polluting his or her space.

16. Since 1871, we've popped more popcorn than anyone else. —*ad for Cracker Jack*

17. Bishop George Berkeley claimed that objects do not exist when they are not being perceived. Though this sounds preposterous, it is hard to refute. How could you prove, say, that the chair over in the corner exists when no one is perceiving it, that is, when no one is looking at it or touching it?

18. I went to watch the Senate deal with the budget crisis. Along the way I was fortunate enough to witness a moment of ironic symbolism in the form of Tip O'Neill (then Speaker of the House of Representatives) getting into a limousine you could hold a senior prom in. —*Dave Berry*

19. No wonder more and more pediatricians are recommending Vicks VapoRub.

20. To the editor: I just finished reading the "Ethics" column, by Nancy Butler, regarding the practice of surgery on unanesthetized infants. According to Butler's credentials, she has never worked in an operating room, and she is not a nurse. Why would you publish a nonprofessional's opinion on ethical matters regarding nurses?

21. Logicians have shown that all the purported proofs for God's existence are fallacious. Therefore, God does not exist.

22. Last time I wrote in favor of gun control, I got letters from people who said I was a communist. Me? A pinko? Come on. You're the guys getting automatic weapons from the commies!

23. Over 450 scientists with a master's or doctorate degree in some field of natural science are now voting members of the Creation Research Society. —*from an anti-evolution pamphlet, "Have You Been Brainwashed?"*

24. Acupuncture has little medical value. It was conceived as a method of treatment by primitive peoples who knew nothing of modern scientific method.

25. Smith argues that we need to build a new city library. He may be right that the old library is outmoded and simply has no room for additional books and periodicals. True, in a recent poll, the majority of respondents indicated a willingness to pay for new library construction. But do you suppose it is just a coincidence that Smith's construction company is one of the major contractors that does business with the city?

26. Easily 95 percent of all UFO sightings in the past 50 years have been successfully explained away. Most turned out to be aircraft, weather balloons,

the moon, Venus, and a few other natural phenomena. Some even turned out to be elaborate hoaxes. It seems likely that the small residue of unexplained cases have some sort of prosaic explanation we have just not figured out yet. Moreover, after all these years there is not one bit of hard evidence, a piece of alien metal or even a clear, indisputable photo of an alien or his or her (or its) spacecraft. It would seem that we have not been visited by aliens from another world.

27. To the editor: The tenets of Marxism say that any means will be justified if the end is achieved as desired. In a democracy or republic, the will of the people must be adhered to as expressed through their representatives in Congress. In sidestepping Congress, Ollie North and his band used the Marxist doctrine to pursue democracy. It doesn't make sense to me either.

28. To the editor: The state of Florida wants to kill Paul Hill for murder because he killed a doctor who performed abortions and one of the doctor's escorts. Hill killed them to stop them from murdering unborn children. How long are we going to go on killing to prevent or avenge killing? Why can't we all get back to the Sixth Commandment: "Thou shalt not kill"?

29. The idea of the soul undoubtedly arose when primitive human beings began to reveal their dreams to one another. Strange and amazing tales were told of events that took place while the "body" rested. The conclusion must have seemed obvious: Something leaves the body during sleep. Thus, the idea that there is a nonphysical part of ourselves that is separated from the body during sleep, and perhaps even death, is but a myth. It is the product of primitive minds trying to make sense of the phenomena we know to be dreams.

30. George Swift, a scholar at the Institute for Creation Research, says that creation science is better received and creation scientists more accepted in Russia. "Communism was tied to evolutionary theory," he notes. "When communism failed, the Russians started seeing the other side of the story. They're hungry for it. They know the other side didn't work out."

31. I know a lot of people out there believe we should do everything possible to keep the terminally ill going. I even understand the concern of churches, hospitals, nursing homes, and doctors. But keep in mind that they stand to lose a great deal of money if they are not able to keep people plugged into those machines.

32. To the editor: Your paper did an admirable job of covering the attack on outcomes-based grade-school curricula by a local conservative group, Project Second Look. Also reported were Project Second Look's connections to groups led by Phyllis Schlafly, Pat Robertson, and others of the Christian far right. I wondered how anyone could be fooled by Project Second Look. But then I realized that only my professional experience (eight years as a teacher, six as a school administrator, and seventeen as a designer of school curricula) lets me see exactly how specious and unfounded the ad hominem attacks and arguments of Project Second Look are. Every great name in education in this century, including John Dewey, Maria Montessori, and Jean Piaget, has advocated some form of outcomes-based education. All of special education has been based on it since the early 1960s. Worldwide, almost every significant researcher in curricula and methods advocates it. Yet Project Second Look opposes it.

Project Second Look is no friend of public education, and no friend of our children.

33. In case you didn't know: A recent Gallup Poll revealed that at least 55 percent of "young persons" accept or believe in astrology. This irks some people, who insist that publications should state, "This stuff is for your amusement only." Ironically, those who attack astrology usually don't understand its basic principles, cannot cast a horoscope, and do not know the difference between sun signs and actual natal charts. Perhaps they should pay attention to philosopher-poet Ralph Waldo Emerson, who declared, "Astrology is astronomy brought down to earth and applied to the affairs of man." —*astrologer Sydney Omarr*

34. To the editor: We need a law requiring five minutes of algebra at the beginning of every church service.

35. To the editor: Alas, it appears that we are doomed to repeat history, as it seems we have not yet learned from it. A group called Crime Stoppers wants to give students rewards for turning each other in (for possessing weapons, drinking, or using drugs in or around schools). And anonymously, to boot.

    It brings back memories of 1930s Germany, where neighbors turned in neighbors and relatives turned each other in. We are supposedly guaranteed by our Constitution to be innocent until proven guilty and, if accused, to meet our accusers.

36. To the editor: Mike Royko's friend is upset about "illegal immigrants" moving onto his land in California. He forgets that "his" land, as well as the rest of California, was stolen from the American Indians and Mexicans.

    Anglo Californians have never apologized for the theft. Indians were put on land the Anglos did not want, and the Mexicans were put to work cutting the Anglo's grass, cleaning his toilets, and acting as nannies to his kids. The Mexicans' cousins from Mexico were put to work picking lettuce and grapes.

    Who asked for papers when they could get away with paying them nothing? Certainly not the state of California, which could collect taxes from them and not have to provide any services. So, are people such as Royko's friend mean-spirited? Yes, really. Unfortunately for the American Indians and Mexicans, Anglos have the money and power, and nothing is going to change.

37. The following is from a letter encouraging college teachers to invite speakers representing the Church of Scientology to address their classes:
    The *Encyclopaedia Britannica* states that "the largest of the new religions is Scientology." There are over 6 million adherents worldwide and nearly 10,000 in your state. Controversial, and vocal, the Church has been feared, praised, attacked, and revered. Why do people like John Travolta, Karen Black, Chick Corea, and John Brodie claim Scientology has improved their lives? Why does Scientology garner the wrath of the APA, AMA, and others?

38. To the editor: Georgie Anne Geyer does not offer an explanation of why conditions are so austere in Cuba except to blame Fidel Castro for having an outsized ego and being willing to sacrifice his people for the revolution.

    Geyer never considers the morality or justice of the 35-year-old U.S. trade embargo on the island nation of 10 million souls. She accepts wholesale that it is OK for America to use its clout to prevent most of the rest of the world from trading with Cuba, despite the severe hardship.

The only explicit justification Geyer gives for her bias is that Castro has failed to "open Cuba to democracy." Well, maybe that is at least partially because of the way democracy is practiced by the United States. We who are so concerned about human rights are the same ones who irradiated 800 people, some without their knowledge or consent, for the sake of a cold war experiment. Who are we to preach human rights?

39. The following is from the testimony of Andrew H. Tisch, chairman and chief executive of Lorillard Tobacco Company, in a class action suit. The suit was filed in the name of a group of people who died from lung cancer presumably caused, as their suit claims, by exposure to cigarette smoke.

Question:

Does cigarette smoking cause lung cancer?

Answer:

I don't believe so.

Question:

Based on what?

Answer:

Based on my understanding of the scientific and statistical evidence that's been presented.

Question:

What is your understanding of the scientific and statistical evidence that's been presented?

Answer:

There's been no conclusive evidence that's been presented that convinces me that cigarette smoking causes lung cancer.

40. For decades, public and private organizations have waged a massive campaign to discourage cigarette smoking. For most of the time, the target of this effort has been the smoker. Recently, however, the emphasis has undergone a major shift. Today there are scientists who claim that cigarette smoke in the air can actually cause disease in nonsmokers. We hear a great deal about "secondhand smoke" and "passive smoking."

But is this new approach wholly motivated by concern for the nonsmoker, or is it the same old war on smoking in a new guise?

These doubts are raised when we recall statements like the following, by a spokesperson for the American Lung Association:

Probably the only way we can win a substantial reduction [in smoking] is if we can somehow make it nonacceptable socially. . . . We thought the scare of medical statistics and opinions would produce a major reduction. It really didn't.

Obviously, one way to make smoking "nonacceptable socially" would be to suggest that secondhand smoke could cause disease. So it is not surprising that we are now seeing a flurry of research seeking scientific support for these suggestions. . . .

Of course, if antismoking advocates want to work for the abolition of smoking, that is their right. We only wish they would come out from behind their secondhand smoke screen. —*from an ad by the R. J. Reynolds Tobacco Company*

B. One way to familiarize yourself with a fallacy is to invent an example. Pick one of the following topics and create an argument that commits at least one of the fallacies discussed in this chapter. Don't allow your fallacy to be too transparent. A well-conceived fallacy should be able to fool people. Give your result to a friend—ideally, one who is not familiar with fallacies—and ask what he or she thinks of your argument. If you have written an effective fallacy, your friend should not have an easy time spotting the mistake.

1. The death penalty should be abolished.
2. Animals have moral rights.
3. We have a moral obligation to be vegetarians.
4. Private citizens should not be allowed to own handguns.
5. All forms of gambling should be illegal.
6. Condoms should be distributed in public schools.
7. Students who sit in the front of the classroom will get the best grades.
8. Personality is reflected in handwriting.
9. We should stop building freeways and build mass transit instead.
10. Professional boxing should be abolished.

C. Pick a topic from the preceding list that is different from the one you chose for Exercise B (or invent your own topic), and write a brief dialogue between two people, Willy and Nilly, in which the topic is debated. In the dialogue, include at least one example of each of the following fallacies of relevance: the genetic fallacy, personal attack, appeal to authority, and appeal to ignorance.

SOLUTIONS

Exercise A

1. *Appeal to authority.* The sheer number of college professors who believe in plant and animal ESP is not relevant evidence of the accuracy of this claim. We are given no reason to believe the professors in question have any kind of expertise in ESP research. What, for example, if the majority of these "experts" teach English or physical education? By the way, can we conclude from this headline that 60 percent of college professors do *not* believe the claim in question?

21. *Appeal to ignorance* and *appeal to authority.* Even if all the "proofs" for God's existence are fallacious, it does not follow that God does not exist. Rather, all that follows is that God's existence has not been established by rational argumentation. The passage also involves a slight appeal to authority in its acknowledgment that "logicians" have discovered the flaws in the purported proofs. "Logicians" here constitute a kind of unsubstantiated group of experts.

CHAPTER SIX

Distortion

When something is inaccurately described, the result is a distorted picture of what actually is the case. **Distortion** can improperly increase the persuasive strength of an argument in two ways. First, an argument can be based on a distorted version of the facts surrounding the topic at issue. Though factual distortion can be inadvertent, it is often calculated. An arguer may intentionally leave out crucial information to make the argument appear stronger than it really is; facts suggesting difficulties for the conclusion may be glossed over or omitted. Arguments that fail to give all the relevant facts or that misrepresent key claims distort in this first way. An argument based on a distorted presentation of the facts invites us to concur in an inference that may be unwarranted. Second, an argument can distort by misrepresenting an opposed view or argument for purposes of criticism. Although the criticism subsequently offered may seem trenchant and insightful, it is nonetheless criticism of a position rigged to be an easy target and not a position anyone might take seriously. In general, then, distortion involves misrepresentation of either the facts surrounding an argument or the views of others. Let's begin by looking at fallacies that depend on distortion of information from the factual background against which an argument is given.

DISTORTIONS OF FACT

There are many techniques by which the factual case on which an argument is based can be distorted. Facts can be omitted or oversimplified. Claims can be couched in terms that make them appear much less suspect than they are, and questionable claims can be left unstated. All such moves leave the impression that things are other than they really are. About any argument, it is a good idea to ask: What facts are missing? What haven't we been told?

Omitting Information

When crucial information is omitted, either intentionally or unintentionally, the result is likely to be a distorted version of the facts relevant in the presentation of an argument. By carefully picking and choosing from the facts surrounding an issue, an arguer can easily turn a weak case into a strong one. The kind of factual distortion that results when information is omitted is particularly insidious. We may not be aware of the omission and will, thus, be in no position to accurately assess the strength of the inference made on the basis of the few facts we are given. Suppose I offered you the following advice:

> If I were you, I'd start hunting for another lawyer, unless you've got plenty of money to throw away. I took your advice and went to see Smith about that little legal problem I had. We talked for about 45 minutes and then, a couple of days later, he phoned me and said to go ahead and sign the purchase agreement on the house. Well, the end of the month rolled around and I got his bill in the mail. Would you believe, he billed me for 3½ hours of work and at an hourly rate that's more than I make in a day?

This argument effectively calls into question Smith's professional integrity. Doubtless, if this is the extent of the story, we have good reason to think about finding a new lawyer. Moreover, you may have no reason to suspect that I haven't provided you with all the relevant details of my dealings with Smith. But suppose, now, a few more facts come to light. Upon examining my bill from Smith, you find the following notations:

Office consultation	.75 hour
Telephone conference with title company	.5 hour
Telephone conferences with escrow agent	.75 hour
Legal research re: tax effect of purchase	.5 hour
Preparation of letter to title company confirming satisfaction of property liens	1.0 hour
Total Time	3.5 hours

Interestingly, this information is not inconsistent with anything I have told you. Nothing here suggests anything I have said is false. However, it now seems Smith may not have overbilled after all. Yet, suppressing the information contained in the bill creates a very different impression.

This example illustrates an important point: *Beware of arguments that are almost too good to be true.* When confronted with an argument so strong it is hard to imagine how anyone could disagree, we need to be suspicious. Something has probably been suppressed or ignored. As a general rule, then, we should be skeptical about the completeness of the facts given in any argument that is seemingly irresistible. Always ask: What facts are missing? What haven't we been told?

Oversimplification   Distortion often stems from an oversimplification of either the facts or issues surrounding an argument. Don't be misled by the context in which the argument in the accompanying cartoon occurs. Although it is given in a humorous setting, this argument seems to take itself quite seriously. As Mallard Fillmore points out at the end, our legal system is "scary." People pursue costly lawsuits against businesses even in circumstances where they have no one to blame but themselves for any damages incurred, encouraged, no doubt, by greedy lawyers. And what makes the system so "scary" is that people often prevail in such suits. The basis for this complaint is an actual case, the case alluded to in the cartoon. A woman purchased a cup of coffee at a McDonald's outlet, spilled it on herself while driving, and got

MALLARD FILLMORE	®	By Bruce Tinsley

(*Source:* Reprinted with special permission of King Features Syndicate.)

burned. She subsequently sued McDonald's, and a jury awarded her nearly $2.9 million in damages, although the cartoon fails to tell us this.

Upon reading this cartoon, most people, I suspect, would concur with Mallard. There is something wrong with a legal system that allows, indeed, encourages this sort of abuse. In the end, we are all going to subsidize these outrageous awards in the form of higher costs for the products we purchase. Mallard's point, though unstated in the cartoon, is undoubtedly that our legal system is in immediate need of reform: Some way must be found to limit the extent of corporate liability in cases brought to the courts by disgruntled consumers.

But consider now a letter from the Ann Landers column that appeared, ironically enough, in my local paper on the same day as the Mallard Fillmore cartoon.

> Dear Ann Landers: I am the attorney who successfully represented the woman who sued McDonald's over spilled coffee. In your recent column on the subject you said, "The once noble profession of law has sunk to a new low." I feel a responsibility to present your readers with some facts about the case.
>
> The woman sued McDonald's for $2.9 million in damages after she spilled hot coffee in her lap while riding in a car. McDonald's coffee historically has been sold at 180–190 degrees Fahrenheit, hotter than that served at most fast-food outlets. My 81-year-old client received third-degree burns and had to spend eight days in the hospital and undergo skin-graft operations.
>
> At 180 degrees Fahrenheit, coffee is unreasonably dangerous. Despite more than 700 reported claims of individuals being burned by McDonald's coffee in the past 10 years, the corporation never consulted a burn doctor to assess risk.
>
> The jury awarded punitive damages to deter McDonald's and other corporations from exposing consumers to unnecessary risk. They considered the severity of my client's injuries, the high number of McDonald's coffee burn cases that preceded this one, and the fact that no effort was made to change

corporate operations. The finding against McDonald's should be hailed as a victory for the consumer. The civil justice system worked the way it is supposed to—to protect individuals from corporate indifference.[1]

Once again, consider Mallard Fillmore's description of this case:

> Hey . . . if a woman can spill coffee on herself and then successfully sue McDonald's for making their coffee too hot . . .

This account leaves the impression the case at issue is just another frivolous lawsuit, one that probably should never have made it into the courts and certainly one in which the settlement was excessive. Yet we can now see that Mallard's description considerably oversimplifies the issues in the case by ignoring several crucial facts. McDonald's, it seems, has persisted in a dangerous practice for a number of years and has chosen not to rectify the situation. Moreover, the woman who sued McDonald's was seriously injured. She did not sue McDonald's, as Mallard suggests, simply because the coffee was too hot. One additional fact, missing from both of the accounts we have examined, is that, of the total damages awarded, only $200,000 was in the form of compensation for injuries. The remainder of the $2.9 million was for punitive damages, that is, damages awarded as a means of both punishing McDonald's and providing McDonald's an incentive to modify its unsafe practices. Not coincidentally, the jury fixed the amount of punitive damages at the estimate of the profits from one day's coffee sales at all McDonald's outlets in the United States.

Once a more complete version of the relevant facts is given, the case begins to look much less frivolous than Mallard insinuates and the argument mounted on its basis much less compelling. Of course, from the fact that Mallard's version of the case is distorted, it does not follow that his conclusion cannot be supported. Even given the preceding facts, the verdict in the McDonald's case seems somewhat excessive. (In fact, the parties to the case later agreed to an out-of-court settlement in which the amount for punitive damages was greatly reduced.) Perhaps our tort system needs to be reformed. Some critics of the system suggest, for example, that awards for punitive damages should be limited to an amount not in excess of three or four times the amount awarded for actual damages.

But before we argue for reform, the need for reform must be documented. Is our current system indeed "scary," as Mallard Fillmore suggests? Are the courts clogged with frivolous consumer lawsuits, and are damages generally excessive? To answer these questions, we would need to look at a good deal of background information. Are awards larger now than, say, five, ten, or twenty years ago? Are there more consumer lawsuits, per capita, now? Is there evidence that manufacturers are producing more dangerously defective products now than in the past and that an increase in lawsuits is, in part, due to this? We would need to look for trends of the sort these questions suggest, not at single cases of the sort Mallard Fillmore has provided us.

Lack of Perspective   The Mallard Fillmore example is not unusual. Arguments are often mounted to advocate changes in policies or practices, and here the potential for

---

[1] Ann Landers, January 16, 1995.

factual distortion is rampant. Someone might argue, for example, that more money needs to be spent on prisons, as a way of countering today's violent-crime rate. Whenever sweeping changes in policy of this sort are advocated, it is worth looking into the factual rationale for that change in an attempt to gain a *historical perspective* on the issue. If we need more prison space, it must be because conditions have deteriorated. Alone, the fact that there is a great deal of crime today does not establish a need for the reform in question. If reform is necessary, it must be because crime is increasing or because available prison space has always been insufficient or has diminished. Thus, an argument that cites the current violent-crime rate yet provides no historical perspective may create a false impression of what the prison situation is today. Without the appropriate comparative data, it is hard to assess the claim that more prison space is needed.

The kind of distortion that can occur when historical perspective is ignored is further illustrated by the following case. Imagine that a poll was taken among several thousand high school students nationwide. The results show that nearly one-half have tried alcohol or other drugs and that one-fifth report continued regular use of either or both. Do we have a pressing social problem on our hands? Here, once again, we need a *benchmark,* some basis for comparison. Assuming the poll is reliable, just how different is the behavior of today's high school students from that of students in the past? If roughly half of all high school students, say, in the past two decades, have experimented with alcohol and other drugs, the poll cannot be taken to suggest a disturbing new trend. If, on the other hand, rates historically have been much lower, the findings of the poll are of some importance. There is increased use of alcohol and other drugs by today's high school students, and we need to begin to formulate a strategy for dealing with the problem. The point here is that, without the appropriate comparative data, the real significance of the poll is difficult to determine.

In the absence of comparative data, then, anyone who attempts to interpret the poll's significance is guilty of distortion by omission. Suppose you were arguing for more funding for an alcohol and drug prevention program in your state. Imagine also that there is no evidence that rates of drug and alcohol use among teens are greater today than in the recent past. You might nonetheless make effective use of the poll by emphasizing its distressingly high numbers yet conveniently omitting any information that might provide the necessary historical perspective.

Comparative data can also be crucial in assessing claims about similarities and dissimilarities between groups. Imagine that we have uncovered data suggesting an alarming difference between the Scholastic Aptitude Test (SAT) scores of public and private high school students:

> On average, the SAT scores of public school students are significantly lower than the SAT scores of private school students.

What is the significance of this difference? Should we take it to suggest that public schools do a less effective job of preparing their students for college-level work than private schools do? Any claim about the significance of this difference depends on how similar the two groups are. If pronounced dissimilarities account for the difference, the preceding claim may be of little significance. If, for example, a large fraction of private schools have entrance exams, the fact that private school students do better on the SAT cannot be taken to suggest that public schools provide less effective education for their pupils. Rather, it seems private schools select their students, in part, on the basis of their ability to do well on tests like the SAT.

Pronounced differences between similar groups usually have some explanation, so we should consider the possible basis for any such difference. An appeal that does not account for the basis of a striking difference should be taken with a grain of salt. Consider the following appeal in which such a difference is exploited:

> What we don't need in this state is a tax increase. What we do need is a reduction in the salary of state employees. Do you realize the average salary for public sector employees in this state is 22 percent higher than the average for people employed in the private sector? I find it ironic that public sector employees want more money and want it to come from people who make a lot less than they do!

How similar are the groups being compared in this example? The comparison tells us very little. Suppose that a much higher percentage of public sector employees than private sector employees occupy positions that generally are highly paid: teachers, doctors, lawyers, engineers, and so on. Suppose also the percentage of minimum-skill, traditionally low-paying occupations is much higher in the private sector than in the public sector. Under these circumstances, the 22 percent difference may signify much less than the passage would have us believe. Once again, the key to coping with a claim like

> Public sector employees make 22 percent more than people in the private sector

is to ask: What facts are missing? What haven't we been told?

Innuendo

Distortion can result from the use of **innuendo** or *insinuation.* In context, most of the remarks we make carry with them what are called **conversational implicatures.**[2] In a typical conversational setting, speaker and audience bring to a claim a number of assumptions; these are the claim's implicatures. So, for example, if you tell me how to get somewhere, I assume you are doing your best to give me accurate information. Unfortunately, the normal implicatures of a claim may not, in some contexts, hold. Suppose I told a class, in which you were enrolled, that some of you have passed the quiz I have just graded and am about to pass back. You will probably—and quite naturally—assume that I'm suggesting some have failed as well. This is, after all, the normal implicature of my remark. But suppose all the students in the class have passed. Though what I have said is not false, I nonetheless have presented a misleading picture of how the class did on the test. Thus, distortion results when a speaker or writer allows a false insinuation to stand by concealing from his or her audience the fact that the normal conversational implicatures of a remark do not hold.

---

[2] The notion of conversational implicature was developed by a philosopher, Paul Grice, in a paper titled "Logic and Conversation," in *The Logic of Grammar,* edited by Donald Davidson and Gilbert Harmon (Encino, Calif.: Dickenson, 1975), pp. 64–153. The importance of this notion in the analysis of the kind of distortion that can result from innuendo was recognized by Robert J. Fogelin in *Understanding Arguments: An Introduction to Informal Logic* (New York: Harcourt Brace Jovanovich, 1978).

Here is a simple example. Suppose you participate in a competition in which, unbeknownst to me, there are but two entrants. You lose. Later, I ask you how you did. "Well," you tell me, "not too bad. I finished second." Although what you have said is not false, it is misleading. My inclination on hearing someone "finished second" is to assume that the person did not finish last and that there were more than two participants. By omitting the fact that there were only two participants, you have misled me by taking advantage of what you know to be the normal conversational implicature of your remark.

Allowing false insinuations to stand can have a considerably more insidious effect. Suppose you are asked to write a letter of reference for an employee, Smith, who you would rather not see leave your company. Smith, it seems, is one of your best and most dependable workers. The normal assumption most of us make is that letters of recommendation or reference will contain all or most of the positive things the writer has to say about the person in question. But suppose your letter reads as follows:

> To whom it may concern:
>
> Smith has worked for me for several years. In that time Smith has rarely been absent from work.
>
> Sincerely yours,

By omitting any additional facts about Smith's performance, you have taken advantage of your reader's natural assumption that your letter contains a relatively complete list of Smith's virtues as an employee. Even better, you have conveyed an entirely misleading impression about poor Smith without saying anything that is false. This tactic is often called *damning with faint praise!*

Anecdotal Evidence

Perhaps the single most common source of factual distortion is the use of anecdotal evidence to create a misleading impression about what is generally the case. Anecdotes carry considerable persuasive force—certainly more than abstract statements of the generalizations they are employed to illustrate. Think once again of the Mallard Fillmore cartoon discussed earlier. The anecdote Fillmore exploits—the lawsuit against McDonald's—is a particularly vivid and dramatic illustration of what Fillmore thinks is wrong with our legal system. It is hard to imagine anybody who would not be disturbed by such a case. Yet we are provided no reason to believe the case is in any way typical. But when anecdotes are given as a way of illustrating a generalization, the tacit assumption is that they are just that—typical—of a general class of events. Even worse, many anecdotes are carefully selected precisely because they represent the extreme case. The one thing they are not is what they are held out to be: typical.

Examples of misinformation by the use of atypical anecdotes are commonplace. Arguments are often mounted for general positions or policies on the basis of just a flamboyant example or two, as in the following cases:

> The welfare system is so out of whack it ought to be junked. Just yesterday I saw a guy buying steak—steak, mind you, not hamburger—with his food

stamps. And did you read the story in the paper about the woman who is pregnant with her seventh child? She's never worked a day in her life and chooses instead to allow the state to support her.

You want to eliminate the federal deficit? It's simple. Cut the waste out of government spending. And don't worry, the fat is there to cut. Any government that can spend sixty-five dollars to buy a hammer has plenty of fat to trim.

Lacking any reason to think the cases cited in these examples typical, we can only assume they have been selected more for their emotional punch than for their ability to accurately represent a problem. As a general rule, we should be suspicious of appeals that rely on anecdotal evidence. Without any evidence to the contrary, a juicy anecdote most likely is nothing more than the worst (or best) example that could be found.

False Precision

Distortion can result when someone uses facts and figures to convey the impression that an approximation is much more meaningful than it really is. I guess, for example, that about half of all Americans are male. I cannot be accused of deceit so long as I make clear that I am just trying to give an approximate answer. However, if I couch my guess in precise numbers, I can lend a considerably different impression. Suppose, instead, I said:

51.3 percent of all Americans are male; 49.7 percent are female.

It now sounds as if I know what I am talking about. Certainly, many people would be less prone to dispute this claim than my earlier guess. I might go a step further by adding a phrase that strikes fear in the hearts of many of us:

The most recent statistical analysis with which I am familiar shows that 51.3 percent of Americans are male.

By simply using words that suggest careful numerical quantification, I have made a guess look to be considerably more like a certainty.[3] In response to either of my claims about the percentage of American males, you should ask me, "On what data do you base your claim?"

Be particularly wary of forecasts that involve a high level of precision:

If current trends continue, the national debt will stand at $29,672 for every American man, woman, and child by the year 2002.

About the future, one thing can be known with precision: Nothing can be known with the degree of precision this claim provides. When predictions and approximations

---

[3] Generalizations like the one just cited are often based on *sampling arguments*—arguments in which an inference is drawn about an entire population based on a relatively small cross section taken from the population. Frequently, media reports of the results of sampling arguments are guilty of a kind of false precision. Samples can provide at best a good estimate of what is the case in the entire population. Yet the media often ignore this fact in reporting sample results. In Chapter 9, we will look at both the techniques involved in sampling arguments and the ways in which false precision can result from misreading the results of such arguments.

exhibit this degree of precision, it is always worth stepping back and asking yourself: How could anybody know this? What information would it take to establish this?

Misleading Qualifiers

It is sometimes necessary to qualify a claim to make it as accurate as possible. If I think there is a fairly good chance it will rain tomorrow, an accurate claim about tomorrow's weather is that it will *probably* rain, not simply that it will rain. As noted in Chapter 2, excessive qualification can lead to vagueness, which, in the context of an argument, can be misleading. The subtle insertion of qualifying words and phrases can exaggerate the importance of the evidence for a conclusion. The following passage is from a pamphlet arguing against a state ballot measure (Measure 16) that would allow physicians to administer lethal drugs to terminally ill individuals who want to end their lives. The pamphlet consisted of a series of quotations from people opposed to Measure 16. Here is one:

> The mission of hospice is to make the lives of the terminally ill fulfilling and comfortable. Measure 16 could offer the terminally ill a lingering, agonizing death that could drag on for days. We can do so much better than that. People should die with dignity, comfort, and peace. I'm voting No on 16.

A cursory reading suggests the drugs that will be administered to hasten death if Measure 16 passes will have tragic consequences. But is that what the passage in fact tells us? Look carefully at the language of the second sentence of the passage. Measure 16 *could* offer a lingering, agonizing death that *could* drag on for days. Only if we overlook these subtle qualifiers does the claim on which the argument is based seem to provide much support for its conclusion. Of course, it does not follow that Measure 16 will not have the consequences mentioned in the passage. Given what the passage actually says, though, we are in no position to draw much of a conclusion about the potential effects of the procedures permitted by Measure 16.

False Dichotomy

A distinction is **exhaustive** if all the things over which it ranges fit under one or the other of its terms.

> Every integer greater than zero is either odd or even

is, thus, exhaustive in that there are no positive integers that do not fit into one of these two categories. Many distinctions, however, are not exhaustive. Consider

> We can go to a movie tonight or stay home and watch TV.

The alternatives set forth here are not exhaustive. Under the general heading "things we can do tonight," there are a number of other options.

A distinction is **exclusive** if none of the things over which it ranges can fall under both of its headings. The preceding claim about the integers greater than zero is exclusive as well as exhaustive since no integer can be both odd and even. Distinctions need not be exclusive. The question

> Are you a student or do you have a job?

presupposes a distinction that is not exclusive. Obviously, one can both go to school and have a job.

A *dichotomy* is a distinction that is both exhaustive and exclusive, like our claim about the positive integers. Dichotomies can form the basis of a reliable type of argument called **argument by elimination,** in which a conclusion is drawn about one of a pair of alternatives based on the fact that the other alternative is not the case. Suppose you have just had your leaky roof examined and are told you have two choices: Either you can repair the leaks and hope no new ones develop or you can have a new roof installed. Once you see the estimate for a new roof, you realize you can't afford a new one. A new roof will cost about five times as much as a repair job. You decide to have the old roof repaired. Your thinking here involves a simple argument by elimination:

> I can either get a new roof or repair the old one and hope it lasts for a few more years. Unfortunately, I can't afford the cost of a new roof, so I guess I will have to get the old one repaired.

The fallacy, **false dichotomy,** occurs when a similar inference is drawn, but on the basis of a distinction that is treated as though it were dichotomous when it is not.

The following argument involves a false dichotomy:

> We really have only two choices. Either we work for a ban on all nuclear weapons or we go on living in a world in which the possibility of nuclear holocaust is ever present. More than a dozen countries already have nuclear arsenals and the number is growing. With constant international bickering, it is only a matter of time before some disgruntled dictator decides to use his or her stockpile of nuclear weapons to solve some petty dispute. Thus, I think we have no choice but to work for total nuclear disarmament.

The conclusion of this argument—that we must work for total nuclear disarmament—follows only if the distinction at its heart

> We must either ban nuclear weapons altogether or face the real possibility of a nuclear war

is exhaustive. If these were the only possibilities, the argument would make good sense. But there may be possibilities other than those included in the distinction. It may be possible, for example, to manage the threat of nuclear war by restricting the number of nuclear weapons or by coercing additional countries into refraining from developing nuclear arsenals. As you can see, the argument appears to be nonfallacious only so long as we are convinced that the distinction on which it turns is a dichotomy. Because the distinction is not dichotomous, the argument is guilty of false dichotomy.

A common tactic is to introduce a distinction in which one alternative is plainly unacceptable as a way of arguing for the other alternative. When the alternatives are not exhaustive, the argument commits the fallacy of false dichotomy. If neither alternative is entirely palatable yet an argument favors one, the fallacy is called **false dilemma.** The point of such an argument is to convince us to choose something we don't particularly want by arguing that the only option is something worse. In the next example, one option is described in terms that leave no question about its acceptability while the other option may not be much better:

CONUNDRUM

In ancient Athens, a mother is said to have given the following advice to her child who wanted to make a career in politics:

If you say what is just, men will hate you; and, if you say what is unjust, the gods will hate you; but you must say either the one or the other. Therefore, you will be hated.

Setting aside the question of whether this appeal is fallacious, can you think of an effective reply the child might have made as a way of avoiding this dilemma?

Make up your mind. You can either take my advice or go ahead and ruin your life.

The conclusion implicit in this argument follows only on the assumption that there are really only two alternatives.

A false dichotomy can be difficult to spot if the distinction on which the argument turns is not explicitly stated. Be particularly wary of arguments that suggest one thing is possible only at the expense of another. Such arguments are nonfallacious only if it is clear that both options cannot both be the case. Consider this argument:

To the editor: I don't usually agree with the President, but I would like to applaud his plan to seek a big cut in the National Endowment for the Arts budget. Something is really wrong with our national values when a war hero freezes to death on the streets of Washington D.C. while a poet gets a $25,000 grant to write poetry. As a libertarian, I would like to see the National Endowment for the Arts eliminated. As a filmmaker, I would like to see some responsibility in the art community.

The author of the argument is opposed to government funding for the arts because any government that would subsidize such nonessential activities when people are freezing to death on the streets has grievously misplaced its priorities. No doubt, few would disagree with the second claim. But is there any reason to think that eliminating the National Endowment for the Arts (the NEA) would result in more spending to alleviate poverty? More to the point, is there any reason to think that the government cannot both fund the NEA and provide a safety net to ensure that people are not homeless? It seems possible that government programs—other than the NEA—could be trimmed as a way of freeing up monies to devote to the eradication of poverty. Thus, the options with which we are confronted in the argument seem to be neither exclusive nor exhaustive. So, we have no reason to believe the claim

Either we fund the NEA or we allow people to live in poverty

is true, let alone that it presents a real dichotomy.

When we are confronted with an argument in which one alternative is ruled out as a way of advocating another, it is always worth pausing to think about the distinction at the heart of the argument. If it is implicit in the argument, take the time to state it clearly. Then consider whether the distinction involves a genuine dichotomy. Is the distinction exclusive? Is it exhaustive? Unless it is both, the argument is probably guilty of false dichotomy.

Slippery Slope

One way of arguing against something is to show that it has unacceptable consequences. Someone might decide to turn down a job offer on the basis of the following:

> If I accept that job, I'll have to take a substantial cut in pay and face an expensive, two-hour commute every day.

If the consequences of a proposed course of action are sufficiently unpalatable, we have a good reason to avoid the action in question. (We might argue *for* a course of action on the ground that it will have advantageous consequences.) However, before accepting such an argument, we must satisfy ourselves that the action and its purported consequences are causally linked. No one, for example, would accept the following as a good reason not to worry about going into debt.

> If I just keep buying lottery tickets, eventually I'll win enough to pay everything off.

A **slippery slope** is a device by which questionable consequences are made to look considerably less so. Slippery slopes gain their name from the fact that they distort by gradually and subtly leading to a highly improbable consequence via a series of intermediate steps none of which, alone, may seem to be particularly questionable. The goal in a slippery slope argument is to lend the appearance of a series of straightforward causal links.

Arguments involving a series of linked consequences need not be fallacious. The following argument, for example, makes perfectly good sense.

> You shouldn't overextend yourself with credit card debt. The more purchases you put on your credit cards, the greater your total monthly debt payments will be. Eventually, you won't even be able to keep up with the minimum monthly payments. Finally, it's all going to catch up with you and you may even have to declare bankruptcy.

Each link in the chain of events outlined in this argument is relatively strong. Thus, it is a safe bet that ever-growing credit card debt eventually will lead to financial insolvency.

Unfortunately, the consequences of an event or action are not always easy to pin down, particularly if they are fairly remote. In a slippery slope argument, the fact that a consequence is questionable is masked by linking it to an action or event via a series of intermediate steps, none of which will be as questionable as the consequence at issue. The aim of such an argument is to come up with a plausible appearing sequence of consequences, each slightly less attractive than the one before. The end result is a consequence so problematic that the claim at issue will seem unacceptable. The following passage takes us down a slippery slope:

> The President's health care plan must be rejected. As I understand it, his proposal would provide government-funded medical care to all citizens, regardless of their ability to pay. Yet, once people get used to the idea of socialized

> **CONUNDRUM**
>
> Distortions of fact occur when crucial information is left out in the process of
> giving an argument. One problem with missing information is that if we don't
> know what it is, we are hardly likely to know it is missing! Based on the fal-
> lacies discussed in this and the previous chapter, put together a brief checklist
> of telltale signs that an arguer may have suppressed or unintentionally omit-
> ted relevant information.

medical care, they will expect the government to provide other services for
nothing. At first, demands will be modest and hardly objectionable: free day
care for working mothers and extended maternity and paternity leave for new
parents. The next thing you know, people will demand free public transportation, food, housing, and clothing. Who knows what's next. If we want to preserve our freedoms and our democratic form of government, we have got to
nip this move toward a socialistic state in the bud.

By a gradual series of steps, we are led to the conclusion that government-funded
heath care will lead to something most people find objectionable—a socialistic state
in which government has almost complete control of our lives.

The way to counter a slippery slope argument is to show that the claim at issue
will *not* have the consequences associated with it. Usually an effective reply will
attack the most immediate consequence; more remote consequences tend to be
highly speculative and thus difficult to either confirm or reject. Against the health
care example, we might point out that just because government provides one service,
meeting one need, it does not follow that other services inevitably will be provided.
We might then point out that the government has provided Medicare, Social Security, and grants for education, for example, for some time now without this leading
to an unquenchable demand for further government intrusions into our lives.

As you can see, the key to responding to a slippery slope is to focus on the purported causal relationships set forth in the premises. The more suspect any of the
links, the more reason to think the argument is a slippery slope.

DISTORTIONS OF THE VIEWS OF OTHERS

The fallacies we have considered so far have all concerned ways in which distortion can
occur in the process of mounting arguments. Distortion can be especially effective in
mounting counterarguments. The final two fallacies for this chapter are about ways in
which a position can be misrepresented so that it becomes an easy target for criticism.

Straw Man (Person!)

A well-argued position may be difficult to counter. A common technique in mounting a counterargument is to distort the position under attack so that it will be more

amenable to effective criticism. This is the fallacy of the **straw man.** The fallacy derives its name from the similarity of a distorted version of a position to a scarecrow. Neither bears much more than a passing resemblance to that which it represents.

One of the most effective ways of creating a straw man is by misstating one of the premises or the conclusion of an argument and then arguing that the distorted version of the claim is problematic. Suppose, for example, that I have argued there is a strong likelihood the company where we work is going to be downsized in the near future. Among other things, I cite the fact that a large corporation has expressed a strong interest in buying our company and that this particular corporation has a history of firing many employees of its new acquisitions. "Nonsense," you reply. "They bought company Z several years ago, and so far they haven't handed out any pink slips." In mounting this criticism, you are guilty of attacking a straw man. The claim you have succeeded in refuting—that the corporation in question never downsizes its acquisitions—is much stronger than the claim I have made in my argument.

The straw man fallacy results when a complex position is oversimplified, as in this passage:

> Liberals seem to think big government can solve all of our social problems. If people can't find jobs, let government create jobs for them. If they can't afford to pay for their own education, why, then, government will pay for it. The poverty of this sort of liberal thinking is shown by the fact that after more than forty years of massive government spending, the problems we as a society face are greater today than ever before.

This passage effectively critiques the claim that government can solve all of our social problems. Unfortunately, there is probably no person—liberal or otherwise—who would subscribe to this claim. Certainly, it does not constitute anything other than a vast oversimplification of the ideology behind what is today called liberalism. Thus, as a refutation of liberalism, the passage is guilty of attacking a straw man.

Perhaps the most scurrilous straw man fallacies are those in which an opponent is saddled with a view that largely ignores anything he or she might have said. Consider the following response from a debate about the need for a national handgun-registration law:

> The arguments you've just heard for more government control of firearms are shameful. Disregard all that rhetoric about the permissibility of gun control under the Second Amendment and the fancy statistics about gun-related deaths. My opponent is guilty of nothing more than scare tactics. He paints for us a picture of a society in which guns are everywhere and where problems are often solved at the end of a "Saturday night special." He should know better, ladies and gentlemen. You don't win an argument by threatening your audience.

Judging by the references to the Second Amendment and to the statistics for gun-related deaths, it would seem the opponent of the author of this passage has advanced a number of arguments. Yet the critique mounted in the passage accuses the opposition of engaging in nothing more than "scare tactics." No doubt the author of the passage is right on one point: You don't win an argument by threatening the audience. But in securing this point, the author has ignored whatever arguments the opposition is trying to advance. In this case, the straw man does not even remotely resemble the position it is put forth as representing. Our debater, it seems, is guilty of the worst sort of straw man fallacy.

An effective and subtle way of creating a straw man is to shift the meaning of a key term or phrase in restating an appeal for critical purposes. (This is a variant of the fallacy of *equivocation,* to be discussed in Chapter 7.) If a key word or phrase occurs in both the original appeal and a distorted reading of that appeal, the distortion will probably go unnoticed:

> All of those people who claim to be "pro-choice" in the abortion debate don't seem to be aware of the contradiction in their position. Or do they really believe pre-born infants would choose to have their lives ended if we could somehow ask them?

People who describe their position on abortion as "pro-choice" believe that a woman ought to have the right to choose whether or not to carry a pregnancy to term. Yet the inconsistency alleged in this passage assumes a very different account of what *pro-choice* means. In fact, it is difficult to say precisely what this second account has in common with the first, other than making use of the term *pro-choice.* The passage seems to want to characterize the pro-choice position as involving a fundamental, if unrecognized, commitment to the right of the "pre-born" to decide their own fate. And lacking any way of knowing what they might want, we must assume the pre-born want to be born. No doubt this is a curious and seemingly inconsistent view, but it is hardly the view of those we would normally think of as pro-choicers.

A technique sometimes used to create a straw man is to focus on a few remarks by the author of a position that, taken out of context, create a distorted version of his or her real position. (This tactic is sometimes called **accent** because parts of a position are taken out of context and given an emphasis they do not deserve.) The following passage is intended to suggest that a well-known evolutionary biologist, Richard Lewontin, holds a view about evolution that can easily be shown to involve inconsistencies:

> As Richard Lewontin recently summarized it, organisms ". . . appear to have been carefully and artfully designed." He calls "the perfection of organisms" both a challenge to Darwinism and, on a more positive note, "the chief evidence of a Supreme Designer."[4]

This version of Lewontin's position makes it look as though Lewontin's views on evolution suffer inconsistencies since, in the final analysis, even evolution requires a "Supreme Designer." When asked to comment on the accuracy of this passage, Lewontin said:

> The point of my article, "Adaptation" in *Scientific American,* from which these snippets were lifted, was precisely that "the perfection of organisms" is often illusory and that any attempt to describe organisms as perfectly adapted is destined for serious contradictions. Moreover, the *appearance* of careful and artful design was taken *in the nineteenth century before Darwin* as "the chief

---

[4] Gary E. Parker, "Creation, Selection and Variation," *Acts & Facts* 88 (October 1980): 2.

evidence for a Supreme Designer." The past tense of my article ("It *was* the marvelous fit of organisms to the environment . . . that *was* the chief evidence of a "Supreme Designer."") has been conveniently dropped . . . to pass off this ancient doctrine as modern science.[5]

Be wary of any version of a view that uses "snippets" taken out of context. The end result is undoubtedly a straw man.

Instances of the straw man fallacy can be difficult to detect, since we must know something of the position that is being misrepresented. Nonetheless, there are often telltale signs that a straw man is afoot. If you suspect that a passage involves a straw man, try first to state the argument or position being criticized. Generally, the result will be a suspiciously simpleminded and vulnerable argument or claim. This is a reliable indicator that a straw man has been built.

Combined Straw Man and False Dichotomy

One way to support a position is to argue that there are no *acceptable* alternatives. However, if the rejected alternatives do not exhaust the field, the argument involves a false dichotomy. If, further, the alternatives are distorted to be susceptible to easy criticism, the argument commits the straw man fallacy. The following passage involves a combination of the straw man and false dichotomy.

> To the editor: A recent letter writer defended Senator Bob Packwood (R-Oreg.) as being pro-choice, not pro-abortion. As an active member of the pro-life movement, I would like to explain why we regard the pro-choice philosophy to be so dangerous.
>
> If a person claims to be pro-abortion, we know two things: The issue is abortion and the person is for it. Often, such people can be convinced by medical, scientific, and biological evidence that a human life is being taken and they may change their minds.
>
> However, the issue for pro-choicers is not abortion at all. The issue for them is choice, and therefore no amount of medical evidence will change their minds. For them, people being allowed to kill other people is simply a matter of choice.

On the face of it, this passage seems intent on establishing that the pro-choice position is not as advertised: Pro-choicers are actually, though they won't say so, in favor of allowing people to choose to kill other people. Here we have an obvious straw man. But the passage does more than this. The way in which its argument is set out suggests that there are really only three positions in the abortion debate: pro-choice, pro-abortion, and pro-life. The first two are plainly untenable, according to the author of the passage. Pro-choicers, for the reason given earlier, are advocates of abortion because they ignore the "medical, scientific, and biological" evidence that abortion involves taking a human life. Considering the alternatives, then, the only tenable position is the pro-life stance. Thus, the argument begins by setting forth a false dichotomy (despite the fact that the passage presents three, not two, alternatives). There are positions not as extreme as those identified in the passage, and there

---

[5] John R. Cole, "Misquoted Scientists Respond," *Creation/Evolution* 6 (Fall 1981): 35.

is also the possibility of a position that combines elements of the three that are mentioned. The argument then commits the straw man fallacy in its characterization of the views it subsequently rejects.

MEDIA WATCH: DISTORTION IN THE COVERAGE OF THE NEWS

Distortion is a fact of life in the coverage of the news. From a never-ending stream of events, those in the business of assembling and disseminating the news must decide what is worth covering and how to cover it. The news media have a limited amount of time and space to fill. The average half-hour television newscast can devote about 19 minutes to the news; the average daily newspaper must restrict its news coverage to about 15 percent of its total space, with total space fixed by the amount of advertising sold. Given these constraints, it is inevitable that many events will not be covered and that those that are covered will often receive superficial treatment. It seems that the picture of reality emerging from the news media cannot help but involve an element of distortion. And this presents us, as consumers of news, with a problem: How can we assess the accuracy of a news story if the information we need to do so is missing from the story? We can't research every story we deem important and, even if we could, we would probably have to rely on other news sources, sources subject to the same distorting pressures we are trying to counter. The one thing we can do is to understand the environment in which news is produced, in particular, the pressures under which the news media operate and the ways in which these pressures influence what is covered and how it is covered. To begin, let's take a brief tour of the news landscape.

News Sources

News sources can be classified by reference to their intended audience, from the global to the local.

■ **International News Media**   Surprisingly, there are no media news sources designed for global consumption. A few newspapers, like the *International Herald-Tribune,* are available in much of the Western world. Television and radio broadcasts are available worldwide, made possible by satellite technology. But none is designed to appeal to a global audience.

■ **National News Media**   These are the sources of news intended for a nationwide audience. They deal in stories judged to be of interest to the entire country. Nearly all the major commercial television networks have news divisions, the most familiar being ABC, CBS, NBC, and CNN. All produce regular, daily news programs, like the *CBS Evening News,* as well as weekly programming, like *60 Minutes* and *PrimeTime Live.* In the United States, there is only one noncommercial television network, the Public Broadcasting System. (Although noncommercial news sources do not run ads, they often receive part of their funding from the business community.) PBS features a nightly news broadcast and several weekly news programs, including *Frontline* and *Washington Week in Review.* There are over thirty nationwide radio networks, but only a few, like the Mutual Broadcasting Network, are devoted to the news. Most news coverage on commercial radio comes from satellite-delivered headline services that provide nothing more than brief encapsulations of major news stories. There are several noncommercial radio news networks, including National Public Radio, Public Radio International, and Pacifica News Radio. All have regularly scheduled news broadcasts, such as NPR's *All Things Considered* and PRI's *Talk of the Nation.* The broadcasts of these networks are generally available only on noncommercial stations. In addition, there are two nonelectronic sources of national news: newsmagazines, including *Time, Newsweek,* and *U.S. News and World Report,* and national newspapers, such as *USA Today* and *The Christian Science Monitor.* A number of local newspapers now publish editions for all parts of the country, among them the *New York Times* and the *Washington Post.*

■ **Local News Media**   These are the television and radio broadcasts and newspapers produced in your area. They specialize in covering stories that originate locally. Whatever nonlocal news they cover generally comes to them from other sources: television network feeds and, in the case of local newspapers, the wire services, like United Press International, the Associated Press, and Reuters International. (The byline on national stories in your local paper will tell you what wire service has provided the copy.) These external sources provide local news outlets with finished stories that are then selected and edited on the basis of time and space available. Television and radio news broadcasts also make use of the wire services. If a radio news story sounds familiar, it may be because you read it in your morning paper.

■ **Specialized News Media**   These are sources of news that are generally available nationwide but that focus on a particular audience. Many have to do with business and government, such as the *Wall Street Journal* and the *Daily Journal of Business.* Many specialized newspapers and magazines provide news on a single topic or theme, for example, *Sports Illustrated, Scientific American, Consumer Reports,* and *People Magazine.* Many interpret the news in light of a particular political ideology, as do *The Nation, Mother Jones, Commentary,* and *The National Review.*

What Makes a Story Newsworthy?

Imagine you have just been hired as the news editor for your local daily newspaper. Yours is a prestigious and important position. Like over 95 percent of U.S. cities that have daily newspapers, your city has only one. Your job, in consultation with your staff, is to decide what will and will not be printed in every issue. Every day, you've got a limited amount of space to fill and an almost unlimited number of stories to choose from. You've got to cover events that happen in your area and, to a lesser extent, national and international events. Most local stories will be investigated and written by staff reporters and "stringers"—people who contribute copy from time to time on events on the fringes of the geographic area you cover. Most national and international stories will be taken from the wire services. What will guide your selection of local news?

In deciding what to print, you will probably rely on the following criteria. First, stories will be selected based on their timeliness; this is a daily paper, so most stories should report on things that have happened within the past twenty-four hours. Exceptions will be made for follow-up stories. Second, stories should pertain to events that are important and that the readership needs to know about. Third, coverage will be balanced in that it will deal with all facets of the local scene: politics, government, education, business, labor, sports, and religion. Finally, coverage will be as thorough as possible, given the constraints of time and resources.

Unfortunately, your career as an editor is going to be short-lived if you rely on the criteria just outlined, for you have ignored one consideration of overriding importance: Your newspaper is a business and your job is to do everything you can to make sure your paper turns a profit. To accomplish this, you've got to attract and keep a large readership. As our brief tour of media news sources suggests, you're facing stiff competition from television, radio, and other news sources. In fact, you are going to have to fight just to keep the audience you already have, as more and more people come to depend on the electronic media for their news. (In 1985 the combined readership of all daily newspapers in the United States was 63,340,320. By mid-1997 it was down to 56,727,902.) Thus, the first and most important consideration for any successful editor is this: *Select stories that will be of interest to your readership and that will attract new readers.* What makes a story newsworthy, then, is its potential attractiveness to the audience. Such stories are called **hard news.**

Hard News

Here is one example of a typical hard news event with which you are probably familiar. This story was covered in *all* the major news media over an extended period of days. On July 17, 1996, TWA Flight 800 went down off the coast of New York, killing all on board. The airliner appeared to have exploded. Within hours, the major news media provided a detailed and remarkably accurate account of the tragedy: when and where it occurred; how many people perished; interviews with eyewitnesses to the event, with people involved in managing the disaster, and with experts who outlined the most probable causes of the explosion. Hard news events, like the crash of Flight 800, are selected because they are deemed of interest to a wide, homogeneous audience. Once selected, they are covered in a fashion that emphasizes aspects of the story that will make the story as compelling as possible. Very few people are going to watch a television report about an event like the crash of Flight 800 in which a reporter simply reads a list of facts about the tragedy, particularly when the competition has live coverage of a correspondent interviewing eyewitnesses and film footage of the aftermath of the crash. Where hard news is concerned, the way in which the story is composed is as important as the story itself. Hard news involves a combination of tried-and-true factors, all aimed at doing one thing: getting your attention and keeping it as long as possible.

■ *Hard news is about the unusual, not the commonplace.* You've got to keep the audience interested and, to keep them interested, you've got to entertain them. And to entertain, you've constantly got to come up with something new, something out of the ordinary. You have heard the adage *"Dog bites man* is not news. *Man bites dog* is." It's true.

■ *A hard news story is about something that has occurred within the past twenty-four hours.* Otherwise, it is not news. Large electronic news organizations like CNN update their stories even more frequently. Events more than a day old retain their news value only to the extent that new information emerges or if they involve a topic judged to be of continuing interest to the audience. The story of the crash of Flight 800 remained in the forefront of the news for several days because new facts and theories about the causes of the crash continued to emerge.

■ *Hard news deals with a discrete event—something that has a definite beginning and ending.* News attracts and maintains our attention because it is exciting; it is about what is happening now. It is hard to get excited about an ongoing story such as the gradual relocation of manufacturing jobs from the United States to other countries where production costs are lower or about a complex issue like a bill before Congress to restrict campaign contributions. A sense of excitement is easier to generate if the focus of a story is a single event—a natural disaster, a particularly tragic accident, or

---

This account illustrates the extent to which factual errors and speculation can creep into a fast-breaking news event. The event in question is the bombing at Olympic Park in Atlanta, Georgia, during the 1996 Summer Olympics.

Getting the Story First . . . Maybe Right

Bill Walsh, Contributing Writer
E-Mail: <u>WillWalsh@aol.com</u>

I did not, of course, witness the actual bomb blast at the Olympic Park last Friday night, but I WAS up watching TV at that time and DID manage to catch the live TV coverage of that awful event. And for those of us who watch the media work, it was fascinating.

I was channel-surfing at 1:30 AM. Jerry Springer (who was doing a show on prostitutes) had just gone to a commercial, so I was flicking the remote, trying to see what else was on. That's how I came upon CNN's coverage of the explosion barely 10 minutes after the actual event.

Atlanta right now probably contains the greatest concentration of live TV technology and more reporters than any city in the world, national and international coverage for the Olympics. I look forward to quick and accurate coverage. That hope ended by 1:30 AM, when a CNN producer on the scene reports that "millions of people are running up the street." Hyperbole and exaggeration. It is not to be the last of it.

Within the first 15 minutes, CNN has obtained a video clip of a German TV crew interviewing some Olympic swimmer at the precise moment the explosion shook the earth and broke glass in the background. I watch as the Olympic swimmer runs for cover and as the reporter and cameraman run outside, towards the explosion. The reporter is asking the cameraman the most important question a reporter can ask while covering a developing story—"Are we on?"

CNN (obviously proud of having obtained the clip) shows it three times within the first half hour.

continued

even a public ceremony, for example. It's even better if a reporter is at the scene to provide an "on the spot, up to the minute" account of what has happened.

On-the-spot coverage of fast-breaking stories is notoriously prone to error. Often, reporters reach the scene shortly after the event has occurred but before too much is known about what happened or why it happened. The pressure to produce a newsworthy story may necessitate the inclusion of much speculation, conjecture, and hearsay, all aimed at making the story come to life. "We don't know exactly what happened or who was involved" is not going to make a compelling story. It's better to speculate about the event and report the views of a few "unconfirmed sources" who do have something exciting to say.

I switch over to NBC. Because they had been covering the Olympics, they have camera crews on the ground and at the site, and they show live pictures of victims writhing on the ground, tending their own cuts and scrapes, or being treated by paramedics. I am angry about the ethics and appropriateness of this. But it's live coverage.

Within the first half hour, NBC reports the rumor that a trash can had exploded. Or maybe it was a transformer. No one is willing to SAY that it was a bomb, but the talk often turns to security issues.

One reporter, tongue-tied (or still in shock), is trying to say that security was taking no chances. Halfway through the sentence, he decides to say that they were taking every precaution. What he winds up saying is that "they are taking absolutely no precautions."

For the first hour or so, both CNN and NBC are showing any images they can get and reporting any scrap of information they can lay their hands on. The Associated Press reports, we are told, 150–200 injuries. One reporter says that there is "blood running down the street." It turns out both of those pieces of information are somewhat overstated.

Trying to be the first with a breaking story leads other reporters to make stupid statements or ask stupid questions. One of them reports breathlessly that "the alleged trash can was next to the tower." Alleged trash can? Another grabs an eyewitness for an interview. Question: "What did the explosion sound like?" Answer: "It was a loud bang."

Shortly after 2 AM, an NBC cameraman staggers onto the makeshift set from where NBC is trying to cover the story. He gives his firsthand account of the police telling him and his partner to move away from a suspicious package on the ground. He looks clearly shaken. His partner was injured, and in an unusual (but touching and responsible) display of sensitivity, he says he doesn't want to give the name of his partner—in case his buddy's family is watching the coverage.

continued

By 2:20 AM, Tom Brokaw is on the air. One hour is not bad time for NBC to have found Brokaw, awakened him, gotten him dressed and prepped, transported to the site, and on the air. The two other networks are still running their usual late-night fare; they still haven't even responded to the story.

Brokaw tries to caution the audience that what they're seeing is "unedited footage," as we're shown injured people on the ground and folks being carried to ambulances. He reports that there are four dead—so says someone who works for the coroner's office. It later turns out that THIS piece of information is also incorrect.

CNN has an interview with the band's sound engineer, who says that he found the suspicious-looking package, looked inside, reported it to police, and then watched them look inside. There's another interview with a band member. CNN shows the footage from the German camera crew a few more times.

I switch between stations, not only trying to see who is saying what (trying to get the story), but paying attention to HOW each is covering the tragedy.

Two hours after the explosion, CBS and ABC are on the air, but they're basically reporting old information. CBS says that there's some footage from a German camera crew "that we're trying to obtain." By this time, I've already seen it six times on CNN.

By 3:15 AM, Robert Gee—a tourist who actually captured the explosion on videotape—is sitting there at the CNN anchor desk and they're running HIS dramatic video footage again and again. I wonder if he has an agreement with CNN already; CNN describes the footage as "exclusive" and Gee's name is prominently displayed every time they run the tape.

continued

Discrete events have the additional virtue of being visually attractive, perhaps the first requirement for both television and newspaper coverage. It is difficult to forget images of the fiery wreckage dotting the night ocean that accompanied the first reports of the crash of Flight 800, the burning oil fields of Kuwait during the Gulf War, or the army of police cars in pursuit of the Ford Bronco in which O.J. Simpson was a passenger. Nothing is less desirable in television newscasts than the "talking head"—a news anchor or reporter reading a story from the prompter against the backdrop of the evening news set. Discrete events are also the easiest and most economical kind of stories to cover. Coverage often requires nothing more than having a reporter at the site of an event. His or her job then becomes simply to report on what has happened. Time and effort need not be expended to do background research or investigative reporting.

At 3:45 AM, CNN reports that they heard from a policeman (who heard it on his police radio) that there are two more "explosive devices" in the park. It becomes clear later that this is inaccurate.

By about 4:00 AM, most of the coverage has calmed down. CNN and NBC have sent reporters to the various hospitals to report on the conditions of the victims and try to interview the doctors treating them. They're starting to decrease the numbers of deaths and injuries, and the interviews with eyewitnesses are taking on a sameness that's less newsworthy than before.

It WAS interesting to watch, certainly. From the initial reports of "millions of people" running through the blood-soaked streets to more accurate reporting of exactly what happened. From an initial hesitancy to call the explosion a bomb through the accumulation of tiny pieces of testimony and evidence that it indeed was one.

NBC had better pictures of their own, but (after all), they had camera crews all over the Olympics anyway. CNN obtained better footage from outside sources. Both networks did their share of reporting rumors and exaggeration before the story finally began to get clear.

None of this is meant to be critical. Although I've never been THAT close to a deadly explosion, I can understand shock. And the burning desire (need?) to be there FIRST with the best information available. I think that individual reporters are to be forgiven their errors (which were probably made in the midst of panic, pressure, and genuine fear).

It was—in the space of a few hours—a telling example of the best and the worst in live coverage of a tragic event. And it remains a valuable lesson to all of us who are reaching towards a greater understanding of the news media and how they work—both good and bad.

It's just the way it is. At least for now . . .

■ *Hard news is personalized.*   We all are attracted to stories of personal tragedy and triumph. Hard news stories almost always involve a "personal interest" hook. If the center of a story is an event, it will be described against the background of personal reactions to the event in the form of interviews with witnesses, victims, and anybody else touched by the event. A front-page story in a recent edition of my local newspaper concerned the findings of a study about "therapeutic touch," the purported ability to heal by massaging the human "energy field." The study claimed that practitioners of therapeutic touch could not perform under tightly controlled conditions. Although this story was doubtless of interest to the small minority of readers who know what therapeutic touch is, it is hardly the stuff of front-page news. The story made it to the front page because the study was done by a nine-year-old girl as part of a science project. With the help of her mother, she wrote up her results and sent

To what extent is the news "personalized"? The Project for Excellence in Journalism and the Medill News Service Washington Bureau conducted a study of the traditional mainstream national news media. They compared coverage in newspapers, television nightly news programming, and newsmagazines. In all, the study examined 6,020 stories in 16 news outlets over a span of 20 years. Among their overall findings were the following:

- There has been a shift toward lifestyle, celebrity, entertainment, and celebrity crime/scandal in the news and away from government and foreign affairs. But infotainment still comes nowhere near dominating the traditional news package.
- There is an even more pervasive shift toward a featurized and people-oriented approach to the news, away from traditional straight news accounts. This tends to make the news more thematic and the journalist more a storyteller and mediator than a reporter.
- The news media are dividing into market-based niches, with the result that a citizen's perception of society can vary greatly depending on the sources of news. Prime-time network magazines, which have replaced documentaries on network television, have almost stopped covering traditional topics such as government, social welfare, education, and economics in favor of lifestyle and news-you-can-use. Newsmagazines that once concentrated heavily on coverage of ideas have moved heavily toward celebrity.

The line between news and entertainment, it seems, is becoming harder and harder to draw.

them to the *Journal of the American Medical Association* where they were subsequently published. As it turns out, the girl was the youngest person ever to have a research article printed in a peer-reviewed scientific journal.

Stories about large-scale events, problems, and issues—a famine or war in a Third World country, the long-term effects of various pollutants, or the strains on the Social Security system brought about by an aging population, for example—will be personalized. Every effort will be made to reduce such stories to a series of anecdotes, illustrating how the problems and issues affect a few individuals. A story about a famine might show or tell the tale of a starving family and then interview a doctor engaged in the relief effort. A story about problems with the Social Security system might detail the plight of a few elderly citizens striving to survive on a severely limited budget. The personalization of a complex story is not, in and of itself, a bad idea. We do want to know the impact of problems and issues on people. But often, news stories are dominated by such anecdotes, to the exclusion of information needed to understand the problem and its causes.

- *Hard news is often staged.*   Many newsworthy events are manufactured for consumption by the news media by parties who want their story told. Such nonspontaneous events are normally scheduled in advance so that reporters and camera crews can be there to cover them. Staged events like speeches, news conferences and brief-ings, press releases, ceremonies, protest marches, and strikes are highly attractive to the media. They are easy and inexpensive to cover and are usually staged in a way to make them attractive as media events. Moreover, the coverage of staged events requires min-imal effort of those doing the reporting. Background information is provided to reporters, and newsworthy figures are often available for questioning. Press releases, both filmed and written, are ready for inclusion in the evening news, with little editing or rewriting needed. The problem with staged events is that the subject of coverage, not the news media, frequently determines what facets of the story are covered. News cov-erage of the Gulf War, for example, relied heavily on information and film footage sup-plied by the Pentagon and disseminated at news briefings run by the military.

■ *Hard news stories play to our interest in the sensational or dramatic.* If we can be shocked, we will stay tuned for the details. Thus, the news is filled with sto-ries involving violence and drama. How often is the lead story on the evening news or in your daily paper about a particularly violent crime, accident, or disaster?

■ *Hard news is tension-filled and thrives on controversy.* One way to keep our interest is to insinuate a kind of dramatic tension between parties to a story. This technique is often used in the coverage of political stories. A bill before Congress is not news. A bill before Congress that is opposed by the President is news. Almost certainly, a news story dealing with such a bill involves interviews with the opposed parties: the President or a presidential advisor is given a few seconds to criticize the bill; an advocate of the legislation, a few seconds to criticize the President. Often their remarks are canned, constructed in advance for media consumption. (Short, pithy "sound bites" have the best chance of being aired.) Stories involving contro-versy have the added advantage of insinuating objectivity on the part of the news media. A reporter who allows opposing points of view to be aired comes across as a disinterested third party, hard at work just getting at the facts.

Although controversy fuels many news stories, rarely are the issues fully aired. Opposed views are oversimplified and reduced to a manageable number, usu-ally two. The goal is to heighten and underline the controversy rather than under-stand the issues. Stories about environmental issues, for example, often grab our attention because we are presented with the picture of two factions at one another's throats: those who want to protect the environment even if it means the loss of jobs and business and those who don't. Controversial issues like this usually involve more than two extreme positions. Often the positions of the disputants are not diametri-cally opposed. But the time and space necessary to make sense of all sides in a con-troversy are just not going to be expended in the production of the daily news.

■ *Hard news is trendy.* Some events remain the focus of media coverage for days and weeks after they have occurred. These are stories dealing with events considered sufficiently interesting to the audience to merit sustained coverage, like the death of Princess Diana; the trial of O.J. Simpson; the bombing of the Murrah Federal Building in Oklahoma City; and the pursuit, by Sammy Sosa and Mark McGwire, of Roger Maris's home run record. Often, in the aftermath of a crime that has clearly captured the public's interest, local news media run follow-up stories for days afterward—interviews with friends, relatives, and neighbors of the perpetrator and the victim and with mental health workers bent on giving us insight into the perpetrator's character. Think how many stories must be ignored by the news media in order to bring us this level of detail in the coverage of a single event and its aftermath. The pursuit of the trendy is not without difficulties. If a story is thought to be sufficiently interesting to warrant sustained coverage, new information must be constantly unearthed that meets the criteria for hard news. Under such pressure, reporters may forgo the kind of accuracy provided by careful fact checking in order to get a story on the air or into print before the competition. (For a detailed example of this, look again at the material in the box on pages 150–153.)

Reading Between the Lines, Seeing Between the Pixels

As consumers of news, we need to understand that some kinds of information about the world around us are going to occupy little space on the media landscape. The news industry thrives on hard news—stories that are simple, personal, dramatic, and visceral and that deal with discrete events. When a big story fits the profile for hard news, it will be covered well and in depth, as in the case of the breakup of the Soviet Union and the impeachment of President Clinton. Dramatic events were happening daily and the media did an excellent job both of keeping us abreast of what was going on and of providing sufficient background information to enable us to understand the larger issues behind the events. Big stories that do not fit the profile for hard news are rarely given this level of attention. For example, one story that has had an enormous impact on our lives in the past decade is one you are probably not even aware of: the growth of multinational corporations and the ever-increasing consolidation of economic power in the hands of an ever-decreasing number of companies. An accurate rendition of even the main features of this important story would need to include a sense of the historical development of corporations, an understanding of the legal benefits accruing to incorporation, and an enormous amount of economic data detailing the growth, ownership, and profitability of today's global corporations. Very few of these details are well known, owing largely to the fact that this story is simply *not* hard news and it is so complex. There is no single event to report, no personal story that will reflect the larger issues. This story has unfolded over a number of years, not days or hours, and requires facts, figures, and careful historical analysis at a level of sophistication that cannot be captured in a few powerful visual images.

In addition to issues and events that do not lend themselves to hard news coverage, there is one type of story that receives little coverage in the news media: stories critical of the news media themselves. Rarely will news stories surface that deal with

- the ownership of the mass media and the extent to which the interests of the owners can compromise news coverage,
- the influence of advertisers in determining the content of the news, or
- the extent to which the output of the news media is orchestrated by external sources.

Ownership of the Mass Media   In the early 1980s, forty-six companies controlled most of the daily newspapers, magazines, television stations and networks, and publishers. By 1990 the number had been reduced to twenty-three.[6] Capital Cities/ABC/Disney is

---

[6] Ben H. Bagdikian, "Global Media Corporations Control What We Watch (and Read)," *Utne Reader,* June/August 1990, pp. 84–87.

now the world's largest media conglomerate owning, among other things, ten television stations and twenty-one radio stations; it also has a controlling interest in ESPN, ESPN2, and several newspapers and a partial interest in cable programming in Japan, Germany, and Scandinavia. When the sources of news are owned by a few large corporations, the potential for distortion is clear. Westinghouse Electric Corporation, for example, now owns CBS. What are the chances the *CBS Evening News* will air a story critical of Westinghouse Electric products or policies?

Given that the mass media are owned and operated by big business, it's no surprise that the point of view of the business world is well represented (and attractively presented for the most part) in the news media. Nor is it surprising that the other half of the business equation—labor—is covered in a very different way. Nearly every major newspaper has a business section in which the business of doing business is detailed. No major newspaper has a regular section devoted to the labor movement or to worker issues. Several national magazines, newspapers, and television news programs (the *Wall Street Journal* and Public Television's *Wall Street Week* are two examples) are about the business of doing business; none centers on worker-related issues. Most news stories involving workers and the labor movement focus on labor strife—strikes and other sorts of labor-management disputes. Thanks to the news media, we are all familiar with the names of the big players in the business world— Bill Gates, Ted Turner, Donald Trump, and Rupert Murdoch, for example. Can you name a single prominent labor leader?

The Influence of Advertisers   As mentioned earlier, the mass media are underwritten by advertising. The news media rarely cover stories critical of sponsors. So, for example, when a daily newspaper is "dummied," spaces set aside for ads are labeled with the names of the advertisers to ensure that no story that might be offensive to an advertiser will appear on the same page. In 1997 the Media Foundation of Vancouver, British Columbia, tried to buy advertising time on the major American TV networks to run a commercial for "National Buy Nothing Day." All the major networks refused to run the spot. Richard Gitter, vice president of advertising standards at General Electric Company, the owner of NBC, explained: "We don't want to take any advertising that's inimical to our legitimate business interests."

Advertising influences the output of the news media in another way. In 1970 a half hour of prime-time television programming averaged about ten minutes of "clutter." (Prime time is programming between eight and eleven P.M.; clutter includes everything but program content: commercials, promotions for other programs, credits, public service announcements, etc.) By 1997 the amount of prime-time clutter exceeded fifteen minutes per half hour on three of the four major television networks: CBS, NBC, and FOX. The fourth network, ABC, averaged just under fifteen minutes per half hour.[7] Non-prime-time programming—like the evening news—is not quite so cluttered though even here the amount of space devoted to clutter is increasing. Commercial radio news programming, as well, is becoming increasingly dominated by advertising. As the time devoted to news coverage diminishes, the tendency toward omission and oversimplification increases.

---

[7] *Brill's Content,* July/August 1998, p. 24.

> *Anyone who's in the magazine business thinks about advertisers when they write about something. And anyone who says they don't is a liar.*
> —John F. Kennedy Jr., editor and publisher of *George* magazine

Manipulation by External Sources   Much of what is covered by the news media comes pre-packaged from external sources—government, political parties and candidates, public relations firms, and advertisers—in the form of press conferences and briefings, news releases, and events staged for media consumption, such as protest marches and the announcement of new products. When, in 1997, the Volkswagen company announced that it was introducing a new version of the VW Beetle, this event was covered in the evening newscasts of all the major television networks. Here, again, the potential for distortion and omission is rampant. The organizations that produce the stories provide just those facts and figures they want to draw attention to. Yet the news media rarely let the audience know when the information contained in a story has been provided by an external source. How refreshing it would be to hear a news anchor end a story with something like this: "Well, that's all I have. We're overbudget and didn't think this event important enough to send out a camera crew, and so we had to rely on the story in the morning paper." Or, "I'd like to tell you more on this story, but I've already covered everything in the press release."

CHAPTER SUMMARY

1. Distortion occurs when something is inaccurately described, generally by omitting crucial facts or by misrepresenting the facts. Fallacies of distortion occur both in giving arguments and in representing the views of others for purposes of criticism.

2. As a general rule, beware of claims that are almost too good to be true. If an argument on a controversial topic makes an airtight case, it probably involves some distortion of the facts.

3. When facts and figures result in an overwhelmingly strong case for a position, you should ask: What facts are missing? What haven't I been told?

4. If an argument is under attack, be on the lookout for the fallacy of the straw man. Generally, if the argument being criticized seems overly simple or obviously fallacious, chances are good it has been misrepresented.

5. Most items reported in the news media are hard news, stories selected because they fit the following profile. Hard news is
   a. about the unusual, not the commonplace;
   b. about something that has occurred within the past twenty-four hours;
   c. about a discrete event;
   d. often staged;
   e. personalized;

f. pitched at our interest in the sensational or dramatic;

g. tension-filled and thrives on controversy; and

h. trendy.

FALLACIES OF DISTORTION

DISTORTIONS OF FACT

Omitting information   Leaving out crucial facts as a means of strengthening the inference of a persuasive appeal. Omitted facts can lead to an oversimplification of the issues in an argument. Often what is omitted is information the audience needs to gain a sense of perspective, information about historical trends, comparative data, and data about similarities and dissimilarities between groups.

> *Example:* The automobile is the least-safe form of transportation. Nationwide, there were more than 800,000 auto accidents reported last year alone.

(This argument fails to provide necessary comparative information—information about accident rates for other forms of transportation.)

Innuendo   Failing to point out when the normal conversational implicatures of a remark do not hold.

> *Example:* Is Jones reliable? Well, he hasn't broken any promises, lately, that is.

Anecdotal evidence   Using carefully chosen but largely atypical anecdotes to convey a misleading picture of what is generally the case.

> *Example:* City workers are overpaid and underworked. Just yesterday I saw a city work crew patching a pothole down the street. Four guys were standing around talking while the fifth one slowly shoveled asphalt into the hole.

False precision   Expressing an approximation or a prediction in overly precise terms or by implying it is backed by competent statistical analysis.

> *Example:* Several recent studies have documented that smokers are 2.37 times more likely than nonsmokers to suffer upper respiratory illnesses.

Misleading qualifiers   Exaggerating the significance of a premise through the subtle insertion of words and phrases used to qualify.

> *Example:* You'd better buy today! These sale prices are good for a limited time only.

False dichotomy   An inference is drawn on the basis of a distinction that is neither exhaustive nor exclusive.

> *Example:* Either we allow people the freedom to buy and own guns unfettered by regulation or we ban them. Do you really want to live in a country where you don't even have the right to keep a gun in the house to defend your family?

Slippery slope   Arguing against something by falsely suggesting that it will have inevitable but unacceptable consequences. The worst consequences may be connected to the thing in question by a chain of hypothetical statements, each new link less acceptable than the one before.

> *Example:* If abortion remains legal, it will become more widespread than it is today and respect for human life will gradually weaken. A country with little respect for human life is likely to adopt other measures allowing the state to decide matters of life and death. Surely, no one would want to

live under this sort of moral dictatorship. Thus, we must do everything we can to make abortion illegal.

DISTORTION OF THE VIEWS OF OTHERS

Straw man   Oversimplifying a position for purposes of subsequent criticism.

> *Example:* If I understand your position, you want the American taxpayer to bail out all of those bankrupt savings and loan institutions. In other words, you want the government to reimburse those wealthy investors and bankers who gambled and lost. That's just great. Once again, the rich get richer and the little guy foots the bill.

Combined straw man and false dichotomy   Defending a position by falsely implying it has only a limited range of alternatives and then arguing against distorted versions of those alternatives.

> *Example:* We must accept either my proposal or your proposal for a settlement of our dispute. Your proposal makes little sense and is open to a number of serious objections, so we ought to adopt mine.

EXERCISES

A. All the passages in this exercise appear to involve distortion. Some may involve more than one fallacy, and some may involve fallacies discussed in Chapter 5. In instances where you are not able to determine the extent of the distortion because you have no real sense of the facts behind the case, try to decide what you would need to know in order to say for sure how the passage distorts. You will find it helpful in difficult cases to begin by determining whether the passage involves an argument or a counterargument. In many cases, it will be helpful to restate the passage as an explicit series of premises and a conclusion.

(Solutions to Exercises 4, 17, and 32 are given on pages 168–169.)

1. To the editor: What good does it do to vote? In the last election we voted to reinstate the death penalty. Now the state courts tell us our vote means nothing: The court says the measure is unconstitutional. I am thoroughly disgusted with our system—a system in which the courts can override the will of the voters—and think voting is a waste of time.

2. If the crisis spread more broadly to emerging markets throughout the globe, which we are all working hard to avoid, the American workers and businesses could be far more severely affected. —*Secretary of the Treasury Robert Rubin, as the Clinton administration pressed for an eighteen-billion-dollar funding package for the International Monetary Fund*

3. If we prohibit the burning of grass stubble by farmers in our state, they will not be able to make a living from their land. They will be forced to sell to developers and land speculators who will then turn our countryside into one big suburban housing tract.

4. There can be little question that the moon can have an effect on our behavior. Look at all the strange and bizarre things police officers, paramedics, and emergency-room personnel report when the moon is full. Crimes, accidents, and even births occur at an astounding rate. Ask any police officer or para-

medic and they will confirm that when the moon is full, their clients all seem to go a bit crazy.

5. *Entry in the captain's log:* The first mate was drunk today.
   Entry in the first mate's log: The captain was not drunk today.

6. To the editor: It is so relieving to see the abortion ban fail. Now women will be safe from back-alley abortions. But if killing our babies is safe, next year we should pass a measure making child abuse legal so that more people will be safe.

7. Do you really believe in that old saw "Equal pay for equal work"? Do you really think that minor league baseball players should make as much as major leaguers? Or that a factory worker who puts in as many hours as the company's CEO deserves the same pay?

8. To the editor: Is this country concerned with President Clinton's abilities in office or his sexual appetite? Monica Lewinsky and the President are accused of having an affair. President Clinton supposedly calls his girlfriend and discreetly asks her not to spread their affair to the media. Fair request!

   It sounds to me that this is not a legal issue but a moral issue. Clinton's promiscuity is really an issue that falls between Hillary Rodham Clinton and himself. Don't we all have something better to do? This country is a little overconcerned with everyone's sexual preferences and experiences.

9. A recent survey of 10,000 physicians revealed that about 25 percent of those who responded reported having problems with depression at some point in their careers. If I were you, I would consider going into some field other than medicine.

10. By the year 2000, two out of three Americans could be illiterate. *—from an ad soliciting funds for the Coalition for Literacy*

11. How do the animal "rights" advocates try to justify their position? As someone who has debated them for years on college campuses and in the media, I know firsthand that the whole movement is based on a single—invalid—syllogism, namely: men feel pain and have rights; animals feel pain; therefore, animals have rights. This argument is entirely specious, because man's rights do not depend on his ability to feel pain; they depend on his ability to think. *—Edwin Locke, "Animal Rights and the New Man Haters," 1997, on the Ayn Rand Institute Web site*

12. It really ticks me off the way the traffic cops in some states pick on out-of-state drivers. Last year on my vacation I was pulled over for speeding in three different states, and in each case I was just driving along with the flow of traffic. It seems clear to me the police want to ticket out-of-staters, knowing full well they are unlikely to come back, a month or so later, to protest in court.

13. Roughly 20 percent of infertile couples who adopt children go on to conceive. It seems clear that many couples who adopt become less obsessed with their reproductive failure, and their newfound peace of mind boosts their chances for success.

14. Many college teachers of English argue that works of nontraditional authors—authors representing minorities and other cultures—should be included in various literature courses. What they don't seem to realize is that by accommodating these no doubt deserving writers, they will have to eliminate

some of the greatest literary figures of Western civilization. I ask you, who should our college students be reading: Shakespeare or some obscure native American storyteller?

15. As part of a heart-healthy diet, the soluble fiber in Cheerios may reduce your cholesterol! —*from the front of a box of Cheerios*

16. Surging sales of stocks and other assets at the end of the last calendar year, undertaken to avoid the onset of higher capital gains taxes, sharply raised the share of income taxes paid by wealthy taxpayers. Figures released Tuesday by the Treasury Department showed that the richest 1 percent of taxpayers paid 26.1 percent of all individual federal income taxes last year, up from the 21.9 percent share the same group paid the year before. The bottom 50 percent of taxpayers paid a slightly smaller share last year—6.4 percent—compared with 7.2 percent the previous year.

17. To the editor: How ironic that the ascendant Republicans have turned "liberal" into an insult. In my dictionary, *liberalism* is defined as "a political philosophy based on belief in progress, the essential goodness of the human race, the autonomy of the individual, and standing for the protection of political and civil liberties." Thomas Jefferson was a liberal. I'm proud to be one too.

    When I hear conservatives herald the "death knell of liberalism," I'd like to think they are just ignorant of history.

18. This society at this time is riddled with toxic substances. According to studies, some of the things that are put in a can of peas or a can of soup are, let's face it, toxic. They are preservatives and the action of preservatives is to impede decay. In other words, those things might be great for the manufacturer as they preserve his product, but they could be very bad for the consumer. —*from an ad for "The Purification Rundown," a pamphlet published by the Hubbard Dianetics Foundation*

19. To the editor: After a peaceful existence in this city during my college and young adult years, I moved east to another big city. There, my husband and I lived in a rehabilitated neighborhood that bordered on what was considered the high-crime area. Many friends questioned how we were able to live there without fear of being victimized.

    Three months ago my husband and I moved back here. We made our home in what we were assured was a comfortable, welcoming, middle-class neighborhood. The first week we were here our car was bashed in by a hit-and-run driver in the middle of the night. When we took it in for repair, we discovered someone had tried to break open the rear driver-side door.

    Not long after that, we were in a parking lot adjacent to a neighborhood theater. After the movie, we had to hustle back to our car when a group of thirty or so teenagers started yelling and making fun of us.

    One recent morning, we discovered yet another broken car window and a damaged ignition switch. Someone had tried to steal our car. In almost every part of town, we are confronted by graffiti on all kinds of surfaces, fixed and mobile.

    We have been here only ninety days and wonder what will happen to us next. What has happened to this city while I was gone?

20. I'm going to start shopping at a different grocery store. Whoever is in charge of inventory at my neighborhood store doesn't know how to do the job, and

I'm no longer willing to be inconvenienced by this sort of incompetence. Every time I've shopped there recently, they've been out of something I needed. And usually it's something that's on sale at a very good price. If they can't do a better job, they're not going to get my business.

21. This year, our average investor realized a whopping 12.2 percent return on investments. Next year, we predict things will be even better. Based on the past five-year performance of our fund, we feel our portfolio will yield no less than a 13.4 percent return on investments.

22. Every dollar we spend to underwrite the military is one less dollar we have to spend on the very real social problems that plague our country.

23. A refugee is a refugee—they all need our help. Thus, if we are going to provide sanctuary for impoverished Cuban or Nicaraguan refugees, then we ought to go ahead and provide it for the thousands of poor Haitians, El Salvadorans, Indochinese, and eastern Europeans. In fact, we might as well open the doors to all the oppressed and downtrodden people of the earth. If we start to accept a few needy Cubans, we'll have to make room for the hundreds of thousands that are sure to follow.

24. The reason you can't have such a thing as a pro-life feminist is because of what we mean when we say "pro-life" and what we mean when we say "feminist." A person who is pro-life wants to see abortion made illegal, whereas a feminist is someone who believes that everyone, even women, deserves the right to self-determination and control over their destiny to whatever extent possible.

25. To the editor: Who has the right to play God? Not the "animal rights" people. I refer to a recent letter decrying the use of animals in laboratory experiments.

    I would like to know where these people were when poliomyelitis was a nationwide epidemic. If not for laboratory animals, it would still be one. Would the animal-rights people like us to return to the days of Hitler, whose scientists experimented on human beings?

    Without experimentation we would still have high mortality rates in childbirth and childhood, and many diseases that are curable today would still be fatal.

    The attitude of the animal-rights people is representative of the general disenchantment with science. People look at the horrors of nuclear war and forget science's role in bringing us electrical appliances.

    I think it is time to stand up and applaud science for all the good it has done for us and all the good it will do in the future, while working toward the elimination of those excesses that are not necessary for competent research.

26. (*In response to 25*) That's just great. You advocate torturing thousands and thousands of animals. And for what? Better electrical appliances!

27. *Corporate recruiter:*   A former student of yours, a Mr. Jones, is applying for a position at our company. He has given you as a reference. First of all, how would you rate Mr. Jones as a student?
    Teacher: Well, he wasn't the worst student I ever had.
    Note: Jones got an A in the one class he took with the teacher.

28. May I direct a question to those who are unwilling to accept my plan for an economic recovery? No doubt, they object to the program cuts I have proposed to

pay for additional tax cuts. But what are the alternatives? If we do nothing, we can look forward to more inflation, more unemployment, and an ever-growing national debt.

29. To the editor: The letter you published from a teen mother is a display of exactly how far we have come in creating dependencies with our attitude toward bailouts. Amazingly, the teen mother commented, "If you take away health care and welfare from teen moms, you take away their choices."

    Take away their choices? Whose choice was it to have sex and become pregnant without adequate preparation for life? Charity does not mean enabling people in their bad decisions. An occasional mistake is one thing, but society is experiencing an epidemic. It's time to end the outrageous, demeaning attitude of those who expect others to pay for their lack of discipline.

30. I'm sorry, but I cannot accept your late paper, even though you became ill last week. You do seem to have a legitimate excuse, but then I suppose every student who asks for an extension would think their excuse valid. And if a professor accepts any excuse at all, he or she will end up accepting late papers from students who missed too many classes, failed to keep up with assignments, or spent their time partying. The next thing you know, a deadline will have absolutely no meaning.

31. If you've read much about the modern theory of evolution, you will have discovered that even its supporters disagree with one another about how evolution works. Ask a punctuated equilibriumist about gradualism sometime. Moreover, there are just too many discrepancies in nature that evolution cannot account for. How, for example, could something as complex as the human eye have developed by natural selection? Early variations that eventually came together as the eye, according to evolutionists, would themselves confer no advantage and so should have been selected out of the evolutionary process. Moreover, there are no good examples yet found of any transitional forms—remains of intermediate species. Given all of these problems, it seems clear that the theory of special creation must be right or at least on the right track. This theory postulates a special, one time only, act of divine intervention in which all the species that populate the Earth were created much as we find them today.

32. People who don't believe in God often try to make their case by pointing out how much gratuitous misery and suffering there is in the world. They argue that any decent person would try to prevent suffering if they could and that the same should be true for God. And since God is supposed to be all-powerful, it follows that God does not exist unless God is exceedingly cruel. What these people don't seem to realize is that a certain amount of suffering plays a necessary role in God's plan for us. One cannot learn to choose to be good, for example, without the possibility of doing the opposite, and this implies doing harm and the possibility of being harmed. Thus, a world without suffering and misery would not be a fit place to accomplish God's purposes.

33. Health is, of course, the major concern of the antismoking Big Brothers—and health care has become a factor in the most serious aspect of their campaigns. With the escalating costs of employee health care, companies are refusing to hire workers who appear likely to have higher-than-average med-

ical bills, and their primary target is smokers. The American Civil Liberties Union (ACLU) reports that an estimated 5 percent discriminate in this area and that the percentage is growing rapidly. Overweight people are also being victimized in the job market. Next in line, according to the ACLU, are social drinkers, persons with high blood pressure or high cholesterol levels, and people with high-risk hobbies, such as skiing or scuba diving. —*from* Philip Morris Magazine, *Fall 1991*

34. The belief that there was once a golden age in public education is as prevalent as it is false. Modern education and degrees are supposed to be less valuable than back when this country had "standards." But the number of students passing advanced placement tests today—tests that give college-level credit for high school work—has risen from 98,000 in 1978 to 535,000 in 1996. Apparently, somebody is learning something in our public schools.

35. To the editor: If we continue on our present course, with criminals being protected by the law instead of being punished, one of two things will certainly happen. People will take the law into their own hands, and we will no longer have law, order, and protection of any kind, *or* the government will take complete control, and we will have lost our freedom. We must impose mandatory sentences for violent crimes with no reduction for good behavior.

36. The following remarks were from a televised debate on whether businesses should pay roughly the same aggregate amount of state taxes as do individual taxpayers.

    I believe that businesses pay more than their fair share in taxes. Look, I own a small business that is a corporation. The corporation pays out a tool tax as well as a tax on the income earned to the county where I do business. We also pay state unemployment taxes, federal unemployment taxes, 50 percent of all Social Security and Medicaid taxes on wages. By the time we pay wages, materials, overhead, and the taxes, there is not a lot left over for the owner.

37. This letter was written during the Gulf War:

    To the editor: There seems to be quite a howl by some to cancel the Super Bowl on the grounds that people should not participate in any event that gives them escape when the war is going on. Well and good. So we cancel the Super Bowl. And close all the theaters, bowling alleys, and amusement parks. Disneyland, golf courses—hey, all those millions of people out there playing golf while our boys are fighting? Why pick on the Super Bowl?

38. To the editor: I just read the article "Criminal Kids: Who Goes to Jail?" and I am disgusted. It states that there are 128 beds in the new $36 million Juvenile Justice Complex. This boils down to a cost of $282,250 for one bed!

39. To the editor: I am disturbed by the report that described my senator as undecided on financial aid for the people of Bosnia. Sadly, she voted for this aid. Yet I have half a dozen letters written to me in the past six months in which she insists repeatedly that she is opposed to funds for Bosnia. So, either my representative is lying to me and countless other voters or she has chosen to abandon a position she has held for close to a year.

40. You keep trying to convince me that I need to start exercising. That's easy for you to say. You don't have to work for a living. If I start spending a couple of

hours every day scurrying around the neighborhood like you, I won't have the time or the energy to get my work done. Better to be a little pudgy than broke.

41. A lot of people say we should legalize cocaine and heroin. It would take the crime out of it and hopefully, as a result, some of the violence associated with it. Besides, the people who are inclined to use drugs are going to do so regardless of its illegality. But the fact that people are going to ignore and break laws is not a valid argument for decriminalization. The state would be sanctioning, even promoting, conduct that is harmful to society. This is similar to today's trendy policies for the free distribution of condoms in our public schools and prisons. We are sending a message that such activity is okay, based on the specious argument that we know the activity is going to occur anyway. We might as well just carry this argument to its logical conclusion: The reason laws are broken is that there are laws. People are going to break the law. They are going to steal, rob, and kill. So what we need to do is to eliminate laws and get rid of the police. That way there will be no crime. The point is that standards of right and wrong and basic decency must be established and maintained. We accomplish this through the establishment of limits on our behavior, which constitutes our law, which descends from the morality and values we deem important and necessary to an orderly and functioning society. —*from* The Way Things Ought To Be, *by Rush Limbaugh (New York: Pocket Books, 1992), p. 53*

42. To the editor: I join with scores of others to defend the President in his latest sex scandal. What he does in the privacy of the Oval Office, Air Force One, or anywhere else is none of our business. His personal life has no bearing on his performance.

    In this same light, former Air Force Lieutenant Kelly Flinn should be given back her wings. Her adultery and deception had nothing to do with her performance as a pilot. She was drummed out of the military for reasons that were her own personal business.

    University professors everywhere, feel free to have sex with your students again. As long as it is in the privacy of your office, it has no bearing on your ability to teach. Corporate executives, get ready to welcome the return of the typing pool, if you know what I mean. As long as your company remains profitable, what you do in the privacy of your office or the boardroom is nobody else's business.

    America must get over its outdated notions of character, morality, and honor. They are vestiges from an earlier, less enlightened time when the economy wasn't so strong and stock market returns were in single digits.

43. To the editor: I come from Germany, and I became an au pair when I was 24 years old. I took my job, which lasted from June '96 to July '97, very seriously and still love "my kids" with all my heart. Right now I am back visiting my host family. I hope that families who are considering an au pair won't change their minds because of the negative publicity from this trial. It is easy to point out one bad case and ignore all the good that au pairs have done and all the joy and happiness that they have brought to "their kids."

44. The following remarks are from a corporate spokesperson when he was asked to comment on the charge that his company was reaping windfall profits from "downsizing" and the sale of the capital assets of a recently acquired company:

> We are charged with making huge profits by firing people and gutting the company we recently purchased. Huge profits? For each of the last five years we have made a profit of no more than 4 percent of net sales in any of our corporate divisions. And the forecast for the coming year is more of the same. Our best estimate is that profits will once again be in the range of 4 percent. We could probably have done better by just putting the money in the bank instead of purchasing the company we are now accused of plundering.[8]

45. There is a grave danger facing mankind. The danger is not from acid rain, global warming, smog, or the logging of rain forests, as environmentalists would have us believe. The danger to mankind is from environmentalism.

    The fundamental goal of environmentalists is not clean air and clean water; rather, it is the demolition of technological/industrial civilization. Their goal is not the advancement of human health, human happiness, and human life; rather, it is a subhuman world where "nature" is worshiped like the totem of some primitive religion.

    If the good of man were the aim of environmentalists, they would embrace the industry and technology that have eradicated the diseases, plagues, pestilence, and famines that brought wholesale death and destruction prior to the Industrial Revolution. They would embrace free enterprise and technology as the only solution to the relatively minor dangers that now exist—minor compared to the risks of living in a nontechnological world.

    By word and deed, they demonstrate their contempt for human life. . . .

    Nature, they insist, has "intrinsic value," to be revered for its own sake, irrespective of any benefit to man. As a consequence, man is to be prohibited from using nature for his own ends. Since nature supposedly has value and goodness in itself, any human action which changes the environment is necessarily branded as immoral. Environmentalists invoke this argument from intrinsic value not against lions that eat gazelles or beavers that fell trees; they invoke it only against man, only when *man* wants something. The environmentalists' concept of intrinsic value is nothing but the desire to destroy human values. *—Michael S. Berliner, "Against Environmentalism," 1997, on the Ayn Rand Institute Web site*

B. A student of yours, Kathy (or Kevin, take your pick), has asked you to write a letter of recommendation to a company where she (or he) is seeking employment. Here are some facts about Kathy:

- Kathy is a few years older than the average student.
- Kathy took three courses with you.

---

[8] This example is based loosely on a case discussed in *How to Lie with Statistics,* by Darrell Huff (New York: Norton, 1954), a most enjoyable account of the ways in which numbers can be used to distort and deceive.

- Her grades were
  Introduction to Business: B minus
  Introduction to Accounting: B plus
  Advanced Accounting: A
- Kathy attended class regularly and handed in all assignments on time.
- Kathy participated regularly in class discussion. Her contributions to class discussions were always helpful, sometimes insightful.
- Kathy met with you often in your office to discuss course material.
- Kathy was well liked by her fellow students.
- Kathy worked outside of class with class members who were having trouble with course material.
- Kathy has a part-time job and is paying her way through school.
- It will take Kathy five years to graduate from college.
- Kathy is divorced and has a young child.
- Kathy's overall GPA is 3.2.

Write two letters, one guaranteed to impress the company, the other designed to ensure Kathy will not get the job. Keep two things in mind in composing your letters. Both letters should appear fair, balanced, and objective and in neither may you lie!

C. Review the discussion of hard news beginning on page 149. Now, watch a half-hour television news broadcast or carefully read the first section of your daily newspaper. Make notes on each story and decide what percentage of the stories qualify as hard news. (A story need not exhibit all the characteristics of hard news to qualify.)

SOLUTIONS

Exercise A

4. *Omitting information.* We need additional facts to understand the significance of the claim being made. Granted, a lot of unusual things happen when the moon is full. But what about other times of the month? Do more or fewer or about the same number of bizarre events take place then? Without this comparative information, it is difficult to know whether the information in the passage supports the claim at issue.

17. *Straw man.* The author of this passage wants to criticize "conservatives" who argue for the "death knell of liberalism." However, the definition of *liberalism* the author introduces is likely very different from what critics of liberalism would give. What conservatives tend to rail against under the rubric "liberalism" is the belief that government, not the private sector, should carry the major responsibility for dealing with social problems. Liberals, on this view, favor a much larger, more aggressive federal government than do conservatives. Note how easy it is for the author of the passage to defend his or her version of liberalism. I doubt there is anyone who would not claim to be a liberal, given this definition.

32. *False dichotomy.* The justification for misery and suffering given in this passage presupposes there are only two alternatives: a world in which there would be no misery and suffering *or* a world containing exactly the amount of misery and suffering we find. On this view, since misery and suffering have an important role to play in our lives, the former option is untenable. So, the latter must be correct. The problem with this argument is that there is another option: a world in which there is just the right amount of misery and suffering to accomplish God's purposes. The passage also seems to involve a *straw man* fallacy. The view being opposed claims only that there is gratuitous, or unnecessary, misery and suffering. Thus, the first option set forth does not accurately reflect the position at issue. The initial challenge is to explain why there is excessive misery and suffering, not why there should be any misery and suffering at all.

CHAPTER SEVEN

Ambiguity and Redundancy

All the fallacies in this chapter involve problems with the meanings of key terms used in mounting arguments. Most of these fallacies turn on the ambiguous use of key words; a word or phrase is used in one way in a premise but in another way in the conclusion or another premise. The final two fallacies involve subtle forms of redundancy. In one, claims introduced as premises simply reassert the conclusion. In the other, claims used as premises are so close in meaning to the conclusion that they will not be accepted unless the conclusion is also accepted.

EQUIVOCATION

Equivocation occurs when a key word or phrase is used in more than one sense in an argument that requires a single, consistent use of the term or phrase. Here is a pretty transparent example:

> An organ is a kind of musical instrument.
>
> The human heart is an organ.
> _____
> The human heart is a musical instrument.

The equivocation involved in this argument is clear. *Organ* is used in two quite different senses in the premises, and so the conclusion does not follow.

Equivocation can be much more difficult to pin down, as in this argument:

> There is really not much point in passing laws against discrimination, for discrimination is just an unavoidable fact of life. We discriminate every time we choose one thing over another, every time we express some preference. Trying to legislate away discrimination makes about as much sense as trying to pass a law against breathing or eating.

In standard form, the argument of this passage becomes

> Discrimination is a necessary element of a human life.
> _____
> Discrimination cannot be eliminated by legislation.

On first inspection, the conclusion of this argument may seem to follow from its premise. But think for a moment about the underlying inference. Someone who advanced this argument must believe that if something is necessary, it cannot be eliminated by passing a law against it. Set out in valid form, the argument is as follows:

> If discrimination is a necessary element of human life, then it cannot be eliminated by legislation.
>
> Discrimination is a necessary element of human life.
> ___
> Discrimination cannot be eliminated by legislation.

When the argument is set out in this form, the equivocation is easier to spot. The premises support the conclusion only on the assumption that *discrimination* means the same thing on each occurrence, in both the premises and the conclusion. Yet, judging by the language of the passage from which the argument was extracted, *discrimination* is being used in two distinct senses. Obviously, there is a sense in which discrimination is a necessary feature of a human life. Discrimination, in this sense, is just the inevitable fact that living means making choices, expressing preferences. This, however, is not what is meant by *discrimination* in the argument's conclusion, where it means the withholding of a person's rights and perhaps opportunities based on his or her race, sex, religion, and so on. And from the fact that one kind of discrimination—the making of choices—is necessary, it does not follow that another kind—the withholding of rights—cannot be eliminated by legislation. Thus, the inference underlying the argument appears to make sense only if we fail to realize that the meaning of a key term has shifted in the move from premises to conclusion.

Often, disagreements turn on an underlying difference of opinion about the meaning of a key word or phrase. **Verbal disagreements,** as such disputes are often called, frequently have a lot in common with equivocal arguments, for the parties to the dispute probably do not realize that they are using key terms in different ways. Although the arguments given by the disputants may not themselves be equivocal, the dispute itself is fueled by a kind of equivocation. Imagine, for example, the following conversation:

> *P:* Did you see that story on TV last night about the little boy who woke up after being in a coma for nearly six months?
>
> *Q:* Yeah, I saw it. Pretty amazing!
>
> *P:* It wasn't just amazing. It was a miracle!
>
> *Q:* Oh, come on. You're exaggerating. The kid just recuperated. Stranger things have happened.
>
> *P:* No. I'm serious. It was miraculous. His doctors had given up on him. They even told his parents there was no hope. But his parents never gave up. They prayed night and day for his recovery. It was a miracle, plain and simple.
>
> *Q:* Look, modern medicine doesn't know everything. Doctors are only human and they make mistakes like the rest of us. This isn't the first time a diagnosis has turned out to be wrong.
>
> *P:* I give up. Can't you just admit that sometimes, when all else fails, prayer is the only answer?
>
> *Q:* People can pray all they want. But that doesn't mean that if they get what they prayed for, a miracle took place. I'm praying that the sun will come up

> tomorrow. Does that mean it's a miracle if it does? Now, if I prayed for the sun *not* to come up and it didn't, then we'd have a real miracle on our hands.
>
> *P:* Now you're just making fun of me.
>
> *Q:* No. I'm serious. At least *that* would be a real miracle.

This conversation could probably continue far into the night without anything getting resolved. The problem is that P and Q have very different views of what *miracle* means. Although neither explicitly defines the term, it is not hard to see where their definitions differ. P thinks of a miracle as a fortuitous and highly unlikely event that appears to have happened in response to prayer. Q, on the other hand, thinks of a miracle as something that cannot have occurred by purely natural means and thus would have required divine intervention. As long as P and Q fail to see that they are using *miracle* in very different ways, their dispute stands little chance of getting resolved.

This last example contains important advice for arguers. If a disagreement appears to be intractable, chances are good there is some underlying confusion about the way in which key terms are being used. It is always wise to pause and try to clarify what really is at issue. Do the disputants genuinely disagree about what constitute the facts or about what conclusion follows from the facts? Or have they just failed to settle on a common definition for some of the key notions used in stating their positions? Resolving the latter question will probably not settle the dispute. But it will make the issues sufficiently clear to improve the chances for making some progress.

Equivocation can be an effective and subtle means of creating a straw man, an argument distorted for purposes of criticism. Imagine that I have advanced an argument in which I claim that all people in this country are equal. You reply, "How can you possibly claim that everybody is equal when there is such a great disparity between the rich and poor?" In fact, I mean to claim only that everybody has equal rights under the law. Your counterargument is directed against a very different claim, namely, that everybody is equal in an economic sense. And, not coincidentally, the version of my view you have given is going to be much easier to knock down than is the view I actually hold. Note that the shift here is not due to a change in the definition of *equal*. Rather, you have subtly shifted emphasis from one phrase using this term to another, from *equal under the law* to *economically equal*.

COLLECTIVE AND DISTRIBUTIVE PROPERTIES

We often make claims about collections of things, as in

> The class did well on the test

and

> Nike shoes are not made in the United States.

But the properties we attribute to things when we make such claims can be of two different sorts. A **collective property** is a property of a group or collection, though not a property of its individual members. Consider the first of our examples:

> The class did well on the test.

Suppose this claim is based on the fact that the class average on the test was 86 percent. Although it is true that the class, taken as a whole, scored 86 percent, it does not follow that any particular student in the class made this score. *Did well on the test* in this example is thus a collective property.

By contrast, a **distributive property** is a property not of the group taken as a whole, but, rather, of the individual members of a group. The claim

Nike shoes are not made in the United States

involves a distributive property. According to the claim, being made somewhere other than in the United States is a property of each and every pair of Nikes. Though the claim is about the collection, shoes made by Nike, it merely states that all members of the collection have the property in question.

Whether a property is distributive or collective can be difficult to determine, since the same phrase may be used to refer to a distribution or a collection, depending on the context in which it occurs. The claim

The New York Knicks are well paid

is ambiguous since it can be understood either collectively or distributively. Collectively, it may be taken to mean that the team, as a whole, is well paid—that the average salary of a New York Knick is pretty high. Distributively, it suggests that each member of the team is well paid.

The next three fallacies all involve a failure to distinguish between the collective and distributive uses of words and phrases when one is attributing properties to collections of things.

DIVISION

Division occurs when an inference is drawn about the members of a group from a claim that involves a collective property of the group, as in the following argument:

We all know that state government is inefficient. Thus, the Department of Motor Vehicles must be inefficient, as well.

Because state government, taken as a whole, is inefficient, it does not follow that every subarea of state government is inefficient, any more than it follows that a particular employee is inefficient because his or her department is inefficient. The criteria we use to determine that a department or an individual is inefficient are different from those we use to decide whether state government, as a whole, is inefficient.

When we speak collectively of a group or collection, we are speaking of an abstraction. Taken collectively, the claim

The New York Knicks are well paid

is about an abstraction—the team, as opposed to its individual members. And the team is not an actual thing, in the sense in which the members of the team are actual human beings. The notion of an abstract entity is tricky. Do we really want to say that abstractions are not things? Suppose I tell you that the investment firm Smith and Jones was fined for insider trading. Surely, the firm is an actual thing, despite the fact that it is an abstraction; we cannot literally see or touch the firm. (We can, of course, literally see and touch the building that houses the firm and the employees of the firm, but neither the building nor the employees are the firm.) We can, however, invest with the firm and the firm can be fined for illegal activity. If we can do things with the firm and if things can be done to the firm, it would seem the firm must be some sort of thing after all. Precisely what kind of thing an abstract entity is—if it is a thing at all—is a deep philosophical question but, fortunately, one we can sidestep.

At least this much seems true of abstractions: When we speak collectively of a group or collection of things, the terms we use to refer to the group are abstract, relative to the individual things the terms describe. Relative to its individual players, the notion of a team, collectively speaking, is abstract. At the very least, the team is a different kind of thing than are its members, and so many of its properties will not be properties of its members. Given that we create abstractions when we generalize about groups of individual things, it follows that we risk committing the fallacy of division when we read properties of abstractions onto the entities over which they generalize. Suppose that I drew the following inference:

The Knicks are the best team in basketball today.

Patrick Ewing plays for the Knicks.

He must be one of the best players in the game.

Perhaps the conclusion of this argument is true. But its truth does not follow from the information in its premises. *The best* applies to an abstraction like the team but not in the way it applies to an individual member of the team. The best team may be the team with the best overall record or the team whose members display extraordinary teamwork. The criteria by which we might judge someone *one of the best in the game* will likely involve a very different set of factors, like individual scoring and rebounding averages.

Arguments that depend on generalizations about the probability of an event often involve division. This version of division is sometimes called the **gambler's fallacy** for reasons amply illustrated by the following case. Suppose I have just flipped a coin and it has come up heads. What are the chances that if I flip it again it will come up heads? Let's consider the odds. If I flip a coin twice, the odds are one in four that both flips will come up heads. Why this is so is easy to see. Given a pair of coin flips, the only possible results are

Flip 1	Flip 2
Heads	Heads
Heads	Tails
Tails	Heads
Tails	Tails

Of these four possibilities, only one contains two heads, and so the odds of flipping two heads in a row are one in four. I have just flipped a heads. And since the odds of

CONUNDRUM

As you are probably aware, auto insurance companies fix rates by such general traits as age and sex. Young male drivers, for example, tend to have more accidents than older drivers, so the rates charged younger male drivers, as a class, are higher. Is this strategy an instance of the fallacy of division? What might a spokesperson for the insurance industry say on this issue?

the coin coming up heads twice in a row are one in four, I have a one in four chance of getting that second heads on the next flip. The argument here is simple and straightforward:

> The odds are one in four that two consecutive flips of a coin will come up heads.
>
> On the first flip, my coin came up heads.
> _____
> The odds are one in four that the second flip will come up heads.

Is this inference correct? If you think it is, you have committed the gambler's fallacy. In fact, the inference in my argument is fallacious. Although the first premise is true, we can draw no conclusion about any particular flip of a coin based on what it says. For any particular flip, the odds are always one in two that it will come up heads (presuming it is a fair coin and there are no tricks involved in the flipping). All the first premise tells us is that in any pair of flips, the chances of getting two heads are one in four; it tells us nothing about any particular event, any particular flip of a coin.[1]

Functional explanations are particularly susceptible to division. What does the heart do? What's the purpose of the thermostat over there on the wall? The answer to questions like these often involve what are called **functional explanations,** explanations that tell us something about the purpose or role a thing plays, often in some larger enterprise. The role of the heart is to pump blood throughout the body. The purpose of a thermostat is to regulate temperature. But from the fact that something fulfills a particular function, we cannot draw any conclusions about the functions of its parts. So, I commit the fallacy of division if, from the fact that the thermostat on my wall regulates temperature, I conclude that one of its parts, say, a small tube of mercury, regulates temperature. Although it is part of a complex system designed to regulate temperature, the tube of mercury itself does not fulfill this function. Similarly, division is involved in the inference from the fact that I am able to think to the conclusion that there must be "thinking" going on in the cells of my brain. No doubt, there is a sense in which the part of me that does my thinking is my brain. But from this it does not follow that the individual parts of that part engage in the same function.

_____

[1] The gambler's fallacy is often explained as an erroneous statistical inference. Events like the toss of a coin are independent in that the outcome of one toss does not affect the outcome of the next toss. Thus, information about the probability of a certain sequence of tosses, like two heads in a row, cannot be used to predict the probability that any single toss will be heads or tails.

COMPOSITION

Composition is the reverse of division. In division, an inference is drawn about the members of a collection, based on a property of the collection, taken as a whole. **Composition** occurs when the inference moves from information about the individual members of a group to a conclusion about the group, taken as a whole. Here is an illustration:

> The company's stockholders did not make much money in profits this year, so the company must not have made much money this year.

To determine whether the company *made much money,* we would need to consider factors such as the percentage of profit on gross receipts, whether or not profits were reinvested in the company or used to expand markets, and so on. From the fact that the company's stockholders did or did not *make much money,* we can draw no conclusion about the financial status of the company. Speaking collectively of the company, *make much money* applies by virtue of a different set of criteria than in speaking distributively of its stockholders. Similarly, from the fact that none of the company's employees made much money, we cannot conclude that the company didn't make much.

Earlier, we noted the ease with which functional explanations can lead to arguments that involve division. Another kind of explanation—reductionistic explanation—is readily susceptible to the fallacy of composition. In a **reductionistic explanation,** the properties of a complex system are explained by reference to the properties of its component parts and their interactions. Often, explanations will be both reductionistic and functional; a thing may be explained by reference to the way in which its parts interact to achieve the function in question.

Reductionism can be an effective and entirely appropriate method of explanation. If I want, for example, to understand how a carburetor works, I would do well to take one apart, trying to understand how its various pieces function in conjunction with one another to accomplish a certain end: the proper mixture of fuel and oxygen. But often, complex systems have properties that cannot be inferred from the properties of their parts alone, and here the efficacy of reductionistic explanation may mislead us. If we conclude that some property of a complex system isn't "real," based on the fact that it is not a property of the parts involved in explaining how the system operates, we commit the fallacy of composition. We would be guilty of composition if we inferred, for example, that water is not really wet because it is composed of nothing more than molecules of hydrogen and oxygen, objects that do not have the property of wetness. Though chemists can account for many of the observable properties of water by reference to how H_2O molecules react under various conditions, it does not follow that wetness is not really a property of water. Wetness is a property of water by virtue of how it feels to the touch and how it tastes, considerations not addressed in the molecular explanation just alluded to.

The lesson to be learned from our discussion of composition and division is not that we should avoid drawing conclusions about groups on the basis of specific cases or vice versa. A generalization is a claim about properties common to some portion of the members of a collection. The properties over which generalizations range are, thus, distributive, not collective. So, for example, from the fact that *all* Nike shoes are made outside the United States, it follows that a particular pair of Nikes is made outside the U.S. Similarly, from the fact that every pair of Nikes we have examined has been made outside the U.S., it *may* follow that all or perhaps most Nikes are made outside the U.S. This last inference may be problematic if, for example, we haven't examined enough pairs of Nikes or if there is something special about the pairs we have examined. But under the right conditions, the inference here may be entirely reliable. Reliable and fallacious arguments—both for and from generalizations—will be discussed in detail in Chapter 9. For now it is enough to note that the problems associated with arguments involving generalizations are different from those that lead to composition and division.

HYPOSTATIZATION

When we falsely attribute properties belonging to the members of a group to the group itself, we are guilty of composition. When we treat the group itself as though it were one of its members, we commit the fallacy of **hypostatization.** Remember, a group or collection is an abstraction. It is not surprising, then, that abstractions lack many of the properties of the things over which they range. Hypostatization usually involves personification, as when groups of people are spoken of as though they were themselves people. How often have you heard politicians claim electoral victory in terms like this?

> By providing us with an overwhelming majority in yesterday's election, the voters expressed their grave dissatisfaction with the policies of the current administration. I'd say the fact that the incumbent received only 45 percent of the vote is a clear indication of the will of the people: Things have got to change.

Now, obviously, a lot of voters expressed their dissatisfaction. But what reason is there to believe that the voters who opposed the incumbent were all dissatisfied for the same or even similar reasons? From the fact that a large block of people voted against the incumbent, it is difficult to conclude much about their collective will. *The will of the people* does not seem to be more than a collection of individual reasons why people have voted as they have. To draw a conclusion about what the *electorate* want or what their votes indicate is thus to attribute to an abstraction—the voters—a property that has no clear meaning in anything other than a distributive sense. Just what could *the will of the people* be, over and above the will of the individual voters?

The sort of oversimplified thinking illustrated by the last example is not uncommon nor is it easy to resist. Having invested an abstraction with the properties of individual things, it is easy to lapse into thinking of the abstraction as though it were just another thing of the sort in question. Claims about abstractions often bring to mind striking images of individual things:

> It is part of the *Russian character* to suffer.

> The *union movement* in this country has become lazy and complacent.

> The *church* is more concerned with profit than with ministering to its flock.

The *House and the Senate* can never seem to agree on anything.

The *American taxpayer* is fed up with the current system.

It is undoubtedly true, for example, that a lot of Americans are disenchanted with our current system of taxation and many would like to see it overhauled. If we are not careful, the claim

The American taxpayer is fed up with the current system

can take on a life of its own: We may begin to think of the *American taxpayer* as just another taxpayer. In so doing, we risk vastly oversimplifying by thinking of what are undoubtedly a myriad of complaints as though they represent a solitary complaint in the mind of a single voter. To argue, for example, that the tax code needs reforming because the *American taxpayer* is fed up is to fall prey to an insidious and implicit instance of the fallacy of hypostatization.

CIRCULAR REASONING

If a claim is to provide support for another claim, it must be distinct from the claim it supports. An argument of the form

$$\frac{C}{C}$$

can hardly be said to provide evidence for C. (Interestingly, the inference in such an argument is unassailable. Obviously, there is no possible set of circumstances under which the premise would be true and the conclusion false!) However, suppose someone gave an argument of the form

$$\frac{P}{C}$$

in circumstances where P asserts the same thing as C, but P is expressed in language that masks the equivalence of P and C. If we fail to see that P only reasserts C, the argument might appear to provide support for C. In these circumstances,

$$\frac{P}{C}$$

would be an instance of **circular reasoning.** In its most basic form, circular reasoning can be highly effective, particularly when the problematic premise is cleverly disguised. Imagine I told you that I am in favor of increasing certain user's fees, like the fees charged to license boats and automobiles and for building and parade permits. I give as my reason the fact that these increases would generate new tax revenue. My reasoning here would be circular. My argument is

User's fees would generate new tax revenue.
_____

User's fees should be increased.

In fact, a user's fee is just one kind of tax, and so my argument says no more than that we should increase a certain kind of tax because that would result in an increase in tax revenue.

Synonymous Descriptions

The use of **synonymous descriptive terms** can be an effective means of creating a circular argument.

> Capital punishment is wrong, because it is immoral and unethical

does nothing more than introduce, in its premise, a pair of synonyms for a key term in the argument's conclusion. *Wrong, immoral,* and *unethical* mean much the same thing. The argument says no more than that capital punishment is wrong because it is wrong.

Circularity can result from the use of language, in the premises, that merely alludes to the fact that there is evidence for or against something, rather than providing any real evidence. Suppose I gave a better argument for user's fees:

> User's fees should be increased because we desperately need tax dollars to fund new programs authorized by the voters and user's fees tax those who can most afford to pay.

Being opposed to the increases I advocate but having no reasons at the ready, you reply:

> I can't agree. An increase in user's fees is unjustified and would be ill-conceived at this time.

What you have done is simply allude to the fact that you think there are good reasons why user's fees should not be increased at this time. But in alluding to the fact that they would be *ill-conceived* and *unjustified,* you have yet to give any real evidence for your conclusion. Thus, your reasoning is circular in that you have done nothing more than reiterate your belief that user's fees should not be increased.

This sort of insubstantial criticism is often prompted by the fact that people need to make quick critical responses without having the time to think things through. Lacking anything much to say about an argument, one can always throw together a few adjectives that suggest the view in question is problematic. When asked by a reporter why he was opposed to turning the U.S. Postal Service over to the private sector, a spokesperson for the Postal Workers Union commented: "Such an action would be inappropriate and unwarranted." This may be right. But lacking substantial argumentation showing why these adjectives apply, this remark is circular. Similarly, anybody who criticizes us on the grounds that we are acting *illogically* or *irrationally* has advanced no case unless he or she gives reasons for thinking these adjectives apply.

Circular Explanations

Explanations can involve a type of circular reasoning even though they are not, strictly speaking, arguments. Though circular explanations are not a type of fallacious argument, they are unacceptable for the same reason circular arguments are unacceptable: Both circular arguments and explanations simply reiterate something we already know.

The point of an explanation is to tell us how or why something happened. "Why did you bring your umbrella?" you ask me. "Because," I reply, "I think it might rain." This seems an adequate explanation. An explanation is circular when it simply redescribes whatever it intends to explain. Suppose you ask me why the check I wrote to you bounced. I explain to you that I didn't have enough money in the bank to cover the check. No doubt you had already figured this out. "I didn't have enough money in the bank to cover the check" is just another way of saying that my check bounced. What you want explained is *why* I didn't have enough money in the bank. If I had said instead, "I miscalculated my checking balance. I thought I had $200, not $2," my explanation would be noncircular, appealing to a fact distinct from the claim it is introduced to explain.

We often ask for explanations when people do things we do not fully understand. Suppose you have just heard that a good friend recently quit his or her job. You might ask, "Why did you just up and quit? I was under the impression you enjoyed it. The last time we talked, you told me you thought it was the most rewarding job you had ever had." Your friend might reply, "I thought it was time for a change." Though intriguing, your friend's explanation says very little. What is puzzling is why he or she wanted this. The explanation you are given does little more than underscore your puzzlement. "Why," you need to ask, "did you think it was time for a change?" Lacking further detail, the explanation you have been given is circular.

We should always be suspicious of **psychological explanations**—claims about why people have done the things they have done—that simply make reference to unspecified wants, desires, wishes, goals, aims, needs, and so on. That someone has chosen to do the thing in question generally implies that he or she believed a want, desire, or need would be met by his or her action. A noncircular explanation of such behavior informs us of how the action was envisioned to satisfy a particular want, desire, need, or whatever. Suppose your friend had gone on to say, "I was no longer challenged by my work there and finally came to realize that I was going to burn out if I stayed much longer." Here is the beginning of an interesting, informative, and certainly noncircular explanation.

BEGGING THE QUESTION

Begging the question is closely related to circular reasoning. In circular reasoning, a variant of the conclusion is given as a premise or a premise is given that says no more than that there is evidence for the conclusion. By contrast, an argument **begs the question** when it introduces as evidence claims that tacitly assume the truth of the conclusion, claims that would be accepted only by those who already believe the conclusion. The phrase *begs the question* is sometimes used to allude to the fact that a person has avoided answering a question. However, an argument that begs the question is one that "begs"—invites—its audience to accept the claim at issue prior to argumentation. Look at the following argument:

> **CONUNDRUM**
>
> We have noted that the following argument is fallacious.
>
> I remember giving a homework assignment.
> _____
> I gave a homework assignment.
>
> Does it follow that all claims, based on memory, beg the question?

People seem to be losing their capacity to distinguish right from wrong. If you doubt this, just look at the increases, in the past decade, in both the divorce rate and the number of unwanted pregnancies that have been aborted.

Think about the inference implicit in this argument. Can we admit that the rates of divorce and abortion have increased and yet deny the conclusion—the claim that people are losing their capacity to distinguish right from wrong? It seems possible that these increases are due to social and economic factors, not some underlying change in moral attitudes. Perhaps, for example, the increased financial pressures that many families now feel are in part responsible for the increased number of divorces. No doubt, someone who gave the preceding argument would reject this explanation. But why? On the grounds that the increases in divorce and abortion rates are *instances* of immoral behavior. Thus, if we accept these increases as evidence for the conclusion, we must also accept that they are examples of a diminished capacity to distinguish right from wrong, a variant of the claim at issue!

One telltale sign that an argument may involve begging the question is this. If, upon hearing or reading an argument, we sense that an arguer is not responding to the point at issue despite the fact that he or she seems to think otherwise, the argument may well beg the question. Now, the point at issue can often be determined by considering what fuels the audience's misgivings about the arguer's position. If the arguer fails to see that the argument does not address these misgivings, he or she is probably begging the question. Suppose that I walk into a class and ask my students to turn in the homework I assigned at the end of the last class period. Several students point out that I made no such assignment; I must be confusing this group of students with another one. I reply by insisting, vociferously, that I distinctly remember making the assignment. My students reply, with equal vigor, that I most certainly did not give the assignment. I go on to insist that I did, giving a detailed account of the things I remember saying. In this context, I am guilty of begging the question, for I have failed to understand what is at issue. No one in the class doubts that I *remember* giving the assignment, at least I hope they don't. At issue is whether my memory of this event is accurate. In insisting that I remember giving the assignment, I do not address this issue. The evidence I do give begs the question, for it assumes as true that which is at issue.

How many times does a question get begged in this cartoon?
(*Source:* © 1997 by Matt Groening. All rights reserved. Reprinted by permission of Acme Features Syndicate.)

Question-Begging Epithets

Biased language can be used to beg the question in a subtle way by stating premises in terms that would be accurate only if the conclusion is granted. Look at the following argument:

> Evolutionists refuse to believe the Bible account of how an infinitely wise and
> all-powerful Creator built this planet and furnished it with every sort of plant

and animal life. Not particularly worried, however, over the fact that they have absolutely no explanation for the origin of life, evolutionists are content to dote on simple theories about one-celled life in a mud puddle evolving to the stature of a man.

At issue in this passage is whether the theory of evolution can explain the origin of life. (Ignore, for now, the fact that the passage involves a straw man in seriously misconstruing the purpose of the theory of evolution—the theory is not intended to explain how life originated.) The passage describes the theory of evolution in terms that suggest it may be mistaken: Evolutionists dote on *simple theories* about *one-celled* organisms in a *mud puddle.* These carefully chosen terms suggest that the theory is much too simple-minded to be correct. The problem is that they apply to the theory of evolution only on the assumption that it is probably mistaken.

Arguments, like the one we have just examined, involve **question-begging epithets.** An **epithet** is a word or phrase used to create a particular picture of a person or thing. Epithets can enrich descriptions by suggesting vivid images of things. Thus, the careful choice of an epithet or two in stating a premise can bias us in favor of the claim at issue in an argument. Suppose I want to convince you that we need to reduce the number of people who work for the federal government. "Big government is inefficient government," I say. If you will only allow me to describe the people whose jobs I want to eliminate as "bureaucrats," you've done half my job for me.

Non-Question-Begging Arguments

We must not be too quick to charge an argument with begging the question. Don't confuse question-begging arguments with arguments merely involving questionable premises. An argument does not beg the question simply because one of its premises may seem at least as questionable as its conclusion. This may simply be a sign that the arguer needs to spend some time backing the questionable claim or finding better evidence. To beg the question, an argument must be shown to involve a premise whose acceptance requires prior acceptance of the conclusion as well.

Nor should we reject an argument as question begging simply because it makes a presupposition about whatever is at issue. A **presupposition** is a belief, usually shared by author and audience, that gives a remark its point. "Sorry I'm late," I say to you. This remark would make little sense if neither you nor I believed I was late. Arguments, as well, involve presuppositions. Here are the conclusions of some of the arguments we have examined:

> The theory of evolution is wrong.
>
> User's fees should be increased.
>
> Discrimination cannot be eliminated.

Clearly, a person would not argue that the theory of evolution is wrong if he or she did not believe there are people who think it is correct. An argument for an *increase* in user's fees similarly presupposes that such fees are now in place. What would be the point of arguing that discrimination cannot be eliminated if discrimination were not a fact?

At first glance, the following dialogue may seem to beg the question. Imagine two people, A and B, engaged in a dispute about the nature of God:

A: God can't possibly be all-knowing.

B: I don't agree. God suffers from no limitations. If there were something God did not know, God would be limited. And this is just impossible.

A: Just hear me out. If God knows everything, God knows everything that is yet to happen. And this means God knows what the future holds.

B: Yes. That much seems right.

A: But this means the course the future will take has already been determined. Otherwise, we could claim only that God is very good at predicting the future.

B: Here I agree with you. God does know the future.

A: But here's the problem. If the future is determined, then we don't really have free will. And if we don't have free will, how can we choose to accept God through Christ? Everything we do has been predetermined, including our choices.

B: I claim only God, not we humans, is all-knowing.

A: It doesn't matter. All you're suggesting now is that we humans may not be aware that we have no free will.

At this point, we might be tempted to interject that both A and B are guilty of begging the question. A and B both seem to assume that there is a God. But this assumption is agreed to only for the sake of the argument—for the purpose of resolving the question of whether such a being could be all-knowing. The question of whether or not there is a God is not at issue in their argument. Thus, A and B cannot be said to beg the question because they assume this. The assumption that there is a God functions as a presupposition of their dispute. Only if A and B grant this assumption is there any point to the arguments they subsequently give.

On occasion, an argument begs the question in circumstances where both arguer and audience are fully aware of what is going on. Such an argument should not be lightly dismissed, for its point may be to **frame the issues** by focusing on what is really at issue in a debate. Suppose someone argued that prayer should not be allowed in the public schools on the ground that it would violate the principle of separation of church and state:

> School prayer violates the constitutional provision for separation of church and state.
>
> ---
>
> Prayer should not be allowed in the public schools.

Now, this argument does seem to beg the question in that its premise would be accepted by those who agree with the conclusion but rejected by those who disagree with the conclusion. However, the disagreement here is not over the *inference* implicit in the argument. No doubt, all parties to the argument would agree that if it is true that school prayer violates the Constitution, then it should not be allowed. The disagreement is going to be over the question of whether the premise is true. Thus, the point of the argument may be to focus on the fact that what is really at issue in this debate is whether school prayer involves a violation of the Constitution. Having framed the issue in this way, of course, the parties to the argument must now provide non-question-begging arguments in defense of their respective views about the constitutionality of school prayer. In such circumstances, we would be wrong to charge the preceding argument with begging the question. The intent of the arguer is not to tacitly encourage the audience to accept the conclusion in the form of a question-begging premise. Rather, the intent is to focus the debate on what is really at issue.

When we suspect that an argument begs the question, it is always a good idea to consider the three possibilities just discussed. Is the argument merely committed to a questionable premise? Have we misidentified an argument as question begging when it merely requires the truth of a presupposition about the conclusion shared by arguer and audience? Is the point of the argument to frame issues without asking its audience tacitly to assume the truth of the conclusion? As these questions suggest, we must make sure we have not misunderstood an argument before charging it with begging the question.

CHAPTER SUMMARY

Equivocation   Equivocation occurs when a key term or phrase is used in more than one sense in an argument that requires a single, consistent use to be inferentially correct.

Example: No news is good news.

Natural disasters are no news.

Natural disasters are good news.

Division   An unwarranted inference about the members of a collection or group based on something that is true only of the collection or group, taken as a whole.

Example: The class did well on the test.

Susan is a member of the class.

Susan did well on the test.

Composition   The reverse of division. An unwarranted inference is drawn about a collection, taken as a whole, based on properties of the individual members of the collection.

Example: Atoms are colorless and odorless.

An apple is composed of atoms.

An apple is colorless and odorless.

Hypostatization   Properties are attributed to a group or an abstraction that apply only to the members of the group or the individual things falling under the abstraction.

Example: The modern multinational corporation has an unquenchable appetite. It wants nothing more than to consume its competitors, dismantle them, and turn their assets into profits for the shareholders.

Circular reasoning   An argument is circular if one or more of its premises reiterates its conclusion.

Example:

It is against the law to willfully take a human life.

Murder is illegal.

An explanation is circular if the explanatory portion merely redescribes whatever is being explained.

Example: The reason he committed suicide was because he had a death wish.

An argument in which the premises merely allude to the fact that there is evidence for the conclusion is circular.

Example:

Your solution would be inappropriate and unwarranted at this time.

Your solution is a poor one.

Begging the question   An argument begs the question when it introduces evidence that assumes the truth of the argument's conclusion.

Example:

The very idea of an uncaused event makes no sense.

Every event has a cause.

Question-begging epithets are descriptive terms used in stating premises that apply only on the assumption that the conclusion is true.

Example:

Every day, opportunistic welfare cheaters rob us of millions of dollars.

The welfare system encourages fraud.

An argument does not beg the question simply because it introduces evidence that is as questionable as the conclusion. An argument in which the conclusion requires the truth of a presupposition shared by arguer and audience does not beg the question. Arguments that introduce premises that would not be accepted unless the conclusion is accepted do not beg the question when they are intended to frame the issues by showing that the conclusion requires the truth of the premise.

EXERCISES

A. Many, perhaps all, of the problems in this exercise involve fallacies of ambiguity or redundancy. Some of the problems may involve more than one. Your job is to decide which fallacy or fallacies each involves. The first thing to do is to get clear on the argument: Give its conclusion and premise or premises. Next, comment in detail on the fallacy it seems to involve. If you are not confident that your diagnosis is accurate, paraphrase the original passage so that it is a clear instance of the fallacy in question. If you find that in doing this you have distorted the original appeal, you are probably on the wrong track and need to reconsider. If the passage strikes you as being nonfallacious, give and defend your reading of the argument. If a passage seems to involve a mistake, but not one that fits neatly under any of our headings, describe in your own words where and how the appeal goes wrong.

(Solutions to Exercises 14 and 34 are given on page 192.)

1. *Car salesperson:* Of course you can afford to buy this car. You can afford to pay $299 a month, can't you?
2. My belief in the divinity of Jesus Christ is based on the events documented in the Bible.
3. *Movie producer:* I'm not going to make small, serious movies. Look at the kind of movies that have been the most successful in recent years. Big blockbusters with lots of action. The movie-going public is just not interested in

thinking about serious matters. When they go to see a movie, they just want to be entertained.

4. I can run a half mile in three minutes, so it follows that if I really put out the effort, I should be able to complete that six-mile race in under thirty-six minutes.

5. The best argument for the existence of God comes from, of all places, science. Science has proven that there are laws of nature, like the laws of entropy and the laws of conservation of mass and momentum. We know that laws require a lawgiver, so it follows that the laws of nature must have an author.

6. *Bill Gates:* If General Motors had kept up with technology like the computer industry has, we would all be driving 25-dollar cars that get 1,000 miles per gallon.

   General Motors spokesperson: Yes, but would you want your car to crash twice a day?

7. Judge Jones shouldn't be appointed to the Supreme Court for the simple reason that he does not have the judicial temperament necessary to sit on the high court.

8. I'm convinced people are being abducted by aliens and used for experimental purposes. I've talked to several people all of whom have been abducted. And they all have told me detailed stories about the bizarre, almost unthinkable, things that were done to them.

9. The federal tax system is a junkyard of loopholes, special exemptions, tax credits, and deductions, all entangled in a chaotic maze of court decisions and special executive rules. That the system needs reforming is obvious.

10. Our expert mechanics can solve all of your repair problems. These highly trained experts have a combined two hundred years of experience working on cars like yours.

11. RECENTLY FOUND DOCUMENT CLOSELY LINKS WALDHEIM TO WAR CRIMES [headline for the following newspaper story]: Vienna, Austria—A West German historian on Saturday said a newly unearthed document linked Austrian President Kurt Waldheim "in the closest way yet" to alleged Nazi war crimes.

12. Our government has no business spending billions of dollars of taxpayers' money on esoteric science projects like the supercolliding super conductor and the Hubblescope. The money for these projects is desperately needed elsewhere.

13. It is ludicrous to charge the major corporations in our industry with fixing prices. The maximum price we can charge for our services is fixed by the federal government.

14. The reason serious crime is such a problem today is clear. People no longer seem to respect the law.

15. The universe is spherical in form . . . because all of the constituent parts of the universe, that is, the sun, the moon, and the planets, appear in this form.
    —*Nicolaus Copernicus*

16. One curious fact from a recent Census Bureau report is that 58 percent of all Americans claim to have voted in a recent election. Yet the fact is that less than 50 percent of all registered voters have actually voted in this period. Why the disparity? Its seems that people tend to overreport their voting habits.

17. Nothing we do in our lifetimes can really matter. At best everything we do will be forgotten within a few years or a few hundred years at most. On a cosmic scale, our lives and even the life of our species and planet are nothing more than a momentary, insignificant blip.

18. Why is there so much unemployment in the country today? Well, the number of people who are unable to find work is on the increase.

19. Prostitution is not a victimless crime, as some would contend. The person who finds it necessary to sell his or her body runs a high risk of becoming the victim of violence.

20. I don't think the way to improve our public school system is necessarily to increase funding. No doubt our schools have some serious problems, with increases in the drop-out rate and decreases in SAT scores. But you can't solve problems as complex as these by simply throwing money at them.

21. *Teacher:* Every college student ought to take at least one course in critical thinking.

    Student: Several of my friends have taken critical thinking, and they tell me very little they learned seems relevant in the real world, outside the classroom.

    Teacher: Well, they must not have been paying attention or studying very hard. The skills you acquire in critical thinking will help you analyze and assess the kinds of reasoning you are going to encounter in everyday life.

22. Don't tell me the theory of evolution by natural selection is true. After all, it's only a theory.

23. We have all heard the slogans: the end of the class struggle, the vanguard of the proletariat, the wave of the future, the inevitable triumph of socialism. Indeed, if there is anything the Marxist-Leninists might not be forgiven for, it is their willingness to bog the world down in tiresome clichés . . . a gaggle of bogus prophecies and petty superstitions. *—President Ronald Reagan, in a speech at the British Embassy*

24. A lot of people complain about the fact that women, on average, are paid much less than men. They say women should be treated as equals in the workplace. But they ignore one indisputable fact. Men and women are not equal, nor will they ever be equal. So don't blame employers because women often don't earn as much as men. If anybody is to blame, it's mother nature.

25. Since arguments are made up of claims and claims are either true or false, it follows that arguments must be either true or false.

26. To the editor: Your article in favor of the proposed new sales tax was right on the money. We desperately need a sales tax in this state. We have suffered long enough because the voters of this state have turned down a sales tax nine times.

27. Reading between the lines as 20th-ranked Southern Cal awaits unranked Oregon in Pacific 10 Conference football, Duck's coach Rich Brooks tries to figure out a way to win in Los Angeles. For starters, the law of percentages may be in Oregon's favor. The suddenly dangerous Ducks, 3-2 after a 30-20 win over Arizona State, are due. Oregon has beaten USC twice in the last 21 years

and once in Brooks's 16 years at the helm, a 34-27 win in 1987 in Eugene.
—*from a story on the sports page of the* Portland Oregonian

28. To the editor: I've had it with our elected representatives. Here we are with the largest deficit ever run up by any nation in history and our elected leaders sit around competing with one another to see who can come up with the most pork for his or her district. Congress is simply out of control and needs to learn to act with discipline and restraint. The only way I can figure to do this is to elect a new Congress.

29. You've shown me the dorm where you live, the library, the gym, the student center, and several classroom buildings, but you promised to show me the college you attend. So, where is it? (This example is loosely based on an illustration given by the British philosopher Gilbert Ryle, in *The Concept of Mind.*)

30. How does mental telepathy operate? By a parapsychological mechanism that does not involve the usual methods by which people communicate with one another.

31. Censorship should not be a bad word. No society can survive without it. I believe the stop sign at the corner is healthy censorship. So there is nothing wrong, in principle, with censoring the use of certain words and phrases in rock and roll music.

32. Forcing law-abiding citizens to register their handguns is not the solution to our crime problem, despite the fact that handguns are used in 150,000 robberies and 100,000 assaults each year in this country. There are well over 50 million handguns in the United States. Assuming that as many as 500,000 crimes are committed each year by private individuals using handguns, and, assuming that a different gun was used in each case, that means less than 1 percent of the existing handguns are used in the commission of crimes. To put it another way, over 99 percent of all handguns are not used for such crimes. Should 99 percent of those who possess handguns be made to pay for the sins of the 1 percent who comprise the criminal element?

33. Those back to nature alternatives like burning wood, trapping sunshine, and harnessing breezes and little waterfalls can't begin to do the energy jobs of a civilization as vast and complex as ours. —*from an ad by Mobil Corporation*

34. A big grocery chain offered to spend up to $1 million to purchase that parcel of land for their new store. I own one-quarter of the property it wanted. So, though the deal fell through because one owner refused to sell, at least I now know how much my land is worth: a cool quarter of a million dollars.

35. To the editor: To end human life or to have a hand in ending human life is in no way compassionate. Compassion means to have sorrow for and to share in the suffering of others. It is very sad indeed to know that so many people have forgotten just who it is who gives life and who makes the decision as to when it will end for each of us. —*from a letter in response to a proposal to allow physician-assisted suicide*

36. The only proof capable of being given that an object is visible, is that people actually see it. The only proof that a sound is audible, is that people hear it: and so of the other sources of our experience. In a like manner, I apprehend,

the sole evidence it is possible to produce that anything is desirable, is that people actually desire it. —*from* Utilitarianism, *by John Stuart Mill*

37. One version of the principle of the uniformity of nature is to the effect that the future will resemble the past in certain key respects. For example, from the fact that the sun has risen every day in the past we are justified in concluding it will continue to rise because in this respect nature is uniform. This basic principle is well established. Literally thousands of years of common-sense experience and scientific experiment all attest to the uniformity of nature over time.

38. That there is no phenomenal necessity in locating consciousness in the brain is further reinforced by various abnormal instances in which consciousness seems to be outside the body. A friend who received a left frontal brain injury in the war regained consciousness in the corner of the ceiling of a hospital ward looking down euphorically at himself on the cot swathed in bandages. Those who have taken lysergic acid diethylamide commonly reported similar out-of-body or asystematic experiences, as they are called. Such occurrences do not demonstrate anything metaphysical whatsoever; simply that locating consciousness can be an arbitrary matter. . . . In reality, consciousness has no location whatever except as we imagine it. —*from* The Origin of Consciousness in the Breakdown of the Bicameral Mind, *by Julian Jaynes*

39. To the editor: After reading the article about school districts testing athletes for drug use, I was surprised that so many people had a problem with the testing. I am involved in high school athletics and I think that testing should be allowed, because when you agree to play the sport, you are also agreeing to follow all the rules. All the testing is doing is enforcing the rules.

40. The following exchange is from a televised debate on the topic of whether or not evolutionists should acknowledge creation. Barry Lynn argues against the resolution and David Berlinski argues for it. Lynn is the executive director of Americans United for Separation of Church and State, and Berlinski is a science writer and the author of *A Tour of the Calculus*. This debate aired on the television program *Firing Line* on December 19, 1997.

> *Berlinski:* My interest in divine creation is negligible, but I do have a scientific question to ask you, in fact, two scientific questions, the second logical. Everyone familiar with paleontological literature, every significant paleontologist, says that there are gaps in the fossil record. Do you have a particular reason for demurring?
>
> *Lynn:* No, but there are gaps in the fossil record—
>
> *Berlinski:* So you agree.
>
> *Lynn:* —of course because the fossil record has only been in existence—
>
> *Berlinski:* I didn't ask whether there was an explanation for the gaps.
>
> *Lynn:* —for about 130—
>
> *Berlinski:* —I asked whether you agreed that the fossil record is full of gaps.
>
> *Lynn:* Of course it has gaps.
>
> *Berlinski:* OK, so to that extent the evidence does not support Darwin's theory of evolution?

Lynn: No, that is absolutely wrong.

Berlinski: It follows as the night the day.

Lynn: Of course not. How could you have a cell, for example, ladies and gentlemen, hundreds of millions of years old, that would leave a fossil record? It would disintegrate, it would quite literally—

Berlinski: I did not insist—

Lynn: —not be able to be found in the fossil record.

Berlinski: I never suggested that there may not be explanations of the gap, but the fact that the fossil record does not on its face support Darwin's theory of evolution is a fact.

Lynn: It does. No, it does. It's just— Your question was—

Berlinski: But it maintains two hypotheses that are in contradiction.

Lynn: —Does it prove everything yet? And the answer is it doesn't prove anything yet, and once again I say, how many times do we have to find those intermediate fossils? How many more steps in the progress—

Berlinski: I gave you—

Lynn: —from ancient horse to modern horse do we have to show you?

Berlinski: —a quantitative answer, what would satisfy a scientifically respectable temperament, and you spurned it. All I am asking for is enlightenment on the significant point. Darwin's theory requires a continuous—a multitude of continuous forms. We do not see that in the fossil record. In fact, major transitions are utterly incomplete. Will you accept that as an empirical fact?

Lynn: You sound like the guy who is writing a story about baseball, comes in the fourth inning, and says, "Well, you know, I am going to write about the fourth inning on; the first three innings didn't happen because I wasn't there to see them." The fact that we can't find every one of those intermediate fossils yet—

Berlinski: We can't find any of them.

Lynn: —in 150—of course we find them.

Berlinski: We can't find any of the major transitional—There is nothing between the fish and the amphibian.

Lynn: It's just that when we find them, Doctor, you say it's still not enough.

B. Pick one of the topics below and create an argument that commits at least one of the fallacies discussed in this chapter. Don't allow your appeal to be too transparent. A well-constructed fallacy will have the power to persuade. Give your results to a friend, ideally one who is not familiar with fallacies, and ask if he or she thinks your argument makes good sense. If you have succeeded in writing an effective fallacious appeal, your friend should not have an easy time spotting the mistake in your appeal.

1. The death penalty should be abolished.
2. Animals have moral rights.
3. We have a moral obligation to be vegetarians.
4. Private citizens should not be allowed to own handguns.
5. All forms of gambling should be illegal.

6. Condoms should be distributed in public schools.
7. Students who sit in the front of the classroom will get the best grades.
8. Personality is reflected in handwriting.
9. We should stop building freeways and build mass transit instead.
10. Professional boxing should be abolished.

SOLUTIONS

14. *Circular reasoning.* This passage attempts to explain why crime is a problem, but the explanation given only reiterates the fact that crime is a problem. To commit a crime is to disobey the law, and so the observation that people are disobeying the law cannot explain the crime problem. What needs explaining is why so many people are disobeying the law, that is, why there is so much crime.
34. *Division.* This one is tricky to diagnose. Taken as a whole, the parcel of land is worth a million dollars. So, each quarter is worth one-quarter of a million dollars provided all parcels are sold to the buyer in question. However, as individual pieces of property—for sale to all bidders—each portion may be worth considerably less. Thus, what is true of the parts—sold to a single buyer—is not true of the parts—sold to different buyers. The problem, then, is that the rate at which the whole gets valued is not the same as the rate at which the individual parts get valued, and this is the reason the argument involves division.

CHAPTER EIGHT

Analogy

You are by now well aware that each chapter of this book ends with a long set of exercises, some of which must seem quite repetitive. Why, you may have wondered, does the author want you to spend so much time doing exercises? Well, learning to think critically is learning to become proficient at a number of skills. In this regard, it is much like learning to play a new sport. Think, for example, of what is involved in learning to play tennis. To play competently, one must master a sequence of discrete skills and then put them all together. One must master the basic strokes—forehand, backhand, volley, and serve—and then the shots—cross courts, lobs, drop shots, service returns, and so on. The only way to become proficient at these skills is through a lot of repetitive practice. You cannot learn to hit a proper backhand, for example, without hitting thousands of practice shots. Similarly, the only way to become a competent critical thinker is by constant repetition of the many discrete skills the critical thinker must have at his or her disposal. Hence, the need for doing a lot of practice problems.

The argument set out in the preceding paragraph is called an **argument by analogy.** The strategy common to arguments by analogy is to establish or explain (or both, as just demonstrated) one thing by reference to its similarity to another. In the previous argument, for example, learning to think critically is compared to learning to play tennis. The point of the comparison in an argument by analogy is to show that what is true of one of the things is true of the other as well. Thus, in the preceding argument we are told that much as one must practice continually to master the skills involved in tennis, so one must practice the skills needed to become a competent critical thinker.

Arguments by analogy deserve special attention because they are common and because of the unusual evaluative difficulties they pose. It is hard to imagine a topic on which an appealing and effective argument by analogy could not be mounted. Yet even the best and most effective arguments by analogy may suffer inherent weaknesses while even the most tenuous may yield interesting insights. As we will discover, appraising an argument by analogy is like nurturing a rare, exotic plant. I'll leave it to you to fill in the details of this particular analogy once you have completed this chapter!

ARGUMENTS BY ANALOGY

Although no two things are exactly alike, things often have common features. When things are sufficiently alike, we say they are of a common type or kind. Apples and

---

CONUNDRUM

When things are sufficiently alike, we say they are of a common type or kind. But often things of a common type admit of a large number of dissimilarities. Both apples and pineapples, for example, are kinds of fruit although they share very few similarities and differ in many ways. Indeed, a case could be made for saying that two things sharing a single characteristic are, in a sense, things of a common type. Both rainbows and pencils are things that occur on Earth. And, as this example suggests, it is hard to imagine any pair of things that could not somehow be construed as members of a single type. Can you supplement the definition we have given of a type or kind in a way that excludes cases of the sort just imagined? If, on the other hand, the definition we have proposed seems right, can you explain why we tend to adopt some classifications by type or kind while ignoring many others? Why, that is, do we think of apples and pineapples, but not pencils and rainbows, as members of a common type?

---

oranges are both kinds of fruit. Red Delicious and Granny Smith are both types of apples. Often, however, we compare things that are not sufficiently alike to be considered members of a common type or kind. Such comparisons are analogical. An analogical similarity is, thus, one that holds between things or states of affairs that are in many respects dissimilar. "You can't make an omelette without breaking a few eggs," we are told, when we protest the loss of farmland required for a new housing development. Making an omelette and building a housing development bear some resemblance to one another, but the analogy here is minimal.

Argument by analogy occurs when such similarities are made the basis for an inference about additional similarities. They take the form

A and B are similar in respects p, q, r, and so on.

s is true of A.

---

s is true of B as well.

The **primary subject,** B, is compared to an **analogue,** A, and a conclusion is drawn about the primary subject on the basis of its similarity to the analogue. In the earlier example, the primary subject is housing, the analogue, an omelette. Often, as in this example, the similarities between the two things being compared will be few—sometimes only a single similarity will be cited. Consider, for example, the following:

> To the editor: To be denied the right of abortion is like being denied the right to drive your car alone. You have room for one or more passengers. Now, there are undoubtedly a lot of people—people who are too old, too young, or too disabled to drive—who would like to ride with someone. But not everybody wants a traveling companion. If a law were passed that said you do not have the right to decide whether or not to drive alone, I'm sure you would be angry and resentful.

In this passage, two states of affairs are said to be similar in at least one respect. Being pregnant and carrying a passenger in a car both require a person to do something for another, assuming, of course, that a fetus has the status of a person. Now, no one would argue that the government has the right to dictate that a driver must carry a passenger when the driver chooses not to do so. Similarly, the passage argues, the government does not have the right to dictate that a woman must carry a pregnancy to term. Put in the standard form for arguments by analogy, the argument goes as follows:

> Being pregnant and driving with a passenger are alike in that both involve doing something for someone else.
>
> No driver should be legally obliged to carry a passenger against his or her will.
> _____
> No woman who is pregnant should be legally obliged to carry the pregnancy to term against her will.

I doubt many people, whether opposed to or in favor of legalized abortion, would be satisfied with this argument. And this brings us to an important question: When, if ever, are analogical arguments acceptable?

ASSESSING ARGUMENTS BY ANALOGY

By their nature, analogical arguments are bound to be less than compelling. If two things are in many respects dissimilar, as are the things likened in an argument by analogy, we may always have some reservation about the appropriateness of the comparison. Analogical arguments are best regarded as providing a kind of tentative, partial support for their conclusions as long as there is no good reason to believe the

---

A well-chosen analogy can be used to make a point briefly and dramatically:

There were an awful lot of people against the automobile, too.
> —physicist Richard Seed on public reaction to his plan to clone babies for infertile couples

Why didn't the special prosecutor ask the most obvious question? "Mr. President, are you a witch?"
> —from a letter to the editor about the Starr Commission's allegations of wrongdoing by President Clinton

This seems a tiny bit like giving Anne Frank a wacky best friend to perk up that attic.
> —Libby Gelman-Waxner, writer, on the Hollywood logic that none of the real passengers on the *Titanic* was interesting enough to make a movie about, so a Romeo and Juliet–style couple had to be created

analogy inappropriate. And this gets us to the meat of the matter: How do we determine whether the analogy at the heart of an analogical argument is appropriate?

Looking for Dissimilarities

An analogy is inappropriate when there are enough relevant dissimilarities between the primary subject and the analogue to raise a serious question about the inference. Arguments based on inappropriate analogies commit the fallacy of **false analogy.** Consider again the last example:

> Being pregnant and driving with a passenger are alike in that both involve doing something for someone else.
>
> No driver should be legally obliged to carry a passenger against his or her will.
> ___
> No woman who is pregnant should be legally obliged to carry the pregnancy to term against her will.

The problem with this argument is that there are a number of glaring differences between the primary subject and the analogue. More importantly, these differences have a direct bearing on the claim that the two cases are alike in the manner described in the argument's conclusion. Even if we grant that a fetus is a person, and thus is like a passenger to its mother, the two cases remain quite different. The most obvious and relevant difference has to do with the potential harm done the "passenger" in the two cases. In most circumstances, if I decide not to give you a ride, I do you no real harm. My right to refuse to give you a ride if I choose is, in large measure, based on this fact. By contrast, refusal to "carry" a fetus will do it great harm. No matter what our view of the moral status of a fetus, we must admit that the potential harm to a fetus renders the comparison at the heart of the argument inappropriate. The cases are not sufficiently alike to shoulder the weight of the inference the arguer wants to make.

Looking for Problematic Similarities

Arguments by analogy can be criticized in another way. The analogy at the heart of an argument can often be used to draw inferences that are in conflict with the conclusion originally drawn. Suppose someone gives an argument of the form

> A and B are similar in respects p, q, r, and so on.
>
> s is true of A.
> ___
> s is true of B as well.

It may be fairly easy to spot a feature of the analogue that the arguer might not want to associate with the primary subject. Using the same analogy, we might argue:

> A and B are similar in respects p, q, and r.
>
> s is true of A.
>
> But t is true of A as well.
> ___
> If s is true of B, then t is true of B as well.

Utilizing the conclusion of this argument, we can go on to argue further:

If s is true of B, then t is true of B as well.

No one accepts that t is true of B.

---

s is not true of B.

The latter argument makes clear that the point of this sort of criticism is not to suggest that t is indeed true of the primary subject. Rather, the point is to bring into question the appropriateness of the comparison between primary subject and analogue. The analogy between A and B is suspect since it can be used to draw a conclusion at odds with the conclusion of the original argument or, at any rate, a conclusion that would be unacceptable to the author of the original argument.

A nice example of this strategy comes from *Dialogues Concerning Natural Religion,* written by the Scottish philosopher and historian David Hume and published in 1779. In this work, Hume criticized a well-known analogical argument for the existence of God. The argument in effect claims that our world must be the product of intelligence and planning because of its similarity to a complicated piece of machinery. According to this argument, if we encounter a machine that is highly complex and efficiently accomplishes a particular task, we should easily conclude that it is the product of human ingenuity and intelligence. Yet the world is, in a sense, a vast and complicated piece of machinery, made up of an almost endless array of simpler machines. And this vast mechanical edifice operates on a level of complexity and at an order of efficiency that dwarfs any human construction. If artifacts require intelligent design, then it would seem only reasonable to infer that our world must have an intelligent designer. Put simply, the argument is this:

Our world is like a bit of machinery in the order and efficiency with which it accomplishes its tasks.

Such machines are the product of intelligence.

Our world is the product of an intelligent entity, God.

Hume criticized this argument by pointing out some rather unsavory conclusions that could be drawn based on the comparison between human constructions and the world.

Consider, said Hume, the inferences we might draw based on the discovery of a marvelously designed and constructed artifact, a sailing ship:

If we survey a ship, what an exalted idea we must form of the ingenuity of the carpenter who framed so complicated, useful, and beautiful a machine? And what surprise we feel when we find him a stupid mechanic who imitated others, and copied an art which, through a long succession of ages, after multiplied trials, mistakes, corrections, deliberations, and controversies, had been gradually improving? Many worlds may have been botched and bungled, throughout an eternity, ere this system was struck out.[1]

---

[1] David Hume, *Dialogues Concerning Natural Religion, Part V.* (Cambridge: Hackett, 1980), p. 36.

Are we to draw similar conclusions about God, based on the resemblance of the world to such an artifact?

In another passage, Hume considers a second similarity between the world and many of the things people construct. The world seems clearly, thinks Hume, to admit of the occasional defect: earthquakes, hurricanes, famines, and so on. Much as we judge the ability of a designer by the quality of his or her work, may we not conclude, claims Hume, that this world is

> the first rude essay of some infant deity who afterwards abandoned it, ashamed of his lame performance; it is the work of some dependent, inferior deity, and is the object of derision to his superiors; it is the production of old age and dotage in some superannuated deity.[2]

Hume's point is not to suggest seriously that God is childlike, over-the-hill, dim, or unimaginative. His point, rather, is to show that the analogy at the heart of the argument can be taken to support a number of conclusions about the nature of God, most of which are at odds with the conclusion of the original argument. Hume is, in a sense, pressuring advocates of the argument to look closer at the analogy on which their argument depends. If the analogy can be taken to suggest such a broad range of curious and even contradictory claims, its value in an argument for any such claim is highly dubious, including the claim that our world is the work of an intelligent deity.

ANALOGICAL REFUTATIONS

Analogies are often used to criticize arguments, and here we must be on the lookout for false analogy. An analogical counterargument attempts to refute one argument by comparing it to another argument, but an obviously unacceptable argument. The strategy is to exploit the similarity as a means of showing that the argument under attack is equally flawed. Refutation by analogy takes the following form:

> Arguments A and B are similar in respects p, q, r, and so on.
>
> Argument A is flawed.
> _____
> Argument B is flawed.

In the following passage, Albert Shanker, then president of the American Federation of Teachers, refutes an argument for minimum-competency exams in math and English for all primary and secondary public school teachers. The argument is based on the premise that this will ensure a high quality of instruction in the public schools. Shanker said of this argument:

> This would be the equivalent of licensing doctors on the basis of an exam in elementary biology or testing accountants on their knowledge of elementary math.

---
[2]Ibid., p. 37.

Which character has done the best job of finding a problematic similarity? (*Source:* © 1997 United Feature Syndicate, Inc.)

Obviously, claims Shanker, no one would accept the argument that licensing for doctors and accountants should be based on such exams, and so we should not accept a similar argument for teachers.

The same considerations should guide the assessment of counterarguments that criticize an argument by comparing it to another, flawed argument. Consider the counterargument discussed above.

> Licensing public school teachers on the basis of minimum-competency exams in math and English would be the equivalent of licensing doctors on the basis of an exam in elementary biology or testing accountants on their knowledge of elementary math.
>
> The latter arguments are flawed.
> _____
> The argument for competency exams for public school teachers is flawed.

As with any analogical argument, we must carefully consider the aptness of the analogy. Are the situations described in this example sufficiently similar to support Shanker's point? To determine this, we would need to know more about the purposes of teacher testing. Is the goal to ensure that all teachers are competent at the level of basic math and English skills? If so, the cases seem to be insufficiently similar to support Shanker's criticism. But if minimum-competency tests are designed to judge a teacher's overall ability to teach, Shanker's counterargument seems to have some basis.

THE USES OF ANALOGY

Arguments by analogy are vulnerable and often constitute easy targets for attack and even ridicule. Yet they are among the most commonly used types of argument. Their appeal stems from the simplicity and clarity they can bring to complex issues and their tendency to stimulate creative problem solving.

Clarity and Simplicity

Arguments by analogy often satisfy our yearning for clarity and simplicity by comparing something complex with a simpler and better understood analogue. And in doing so, they can be quite seductive but also quite misleading. Someone, for example, who is opposed to deficit spending and the growing national debt might register his or her misgivings in an argument like the following:

> If I spend more than I make, I will have to go into debt, and if I continue with this practice long enough, my total indebtedness will finally reach a point at which I won't even be able to keep up with the interest payments and will probably have to declare bankruptcy. The government's policy of spending more than it takes in must be brought to a halt by raising taxes, or cutting spending, or doing both. If left unchecked, the current policy of deficit spending by our government is going to lead to disaster just as surely as it would if you or I were consistently to spend more than we make.

The analogy here is striking, but, unfortunately, it vastly oversimplifies the issues involved in government economic policy. In one or two respects, the economic realities faced by governments and individuals are the same. But there are a number of crucial dissimilarities between the two, including the ability of governments to set economic policy and to control interest rates and the money supply. The question of whether governments should and can effectively engage in deficit spending cannot be fully addressed by comparing a national economy to the economic realities faced by an individual. The preceding argument is quite appealing in that it provides a simple and easy-to-comprehend solution to a difficult, complex problem. Precisely for this reason, it is tempting to accept such arguments if only because of the false sense they provide us that they have brought clarity and simplicity to a complex issue.

Case-by-Case Analysis

Analogical reasoning can be genuinely edifying and in many circumstances may be the best analytic tool we have at our disposal. **Case-by-case analysis** is indispensable in dealing with many issues in the study of law, morality, and history, for example. In this method of analysis, problematic cases are compared to a variety of similar but clearer cases. A historian might attempt to understand recent events by comparing them to similar events from an earlier time, events that are now more fully comprehended. In our courts, new cases are often decided by reference to the decisions struck in other cases; where the cases are sufficiently similar, similar decisions will follow. Consider, for example, a case that came to court recently in the area where I live.

A local department store ran a promotion that involved sending "scratch-off" tickets to thousands of its customers. Many of the tickets guaranteed a certain percentage off the price of all purchases, provided the ticket was scratched off in the presence of a store cashier after the purchases were rung up. Most of the winning tickets awarded 5, 10, or 20 percent off. Many awarded nothing. But one of the tickets, so the promotion promised, awarded the winner "100 percent off" on all purchases. As it turned out, the winning ticket was defective. The person who received it was able to make out the "100" by carefully holding the ticket up to the light. Overjoyed at this discovery, the excited ticket holder rushed to the store and proceeded to load up several dozen shopping carts with expensive merchandise: TVs, stereos, computers, and the like. Employees of the store noticed this peculiar behavior and called the manager. The holder of the winning ticket informed the manager he was confident he had the winning ticket and so intended to make the best of his good luck. Not knowing what to think, the manager did nothing. When all purchases were rung up, the total came to more than $75,000, and when the ticket was scratched off, the number "100 percent" did emerge. At this point, the winner realized he was going to need a truck to haul away his winnings and made arrangements to come back the next day, since it was by now past closing time. To make a long story short, the store manager consulted the owners and a decision was reached. The store would allow the winner $5,000 in merchandise of his choice but no more. As you may suspect, the winner sued the department store.

How would you decide this case? Should the department store be made to honor the winning ticket? Or does the store have the legal and moral right to limit its losses on the ground that the promotion clearly specified that winners were not to know the amount of their discount until after purchases were rung up? The way to think about this case is by comparing it to similar cases where the proper decision seems clearer. Consider the following situation.

Suppose we are playing poker and I have carefully arranged the seating so that I can see your cards reflected in a mirror behind you. Any winnings I might realize via this arrangement would clearly be the result of cheating and so would be undeserved. Isn't this similar to what happened in the case at issue? The winner was privy to a kind of information that was not allowed by the rules of the promotion—information available to no other customer. The similarities here suggest that the winner should be happy with the settlement offered by the store's owners.

No doubt, the owners of the store would appreciate this analogy. But other clear cases come to mind. Suppose now we are playing poker and, in a particularly big hand, you inadvertently expose several of your cards. Unbeknownst to you, I can see your cards and realize I have the winning hand. I bet everything I have, you match my bet, and, of course, I win. Though I commiserate with your unfortunate luck, I am under no obligation to return your money. I've won fairly despite the fact that I knew in advance I was going to win, and so I have the legal (we were playing in a licensed casino) and moral right to my winnings. The similarity to the case at issue seems clear here. Though the winner did have information that guaranteed a big win, he did not gain it by any sort of skulduggery. The department store, it would seem, like the poor loser in our second analogous example, must bear the brunt of its mistake.

Neither of the analogous cases we have examined suggests how the case at issue ought to be resolved, though they have at least stimulated our thinking and have begun the process of clarification. With this start, you can undoubtedly think of other cases or modifications to the previous two that might be brought to bear in attempting to clarify our problematic case. (If you want to think about this case, don't try to solve it by placing the responsibility on the company that printed the defective ticket. By the time this case came before the court, the printer was out of business!) The point illustrated by the analogies introduced here is only that case-by-case analysis—thinking of a problematic case in terms of an analogy with other, clearer cases—can be an effective tool in dealing with novel situations.

Problem Solving

Analogical comparisons can also serve as a stimulus to creative problem solving. In particular, novel explanations are often suggested by the process of drawing an analogy between something that needs explaining and something similar that is more fully understood. Some of the first attempts at understanding the biological basis of memory, for example, likened the part or parts of the brain involved in memory storage and retrieval to a tape or video recorder. Information must be "recorded" on some medium in the brain, so it was hypothesized, and some part of the brain must function as a "replay" mechanism. Early researchers then began speculating about how the brain might accomplish these tasks. Unfortunately, the solution suggested by this analogy turned out to be largely untenable, as research began to document the ways in which memory actually works. Yet, even here, the analogy proved to be of some use, for points of dissimilarity between brain and tape recorder themselves suggested the need for a better model. One glaring dissimilarity was the "point of view" problem. When a videotape is replayed, what appears on the TV screen are events exactly as recorded. If memory operates like a video recorder, recalled experiences should be "seen" just as they were recorded. Yet, when people remember events, they typically "see" them from an outside perspective in which the person doing the remembering is an actual participant in the remembered scene. In recalling things, it seems we do not simply reexperience the visual and audio impressions that were the basis of the memory. Thus, memory has a reconstructive element to it that is lacking in various tape-recording processes. In science, a lot can be learned by discovering that something is not the right answer. The discovery that memory does not operate like a tape recorder suggests something important that subsequent explanations of memory must include: some mechanism for the reconstruction of remembered events.

WORKING THROUGH ARGUMENTS BY ANALOGY

Analogical arguments are among the most difficult to assess in an evenhanded way. Points of dissimilarity are usually plentiful and easy to spot. But, as we have seen, analogical reasoning has the potential to provide insight and to help us clarify problematic situations. So, it is crucial that we treat analogical arguments in a sympathetic manner. In evaluating the strengths and weaknesses of an argument by analogy, the following strategy should enable us to arrive at a fair and balanced assessment.

Determine What Is at Issue

What is being argued for or against? Analogies frequently suggest many points of possible similarity and dissimilarity, and the claim that is being defended or countered may not always be explicitly stated. It is easy to discover a similarity between two things, remark it, and yet only vaguely allude to the lesson to be drawn from the comparison. When it is unclear what is being argued, the way to proceed is by restating the argument in standard form:

A and B are similar in respects p, q, r, and so on.

s is true of A.

---

s is true of B as well.

If we can isolate the primary subject and analogue, the basis for the claim that they are similar, and the additional point of similarity at issue, we can then arrive at a clear formulation of the conclusion.

With this in mind, consider the following passage in which the point at issue is not clear:

> To the editor: Like a person trying to shake a lethal heroin addiction, the cost to the American economy's withdrawal from being dependent, as much as it is, on the production of nuclear weapons is a high one. Built on utter misuse, dependence in both cases creates a frightening euphoric illusion of security. Like an addict, however, we should not allow the pain to stop the withdrawal process; the only alternative is a continued lulling of this nation's people and their economy into collective insanity and death.

The author of this passage is interested in saying something about the dependence of the American economy on the production of nuclear weapons and the problems we will face if we halt the production of these weapons. America's economy, it seems, is dependent on industries that produce nuclear weapons, much as a heroin addict is dependent on heroin. But what follows, according to this passage, on the basis of this comparison? That we should stop manufacturing nuclear weapons? That we no longer need nuclear weapons? That our economy is seriously ill? What, in other words, is really at issue in the passage?

Let's put the argument in standard form by focusing on the points of similarity between the primary subject and the analogue:

> The dependence of our economy on the production of nuclear weapons is similar to the dependence of an addict on heroin in the following ways:
>
> First, both heroin and the production of nuclear weapons cause a kind of euphoria, the latter a sense of economic security brought about by a flourishing industry.
>
> Second, both involve withdrawal pains, the latter due to the potential economic downturn when a whole industry shrinks.
>
> Third, in both cases, continued dependence will lead to disaster.
>
> Withdrawal from heroin addiction is in the best interest of the addict.
>
> ---
>
> Withdrawal from the production of nuclear weapons is in the best interest of the economic health of our country.

This formulation involves some claims that are not explicitly stated in the original passage. The third point of similarity between primary subject and analogue is only implied in the last sentence. Also, the conclusion is not explicitly given in the original wording. Nevertheless, the conclusion we have identified does seem to be the claim best supported by the points of analogy at the heart of the passage. Having isolated the argument's conclusion, we now see that the original passage is intended as a counterargument. Withdrawal from the production of nuclear weapons is in the best economic interest of our country. But who would disagree? Plainly, those who would argue that the economic health of our country is in part dependent on the nuclear weapons industry. The point of the passage, it seems, is to undermine the argument for continued production of nuclear weapons by acknowledging the dependence of our economy on the nuclear weapons industry and then countering by pointing out how this dependence is like an addiction. And, as with most addictions, the risks of continued dependence far outweigh the costs of withdrawal.

Perhaps this is not the definitive reading of the passage; it may not reflect precisely the author's thinking. This may be because the author has not thought through the analogy. Struck by the similarity between our economic dependence on the production of nuclear weapons and the dependence of an addict on heroin, the author may not have given much thought to the precise terms of his or her conclusion. And this underscores the need, in both giving and assessing arguments by analogy, to be clear on precisely what is at issue. It is easy to become so enamored of an analogy that we end up spending our time trying to find further points of similarity while losing track of the reason for venturing the analogy in the first place.

Determine Whether the Argument Depends on the Analogy

Often, analogical similarities are cited to illustrate the rationale behind a claim rather than to provide an argument for the claim. Such an argument is not an argument by analogy in that it does not *depend* on the analogy. Generally, such arguments can be restated without reference to the analogous situation. Look, for example, at this argument:

> Despite recent demands that criminals serve longer sentences, there are good reasons to keep prison sentences to a minimum even for violent crimes. Obviously, convicted criminals should be punished for their crimes, and this is particularly true for crimes of violence. But part of the goal of incarceration is rehabilitation. If we keep people in jail for too long, they become dependent on institutional care and stand little chance of succeeding when they are finally released. It's kind of like baking a cake. When the cake is baked, you've got to take it out of the oven. Otherwise, it will get burned beyond repair.

The point of this passage is not to argue that prison sentences ought to be kept to a minimum on the ground that excessive sentencing is like overbaking a cake. The argument does not depend on this analogy. Rather, the analogy is a picturesque way of reiterating a crucial premise of the argument: If a person is incarcerated for too long, chances of successful rehabilitation diminish.

In general, then, if an argument that makes use of an analogy can be restated without mention of the analogy, it is not an argument by analogy. From a critical point of view, it is crucial that we determine whether or not an argument involving an analogy actually requires the analogy. If it does not, criticism based on problems with the analogy will be irrelevant. The fact, for example, that prisoners have little in common with cakes does not suggest anything wrong with the preceding argument. By contrast, an argument that depends on an analogy—an *argument by analogy*—cannot be restated without reference to the analogy. The point of the argument is to suggest that something is the case in one situation precisely because it is true in another, similar situation. If the analogy does not hold, the argument fails. Thus, once we have determined that an argument depends on an analogy, criticism can properly focus on the appropriateness of the analogy.

Look for Important Points of Dissimilarity

Here we need to think about two possibilities. Consider, once again, the form of arguments by analogy:

> A and B are similar in respects p, q, r, and so on.
>
> s is true of A.
> _____
>
> s is true of B as well.

First, are there facts about the primary subject, B, that suggest s is not one of its features? In an example discussed earlier, nuclear weapons production was compared to drug addiction. Are there differences between the two situations that suggest the conclusion of the argument does not follow—differences that suggest it is not the case that our economy needs to "withdraw" from the production of nuclear weapons? What, for example, of the fact that drug addiction has no beneficial consequences? Can the same be said of the segment of our economy involved in the production of materials for nuclear weapons? And does this difference make a difference?

Second, are there facts about the analogue that yield conclusions about the primary subject inconsistent with the argument's conclusion or unacceptable to the argument's author? Grant, for a moment, the analogy between the economy and an addict. Grant that our economy is addicted to the production of nuclear weapons. Often, addicts need to be coerced, sometimes by force, into kicking their habit. Should we therefore pass laws making illegal the production of materials required for nuclear weapons? Addicts are sometimes given drugs to ease the withdrawal process. Should we therefore subsidize the nuclear weapons industry if this is needed to halt nuclear weapons production? Should we get the industry through its economic withdrawal pains by paying companies not to produce nuclear weapons, much as we pay farmers not to grow crops? An analogy can be effectively undermined by showing that it leads to consequences unforeseen by the argument's author, consequences inconsistent with the conclusion he or she favors.

One final point needs to be heeded in working with arguments by analogy: *Be sympathetic!* Don't go out of your way to misconstrue the analogy. Points of dissimilarity can be found in every argument by analogy. Try to limit your thinking to points of similarity and dissimilarity that have a direct bearing on the claim at issue. The point of an argument by analogy is to bring to our attention important similarities between the primary subject and the analogue. Don't begin your analysis by assuming that nothing is to be learned because the similarities are only analogical. When you give an initial paraphrase of an *argument by analogy,* make it as plausible as possible, by attempting to take the similarities seriously. Only then will it be possible to level insightful criticism.

CHAPTER SUMMARY

1. In an argument by analogy, the similarities between two things or states of affairs are made the basis for an inference to other similarities. Arguments by analogy take the form

   A and B are similar in respects p, q, r, and so on.

   s is true of A.
   _____

   s is true of B as well.

   In this pattern, B is the primary subject and A is the analogue.

2. Analogical refutations claim that one argument is flawed because of its similarity to another, more obviously flawed argument.

3. The fallacy **false analogy** occurs when there are too few similarities between primary subject and analogue to bear the weight of the inference or when there are sufficient dissimilarities to undermine the inference.

   Example: Colleges should pay students for getting high grades. After all, businesses handsomely reward their top people with bonuses and commissions when they perform well, and this policy has a beneficial effect on productivity.

   Analysis: It is hard to find any real similarities between these two situations, other than that both students and employees are, in a sense, judged by their performance. There is, however, an important dissimilarity between the two cases. Students are not employees, and so financial rewards would not be based on monies earned by students for their schools, as are employee bonuses and commissions.

4. Arguments by analogy are often vulnerable to criticism by extension of the analogy. The strategy in this form of criticism is to show that the primary subject and the analogue are similar in ways that lead to other inferences in conflict with the conclusion of the argument under attack.

   Example: Colleges should pay students for getting high grades. After all, businesses handsomely reward their top people with bonuses and commissions when they perform well, and this policy has a beneficial effect on productivity.

   Analysis: Employees who perform poorly are often fired. Should we therefore "fire" students who perform poorly as well as reward those who perform well?

5. Arguments that use analogies as illustrations are not instances of argument by analogy and should not be criticized on the basis of points of dissimilarity. If an argument involving an analogy can be accurately restated without reference to the analogue, it is not an argument by analogy.

6. In evaluating an argument by analogy, follow these steps:
   i. Determine whether the argument depends on the analogy.
   ii. Determine what is at issue by putting the argument in standard form.
   iii. Look for important points of dissimilarity—crucial features of the primary subject but not the analogue and features of the analogue that yield conclusions about the primary subject at odds with the argument's conclusion.

iv. Don't go out of your way to misconstrue the analogy in order to mount flashy criticisms. Concentrate on important points and be sympathetic in reading and structuring the argument.

EXERCISES

A. The passages below all involve analogies. For each passage, do the following:
   i. Decide what is at issue.
   ii. Determine whether the point of the passage is to mount an argument or a counterargument.
   iii. Identify and clarify the primary subject and analogue.
   iv. Decide whether the analogy is integral to the argument.
   v. If it is, put the argument in standard form for analogical arguments. If it is not, restate the argument in terms that make no reference to the analogy.
   vi. Appraise the argument by commenting on relevant points of similarity and dissimilarity between the primary subject and the analogue.
   vii. When appropriate, comment on further points of similarity that might be used to undermine the original argument.

In your analysis, be as sympathetic as possible. If you believe a passage involves a particularly incisive or appropriate analogy, defend the argument against the most likely criticism of the analogy.

(A solution to Exercise 4 is given on page 212.)

1. Do you really believe banning handgun ownership would significantly reduce murders and robberies? Did banning booze significantly reduce drinking?

2. The National Rifle Association has done a good job of persuading its members that gun registration is the first step to confiscation of all weapons. Nonsense. Americans register, among other things, their dogs, cars, and the birth of their children. Yet confiscation of dogs, cars, and children has never been a problem.

3. The reason we need a state income tax is to provide for a more stable source of funding. Currently, we operate on the basis of a sales tax and a tax on property. But a stool with only two legs will not stand for long. A third leg is needed for stability, in the form of a state income tax.

4. Actually, it is a healthy idea to scream, yell, and use taboo language now and again. These are appropriate and effective ways of venting anger, which, if left unexpressed, may finally explode in the form of violence.

5. To the editor: The argument is forever made that because many students at private schools receive federal financial aid, the schools are, ipso facto, public schools and so should be subject to government regulation. This argument is fatuous. For example, if a food-stamp recipient buys groceries at Safeway, does this make Safeway a public entity whose policies and management are to be directed by the government? Let's get serious.

6. To the editor: I am disappointed by your headline "Unborn Child Has Rights in Lawsuit, Appeals Court Says." The phrase *unborn child* was created by anti-abortion advocates as a rhetorical device to gain sympathy for their cause. You should report facts in clear, simple, neutral language. It's called a "fetus." We don't refer to eggs as unhatched chickens, nor do we refer to logs as uncut two-by-fours.

7. To the editor: When you force-feed a neutered rooster, it becomes a capon and a delicious dinner at that. The President should keep that in mind when he pleads for continued force-feeding of the military on an inflated defense budget, ignoring the waste already existing. Such a military cock on the primrose path is not going to scare even the chicks in the barnyard. Let it scratch for a living like everyone else and maybe it will develop into a battling bantam.

8. Be a hero, save a whale
   Save a baby, go to jail —*bumper sticker*

9. To the editor: Several articles recently have concluded that watching or playing violent television shows or video games causes violent behavior. Your most recent article, "Pulling the Plug on Video Violence," even included a sidebar filled with "tips on limiting your child's exposure to violence."

   Finally, people are beginning to realize what ails our society: It's television, stupid. There's just one little problem with that approach. Television is addictive. Limiting TV watching is like putting filters on cigarettes. At best it's a feeble attempt to remedy the problem; at worst, it solves nothing.

   People have said that nicotine is the most addictive substance known to man. But that's incorrect; television is. The only way to solve the video violence problem is to unplug the plug-in drug.

10. Imagine you are a bomber pilot, on a practice run. You are about to drop a bomb when you notice a shack. Now, you have no idea whether anybody is actually inside the shack, but wouldn't you pull back until this could be determined, one way or the other? Wouldn't this just make good sense? Well, the same holds for abortion. Maybe we can't say for sure whether the fetus is a human being, but until we know, shouldn't we err on the side of safety?

11. If architects want to strengthen a decrepit arch, they increase the load that is laid upon it, for thereby the parts are joined more firmly together. So, if a therapist wishes to foster their patient's mental health, they should not be afraid to increase that load through a reorientation toward the meaning of one's life.[3] —*from* Man's Search for Meaning, *by Viktor E. Frankel*

12. Stephen Jay Gould on the claim that the D4 gene is responsible for about 10 percent of novelty-seeking behavior:
    First of all, the D4 gene, by itself, exerts only a weak potential influence on novelty-seeking behavior. How can a gene accounting for only 10 percent of the variance in a trait be proclaimed as a "gene for" the trait? If I decide that 10 percent of my weight gain came from the calories in tofu (because I love the stuff and eat it by the ton), this item, generally regarded as nutritionally benign, does not become a "fatness food." —*from "The Internal Brand of the Scarlet,"* Natural History, *March 1998, p. 76*

13. Do you believe this proposal to distribute condoms in the public schools? Our educational leaders say, "They will have sex, ergo give them condoms." Never

---

[3]My indebtedness to S. Morris Engel for citing this example in *With Good Reason: An Introduction to Informal Fallacies,* 5th ed. (New York: St. Martin's Press, 1994).

mind maturity or competence of users, reliability of product or effects of misuse. Students will also have beer or cigarettes if they want. Are these next for free handouts? Distribution of condoms in schools is bad logic and bad policy.

14. Though well over 90 percent of all UFO sightings can be explained away, the remaining must be taken seriously. To do otherwise would be like a drug company saying that since 90 percent of the drugs we have tried are ineffective in treating AIDS, the remainder need not be taken seriously as a possible cure for AIDS.

15. Preserving NATO after the dissolution of the Soviet Union makes as much sense as continuing chemotherapy after the cancer has gone into remission. At best it is wasteful and expensive; at worst, provocative and nauseating. Let a united Europe deal as it will with the liberated republics, but as for America, let NATO be no more.

16. There seems to be a misconception that something truly psychic would need to be 100 percent accurate or always capable of being measured beyond chance. Unfortunately, this is simply not the case. In a sense, a psychic is like an expert fisherman. An individual trained in the sport of fishing, with years of experience and a great deal of knowledge about the activity, has a better chance of catching a fish than does the average person. However, every time the individual goes fishing, he is not necessarily successful. That does not mean, however, that his "score" in comparison to others over time cannot be measured to exceed random chance. The same is true of an ethical psychic like Edgar Cayce.

17. The U.S. secretary of education recently released state-by-state comparisons of how well public schools in the fifty states are doing. Compared were, for example, percentages of students taking college placement exams and subsequent scores. Florida's education commissioner, Ralph Turlington, said the rankings represented a breakthrough in motivating states. "If you removed all the scorecards from the nation's ballparks, attendance would drop and the interest of the players and even the coaches would diminish," he said. Education, however, is not a ball game, and measuring performance as if it were is a perilous path to improvement, especially since the rules of the game vary so much within states as well as from state to state.

18. Now let's take a look at capitation and how it works. As you know, instead of your doctor getting paid every time he does something for you, capitation means he gets a flat fee per month for you, and whatever he spends out of that fee, he loses. On the other hand, whatever he doesn't spend, he keeps. HMO executives spin the argument and say they now pay their doctors to keep you healthy. On the surface, it doesn't sound that devious. But let's take a closer look at this arrangement another way.

Suppose a man makes a contract with his neighbor that he'll buy her groceries every month. The neighbor will give him $100, and he'll go to the store and buy her food. But here's the catch: *Whatever's left over from that $100 is his to keep.* Now you can imagine that the neighbor would like him to buy the best food he can for that $100. But if he buys all the things she wants, he could end up spending the entire $100 or more, leaving him nothing for his trouble. *So he has to decide how to balance what's good for his neighbor against how much money he wants to keep for himself.*

So he buys her hamburger or liver instead of steak this month. And he decides she really doesn't need peanut butter this month. And that she can get more servings from powdered milk than she does from bottled milk. In the end, he spends $55 and keeps $45. The neighbor may gag on the food he bought, but he was careful to meet her minimum nutritional requirements!

In the case of capitated HMO medicine, you end up giving your "grocery" money to the primary-care doctor, who in turn has to make these same difficult decisions: *How much health care do I give the patient, and how much do I want to keep for my trouble?*

How many of you would actually allow your neighbor to do your grocery shopping under these conditions? If so, why do you let your doctor operate like this? Now can you see why gatekeepers might want to keep you from specialists, tests, hospital stays, and procedures?[4]

19. To the editor: Your editorial decrying the National Endowment for the Arts' funding restrictions contains a puzzling usage of the term *censorship.*

Let me illustrate by example: If I walked into an art gallery with my checkbook and told the proprietor I was only interested in buying artwork that wasn't lewd or indecent—by whatever prudish or tasteless criteria I chose to apply—would I be guilty of censorship? Of course not. The artists whose works I disapprove of are still perfectly free to paint what they wish and display it or sell it as they see fit. Likewise, I am free to spend my money as my own tastes dictate.

What you complain about isn't censorship at all. It's accountability to the client who commissioned the work, in this case, Uncle Sam. Like most Americans, I support artists' right of free expression, but not necessarily at taxpayer expense. While I don't agree with some of the restrictions being placed on NEA endowments, it seems outrageous that artists should demand this money without accountability to the patron. And it's especially irritating to see them wrapping themselves in the Constitution and crying "Censorship!" when all they really want is a government handout without strings attached.

Let's not confuse a free country with a free lunch.

20. Atheism can be more positively defended in the following way. We can properly claim to know that many things are not so if reasons have not been offered to support the claim that they are so. For example, I am able to claim that I know my friend Frank is not at home precisely because there is no reason to believe that he is at home. There is no noise coming from his house, the lights are out at the time when he is usually awake, his bed is empty, and so forth. Everything seems to count for my belief and nothing against it. I

---

[4]Gordon Miller, *Speak Now or Forever Rest in Peace: The Very Real Dangers of HMOs and What You Can Do About Them* (Salem, Oreg.: Gordon Miller, 1997), pp. 50–52.

could discover that I was mistaken, but the possibility of error exists for virtually any knowledge claim one might make.

The parallel between the belief that Frank is at home and the belief that God exists is an exact one. If Frank is at home, there will be evidence indicating this state of affairs. On the other hand, if there is no evidence that he is at home, one can claim to know he is not at home. Similarly, if God exists, there will be evidence of this: signs will emerge which point to such a conclusion. However, if there is no evidence that He exists, then one can claim to know that God does not exist. It could be claimed that God exists but has simply left no evidence upon which to base the claim. But such a statement would be much like saying that Frank is at home yet there is no evidence of his presence. Neither claim seems plausible. Frank is normally involved with his house in various ways and if there is no evidence of involvement, one can assume that he is not at home. Presumably, God is even more involved with the world than Frank is with his house—after all, God designed and created the world. Therefore, if the evidence of God's involvement with the world is no more compelling than that of Frank's present involvement with his house, then one is equally justified in claiming that God does not exist as one is in claiming that Frank is not at home. [*Note: You will need to think about a fallacy discussed in an earlier chapter to solve this problem.*] —*from* The Atheist Debater's Handbook, *by B. C. Johnson (Buffalo, N.Y.: Prometheus Books, 1983), pp. 14–15.*

B. Below are ten claims in defense of which you are by now more than proficient. Once again, pick one, or devise a claim of your own, and give a plausible argument by analogy for the claim. The operative word here is *plausible.* Try to come up with an analogue that can withstand the sort of criticism we have discussed in this chapter.
   1. The death penalty should be abolished.
   2. Animals have moral rights.
   3. We have a moral obligation to be vegetarians.
   4. Private citizens should not be allowed to own handguns.
   5. All forms of gambling should be illegal.
   6. Condoms should be distributed in public schools.
   7. Students who sit in the front of the classroom will get the best grades.
   8. Personality is reflected in handwriting.
   9. We should stop building freeways and build mass transit instead.
   10. Professional boxing should be abolished.

C. The passages below all appear to involve moral dilemmas. For each passage, invent a number of cases that are similar but clearer. Be sure to consider cases on both sides of each issue. Your goal is to reach a decision about what you should do by comparing the dilemma to other, similar cases where the course of action is clearer.
   1. Standing in line for a movie, you overhear a conversation between the two people behind you, neither of whom do you know. Their conversation is filled with particularly vile racial epithets. Should you say something to them?
   2. The employee handbook for the company where you work says that employees are permitted to take up to three days of "personal leave" with pay each year.

No reason need be given the employer when personal leave is taken, but the handbook specifies such leave may be used only for "bona fide reasons," for example, to look after a sick child or to deal with an emergency. You haven't had a vacation for several months and feel that you need a day for rest and recuperation, though you are not sick. Should you take a day of personal leave?

3. The checker at the supermarket has just rung up an item from your shopping cart at $2.99. In fact, the checker has made a mistake. The item is ticketed at $29.99. Are you going to bring this mistake to the checker's attention?

4. A friend has confided in you that he (she) found a wallet containing a substantial sum of money as well as the identification of the owner. Your friend goes on to say that though he returned the wallet through the mail, he kept most of the money. The friend tells you the name of the wallet's owner: a rather wealthy person well known in the community. Your friend is steadfast in refusing to give the money back. Should you break the confidence and tell the person?

5. According to the federal tax code, you may deduct up to $500 for charitable contributions of things other than money. You are allowed to deduct "fair market value" for the merchandise you donate. Recently you dropped off a couple of shirts, a few knick-knacks, and several dozen old CDs and LPs at the Goodwill shop. The person who accepted the goods gave you a receipt for tax purposes, but left blank the section calling for a description of donated goods and their fair market value. The receipt is signed and dated. You are now doing your income taxes and could use a $500 deduction. Are you going to fill out the tax receipt to exaggerate the value and nature of the goods you have donated?

SOLUTIONS

Exercise A

4. This example is quite interesting because the analogy at its heart is only hinted at. The primary subject is, of course, anger. Anger should be vented in acceptable ways. Otherwise, pressure will build up and may explode in the form of violent behavior. The terms *vented* and *explode* suggest the analogue is some sort of pressurized device, like a steam boiler. To keep pressure from reaching a point at which the boiler will explode, it may be necessary to vent a little pressure now and then. Indeed, most pressurized devices contain a safety valve designed to do just this. So, anger is like the contents of a pressurized container, and yelling and screaming are like a safety valve. By releasing a little emotional pressure now and then, we can keep our anger at a safe level.

The argument seems to depend on the analogy, for it would be difficult to state without reference to some sort of pressurized system. Indeed, without such reference, there would be nothing to the argument. An important point of dissimilarity lies in the fact that human emotional make-up is so much more complex than a simple pressurized system. By the way, much psychological research suggests this analogy is inappropriate. It turns out that anger tends to increase, rather than diminish, when vented in the ways suggested in the passage. A much more effective way of coping with strong emotion is to try to calm down. It seems we are not much like a simple pressurized container after all.

CHAPTER NINE

Generalizations and Causes

Two familiar kinds of claims play a prominent role in much of our reasoning. Suppose you and I decide to go out for dinner. You suggest a particular restaurant. "You must be kidding!" I reply. "The place is always packed. We'll starve before we get seated." One of the claims I have made is a generalization:

> The restaurant in question is always packed.

"That's hard to believe," you respond. "The food's not that good." "I know, but the place was recently listed in the newspaper as one of the best restaurants in the city," I go on to explain. This last claim

> The place was recently listed as one of the best restaurants in the city

explains why the restaurant is crowded by offering a possible cause. The fact that it got a rave review in the newspaper is, I suspect, the reason the restaurant is always crowded. In this chapter we will look into the methods by which these two types of claims—generalizations and claims about causal relationships—can be established. We will also consider common fallacies associated with each.

GENERALIZATIONS

A **generalization** is a claim about features common to a collection or group. A generalization can be to the effect that *all* the members have the feature(s), as in

> Every student in this class is twenty-two years of age or younger.

Conversely, a generalization may claim that *none* of the members of the group or collection has a feature(s), as in

> Nobody will live forever.

Generalizations are often limited in scope, claiming that a portion of a group or collection has or lacks a feature(s).

> Most sociologists are Marxists,

> A few professional tennis players have college degrees,

and

213

The vast majority of all Americans do not speak a foreign language

are examples of limited generalizations.

Like other kinds of claims, generalizations can be true or false, plausible or unlikely. What would it take to decide about the status of a general claim? Consider one of the preceding examples:

Every student in this class is twenty-two years of age or younger.

We could test this generalization for accuracy by checking with each student to find out his or her age. If any student is over twenty-two, the generalization is false. Limited generalizations can be tested as well.

Nearly every student in this class is twenty-two years of age or younger

would be true if it turned out that no more than a few of the students were over twenty-two. Of course, a generalization to the effect that *most* students are twenty-two or younger would be trickier. To decide about its truth or falsity, we would have to determine what constitutes *most*.

Unfortunately, this sort of exhaustive investigation is not always the most efficient or practical way to proceed. If a generalization is about a large group of things or events, it will be impossible to investigate each and every individual case, to determine whether the generalization holds. The evidence for most generalizations is obtained from a process with which you are probably already familiar: sampling.

Sampling Arguments

A **sample** is a limited group selected from a larger population. Suppose that I pick a dozen or so apples from the apple bin at my local supermarket. I discover that each apple in my "sample" is rotten. I might then conclude that all the apples in the bin are rotten. My sampling argument thus goes as follows:

All of the sampled apples from the bin are rotten.
_____
All of the apples in the bin are rotten.

If I had discovered instead that half of my dozen apples were rotten, I might have reasoned

Half of the sampled apples are rotten.
_____
Half of the apples in the bin are rotten.

We can generalize over these examples and give the form that all **sampling arguments** take:

X percent of the sampled A's are B's.
_____
X percent of all A's are B's.

If X turns out to be 100 percent or 0 percent, the conclusion drawn will be, respectively, that

I've just hired you to take a census of the rainbow trout in a small pond I own. The good news is that all the fish in the pond are rainbow trout. The bad news is that you can't drain the pond and count the fish. You've got to take a sample. Can you figure out a way, using sampling, to give me an accurate estimate of the number of fish in my pond?

All A's are B's.

and

No A's are B's.

In context, sampling arguments often do not explicitly reflect the form we have given. I might, for example, give the following argument for a generalization mentioned earlier:

That restaurant is always packed. Every time I have been there, it's taken at least forty-five minutes to get seated.

Although I have not explicitly mentioned samples and populations or anything of the sort, my argument is nonetheless an instance of the pattern given earlier. My sample is composed of my past visits to the restaurant, and on the basis of my sample I generalize that the restaurant is always as busy as it was on those occasions when I have been there.

Requirements for a Reliable Sampling Argument

Sampling arguments are not uniformly reliable, as this last example suggests. Unless I spend a remarkable amount of time at the restaurant in question, it seems likely that my sample is insufficient to establish the general claim I have made. Suppose that I have eaten at this restaurant only a few times and always early in the evening on Fridays or Saturdays. From the fact that the restaurant has been packed at peak business hours on the few occasions I have observed, it hardly follows that the restaurant is always packed. To be reliable, a sampling argument must satisfy three requirements.

The Sample Must Be Sufficiently Large   Just how large is large enough is a hard question to answer. Common sense suggests that the larger the sample, the greater the chances the sample will mirror the population from which it is drawn. So, as a general rule, a small sample will be unreliable and we should usually be suspicious of a generalization based on only a few instances. (There are exceptions to this rule: A single taste may be sufficient to determine that the stew needs more salt.) Common sense aside, the question of what constitutes a sufficiently large sample depends on the level of precision desired in the generalization, particularly when the population is large.

Consider an example of one common use to which sampling arguments are put: polling. A group of voters are asked whether they intend to vote for candidate X or Y. Sixty percent of the voters sampled respond that they intend to vote for X, 30 percent for Y, and 10 percent are undecided. How sure can we be that 60 percent of the electorate will actually vote for X? If you have read the results of polls like this, you have probably encountered the phrase **margin of error.** A media report of a sample usually includes a remark to the effect that "the margin of error for the sample is plus or minus P percent." What this means is that there is a P percent chance that the results of the sample are inaccurate. The notion of margin of error is essential to an understanding of the significance of sample size.

Mathematicians have spent a good deal of time investigating the logic of sampling arguments. In particular, they have made some interesting discoveries about situations like the following. Suppose we know that the frequency of a trait in a population is 50 percent. To follow our voting example, suppose we know in advance that 50 percent of the electorate favor candidate X. Suppose in addition that we sample the opinions of 100 voters at random. A sample is random if every member of the population stands an equal chance of being picked. (We will have more to say about the importance of randomness in sampling in just a bit.) What mathematicians have been able to show is that a high percentage of all possible sample outcomes lie within a narrow range—the larger the sample, the narrower the range. Now, our sample of 100 voters may contain anywhere from 0 to 100 voters who favor X. Yet, of all possible sampling outcomes, about 95 percent contain between 40 and 60 voters who prefer X. All this means is that if we took a large number of samples of 100 voters, 95 percent of our samples would probably contain between 40 and 60 voters who favor X, provided of course that 50 percent of the sampled population favor X. If we had sampled 1,000 voters instead, we would have discovered that 95 percent of our possible sample outcomes lie in the interval between 470 and 530 voters for X.

Table 9.1 summarizes the intervals for a number of common sample sizes when the frequency of the sampled characteristic in a population is 50 percent—where half do and half do not have the characteristic. Our choice of the interval containing 95 percent of all possible sample outcomes is somewhat though not entirely arbitrary. We could, for example, just as easily have settled on another interval, say,

TABLE 9.1   Ninety-five percent confidence intervals for common sample sizes

Sample Size	Interval Containing 95% of All Possible Sample Outcomes
25	7–18
50	18–32
100	40–60
250	110–140
500	230–270
1,000	470–530
1,500	720–780

the interval containing 80 percent of all possible outcomes. If we had done so, we would have found it to be much narrower than the interval in Table 9.1, the interval containing 95 percent of all possible outcomes. For a sample of 100, 80 percent of all possible outcomes fall between 43 and 57; for a sample of 1,000, between 480 and 520. Note that as we decrease the interval size, the range of outcomes under the interval diminishes for obvious reasons: The interval containing 80 percent of the possible outcomes has fewer values than does the interval containing 95 percent. But in polling, as well as in much scientific research, 95 percent is the proportion most frequently used in reporting results, and it is this number that is usually reflected in reports of margin of error. Unless we have information to the contrary, it is safe to assume that a reported margin of error is figured on the basis of the intervals in Table 9.1.

Margin of error is usually reported as a percentage, and we can easily convert Table 9.1 to reflect this. The information in Table 9.2 can be quite useful. If we read of a poll in which the margin of error was reported to be "+/–4 percent," we could conclude that about 500 subjects must have been sampled. Sometimes, reports of margin of error will mention **level of significance.** This phrase refers to the percentage of sample outcomes contained in the +/– interval. A generalization based on the level of significance given in Table 9.2 will be "statistically significant at the .05 level" because, if 95 percent of all possible sample outcomes lie within the interval, only 5 percent, or .05, lie outside the interval. Hence, in a sample of 500, chances are only 5 percent that the population from which the sample was taken will vary more than 4 percent from the sample result. (If we had decided to use a smaller interval, say, the interval containing 80 percent of all possible outcomes, our margin of error would have been smaller. But, then, we could be only "80 percent sure" that the result mirrored the proportion in the sampled population.)

Now let's apply what we have discovered about the logic of sampling to our voting example. We do not know the percentage of voters who favor candidate X, and so we take a random sample of 100 registered voters. Sixty percent of those polled report that they favor X. Table 9.2 tells us that the interval containing 95 percent of all possible sample outcomes is roughly 10 percent in either direction.

TABLE 9.2 Margins of error for common sample sizes

Sample Size	Approximate Margin of Error*
25	+/–22%
50	+/–14%
100	+/–10%
250	+/–6%
500	+/–4%
1,000	+/–3%
1,500	+/–2%

*The interval surrounding the actual sample outcome containing 95% of all possible sample outcomes.

From this we can conclude that we are 95 percent sure that somewhere between 50 percent and 70 percent of the voting population favor candidate X. When the percentage of those sampled having the characteristic in question is very high or very low, the intervals in Table 9.2 will be off a bit; the range of possible outcomes on the + and − side of the sample outcome will differ slightly from one another. But we need not be concerned with this small inaccuracy. The intervals in Table 9.2 are only approximate and are intended to provide only a rough sense of the level of precision we can expect from samples of various sizes. Unless sampling results are very near 0 percent or 100 percent or the sample is quite small, the numbers in Table 9.2 provide a fairly accurate approximation. If, for example, our result had been that 70 percent of the sample favored X, the interval would have remained very close to +/−10 percent.

The Sample Must Be Representative   We have decided to poll the voters in our state about their preference in the race involving candidates X and Y. We want a result that will be accurate with a margin of error of no more than +/−3 percent, so we need to sample about 1,000 voters. Since we don't have a lot of time and money, we decide to focus on a large and convenient group of voters. As luck would have it, Y's party is holding its convention this weekend and so we do our polling there. We take a random sample of the preference of 1,000 attendees and our results are spectacular: Fully 97 percent of the voters sampled favor Y! Here, despite the fact that our sample is quite large, our result is undoubtedly inaccurate. Our sample is not *representative* of the general population of eligible voters. A **representative sample** reflects characteristics of the sampled population that might make a difference to the outcome of the sample. Thus, a representative sample of voters should contain roughly the proportions of political party membership found in the voting population, since party membership generally influences a voter's preferences. A sample that reflects important differences that can influence the outcome is said to be **stratified.** Thus, in many cases, a representative sample needs to balance both randomness and stratification. Although our sample was random, it was not well stratified since every subject likely was a member of a single party.

Precisely what constitutes a representative sample depends on the nature of the things being sampled. If we are sampling voter preference, party membership will be an important consideration as will be age, gender, and income level. If we are using sampling as a means of quality control in the manufacture of a product, we may still need to stratify our sample of products. Suppose we want to determine how many defects occur per thousand units of product. To ensure a representative sample, we need to think about differences in the production process that may contribute to the overall defect rate. It seems likely, for example, that workers might be more effective early in their shifts and early in the work week and that workers in one area of the plant may be more efficient than workers in another area. With all of this in mind, we can easily settle on a procedure that will pick a fairly large number of units at random from various locations in the factory, at various times of the day, and over a series of days.

Do you want to learn more about the techniques used in taking samples? If you are on line, visit the Gallup Organization Web site—www.gallup.com. The Gallup Organization is the oldest and largest company in the United States that specializes in public opinion polling. At the Gallup Web site, you will be able to look at the results of many recent polls. You will also be able to find out more about the methods by which samples are selected, questions framed, interviews conducted, and results assessed.

The Techniques Used to Elicit Information Must Be Unbiased   The wording of the questions asked in a sample of people can influence their responses. The following case illustrates the way in which biased language can affect the way people respond to a question. U.S. Senator Orrin Hatch, of Utah, wanted to find out how voters feel about unions and their legal right to strike. One of the questions on his survey was this:

> Are you in favor of allowing construction union czars the power to shut down an entire construction site because of a dispute with a single contractor . . . thus forcing even more workers to knuckle under to union agents?

Even if Senator Hatch's questionnaire had gone out to a large and randomly selected sample of voters, his results would be questionable, for it is hard to imagine anyone who would respond that they were in favor of this practice. We should be suspicious also of questions asked on particularly sensitive issues, but asked in a setting that does not guarantee anonymity. Suppose a pollster approached you on the street and asked:

> On average, how many times per week do you say something that is not entirely true?

I can't imagine many people would feel comfortable in responding to this question face-to-face, and so chances are good many people would underreport the extent of their lying, that is, if they responded at all. Another interesting fact about this question is that it would be very hard to answer accurately under any circumstances. Short of keeping a record of the lies one tells, how would one go about accurately estimating their number? The lesson of these last examples is that when a poll is on a sensitive topic, we need to know both what questions were asked and the conditions under which the poll was taken if we are to arrive at any sense of its reliability.

FALLACIES INVOLVING GENERALIZATIONS

Three fallacies are often committed in conjunction with arguments involving generalizations. The first, hasty generalization, occurs when a generalization is made on the basis of insufficient information. The other two, stereotypical thinking and special case, occur when an improper conclusion is drawn about a specific case based on a general claim.

Hasty Generalization

Our discussion of sampling suggests that **hasty generalization** can be the product of a number of difficulties. A generalization may be based on a sample that is too small. It is not unusual for people to make generalizations based on nothing more than a few confirming instances. The first generalization we considered in this chapter is a good example. You will recall that I suggested we not eat at a particular restaurant because it is "always packed." If I have been to this restaurant only once or twice, I am guilty of basing a generalization on a sample that is too small to be reliable. In addition, an argument for a generalization commits the fallacy of hasty generalization if it is based on an unrepresentative sample. My generalization about the restaurant makes this mistake as well, for I visited the restaurant only at peak business hours.

Hasty generalization can result from biased survey techniques or questions. Suppose that I decide to poll a number of customers at the restaurant about their past experiences there. If I select the people who appear the most disgruntled and so are the most likely to take the time to answer my questions, my sampling technique has a built-in bias in favor of the result I believe true. Finally, hasty generalization occurs when a generalization is not properly qualified. If we survey twenty-four voters and find that half favor a particular candidate, we commit the fallacy of hasty generalization if we fail to point out that, as far as we can tell, somewhere between roughly a quarter and three-quarters of the voters favor the candidate in question. Further, we must admit that there remains about a 5 percent chance that this result is wrong, even if the sample is entirely representative. Hasty generalizations of this last sort are guilty of a fallacy discussed in Chapter 6, false precision. If we were to report, in the example just cited, that *50 percent of the voters* favor the candidate in question, we would be drawing a conclusion far more precise than the survey entitles us to draw.

Whenever we encounter evidence for a generalization, it is worth asking a series of questions to determine whether the evidence involves the fallacy of hasty generalization:

> How large is the sample?
>
> Is the generalization qualified to reflect sample size?
>
> Is the sample representative?
>
> Has the sample included any necessary stratification?
>
> Were the sample subjects randomly selected?
>
> Were the survey techniques unbiased?

If the answer to one or more of these questions is "no," the argument for the generalization is guilty of hasty generalization. Bear in mind that samples can provide at best a good approximation of what things are like in a population. We may be "95 percent sure" that a sample outcome is correct within the margin of error for a sample of the size in question. But the statistical precision of this sort of claim must be understood in light of the many problems that can confound the process of sample taking.

Stereotypical Thinking

By their very nature, generalizations apply to individual cases. If I know, for example, that nearly every resident of Sun City is retired and if I know that X lives in Sun City, I can conclude that X is probably retired. But this sort of inference can be dangerous and is often unwarranted. First of all, many generalizations, particularly about people, are unfounded stereotypes, based more on prejudice and expectation than on careful investigation. We meet a person who strikes us as being unusually arrogant and subsequently discover she is a brain surgeon. "Ah," we speculate, "brain surgeons are prima donnas and this explains her arrogance." But not all generalizations, nor even all stereotypes, are unfounded. Yet, even if a generalization is true, subsequent inferences based on the generalization are risky. This is because generalizations, particularly about people, tend to focus on a single characteristic. The result is a picture that probably resembles no individual person. Think of the following stereotypical generalizations:

Teenagers are reckless drivers.

Fundamentalists are intolerant of other religions.

Women are emotional, men analytic.

The Irish drink too much.

Even if one or more of these stereotypes has an element of truth to it, very little follows about any individual falling under the generalization. Perhaps some teenagers are reckless drivers and some fundamentalists are intolerant. But knowing only that an individual is a teenager or a fundamentalist, we have little reason to suppose he or she fits these stereotypes. The fallacy, **stereotypical thinking,** occurs when we characterize a person by applying a stereotype without considering his or her individual quirks and traits.

Advertisements often rely on stereotypical thinking to sell their products.

A good example is a recent newspaper ad for Formula 409 Carpet Cleaner. Unfortunately, the makers of Formula 409, The Clorox Company, refused permission to reprint the ad so the following description will have to suffice. The ad features a "typical" homemaker kneeling on a spotless carpet, which, judging by the work gloves she is wearing and the can of Formula 409 next to her, has been recently cleaned. She is a slim, attractive woman in her mid-thirties, dressed in slacks, a blouse, and a sweater, and is proudly pointing to the carpet. Superimposed over the top of the picture is the phrase "A Better Carpet Cleaner!" You will probably not be surprised to hear that homemakers are the people most likely to purchase Formula 409. Stereotypical lines are seldom crossed in advertising. Beer ads, for example, are not going to feature images of homemakers like the one in the Formula 409 ad. Nor are we likely to see a Formula 409 ad featuring a middle-aged male—dressed in jeans, sweatshirt, and a baseball cap—beaming proudly at the job he and his can of Formula 409 have done on the floor of the room where he and his buddies are watching a football game.

CONUNDRUM

Generalizations can be falsified by finding counterexamples, as in the following case. The claim

(1) All ravens are black

would be false if we could find at least one nonblack raven. Confirmation of (1) would be more time consuming. If we were to examine a large number of ravens and find that all of them were black, we would have at least some initial sense that (1) is true. The greater our sample, the more confidence we would have in (1). In general, then, it seems that the confirmation or rejection of (1) depends on whether there are any nonblack ravens and nothing else. But consider a different way of saying what (1) says:

(2) No nonblack thing is a raven.

The equivalence of (1) and (2) follows from the fact that if all ravens are black, then no thing that is not black can be a raven. But if (1) and (2) are equivalent, anything that would confirm (1) would confirm (2) and vice versa. But a piece of purple chalk, for example, would be just the thing that might lead to the confirmation of (2): It is nonblack and it is not a raven! Must we, therefore, conclude that (1) can be confirmed not only by black ravens but by anything that is neither black nor a raven?

Special Case

Inferences based on generalizations are susceptible to another fallacy. **Special case** (sometimes called **sweeping generalization**) involves the unwarranted application of general rules or policies. In most cases, for example, it makes good sense to refrain from making important decisions in a hurry. We do well, as a rule of thumb, to take our time and think things through before deciding. In an emergency, however, it may be important to make a decision quickly, with little deliberation. Such circumstances are not at all the kind envisioned in the general rule "Don't make important decisions in a hurry." To take another example, a soldier who justifies doing something illegal on the ground that "I was just following orders" commits the fallacy of special case. Although, in general, a soldier ought to follow orders, an exception is made for orders that clearly countenance something illegal.

In Chapter 7, we discussed two other fallacies involving generalizations, division and composition. Don't confuse these two with hasty generalization and special case. Division occurs when a fallacious inference is drawn about the members of a group based on something that is true only of the group as a whole. Division results from a failure to see that a key word or phrase applies in one way to the individual members of a group and in another way to the group itself. ("Dogs live on every continent and Fido is a dog, so Fido lives on every continent" is a simple example of division.) By contrast, special case occurs when there is something unusual about an individual case that disqualifies it from inclusion under a generalization, but there will be other cases to which the generalization does apply. So, in division the problem stems from applying something true of a group to its individual members; in special case, the problem is that we are applying the generalization to the wrong sort of case.

A similar contrast can be drawn between composition and hasty generalization. Composition occurs when a fallacious inference is drawn about a group as a whole based on something that is true only of the group's individual members. ("Every member of the Knicks is an accomplished basketball player, so the Knicks as a whole are an accomplished team" is an example of composition.) The problem in composition is not that the inference is based on a sample that is too small or unrepresentative. Yet this is precisely the problem in hasty generalization; a generalization is based on insufficient evidence. By contrast, when a general claim is the result of composition, the problem is a failure of language, not fact.

REASONING ABOUT CAUSES

Claims about the causes of things can play an important role in our daily lives. When we want to understand why something has happened, we often need to get at its cause or causes. My street flooded recently, during a heavy rain. Why? Because the storm drain was clogged with leaves washed into the street by the rain. After this was figured out, the problem was easy to solve. This example is typical of what comes to mind when we think about the notion of a cause: a prior event responsible for the effect in question. But causes can have a number of features not illustrated by this case.

First, causes are not always singular: An event may be the product of several causal factors. We learn that a friend has failed an important exam. He tells us he was so nervous he had a hard time concentrating and admits also that he did not spend enough time studying the material. Lack of sufficient study time here is one factor but not the whole causal story. Second, causal factors can be preventive. If aspirin stops your headache, there is a causal relationship between your headache and the aspirin. Finally, causes often pertain to general classes of events. It is well known, for example, that cigarette smoking causes lung cancer. What this means is that smokers in general are at risk of contracting lung cancer.

This last point suggests the extent to which scientific investigation involves the search for causes. Perhaps the central goal of science is to expand our understanding of both ourselves and nature. One crucial way of advancing this understanding is by getting at causes of a thing or an event. And this is generally done in science by speculating about the causes of something and then finding some way to test these speculations. If anything deserves to be called "scientific method," it is the simple strategy just sketched.

TESTING FOR CAUSAL LINKS

Consider a claim about a possible causal connection:

Excessive caffeine consumption causes severe depression in many people.

How might we test this claim? We might begin by asking a lot of people who consume a lot of caffeine if they tend to get depressed. But before proceeding, we need to clarify the notion of "excessive consumption." Suppose we discover, after asking a number of people, that about a third of those who consume three or more caffeinated drinks a day admit they have a serious problem with depression. Although this is an interesting result, it does not establish a causal link between caffeine consumption and depression. What if it turns out that roughly a third of all people—both those who do and those who do not consume excessive amounts of caffeine—report a similar problem with depression? Moreover, what if there are factors other than caffeine consumption that account for the depression in some of the people we have interviewed? Unfortunately, until we have addressed these possibilities, we can arrive at no realistic sense of the extent (if at all) to which caffeine consumption and depression are causally linked.

Imposing Controls

To account for these possibilities, we need to find some way of comparing our heavy caffeine users with people who do not use much caffeine yet who are like our heavy users with respect to other causal factors for depression. These requirements are the essence of the notion of a **controlled experiment.** The basic idea is to create a set of experimental conditions that include a way of controlling for extraneous causal factors. In our example, control will be provided by the comparison group we have just envisioned.

Let's see if we can improve on our original "experiment" by imposing a few controls. Imagine we have the time and resources to track a large group of people for a number of years. At the beginning of our experiment we select a large group of subjects, all of whom consume three or more caffeinated drinks per day. We then divide our subjects into two groups, making sure that a similar percentage of each group suffers from depression. We might hire a psychologist or two to make this determination. Next (and this is the hard part!) we convince the members of one group to restrict their use of caffeine. In the jargon of the causal researcher, the group who continues to use caffeine is called the **experimental group,** the restricted users, the **control group.** The suspected cause, caffeine, is the **independent variable,** while the effect is the **dependent variable.**

After several years, we call in all subjects and have our psychologists interview them. Suppose we had tracked 200 subjects, 100 each in the experimental and control groups. We now discover that 24 percent more of the experimental group than of the control group are clinically depressed, according to our experts. Does our experiment suggest that excessive caffeine consumption causes depression? Note that a new wrinkle is built into our results. We now need to grapple with the fact of different levels of the dependent variable, depression, in our two groups. Is a 24 percent difference enough to make a difference? That is, does a 24 percent difference show a definite causal link? Unfortunately, these questions are too complex to answer in a simple and nontechnical way. But our earlier discussion of the statistical considerations involved in assessing samples can tell us how these questions can be resolved.

Assessing the Results

In a sense, our experimental and control groups are samples. Remember, the claim we are investigating is that excessive caffeine consumption causes depression, not only among our subjects, but among the population at large as well. Table 9.2 (p. 217) reveals that for a sample of 100, the margin of error is +/–10 percent. This suggests that the difference in our two groups is probably meaningful. If, say, 50 percent of the experimental group suffer depression, we can be relatively confident that no less than 40 percent of the sampled population suffer depression. And if 26 percent of the control group are depressed, we can be similarly sure this is true of no more than 36 percent of the sampled population. The fact that there is no overlap between these two intervals suggests we have found a real difference in the sampled populations: There is only about a 5 percent chance that the difference we have detected is due to sampling error. (Remember, our figures for margin of error are based on an interval containing 95 percent of all possible sample outcomes.) When researchers report their results, they often refer to such differences—differences that are probably not due to sampling error—as being **statistically significant.**

If we had instead found a much smaller difference between the levels of depression in our experimental and control groups—say, a 6 percent difference—we might have been tempted to conclude that there is no causal link between caffeine consumption and depression. But we must be careful here. For samples of 100, a difference of 6 percent could easily occur even if there were no real difference in the sampled populations. However, it is also possible that there is a real difference in the sampled populations, but a difference too small to measure reliably in samples of the size we are using. Thus the conclusion we are justified in drawing, given a 6 percent difference in the samples, is that we have no evidence for a causal link, not that there is no link between the two factors. If caffeine is indeed a causal factor for depression, its effect is too small to detect in a study of the size we have undertaken. A small difference or no difference in the levels of effect in the two groups is often reported as being **not statistically significant.**

As you may suspect from our discussion of the relationship between sample size and margin of error, the amount of difference in the dependent variable needed to suggest a causal link shrinks when the size of the experimental and control groups increases. In general, then, the larger the groups, the smaller the difference required in levels of the effect to suggest a causal link; the smaller the size of the groups, the greater the difference required to reach a result that is statistically significant.

The intervals provided in Table 9.2 (p. 217) can give us a rough approximation of whether a difference in sample outcomes is significant, but they are also a bit misleading. The percentage difference required to achieve "statistical significance" when two samples are compared is generally a bit less than the difference suggested in Table 9.2. For example, a difference of just over 13 percent will be statistically significant for samples of 100 or so. (The required difference decreases even more when the sample frequencies are near 0 percent or 100 percent.) By contrast, Table 9.2 suggests that a 20 percent difference would be required. The amount of overestimation of interval size in the table decreases as sample size increases. Table 9.2 suggests a 6 percent difference is required to achieve statistical significance for samples of about 1,000, when in fact just over a 4 percent difference is sufficient. We can correct for the inaccuracy in Table 9.2 if we adopt the following rules of thumb when comparing sample proportions. If a difference exceeds the intervals given in the table, it is statistically significant. If there is some overlap of the intervals (if the intervals have less than a third of their values in common), the difference is probably statistically significant. But if there is a good deal of overlap (roughly, more than one-third of all values), the difference is not statistically significant.

So, we have tracked 200 subjects for several years and have found a 24 percent difference in levels of depression in our two groups. We have established a statistically significant link between caffeine and depression. But we are not yet ready to conclude that there is a causal link! The results of our experiment must be assessed in light of one crucial qualification.

The credibility of our results is completely dependent on our ability to control for other factors that might lead to depression among our subjects. In a "real world" experiment like the one we have outlined, we need to worry about the influence of other potential causal factors. This is why scientists are happiest when they can carry out their experiments in the artificial but immensely more controllable environment of the laboratory. Often, laboratory experiments designed to determine how suspected causal factors influence humans are carried out on animals instead. Much cancer research, for example, is carried out on animals specifically bred for research purposes. One reason animals are preferred as experimental subjects is that the environment in which they live can be completely controlled.

Note that claims about causation in humans based on results found in laboratory animals involve an implicit argument by analogy. Suppose a study shows that caffeine causes a certain level of bladder cancer in laboratory-bred mice. The claim that caffeine causes bladder cancer in humans assumes the correctness of the following argument:

> With respect to most carcinogens, laboratory mice and humans are alike.
>
> Caffeine causes bladder cancer in laboratory mice.
> _____
>
> Caffeine causes bladder cancer in humans.

As with any argument by analogy, the correctness of this argument depends on the extent of the similarities and the lack of relevant dissimilarities between primary subject and analogue. If, indeed, just about everything that causes cancer in laboratory mice also causes cancer in humans, the argument is a good one.

Types of Causal Experiments

There are three basic strategies that can be employed in carrying out a causal experiment. Which strategy researchers choose often is determined by the time and funds available to carry out the experiment and the nature of the link being tested.

Randomized Causal Experiments   These experiments, generally carried out under tightly controlled and somewhat artificial conditions, typically involve fairly small experimental and control groups. The example we worked through in the previous section is a randomized causal experiment.

CONUNDRUM

Is something amiss in our account of what it takes to establish a cause-effect relationship? Ideally, if A causes B in C's, then all C's exposed to sufficient levels of A should contract B. If B does not invariably occur when C's are exposed to A in sufficient amounts, then what sense is there to the notion that A causes B? Can it really follow, for example, that smoking cigarettes causes lung cancer when even heavy smokers do not invariably contract lung cancer?

Prospective Causal Studies   Causal experiments cannot always be carried out in the artificial confines of the laboratory, where small groups of subjects can be randomly assigned to the experimental and control groups. Often, large-scale causal studies involve segments of the real population. A study may focus on segments of the population who either have or lack a suspected causal agent, tracking the two segments over time to see if different levels of the effect emerge. Studies of this sort are called prospective causal studies. To do a prospective study of the suspected link between caffeine and depression, we might begin by isolating two large groups of people, only one of which consumes excessive amounts of caffeine. If there is a link between caffeine and depression, we would predict that, over time, more members of the experimental group—the caffeine consumers—than of the control group will become clinically depressed.

Retrospective Causal Studies   This sort of study focuses on segments of the population who have and lack the effect under investigation, looking into the histories of the subjects to see if there are significantly different levels of the suspected causal agent. A retrospective causal study of our suspected link would involve checking the background of two groups—people who are clinically depressed and people who are not—in an attempt to discover if there is a higher level of caffeine consumption in the experimental group.

Advantages and Disadvantages   There are advantages and disadvantages to each type of causal experiment. Randomized experiments—experiments in which like subjects are randomly assigned to experimental and control groups before the experimental group is exposed to the suspected cause—offer the greatest chances for the control of extraneous causal factors. In both retrospective and prospective studies, there is always a chance that extraneous factors will be represented at different levels in the experimental and control groups. The influence of other causal factors can be reduced by identifying and eliminating people subject to these other factors. In a prospective study of the effects of caffeine consumption on depression, we might, for example, equalize the number of subjects in each group prone to known causes of depression. But the possibility of influence by extraneous causal factors cannot be entirely eliminated, short of the kind of randomized process for assigning subjects to experimental and control groups rarely available outside the laboratory or in very small studies. The major advantage of prospective and retrospective studies is that they can be done with large numbers of subjects, thus increasing the chances they will be reliable samples. Retrospective studies have the added advantage that they can be carried out quickly, since information about the suspected effect is available at the time the study is begun. This advantage is responsible for the biggest deficiency in retrospective studies: Because all members of the experimental group have the effect being studied, it is very difficult to rule out the possibility that factors other than that being studied may be responsible for much of the effect.

CAUSAL FALLACIES

People often draw conclusions about causal links on the basis of evidence much less compelling than that provided by a controlled experiment. Not surprisingly, many inferences to causal links are fallacious; the information on which the inference is drawn falls short of that required to establish a causal link. In particular, three kinds of mistakes are commonly committed in arguments about causes:

- mistaken inferences from a correlation between two factors to the claim that they are causally linked,
- mistaken inferences from the fact that one thing occurs before another to the claim that they are causally linked, and
- failure to impose controls.

In many cases, the inference to a causal link seems plausible only because rival explanations for the data are overlooked. Often, showing that a causal inference is fallacious involves getting at the real explanation for the evidence that has prompted the inference to a causal link. In what follows we will detail the kinds of explanations typically overlooked in each of the three types of mistakes.

Inference from a Correlation to a Causal Link

When two factors are correlated, they are not necessarily related as cause to effect. A **correlation** is a statistical comparison of the frequency with which two or more factors occur or the frequency of a single factor in two or more groups. The simplest sort of correlation is the latter. To say that a correlation obtains between two things, A and B, is just to say that B occurs at a different frequency among A's than among non-A's. Correlations can be positive or negative. A positive correlation exists, for example, between marijuana use and cigarette smoking if a higher percentage of smokers than nonsmokers use marijuana. To claim a negative correlation between the two is just to claim that a lesser percentage of smokers than nonsmokers use marijuana. Correlation and causation are not entirely unrelated notions. If there is a causal link between two factors, they will be correlated. But from the simple fact that two factors are correlated, it does not follow that one causes the other. The inference of a causal link based only on the evidence of a correlation is fallacious. Many correlations do not reflect an underlying causal link.

Suppose, for example, we discovered the following evidence for a crucial tenet of astrology: the position of the sun and planets at the time of a person's birth can have an influence on the development of personality. The evidence is from a study that claims more M.D.'s are born under the sign of Sagittarius than under any other astrological sign. There is, in other words, a positive correlation between being a Sagittarian and being an M.D. Before we rush to the conclusion that there is a causal link between the two, we need to consider another possible explanation of the correlation. The most likely is that it is just a coincidence. If we look at a number of people in a single profession, we will probably find a few interesting correlations provided we have enough detailed information about the people at our disposal. (We might discover, for example, a positive correlation between playing handball and practicing law. All this would require is evidence that lawyers, on average, put in more time on the handball court than do other people. Who knows what we might be able to find if we look hard enough!) Doubtless, many correlations are due simply to the fact that if just about any group is split in two, some characteristics will occur at different proportions in the two subgroups. When the original group is small, there is an increased chance of finding these sorts of differences. Suppose our study of the astrological signs of M.D.'s involved only a few dozen subjects. Chances are exceedingly slim that the same number of subjects will fall under each of the twelve astrological signs. Thus, the odds are very good that we will find a correlation somewhere in the data. But clearly, any correlation we find will be the result of a happy coincidence, not a causal link.

A correlation need not be taken as evidence of a direct causal link even when it is not due to mere coincidence. A study, for example, might reveal a positive correlation between attendance at a private high school and Scholastic Aptitude Test (SAT) scores: Students who attend private high schools achieve higher SAT scores on average than do students who attend public high schools. Here, we must not be too quick to assume a causal link—that the quality of instruction at private schools is responsible for the higher SAT scores. The correlation may be due to some *third factor* (or complex of factors). It may be that private schools tend to attract students who are academically better prepared than are public school students. Or it may be that parents who are sufficiently interested in the academic careers of their children to send them to private school also tend to do more to encourage their children to study. I'm sure you can think of other rival explanations. The lesson of this example is that the evidence of a correlation alone is not evidence of a direct causal link. One factor may be correlated with another, and there may be some connection between the two, yet the first may not be the cause of the second. Some additional causal factor(s) may be needed to explain the correlation.

One final difficulty may beset an inference from a correlation to a claim of causal connection. As it turns out, positive correlations are symmetrical. If A is positively correlated with B, B is, in turn, positively correlated with A. If more cigarette smokers than nonsmokers use marijuana, it is also the case that more marijuana users than nonmarijuana users smoke cigarettes. This suggests we should consider the possibility that cause and effect are reversed when we are presented with the evidence of a positive correlation. In our previous example, it is possible that cause and effect have been reversed. The correlation between SAT score and attendance at private schools may just be due to the fact that, for admission, private schools require an SAT score above the average public school score!

The correlations we have considered so far have involved a single factor, split between two groups. But correlations can also be found between pairs of characteristics within a single group. Correlations of this latter sort are often called **concomitant**

variations. If we examined, for example, a large number of parents, we would find a concomitant variation between height of parents and height of their offspring. The correlation would be positive: Taller parents tend to have tall children. (If the correlation were negative, we would have found that the taller the parents, the shorter their children, as a general rule.) A perfect correlation would be a one-to-one correspondence between one trait and an increase or decrease in another. So, if we found that, without exception, the taller the parents, the taller their offspring, we would have evidence of a perfect correlation. Most correlations, however, are imperfect. Although, in our example, we may find a positive correlation between height of parents and their children, the correlation will be imperfect. Some tall parents will have relatively short children, and some short parents will have relatively tall children.

Concomitant variation can be a useful tool in discovering possible causal connections. If increases in one factor are fairly systematically matched by increases or decreases in another factor, we may have some initial evidence of a causal link. Many variations, however, do not indicate a causal link. The problem is that a remarkable number of entirely unrelated things tend to vary in regular sorts of ways. There has been a dramatic increase in the number of television networks in the past twenty years. At the same time, there has been a corresponding increase in mini-van ownership. What do you suppose the explanation is? A causal link? Some overlooked third factor? The most plausible explanation is that we have isolated two entirely unrelated trends that happen to be going in the same direction at the same time. So, though concomitant variation can be a useful tool in causal research, we need to be skeptical in those cases where the variation is so superficial it is likely due to coincidence.

Predictions are often made on the basis of imperfect concomitant variations, and here we must be wary of the **regression fallacy.** When two factors are imperfectly correlated, extreme values of one will frequently be matched by less extreme values of the other. Remember, in an imperfect correlation we would expect to find the extreme values of one factor paired with a range of values for the other, and vice versa. So, for example, although tall parents will often have children as tall as or taller than them, some tall parents will have children shorter than them. Extremely tall parents will be less likely to have children equally tall or taller than are parents who are tall but not extremely tall. The regression fallacy occurs when we fail to recognize the effects of statistical regression and go on to offer an explanation for the apparent mismatch between the extreme values for the two factors. Imagine, for example, that we live in an area of the country where there is a lot of rain. We might find a positive correlation between rainfall levels and serious auto accidents. However, a careful look at the data will probably reveal that the greatest number of accidents *do not* occur on the days with the greatest rainfall. We commit the regression fallacy if we speculate about the explanation for this. *Maybe people, being aware of the danger of driving in heavy rain, are more cautious on particularly rainy days.* In fact, the phenomenon we have discovered is probably due to nothing more than the kind of regression that accompanies extreme values of one factor.[1]

---

[1] For an excellent discussion of the regression fallacy, see Chapter 2 in *How We Know What Isn't So: The Fallibility of Reason in Everyday Life* (New York: Free Press, 1991).

Inference Based on Temporal Succession

If one event is the cause of another, the causal event obviously must occur first. But the fact that one event precedes another does not show that the former is the cause of the latter. In most circumstances, we would not mistakenly think that simply because one thing precedes another, the former must have caused the latter. But the temptation to infer a causal link increases dramatically when something remarkable is preceded by something equally remarkable. We all have had experiences like this: We are thinking about someone—a friend or relative—and, shortly thereafter, the phone or doorbell rings or a letter arrives. It is the person we were thinking about! Many psychics believe this sort of case provides striking evidence of "precognition," that is, an ability to "see" the future. In fact, such cases are probably due to the fact that two unusual but unrelated events have occurred at about the same time. When something remarkable happens, it is only natural to wonder about its causes, and it does not seem unreasonable to think that something remarkable must have an equally unusual cause. Moreover, we tend to remember the unusual, not the ordinary. If something unusual comes to mind, something that happened shortly before the event we are thinking about, the thought that they are linked is difficult to resist. Many superstitions are probably based on this sort of occurrence. Something out of the ordinary happens—perhaps a black cat crosses your path. And then another peculiar thing takes place, a remarkably bad bit of luck. The fact that the two events are out of the ordinary and that one occurred on the heels of the other makes it all too easy to conclude they are causally related.

Of course, temporal succession may provide some initial reason to suspect a causal link. But what is generally required to establish such a link is some sort of evidence the events are related, something in addition to the fact that the first preceded the second. One morning not long ago, I picked up my telephone only to discover that the line was dead. I checked with the neighbors and their phones were all in order. Finally, it occurred to me that I couldn't remember whether I had paid my phone bill. Looking over my checkbook register, I found, much to my dismay, that I had overlooked my last three monthly phone bills, something I had never done before. In these circumstances, it seems entirely reasonable to conclude that my failure to pay my phone bill prompted the phone company to disconnect my service. But note here that I have some reason, in addition to the fact that the one event preceded the other, to suspect a causal link: Unfortunately, phone companies have the nasty habit of taking extreme measures when customers fail to pay for their services.

Failure to Impose Controls

This mistake is reminiscent of a fallacy discussed in Chapter 6, omitting information. It occurs when we note what seems an unusually high (or low) frequency with which one factor is associated with another and then conclude there must be some causal link between the two. Now, there may indeed be a link between the two. But to decide about this, we need some sense of what happens in instances where the second factor occurs in the absence of the first. We need, that is, the kind of benchmark a control group can provide. Lacking this additional information, we cannot conclude much about the nature of the relationship between the two factors.

You have probably heard the claim that a high number of violent crimes are committed when the moon is full. What do you suppose is the explanation? Before attempting to answer this question, we need more information. What is the rate of violent crime when the moon is *not* full? If it is roughly the same, our little puzzle requires no further explanation. It is amazing how often people assume a causal link, without first stopping to think about the kind of benchmark information needed to substantiate a link. Over the years, I have noticed that the students enrolled in my courses who attend class regularly tend to achieve high scores on my exams. No doubt this is a testimony to my teaching ability.

MEDIA WATCH: SCIENCE IN THE NEWS

The amount of information produced by the scientific and technological community is staggering. Worldwide, there are more than 30,000 periodicals devoted to some area of science or technology. These periodicals, along with thousands of scientific conferences each year, constitute the forums in which new research is made public. Most scientific journals are peer reviewed, which means submitted papers are reviewed and criticized by experts in the field prior to publication. It is not unusual for a paper to be sent back to its author(s) for further research or revision. A typical journal article may run to dozens of pages; the issues raised and discussed may be complex and technical, and conclusions will often be tentative and carefully qualified. The news media, thus, face some real problems in deciding what science stories to cover and the level of coverage. How can an important story be translated into terms the lay reader can understand and yet remain brief enough to retain the kind of immediacy and excitement required for hard news?

Most newspapers, newsmagazines, and television news organizations employ science writers and editors. A few television programs, including *Nova* and *National Geographic,* and popular magazines, such as *Scientific American* and *Popular Mechanics,* focus on science and technology. For the most part, the news media do a good job of reporting the few major scientific stories they choose to cover. New discoveries and breakthroughs are given ample coverage, often in terms that are accurate and understandable to the public. Perhaps the most notable scientific breakthrough of the '90s was the cloning of a sheep, Dolly, by an English veterinary scientist, Dr. Ian Wilmut, in 1997. The story was covered in depth in all the news media. The technology involved in cloning and the implications for future research were carefully explained; the moral issues involved in the notion of cloning a human were explored in depth.

One type of scientific story, however, deserves special mention. The news media regularly run stories about causal research, usually research that may have an immediate impact on the reader or viewer, such as medical research. Recent issues of my local newspaper, for example, included several stories about medical research, under the following headlines:

Studies Find Chiropractic Treatment of Marginal Benefit

Children Afflicted with Allergies More Prone to Behavior Problems

Depression's Link to Heart Disease Doubles as Stroke Risk, Study Says

Just what is science? And what is technology? These are hard questions to answer given the wide range of activities in which scientists engage. From a theoretical point of view, the sciences are unified around a single theme: The job of the theoretical scientist is to advance our understanding of some part of the natural world. Technology is science applied to the solution of practical problems via technical innovation. What is the subject matter of science? Even harder to say. Perhaps the best answer is provided by the following list. These are the divisions of the American Association for the Advancement of Science, the largest and most prestigious scientific organization in the United States. The divisions represent current thinking about the broad subject areas that, taken together, map out the domain of science.

Agriculture, Food, and Renewable Resources
Anthropology
Astronomy
Atmospheric and Hydrospheric Sciences
Biological Sciences
Chemistry
Dentistry
Education
Engineering
General Interest in Science and Engineering
Geology and Geography
History and Philosophy of Science
Industrial Science and Technology
Information, Computing, and Communication
Linguistics and Language Science
Mathematics
Medical Sciences
Neuroscience
Pharmaceutical Sciences
Psychology
Social, Economic, and Political Sciences
Societal Impacts of Science and Engineering
Statistics

The Effect of Education on Health Holds True in the Aged, Study Finds

Researchers Find Link Between Religion and Lower Blood Pressure

Each story gave a brief rundown of the research that was undertaken and the apparent results. Unfortunately, each of the stories managed to omit much of the key information needed to fully understand and appreciate the significance of the research. Yet, these stories are fairly typical of the kind and level of coverage given causal research in the mass media. Here, for example, is the complete text of one of the stories.

Researchers Find Link Between Religion and Lower Blood Pressure

The religiously inclined don't necessarily have to wait for the hereafter to reap the rewards of faith, health researchers say. In the latest of a series of studies on the theology-biology link, researchers at Duke University discovered a connection between church attendance, Bible study, and blood pressure. Religiously active older people tend to have lower blood pressure than those who are less active, the researchers concluded.

But anyone hoping to take advantage of the links had better practice religion the old-fashioned way. One finding was that people who tuned in to religious television and radio had higher blood pressure than those who did not. The researchers examined the health and habits of almost 4,000 randomly selected people 65 and older in an overwhelmingly Protestant area of North Carolina during a six-year period. People who attended religious services at least once a week posted lower readings than those who attended less often.

The twenty-four page article on which this story was based was published in the *International Journal of Psychiatry in Medicine,* in July 1998, with the title "The Relationship Between Religious Activities and Blood Pressure in Older Adults." The article was coauthored by six scientists, four of whom were medical doctors.

Note first that the newspaper headline has more punch than the title of the journal article. A *link* between two things is, presumably, of more interest than a mere *relationship.* Also, the headline mentions only the link between religion and blood pressure rates; it omits an important qualifying phrase from the title of the journal article, "in older adults." Does the study actually establish a link between religion and blood pressure as the headline claims? Relying simply on what is in the news report, we are in no position to say. Although we are told the age of the experimental and control subjects and where they live, we are given no information about the extent to which other factors were taken into consideration. If the population of the area is "overwhelmingly Protestant," how did the researchers manage to "randomly" select experimental and control groups of approximately equal size? Or did they? We don't know. Look at the report of the results of the study. The experimental group subjects "posted lower readings" than the control group. How much lower? Low enough to be highly unlikely if there is no real link between church attendance and blood pressure? Even assuming the study has uncovered a statistically significant difference between the blood pressure measurements of the two groups, no explanation is given for the link. It may be due to a third factor. The last sentence in the story gives us a clue that we may be on the right track here: Regular church attenders have lower blood pressure than those who do not attend regularly. Perhaps a number of nonattenders don't attend because they have health problems.

All the questions we have just raised are patiently and carefully answered in the original journal article. The difference in blood pressure rates for the two groups was statistically significant, though it was not a large difference. (The difference was reported as "small but significant.") The experimental and control groups were controlled for age, race, gender, education, physical functioning, and body mass index. The researchers considered a number of possible explanations for the apparent link, among them, the one ventured in the newspaper story. (Among the five possible explanations they considered, one of the more interesting was that religious people tend to be more compliant and so would be more likely to follow the recommended medical treatment.) The researchers were careful to conclude that there appears to be a link between blood pressure and church attendance but that more research is needed to establish this. They also concluded that the explanation for the relationship is not fully understood.

As this example suggests, it is always a good idea to pause and think critically about the details of popular media accounts of causal research (the facts and figures that are missing as well as the ones that are included!). As a rule of thumb, the briefer the story, the more likely it is to have omitted facts and figures necessary for us to know what to make of the study. Beware also of the headlines accompanying such stories. Chances are good the results of the study have been exaggerated simply to attract our attention.

The following essay is by Dr. Marcia Angell, executive director of the *New England Journal of Medicine.* It seems we Americans tend to do a poor job of estimating health risks even when we have at our disposal the information needed to determine that risk. As you will see, Dr. Angell believes the news media contribute to this problem via their tendency to exaggerate and over-simplify in covering medical research.

Americans follow news of medical research as closely as sports or the stock market.

We are particularly avid for new findings about the health effects of diet and how we live, because we've come to believe no one gets sick anymore just because of bad luck.

Instead, we see health as mostly a matter of doing the right things, with the corollary that illness is a failure of some sort.

If we can keep up with all the new research and change our habits accordingly, we will stay well.

At the *New England Journal of Medicine,* where I am executive editor, we often witness the impact research papers can have on the general public.

No sooner do we publish a study than news of its conclusions, but virtually none of its qualifying details, hits the airwaves. Within 24 hours, millions of people consider exercising and eating fewer egg yolks or more oat bran to fend off disease.

This meritocratic faith ignores one critical fact: Science has hardly begun to touch the big medical mysteries about diet and lifestyle. We simply do not know much about what is risky and what isn't.

What we do know often is distorted or misinterpreted. Most Americans are not good at distinguishing big risks from little ones, or risks based on solid evidence from those that aren't. We're likely to react to all reported risks in the same way, or choose which to respond to, on the basis of irrational fears or the prominence given them on the 6 o'clock news.

continued

Our problems in evaluating risks were evident in the controversy about mammograms for women in their 40s. In January, many people were outraged when a National Institues of Health panel of experts didn't recommend regular mammograms for women in this age group.

The panel reviewed the evidence and concluded that regular mammograms from 40 to 49 would at best save the life of only one woman among every 1,000 screened. Offsetting that benefit would be the increased risk of cancer from the extra radiation, perhaps three more cancers for every 10,000 women screened.

So small would be the payoff of regular mammograms at this age that the risks of driving the car to get them might outweigh the benefits of the test.

Despite the complexities and ambiguities, many people reacted to the panel's statement as though its members had callously sentenced large numbers of women to death from breast cancer.

The reaction was so intense that in March a second panel reversed the first one's recommendation.

One reason for the outrage was the disproportionate fear of this disease. Even though breast cancer is the most common cause of cancer death in women in their 40s, the disease has affected fewer than 2 percent of women in this decade. After the age of 50, the death rate from breast cancer rises rapidly, but during a woman's lifespan, it lags behind lung cancer deaths and never comes close to the death rate from heart disease.

Heart attacks kill about six times as many women as breast cancer. Still, many women fear breast cancer far more. Because of this fear, the risk seems much larger than it is.

Not only are our fears often disproportionate to the size of the risk, but they might have little to do with whether there is good evidence of any risk.

Some risks are a lot better grounded than others. The evidence that smoking cigarettes causes lung cancer is incontrovertible. It has been found consistently in multiple studies of various types over many years. But not many risks are established by such clear-cut evidence.

Smaller risks might be difficult to demonstrate, and often the research is inconsistent or even contradictory. One research study indicates a risk; another on the same subject does not.

What is a health-conscious American supposed to believe?

Seeking the Quick Fix

A big part of the problem is unrealistic public expectations. Many people want science to provide quick, unequivocal answers with immediate implications— not just get it right, but get it right the first time. If only it were that easy.

Unfortunately, inconsistency is common in medical research, particularly epidemiological research about diet and lifestyle. Such studies are exceedingly difficult, and often factors that can't be controlled distort the results.

continued

Instead of becoming frustrated or feeling betrayed by the disagreements, we should see them as a message to be more cautious about accepting the results of any study in the first place. Inconsistency teaches scientists to be cautious, and there is no reason why the public can't learn the same lesson.

In general, scientists and doctors do not embrace the conclusions of one epidemiological study until they are supported by other studies. Only with a fairly large body of evidence are we able to evaluate risks. When multiple studies still can't give an answer, the risk being studied is probably small— or nonexistent.

Journalists, and even scientists, are partly responsible for the way risks are inflated or distorted in health news. Not surprisingly, news of a big risk attracts more attention than news of a small or uncertain one. Reporters naturally would rather have a story that attracts notice than one that doesn't.

The quality of health reporting is highly variable. Some of it is excellent, but many reporters succumb to the temptation to exaggerate. Even if reporters are appropriately circumspect, their headline writers might have other ideas and blow medical stories out of proportion. (The word *breakthrough* is a favorite of headline writers.)

The sound-bite culture of television lends itself to hyperbole, and scientists and their research institutions are increasingly seeking the limelight. Public-relations offices distribute inflated news releases of research results, and scientists are pressured by their institutions and professional societies to present their findings to the media.

Under these circumstances, some researchers find it difficult to resist overstating the significance of their work.

Different Expressions

The way risks are expressed, by scientists and journalists, also influences their impact on us. Framed in a certain way, a small risk can look big. Take the study that found postmenopausal estrogen is associated with a 30 percent increase in the risk of breast cancer. That sounds like a lot.

But the same risk can be expressed in much less alarming ways. For example, because we already know 3 percent or 4 percent of postmenopausal women will get breast cancer in the next 10 years, we could say this study shows estrogen increases the risk to 5 percent.

To put it another way, if you are a postmenopausal woman trying to decide whether to take estrogen, this study shows that your chances of remaining free of breast cancer for 10 years would decrease from more than 96 percent to about 95 percent.

These equal ways of expressing the same finding have different psychological effects, even though they're saying the same thing.

There's another reason for confusion about risks: Without anyone admitting it, the focus in health care is shifting from the individual to whole populations,

continued

and that changes how risks are assessed. The new emphasis on groups is partly a result of increasing concern about national health care expenditures and the cost of covering people through managed care.

Payers of benefits want to know what health recommendations will make the biggest difference to the group as a whole. But risks and benefits that are important across a large population are not necessarily of much importance to an individual.

For example, a research study a decade or so ago showed that using a drug to lower blood cholesterol in middle-aged men with high cholesterol levels reduced their seven-year risk of heart attacks from 8.6 percent to 7 percent.

Although this tiny improvement might not seem worthwhile to an individual, particularly if it means taking a drug with side effects, when spread over the estimated 1 million to 2 million Americans with similar cholesterol levels, it could account for about 32,000 fewer heart attacks during the first seven years.

The switch in emphasis from personal to public health gives individuals exaggerated notions of what changes in diet or lifestyle can do.

Many people believe high blood levels of cholesterol are virtually a death sentence, while low cholesterol means they will be forever free of heart disease. They hear the public health message and unthinkingly apply it to themselves, making great changes in their habits and diets for little individual gain.

What Does It Mean to Me?
So what should we make of the constant bombardment of news about health risks? The short answer: We should be a lot more wary.

Unless the risk is large, the results make sense and the change in lifestyle would be minimal, there is no reason to change habits on the basis of one study. We should wait until the risk is confirmed by other research, then ask ourselves how the findings apply to us.

We also should remember medical journals publish works in progress for other scientists and doctors. The papers are not meant as the final word for the public.

We all want to believe changes in the way we eat and live can greatly improve our health. But with our current state of knowledge, the likelihood is—with a few exceptions such as giving up smoking—many, if not most, changes will produce only small effects (and large profits for the burgeoning industries that thrive on health promotion).

There's more to life than fretting about health risks.

CHAPTER SUMMARY

1. A **generalization** is a claim about features common to a group or collection. Generalizations can be claims to the effect that all or none of the members of the group have the feature(s) in question. Limited generalizations claim that a portion of the group have or don't have the feature(s) in question.

2. A generalization can be established by investigating the things over which the general claim ranges. This is most often accomplished by sampling. **Sampling arguments** take the form

X percent of the sampled A's are B's.

X percent of all A's are B's.

The results of a sampling argument should be qualified to reflect margin of error. **Margin of error** is based on sample size and provides information about the chances a sample mirrors the population from which it was taken.

3. To be **reliable,** a sampling argument must satisfy three criteria:
   i. The sample must be sufficiently large.
   ii. The sample must be representative of the population from which it is taken. To ensure representativeness, each member of the sample must be drawn at random, subject to any necessary stratification.
   iii. Techniques used to elicit information from the sample must be unbiased.

4. Causes may pertain to singular events or to classes of events. They may be causative or preventive, and a single event may be the result of several causal factors. Causation is not an all-or-nothing business. Not everything exposed to a causal factor will necessarily come to have its effect.

5. Two factors, A and B, are correlated when B occurs at a different frequency in A's and non-A's or when a regular variation in A is matched by a fairly regular variation in B. Correlations of the latter sort are called concomitant variations. Alone, the evidence of a correlation is not sufficient to establish a causal link.

6. The first step in trying to decide whether a causal link exists between two events is to think about rival explanations for the effect. The apparent link may be due to coincidence. The link may be real but explicable in terms of other, intervening factors. Occasionally, cause and effect may be reversed.

7. The method by which causes are most often investigated is the causal study. In a **causal study,** subjects who have the suspected cause (the experimental subjects) are compared to others (control subjects) who lack it, in an attempt to determine whether different levels of the effect obtain. The effectiveness of a causal study is entirely dependent on the degree of success in controlling for other factors that might result in the effect under investigation. The results of a study are reported as **statistically significant** when a difference in levels of effect is unlikely to be due to sampling error.

8. Three common types of causal studies are
   i. *Randomized experimental studies:* A single group of like subjects is randomly divided into experimental and control groups and only the experimental group is subjected to the suspected causal agent.

    ii. *Prospective causal studies:* Groups are selected who have and lack the suspected cause and are tracked over a period of time to see whether different levels of the effect emerge.

    iii. *Retrospective studies:* Groups are selected who have and lack the suspected effect. Their histories are checked in a search for different levels of the suspected cause.

The most reliable evidence of a causal link is provided in randomized studies; the least, in retrospective studies.

9. Be wary of popular media reports of causal studies. Such reports tend to leave out important facts and figures and often exaggerate the significance of the findings.

FALLACIES INVOLVING GENERALIZATIONS

Hasty generalization   Occurs when a generalization is based on a sample that is too small, unrepresentative, and biased. Hasty generalization also occurs when the generalization is not properly qualified in light of the statistical evidence provided in the sample or when a generalization is based on anecdotal evidence.

    Example: In a random poll of 500 people taken recently in Grants Pass, Oregon, 82 percent of those interviewed said the federal government should not reduce the amount of public land available for logging. Clearly, a vast majority of Americans favor current logging policies. [*an unrepresentative sample—all the people polled live in an area economically dependent on logging.*]

Stereotypical thinking   Thinking about a person in terms of a stereotype rather than individual characteristics.

    Example: He can't be too intelligent. He's on the football team.

Special case   A conclusion is drawn about an individual case that, for some reason, is not the sort of case the generalization is designed to encompass.

    Example: Sorry. You can't borrow my car just because you've got to get your husband to the emergency ward. Ben Franklin said it best: Neither a borrower nor a lender be.

CAUSAL FALLACIES

Inference from a correlation to a causal link

    Example: Don't tell me religion isn't an important source of moral value. Studies show that in the past two decades church attendance has declined dramatically in this country. At the same time, there has been a steady increase in divorce, illegitimate births, and violent crime.

Inference based on temporal succession

    Example: Last night I dreamed that we would have a surprise quiz in class today. And guess what? When I walked into class this morning, my teacher announced that we were going to have a quiz. And this is not the only precognitive dream I've had.

Failure to impose controls

    Example: There's got to be something to chiropractic medicine. A study done recently revealed that 70 percent of all people who go to chiropractors for low-back problems report significant improvement within thirty days.

EXERCISES

A. Many of the passages below involve fallacious arguments both for and from generalizations and for the existence of causal links. Some involve misapplications of the statistical concepts discussed in this chapter rather than a specific fallacy. Some passages contain more than one problem, and you may find instances of fallacies from the previous chapters as well. First, decide whether the argument of a passage involves a generalization or a purported causal link. Next, give an explicit statement of the argument's premises and conclusion. Then comment on the mistake(s) you suspect the argument commits.

   i. Decide what is at issue. Is the passage about a generalization? A causal link?

  ii. Put the argument in standard form for arguments of the appropriate type when possible. In any event, give an explicit statement of the argument's premises and conclusion.

 iii. Comment on the fallacy or fallacies you discern in the passage.

(Solutions to Exercises 3 and 30 are given on page 249.)

1. Over the years, I have noticed that the students enrolled in my courses who attend class regularly tend to achieve high scores on my exams. No doubt this is a testimony to my teaching ability.
2. You don't know how long to cook pasta? Call Gino. He's Italian.
3. Yesterday, as I walked into my office, I noticed somebody leaving whom I didn't recognize. And when I looked for my briefcase later that day, I couldn't find it. All I remember about the guy who took it was that he was about six feet tall, had long blond hair, and seemed to walk with a limp. He shouldn't be too hard to find.
4. People over age sixty-five tend to be very poor drivers. How often have you passed a car meandering along in the fast lane, only to discover a little gray-haired man or woman hunched intently over the wheel?
5. Whoever is elected President in the year 2000 had better be very careful. Only a fool would ignore the fact that every President since Lincoln who was elected in a year ending with "0" either has died while in office or has been the victim of an attempted assassination.
6. One thing I know for sure. The next time I get a chain letter, I'm sending it on. I got one last week that said bad luck would come my way if I didn't mail the letter to others. I ripped it up and guess what happened. The next day I was laid off. Better safe than sorry, I say.
7. The clerks at the music store down the street are incompetent. I went in a couple of days before Christmas to buy a few CDs and it took me half an hour to get any service. What do they do? Spend half their time on coffee breaks and the other half gossiping with one another?
8. If strong law enforcement really prevented crime, then those areas where community policing were in effect would be the least likely to have high crime rates. Actually, the reverse is the case, for in those areas with high concentrations of police, serious crimes of all kinds are more common than in other areas where police visibility is much lower.

9. It really ticks me off the way the traffic cops in some states pick on out-of-state drivers. Last year on my vacation I was pulled over for speeding in three different states, and in each case I was just driving along with the flow of traffic. It seems clear to me the police want to ticket out-of-staters, knowing full well they are unlikely to come back, a month or so later, to protest in court.

10. I know, smoking and drinking have their risks particularly if, like me, you are a bit out of shape and a tad overweight. But everything in this life involves a risk. If you play golf, you can be struck by lightning or an errant golf ball. If you are driving to work, you could get in a wreck. But we don't tell people "Don't play golf or drive your car, because these activities can be hazardous to your health."

11. This city never had so much trouble with drugs and street gangs until Hacko was elected mayor.

12. The second law of thermodynamics informs us that everything tends toward a state of randomness and disorder, over time. So, there is no sense trying to keep your house straightened up. It's just going to get more and more disordered as time goes on.

13. The experience of our public schools over the past ten years or so shows the futility of offering courses in sex education. Throughout the '80s and early '90s, the rate of sexually transmitted diseases and teen pregnancies has increased just as has the number of high schools offering courses in sex education.

14. I swear, our local daily paper must have been taken over by the *National Inquirer.* Lately, it's been filled with nothing but sex and violence. In last night's paper, there were five stories in the first section alone that were about lurid sex scandals and violent crime.

15. **Gap Between Candidates Narrows**

    In a poll taken only three weeks ago, mayoral candidate Smith was reported to lead her opponent, Jones, by 12 percentage points. Fifty-two percent of those polled favored Smith while 40 percent favored Jones with 8 percent undecided. A new poll taken this week now reveals that Smith's lead is shrinking. The new poll found that only 50 percent favor Smith while Jones is supported by 43 percent. The gap between Smith and Jones has narrowed by 7 percent in just over two weeks. With the election still more than a month off, it looks like a dog fight.

16. Just last week a student turned in an incredibly sloppy and poorly researched term paper. But, then, what do you expect? He's a P.E. major.

17. There must be something wrong with this coin. It must not be balanced or something. I flipped it half a dozen times and it came up heads on five out of the six flips.

18. The amount of TV a child watches, it seems, is directly linked to scholastic achievement. In a recent study, two large groups of children were examined, all of whom attended school in a large urban school system. The children were asked to have their parents fill out a questionnaire about their TV-watching habits. Children who watched more than three hours per day, as it turned out, had much lower grades and aptitude test scores, on average, than did those children whose parents reported they watched less than three hours of TV per day.

19. I'm going to start shopping at a different grocery store. Whoever is in charge of inventory at my neighborhood store doesn't know how to do the job, and

I'm no longer willing to be inconvenienced by this sort of incompetence. Every time I've shopped there recently, they've been out of something I needed. And usually it's something that's on sale at a very good price. If they can't do a better job, they're not going to get my business.

20. Everybody knows it's best to get a good night's rest before an important exam. I admit I haven't really studied much for my exam, but it's almost 11 P.M. and my final is scheduled for 9 A.M. tomorrow. Time to knock off and go to bed.

21. To the editor: I strongly disagree with the position your newspaper has taken on the issue of dissemination of blood-alcohol test results by emergency room staff. Our health care providers should not become health police. Fortunately, both state and federal law protects persons whose blood-alcohol levels are tested from disclosure of those results to the police. Such protection of patient confidentiality has long been understood to be a necessary component of the therapy a patient needs. If patients come to believe that they cannot talk openly to their doctors and cannot freely authorize their doctors to run tests necessary for their health and safety, patients will feel compelled to be dishonest and to refuse to authorize tests.

    There can be but one legitimate role for the health care provider, whether doctor, nurse, phlebotomist, or lab technician. That role is to treat and cure the patient.

    Consider how you would feel if your disease suddenly became so socially unacceptable as to be illegal. How would you feel if you were forced to choose between obtaining effective health care and giving the police evidence that you had your disease? Keep medical test results from the police.

22. To the editor: Concealed-weapons permits and firearms are up; crimes of rape, robbery, and burglary are down in our state—even though the population has increased. One wonders if criminals are concerned about encountering more people able to defend themselves and their homes, causing some criminals to change their professions. Perhaps there is some truth to the pro-gun/self-defense theory in an increasingly violent society.

23. Many people believe that we can cut down on the number of accidents by reducing the speed limit. However, a careful examination of the fact reveals that this is not the case. Consider these statistics from the National Highway Traffic Safety Administration about the speed involved in U.S. automobile accidents in 1993:

20 mph or less	2.0%
25 to 30 mph	29.7%
35 to 40 mph	30.4%
45 to 50 mph	16.5%
55 mph	19.2%
60 to 65 mph	2.2%

Note how few accidents occurred at high speeds. Note also that it is much more dangerous to drive at moderate rates of speed.

24. In William J. Bennett's "The Index of Leading Cultural Indicators," the graph for violent crimes since 1960 takes off like an airplane, as do the graphs for juvenile arrest rates, teen pregnancy (that's more like a rocket trajectory), births to unmarried women, child abuse, teen suicide, single-parent families, and daily television viewing. Meanwhile, SAT scores, the numbers of children living with both biological parents, and infant survival rates all plummet as if the airplane just ran out of gas.

25. To the editor: In more than thirty years of driving trucks over the road, I have lost count of the people I have pulled out of wrecked vehicles, including some that were on fire. Once I pulled a nineteen-year-old girl out of an overturned car that was on fire. Fortunately, she had not had her seat belt buckled, or she would have been trapped in that mess.

    Another time I saw an auto dragged out of a lake. Inside were a mother and a ten-year-old boy, both with their seat belts fastened.

    From years of on-the-scene observations, I have seen the other side of the seat-belt controversy. There is no doubt that on many occasions lives were saved by seat belts. However, from what I have seen over the years, and not from easily obtained statistics, not enough lives are saved to justify making the wearing of seat belts mandatory.

26. UFOs must be propelled by some sort of electromagnetic source. On the night of the big power blackout in New York City, there were a number of reports of UFO activity in the area.

27. We have a basic moral obligation not to divulge information given to us in confidentiality. If you tell me something you don't want anybody else to know, and if I agree to keep what you tell me confidential, I have a duty to remain silent. Thus, your honor, I must refuse to tell the court what my friend, Smith, confided in me about his relationship with Jones the night before Jones was murdered.

28. I have noticed that every time I have to deal with a large bureaucracy I end up talking with some mid-level management type who doesn't seem to have the slightest idea what is going on. This kind of incompetence seems to plague every large organization, be it public or private sector. The reason, of course, is quite obvious. As the Peter Principle tells us, people tend to rise to their level of incompetence. Once a person is promoted to a position where he or she is incapable of doing the job, they are stuck for the remainder of their career—stuck doing a job they are incapable of doing well. And this is why, when you get on the phone with a bureaucrat, you might as well give up.

29. Everybody has the right to turn a fair profit from their labors. So, where is the harm in city councilman Edwards's construction company getting the contract to build the new city hall? Edwards has to make a living like everybody else, and I have no doubt his bid was competitive.

30. Soviet radio commentator Vladimir Pozner was interviewed recently by *Advertising Age* about his impression of U.S. advertising. Pozner called attention to what he considered the false claim that tobacco advertising causes people to smoke. "There is no advertising of cigarettes or alcohol on Soviet TV and no advertising of alcohol and cigarettes in magazines or newspapers. But you know as well as I that there is drinking and smoking in the

Soviet Union," Pozner said "I know that advertising has nothing to do with it. The lack of advertising in no way hurts sales of liquor and tobacco, which are state monopolies."

31. A remarkable fact is that many of the great scientists and mathematicians in history have had a deep and abiding interest in music. Einstein, for example, was a devoted amateur violinist, and Newton was said to have been fascinated by the mathematical structure of musical compositions. If you want your child to pursue a career in science, you would be well advised to do everything you can to develop his or her interest in music.

32. Don't tell me I don't know how to pick a winner at the race track. I've had at least a dozen big wins in the past few years.

33. Arturo Toscanini died a few weeks short of his 90th birthday. Leopold Stokowski died at age 95. If you think of symphony conductors as a long-lived group, you are correct. According to a major life insurance company study of 319 conductors living in 1990, 21 were 80 years or older, and 3 were over 90 years old. The study also found that the average life span of a conductor was several years longer than that of people in other occupational groups. The insurance company concluded: "The exceptional longevity enjoyed by symphony conductors lends further support to the theory that work fulfillment and recognition of professional accomplishments are important determinants of health and longevity."

34. In describing his life and the lives of others he met while in prison for similar crimes, Ted Bundy stated that, without exception, the catalyst for these terrible crimes was heavy exposure to hard-core pornography. Can there be any question of the connection between violent crime and pornography?

35. That dowser I hired to tell me where I should drill for water was just amazing. She walked around my property for over an hour with a forked stick pointed straight out in front of her. Then, all of a sudden, the point of the stick started moving and finally pointed right at the ground. I hired a drilling company to bore a hole right at that spot. And wouldn't you know it. They hit water only 250 feet down!

36. *Baseball announcer:* Unbelievable. Look who's up first this inning. The guy who made the spectacular play to end the last inning. Isn't it amazing how often this happens? A guy makes a great play and he comes to bat first the very next inning![2]

37. Like me, a lot of my friends are into exercise. And, like me, they rarely miss a day of work due to illness. Too bad everybody isn't aware of the fact that exercise can keep you healthy.

38. I can't believe Jones's college GPA is only 2.9. Her SAT score was in the top 2 percent for the nation. Obviously, she's just not working very hard.

39. The editors of *Reader's Digest* magazine wanted to test the honesty of the average American and so they conducted the following test in 1995. One hundred and twenty wallets containing $50 each were dropped on the streets

[2] This example is cited in Gilovich, *How We Know What Isn't So: The Fallibility of Reason in Everyday Life,* p. 69.

and shopping malls, restaurants, gas stations, and so on in 12 cities. Included in each wallet was a name, address, phone number, family pictures, and coupons. Of the 120 wallets, 80 were returned with all the money. Here is a breakdown of the results:

Seattle, Wash.	9 of 10 returned
Meadville, Pa.	8 of 10 returned
Concord, N.H.	8 of 10 returned
Cheyenne, Wyo.	8 of 10 returned
St. Louis, Mo.	7 of 10 returned
Boston, Mass.	7 of 10 returned
Los Angeles, Calif.	6 of 10 returned
Las Vegas, Nev.	5 of 10 returned
Dayton, Ohio	5 of 10 returned
Atlanta, Ga.	5 of 10 returned
Houston, Tex.	5 of 10 returned

In response to a query from Ann Landers about the results of the study, a spokesperson for *Reader's Digest* summed up the study as follows:

> Small towns scored 80 percent returns and proved to be more honest than larger cities, with the exceptions of Seattle. Women, it turned out, were more honest than men—72 percent to 62 percent. Young people posted the same overall return rate—the same as the overall rate.[3]

40. Now that you have just about completed this book, you will be pleased to hear that students who have taken this course before you report it is one of the most useful, relevant, and clearly written texts they have had the pleasure to read. I ought to know. I make a point of asking my students about this book once they have completed their course work.

B. The passages below are all taken from popular media reports on causal research. For each passage, answer the following questions:
- What causal hypothesis is at issue?
- What kind of experiment or study is being reported on?
- What crucial facts and figures about the study are missing from the story?
- Given the information at your disposal, what conclusion can you draw about the study? Do you have sufficient information to decide what has been established?

(A solution to Exercise 7 is given on pages 249–250.)

1. Sex offenders are commonly thought to have a high rate of repeat offenses, but a review of 61 studies found that more than 80 percent of the offenders did not commit another sexual crime. Of the more than 23,000 sex offenders whose cases were reviewed, only about 20 percent were found to have committed another offense after four to five years in the community, said R. Karl Hanson, a psychologist in the Corrections Research Department of the Solicitor General

---

[3] "Dear Ann Landers," November 24, 1966.

of Canada. "Those that did reoffend were found to have more prior sexual offenses . . . and had not completed their treatment," he reported in the *Journal of Consulting and Clinical Psychology.*

2. Boys in elementary school who come from more crowded homes have a greater psychological response to stressful situations and wind up taking more days off from school because of illness, research shows. Catherine H. Johnson-Brooks of the University of Colorado and her colleagues reported in the September issue of *Psychosomatic Medicine* that their "analyses indicate that a chronic stressor, such as greater household density, is related to larger increases in cardiovascular responses to stressful circumstances." The researchers monitored the heart rates and blood pressures of 81 sixth-grade boys while the boys completed a series of stressful tests, including mental arithmetic. Information on the boys' homes and the number of days they missed school because of illness came from answers to a questionnaire their mothers completed. The study found that boys from homes that were more crowded than the average showed greater changes in heart rate and blood pressure and more sick days.

3. New research in mice shows that stress caused by changes in social interactions can stimulate a dormant herpes virus to resurface. In a series of experiments at Ohio State University, 40 percent of mice with latent herpes had their virus reactivated when their social structure was reorganized, leading to conflicts among the mice. The virus was most prevalent in the dominant mice, which were involved in the most aggressive social interactions. Mice that had been infected with the herpes virus were subjected to two stressful situations: restraining the animals for portions of eight days and reorganizing the social hierarchy by placing a dominant mouse in a new cage. Only the social reorganization resulted in a significant reactivation of the virus. The findings were published in a recent issue of the *Proceedings of the National Academy of Sciences.*

4. Depression has long been linked to heart disease, but a 29-year study of more than 6,500 people showed that it also significantly increases a person's risk of stroke. People who had five or more symptoms of depression were 66 percent more likely to have a stroke than people who were not depressed, said Susan A. Everson of the Public Health Institute in Berkeley, California. Symptoms include mood disturbances, negative self-concept, loss of energy, and problems with eating and sleeping.

5. Elderly people with higher levels of education are move active, smoke less, are less heavy, and feel a greater sense of control over their lives than their less well educated peers, a study of healthy older adults revealed. The researchers from Harvard and the University of Southern California interviewed nearly 1,200 men and women in their 70s from New Haven, Conn.; East Boston, Mass.; and Durham, N.C. The link between education and health-related factors suggests "that social disparities may continue to affect health outcomes in late life," the researchers said in the September issue of *Psychosomatic Medicine.*

6. In a dramatic and controversial finding, a team of psychologists has reported that left-handed people live an average of nine years less than right-handers. The researchers examined the death certificates of 1,000 randomly selected people. In each case, they contacted next of kin and asked which hand the deceased favored. The results shocked the researchers. The average age of

death for the right-handers in the sample was 75 years; for the lefties, it was 66 years. Among men, the average age of death was 72.3 for right-handers and 62.3 for left-handers. It looks as though longevity is somehow connected to whatever parts of our genetic make-up control which hand we favor.

7. Victims of rape and other serious crimes are at high risk of developing emotional disorders, including post-traumatic stress disorders, depression, phobias, and obsessive-compulsive disorder, a study of nearly 400 women reveals. The effects are strongest for rape and other life-threatening crimes, while robbery and burglary were not linked to an increased risk of any mental disorder, the researchers reported in the fall issue of the *Journal of Traumatic Stress.*

    The researchers interviewed 391 women from Charleston, South Carolina, about their experiences with crime and their mental health symptoms. About three-quarters of them had experienced at least one crime—23 percent had been the victim of rape, 10 percent had been physically assaulted, about 6 percent had been robbed, and 13 percent had experienced a burglary while at home.

8. Lithium, which is widely prescribed for manic-depressive disorders, may be the first biologically effective treatment for alcoholism. The new evidence indicates that lithium appears to have the unique ability to act on the brain to suppress an alcoholic's craving for alcohol. A recent study involved 84 patients, ranging from 20 to 60 years of age, all of whom had abused alcohol for an average of 17 years. Eighty-eight percent were male. Half the patients were given lithium while the other half were given a placebo, a chemically inactive substance. Seventy-five percent of the alcoholics who regularly took their lithium pills did not touch a drop of liquor for up to a year and a half during the follow-up phase of the experiment. This abstinence rate is at least 50 percent higher than that achieved by the best alcohol treatment centers one to five years after treatment. Among the alcoholics who did not take their lithium regularly, only 35 percent were still abstinent after 18 months. Among those who stopped taking the drug altogether, all had resumed drinking by the end of six months.

9. A large new study produced strong evidence that moderate coffee drinking doesn't increase the risk of heart disease. The study of over 45,000 American men by researchers at Harvard University School of Public Health goes a long way toward exonerating coffee as a heart risk factor.

    The researchers queried the men—a group of health professionals age 40 to 75—in 1986 about their coffee-drinking habits. They followed the men for two years and found that men who drank even as much as three or four cups of coffee a day had no higher risk of developing heart disease than those men who drank no coffee at all.

10. Children born in the summer may stand a greater chance of developing dyslexia, a reading impairment that afflicts up to 9 percent of children in the United States, a new study suggests. Richard Livingstone, a psychiatrist at the University of Arkansas for Medical Sciences, reviewed data on 585 boys born between 1948 and 1970 who were referred to a university psychiatric clinic. (Not enough girls attended the clinic to allow for an analysis of their disorders.) A total of 173 boys were found to have dyslexia. Boys born in May, June, or July displayed more than twice the risk of developing dyslexia as boys born in any other month. Births in these three months accounted for

40 percent of dyslexia. Livingstone theorizes that the pattern may result from the exposure of women in the second trimester of pregnancy to influenza or other viral diseases during the late winter.

C. The following problems are intended to challenge your comprehension of the standards for good argument of the two types we have investigated.

1. A key claim in a recent, controversial book on race, intelligence, and social status, *The Bell Curve,* is that

    Highly skilled, high paying jobs require a high IQ.

    Can you devise a strategy for determining whether this generalization is or is not true? That is, can you come up with a sampling argument to test the veracity of this claim?

2. A common belief on the part of many college students (and many college teachers!) is that students who sit in the front of the class tend to do better. Devise a randomized causal study, a prospective causal study, and a retrospective causal study to investigate the purported link between seating location and academic success. In designing your studies, consider ways of controlling for other suspected causal factors.

SOLUTIONS

Exercise A

3. *Fallacious causal inference.* More precisely, the fact that one thing occurs before another is taken as evidence the first is the cause of the second. I saw somebody leave my office, discovered the missing briefcase, and immediately concluded that the person I saw must have taken my briefcase. In fact, something very much like this happened to me a few years ago. I was a little embarrassed to find my briefcase in my car later that day.

30. Pozner has performed a kind of "real world" causal study. He claims that advertising does not have an effect on alcohol and cigarette consumption and bases this claim on a comparison of two countries, only one of which allows advertising. The fact that Soviet citizens as well as Americans smoke and drink is taken to be evidence that there is no causal link between advertising and cigarette and alcohol consumption. The big problem is with Pozner's control group, the citizens of the (former) Soviet Union. He provides no reason to believe there may not be other factors that influence smoking and drinking or that the factors are equally represented in both populations. Pozner is guilty of a *fallacious causal inference.*

Exercise B

7. *What causal hypothesis is at issue?* The hypothesis is that rape and other life-threatening crimes cause emotional disorders.

    What kind of experiment or study is being reported on? It is hard to say. Were the researchers looking into the background of women who suffered emotional disorders? If so, the study is retrospective. Did they look just for evidence of these two factors in a large group? If so, all the study has uncovered is some initial evidence for a correlation between being the victim of a violent crime and suffering a mental disorder.

What crucial facts and figures about the study are missing from the story? The passage gives us sufficient information to determine what sort of study was undertaken. No mention is made of experimental and control groups. We also get no information about the mental health of the 25 percent who had not been victims of serious crimes nor about differences in the mental health status of those who had been victims of crimes not classified as life threatening

Given the information at your disposal, what conclusion can you draw about the study? Do you have sufficient information to decide what has been established? This story is so sketchy that we can conclude very little. Given the lack of information about those women who were not victims of serious crimes, we cannot even decide whether the study uncovered evidence of a correlation. Of course, this does not mean that the study was poorly designed or carried out. The report on the study, however, is quite poor.

CHAPTER TEN

Reason, Rhetoric, and Emotion:
The Fine Art of Manipulation

The use of argument is but one method of getting others to do and believe things. Persuasion can also be accomplished by manipulation, the topic of this chapter. We engage in **manipulation** when we attempt to secure compliance by means the audience we are intent on influencing is not aware of, rather than by the give-and-take of argument. Manipulation can be difficult to detect, for although it is by nature coercive, it is not overtly coercive. A threat, for example, is much too obvious to be manipulative. Rather, we are being manipulated when we are subtly steered in the direction of a particular decision, though in such a way that we believe the decision to be our own.

Strictly speaking, this final chapter is slightly out of kilter with the aims and interests of a book on fallacious reasoning. The persuasive techniques we will examine can and often do succeed when they should not. This much they have in common with fallacies. Nevertheless, we cannot really classify them as fallacies. A fallacy is an argument, albeit a mistaken one. Manipulation, by contrast, is a distinctively nonargumentative method of persuasion.

Manipulation can appeal to our rational faculties or to our emotions. A type of rational manipulation occurs, for example, when an arguer attempts to get the audience into a frame of mind that will predispose them to accept his or her argument. This can be accomplished in a number of ways; one of the more effective is to convince the audience of the arguer's objectivity. If I can get you to trust my judgment, I can probably get you to trust my arguments. Or manipulation can have just the opposite effect; it can involve an attempt to undercut the veracity or objectivity of an opponent. Manipulation can involve a kind of misdirection, getting the audience to overlook deficiencies in a presentation by directing their attention elsewhere.

The techniques just mentioned all involve manipulating the rational sensibilities of an audience. Common sense suggests, for example, that the appeals of an objective, disinterested presenter are more credible than those emanating from a biased point of view. To insinuate objectivity on the part of the arguer, or bias on the part of an opponent, is to exploit our instinctive sense of what credible persuasion should involve. But manipulation does not always play on our rational sensibilities nor need its goal simply be to gain a rhetorical advantage. Manipulation can and frequently does involve bypassing our rational faculties by appealing directly to our emotions.

Perhaps you have been on the receiving end of this sort of manipulative appeal: "Of course, it's up to you to decide whether to go to college. But I'm sure you are aware how much it would mean to your father if you went on to get your bachelor's degree." This appeal operates by exploiting your feelings for your father as a means of gently pushing you in the direction of a particular decision. The author of the appeal is trying to influence your decision by playing on the guilt you will no doubt feel if you disappoint your father. We could, of course, represent this appeal in premises-conclusion form.

> If you don't go to college, you will disappoint your father.
>
> You don't want to disappoint your father.
> _____
>
> You should go to college.

But representing it this way doesn't give us a real sense of what is going on or why the appeal is effective. The author's aim is to exploit your feelings for your father, not to provide you with a set of reasons you ought to go to college. Thus, to understand the appeal we must consider how the appeal is designed to achieve its intended effect.

Don't be misled by the fact that manipulation operates by influencing the rational sensibilities and emotions of an *audience*. What comes to mind when we think of an audience is generally a sizable group. The target of a manipulative appeal may be as large as a nation, in the case of the appeals made in the heat of a political campaign. But it may consist of a single person, as in a one-on-one sales pitch or the kind of appeal just discussed. As we investigate fallacies of manipulation, we will be concerned to understand exactly how such techniques work. To do this, we must learn to shift our point of view in order to see things from the audience's perspective. This should not be difficult to accomplish, since we are all, from time to time, victims of manipulation.

EMOTION AND REASON

Our decisions are often influenced by our feelings. I might, for example, decide to contribute to a charity out of a sense of compassion for those the funds will help. Or I might mow the lawn of the elderly lady next door, partly because I felt guilty when I watched her struggle to mow the lawn a few weeks ago. But are we acting rationally when we allow our emotions to influence our decisions? This question suggests a certain picture of the relation between the rational and emotional elements of our personalities, a picture that implies a tension between the two: A *rational* decision is one arrived at after carefully weighing the facts. To be rational is to be cold, objective, impersonal, and logical. The "human element" is absent from a decision based on entirely rational considerations. By contrast, a decision based on *emotion* often ignores the rational. Such decisions are based on "gut reactions," "hunches," and what our hearts tell us to do. When facts and feelings are at loggerheads, feeling wins out.

Taken one way, this picture can be profoundly misleading. Captain Kirk and Mr. Spock aside, people do not fall into two broad types: those whose lives are dominated by feeling and those dominated by thought and rational reflection. Nor do the majority of our decisions present us with a dilemma—trust your feelings at the expense of reason or vice versa. But taken another way, the picture contains an important insight about the relation of emotion and reason. Many of our decisions will be influenced by both reason and feeling, and occasionally there will be a conflict between the courses of action suggested by the two. But the attendant tension between reason and emotion serves an important function.

Reason, if left unchecked by feeling, can lead us to undervalue the concerns and interests of others affected by our decisions. In making responsible decisions, we must be able to envision how those whom our actions will impact might feel; this we do by imagining how we might feel in similar circumstances. Moreover, our deepest moral commitments—to fairness, decency, openness, and the like—have a distinctly emotional component. We believe in fairness in part because we have a deep emotional attachment to this notion. Instances of unfair treatment often prompt a decidedly emotional response that predisposes us to resist appeals inconsistent with our basic sense of fairness.

Much the same can be said for emotion, unrestrained by reason. We meet somebody and our initial "gut" reaction is that there is something about him or her we don't like. Yet, more often than not, such impressions turn out to be unfounded. And here lies a real danger of allowing decisions to be controlled by emotional reaction. If my instincts tell me, for example, that there is something untrustworthy about a candidate for public office, I will be unlikely to give that candidate a fair hearing. Emotion, it seems, can benefit by the occasional course correction reason can provide.

EMOTIONAL MANIPULATION

Not long ago, I decided to buy a new vacuum cleaner and so made a trip to a local appliance store. The salesperson who greeted me told me a little about a number of brands and models and then suggested that a particular, rather expensive, model was just what I needed. I was not convinced; I have bought cars that cost less. The salesperson, sensing my disenchantment, proceeded to give me a half-hour demonstration of the abilities of this and another, less expensive, model. He spread dirt and debris on the showroom floor and demonstrated the superior cleaning ability of the more expensive model. He cleaned under couches and chairs, up and down steps. He vacuumed pillows, chairs, throw rugs, drapes, and blinds, all with great enthusiasm for his favored model. I must confess, I was impressed. "Anyone who would work this hard deserves to make a sale," I thought to myself. "And anyhow, this machine looks to be a pretty good one." As you have probably guessed, I did purchase the more expensive vacuum cleaner, plus an amazing assortment of attachments. Looking back on the episode, I now see I was manipulated by a clever, sophisticated salesperson. Although at the time of the transaction I believed my decision was purely rational, it was prompted more than anything else by a desire to reward the efforts of the salesperson. He worked so hard at his demonstration and was so enthusiastic about his product. He certainly would have been deeply disappointed had I rejected his professional advice, or so I thought. You don't suppose, do you, that the salesperson had any idea these thoughts might be running through my mind?

Appeals like the one just described attempt to influence our decisions by exploiting our feelings, not by advancing a discernible argument. Was the vacuum cleaner a good buy? A good product? Maybe. But my decision to purchase the vacuum cleaner was not made on the basis of the answers to these questions; it was made, ultimately, on the basis of my feelings. Situations like this are not uncommon. You have no doubt watched countless TV commercials designed to manipulate our feelings and little more. A telephone company might, in the space of a thirty-second commercial, paint a warm and moving portrait of an extended family bound together by the link of their holiday phone conversations. We like what we see and hear, and we sympathize with the players in the little mini-drama as it unfolds before us. "Reach out and touch someone," we are told as the drama comes to an end. So, why should we purchase our long-distance phone service from this particular company? Does it charge less than other companies? Does it provide better service? The TV ad conspicuously avoids answering these important questions. But, of course, the intent of the ad is not to make a factual case. It is designed to elicit a particular emotional response, nothing more.

Emotional appeals are often intertwined with arguments, particularly arguments on highly charged topics, like abortion, animal rights, and physician-assisted suicide. When we encounter an argument on such a topic, it is worthwhile trying to determine whether the arguer is engaging in emotional manipulation. Consider this lengthy argument:

> Should the terminally ill have the right to decide the moment of their own death and to be assisted, if necessary, in bringing their life to an end? At the age of ninety-three my grandmother suffered a final debilitating stroke, which left her paralyzed from the waist down and unable to control many of her bodily functions. After that day she lived in constant, intractable pain. We all knew the end was near. And so did grandmother. One morning shortly after her stroke, in a moment of complete lucidity, my grandmother calmly informed me she wanted to bring an end to her suffering. She said she had lived a good and full life but that she was tired of fighting and she felt that her time had come to leave this world. I know my grandmother well; this was not a spur-of-the-moment decision. She had lived an active life and wanted to make this one final choice. Yet her doctor and family could do absolutely nothing other than stand by and watch her suffer. In the ensuing weeks, my grandmother was never again completely lucid. Every once in a while she would open her eyes and look in my direction. I will never forget that look. She was pleading with me: Please let this end. I wish I could say her death was serene and peaceful, but it was not. My grandmother's last few days were filled with pain and helpless struggle against the inevitable. Her death did not come with the kind of dignity she so desperately wanted. As for me and my family, we firmly believe her life was over long before that moment at which her struggle finally and mercifully came to an end.

This passage is moving and no doubt accurately records the facts of the incident it relates. Although the story it tells is emotionally charged, the passage does not seem to be designed simply to arouse our sympathies. Nevertheless, as an argument for the legalization of assisted suicide for the terminally ill, it does seem to be manipulative. We are provided a single, heart-wrenching example in which many would agree that ending a life would be the decent, humane thing to do. But if what is at issue is a policy allowing for assisted suicide, a single case provides a very weak rationale. A number of important issues would need to be addressed in an argument for the legalization of assisted suicide. What exactly is being proposed? Just how near to death

> **CONUNDRUM**
>
> Emotional manipulation can be a powerful persuasive device, even in the absence of argument. One troubling feature of manipulation is that it tends to be deceptive; to manipulate an audience into making a decision is to circumvent the need for rational deliberation or choice, often without the audience being aware of what is going on. In most cases, we would deplore this kind of tactic. But are there circumstances in which we would be morally justified in engaging in emotional manipulation and, hence, deception?

need one be before assisted suicide is permitted? What guarantee is there that such a policy would not be abused, particularly in the case of the terminally ill who are not competent to make life-ending decisions? Would others—family members or physicians—be allowed to make such decisions for incompetent patients? What of the liability of those who assist in ending a life?

The net effect of the appeal contained in the preceding passage is to encourage us to formulate our view on assisted suicide without considering these crucial issues. To make matters worse, the emotive force of the case that dominates the passage is likely to discourage reasoned inquiry on the issues. Any response, for example, that disagreed with the sentiment so movingly expressed by this passage would seem cold and calculating. What kind of person could argue against a policy that would have allowed the grandmother to end her suffering with dignity? Though it seems unlikely that the author of this passage intended to manipulate his or her audience, the net effect of the appeal is to elicit an emotional response and little more. The appeal of the passage is, thus, to a large extent irrelevant to the larger issue of permitting assisted suicide. Understanding this, we can attempt to clear away the emotional debris and begin to search for the arguments that need to inform our view on this very difficult matter.

Although just about any emotion can be used to manipulate the sensibilities of an audience, three are particularly common and effective: fear, vanity, and our sense of pity, compassion, or sympathy for the plight of others.

Appeals to Fear

There is nothing irrational about acting out of fear. I might install smoke detectors on every floor of my house, partly out of fear for the potential disaster a fire could cause. Decisions based partly on fear of what may happen may be prudent and entirely rational. My tax accountant, for example, might convince me not to exaggerate my income tax deductions on the ground that I will probably be audited by the Internal Revenue Service; she may even insinuate that she has a duty to cooperate with the IRS if I am called in for an audit.

The use of fear to manipulate our decisions can be quite subtle. Advertisements often take advantage of our fears and insecurities. The implicit message in many ads for personal hygiene products is that we will be less attractive to others if we do not use the breath mint, deodorant, or whatever. Nothing explicitly claimed in such ads says this. Imagine a deodorant ad that includes the line "If you don't use our product, you will smell bad and offend your friends." Instead, the message is conveyed by carefully selected images and, often, innuendo. A TV or print ad shows a picture of a happy, handsome young man taking a shower and scrubbing away with a well-known deodorant soap. The subtle implication is that if you want to be like this guy, you need to use the product in question.

Ads that emphasize the popularity of a product attempt to exploit our concerns about not being accepted. Wear this brand of jeans or drive that model of car and you will be accepted and admired by your peers! Why do I need a phone in my car? One particularly manipulative television ad pictures a women sitting in a parked, disabled car late at night in a secluded and threatening spot. To make matters worse, a violent storm is in progress. Fortunately, she has a car phone and so is able to call for help. As the ad ends, we see a brightly lighted tow truck save the day. That's why I need a car phone.

Appeals to Vanity

Vanity can be a particularly effective tool for manipulation. Appeals that play to our vanities are often called **snob appeal.** Ads that emphasize that a product is not for everyone are good examples of snob appeal. The mustard that is only for those of discriminating taste and the athletic shoes for the really serious runner play to the vanities of the audience for the ads. I once received a letter from a textbook publisher. The aim of the letter was to convince me to adopt one of its books in a class I teach. In other words, it was a sales pitch. The letter opened:

> Dear Professor Carey:
>
> I am writing to invite you to become a member of the editorial board that is being appointed to evaluate the current edition of . . . . Two well-qualified professors in each region of the nation will be serving on this board. By accepting this invitation, you will join a distinguished group of educators.

Of course, to join this distinguished group, I would have to order a large number of copies of the book in question. Quite a compliment. But at any rate, if I bite, I'll be joining a select group. Only two well-qualified professors from each region of the nation will be selected to serve with me on the editorial board. By the way, just how big do you suppose a "region of the nation" is? My guess is that any place where two "well-qualified" professors order the book in question constitutes a region.

Appeals to Pity, Sympathy, and Compassion

If we see someone suffer an embarrassing or disappointing moment, we naturally feel sympathy for him or her. If the suffering is more prolonged or intense, we may feel pity or compassion, depending on how closely we identify with the object of our feelings. I may feel pity for one whose plight I know I will never experience but compassion for those whose suffering I have some capacity to share.[1] Manipulation

---

[1]For a more detailed treatment of the differences among appeals to pity, sympathy, and compassion, see *Appeal to Pity—Argumentum ad Misericordiam,* by Douglas Walton (New York: State University of New York Press, 1997).

that exploits our sense of pity, sympathy, or compassion takes advantage of these human tendencies. A student who asks a teacher for an extension of a due date for a term paper on the ground that "I'm under a lot of stress right now at home and just need a little more time to get things together," engages in a not-so-subtle form of emotional manipulation. Whether this appeal is designed to exploit the teacher's sense of pity, sympathy, or compassion depends on how the student understands his or her relationship to the teacher.

Many advertisements for charitable causes attempt to exploit our sense of pity. Sympathy and compassion can play a role in such appeals, but pity seems the dominant theme since we are generally asked to contribute to those whose plight is genuinely tragic and whose lives are very different from our own. I recently received a letter from an organization called Doctors Without Borders, USA, Inc. The letter begins:

> Dear Friend,
>
> The tortured African country of Rwanda may no longer dominate the TV news every night, with those horrific pictures of countless bodies. But in the wake of devastating civil war and genocide, let me assure you that Rwanda's agony is far from over—and that is why our volunteers are still there, fighting every day to ease the pain. The scope of suffering is appalling. One of every fifteen Rwandans has been killed—a catastrophe of such magnitude that in a nation the size of the United States, it would mean more than sixteen million dead! Three out of seven Rwandans are homeless and must rely on humanitarian aid to save them from starvation, disease, and despair—and therefore they depend on you and others like you to support humanitarian organizations such as ours.

As you might suspect, the letter goes on to ask for contributions to pay for much-needed medical supplies and services:

> To continue our work, we depend on financial aid from others who share our concern. Your contributions can help us to continue and to give us the moral strength to go on under dangerous and depressing conditions. Together, we can show the world that some of us do care. Please accept our sincere thanks for any help you can give us.

Included with the letter are a series of intensely disturbing and moving photographs, many of thin and emaciated children and of the elderly. All are clearly the victims of almost unimaginable suffering. Several pictures feature doctors and nurses valiantly at work, giving aid to needy Rwandans.

Appeals like the ones in this letter and its accompanying pictures can very effectively play on our sense of pity and perhaps compassion for the plight of others. However, we must not be too quick to reject such an appeal as nothing more than a sales pitch calculated to exploit our feelings. It is hard to imagine any appeal for funds to alleviate the suffering in Rwanda that would not elicit some powerful emotional responses. To its credit, the letter from Doctors Without Borders does not seem to be designed simply to exploit these very natural responses. The letter goes on to document the fact that Rwanda does not have the resources to do much of anything about the plight of its people and that, short of voluntary humanitarian efforts, the suffering in Rwanda will not be abated. Although it gives rise to powerful feelings, the letter does not seem designed simply to take advantage of this.

Enclosed with the material from Doctors Without Borders was a card on which to check off the amount of money to be donated. Options ranged from twenty to five hundred dollars. In very small print at the bottom of the card was the following:

> Unless otherwise noted, your gift will be used by Doctors Without Borders for the project(s) that Doctors Without Borders determines is in need of funds.

This caveat suggests that there may be some manipulation lurking in the appeal. No doubt, there are many places in this world where people suffer and where the assistance of Doctors Without Borders is needed. But the appeal of the letter focused exclusively on Rwanda. The fact that funds are being solicited for use elsewhere makes it look as though the situation in Rwanda may have been selected in part because of its emotional power. A slightly less manipulative approach would mention all the purposes for which donations will be used and perhaps provide an accounting of the percentage of funds donated that are actually devoted to medical supplies and services, not to more fund-raising.

As the last example suggests, the question of whether an argument is guilty of emotional manipulation can be difficult to sort out. As a general rule, an argument is not guilty of emotional manipulation simply because the case it makes gives rise to strong feeling. Rather, manipulation occurs in those arguments that are designed expressly to evoke a particular emotional response. Whatever "facts" are cited are introduced not so much to provide a rationale for the argument's conclusion, but, instead, to push the emotional buttons most likely to illicit the desired response.

REASON AND RHETORIC

Rhetoric is the study of persuasion, particularly the techniques a speaker or writer can use to enhance the persuasive power of his or her arguments. An argument that is poorly written or disorganized will not have much persuasive punch, no matter how strong the evidence provided in its premises. A speaker who is clear, forceful, dynamic, and entertaining stands a much better chance of winning over the audience than one who is obscure, tentative, and dry. Thus, when properly deployed, various rhetorical techniques can be an effective adjunct to a well-reasoned argument. Unfortunately, a skilled rhetorician can often do a lot to persuade his or her audience by the use of rhetoric alone. Speakers and writers who engage in such tactics are guilty of **rhetorical manipulation.**

RHETORICAL MANIPULATION

As noted earlier, to engage in manipulation is to attempt to secure the compliance of an audience by means other than argument and, moreover, by means that may go unnoticed. Rhetorical manipulation can take advantage of a number of strategies. An arguer can try to win the allegiance of his or her audience prior to mounting an argument. In the context of a debate, a speaker might say things to undercut the credibility of his or her opponent. A skilled debater may even be able via a clever rhetorical ploy to direct the audience's attention away from deficiencies in the case he or she is attempting to mount.

Several of the rhetorical techniques we will examine have much in common with two of the fallacies of relevance introduced in Chapter 5: personal attacks and appeals to authority. One very effective way of manipulating the sensibilities of an audience is to make them aware of the speaker or writer's expertise. Another is to find a way to bring into question an opponent's expertise. The former can sometimes be accomplished by an appeal to authority, the latter by a personal attack. Our concerns in Chapter 5 were, first, to acquire a sense of why such claims are often irrelevant to the arguments in which they occur and, second, to distinguish between legitimate and fallacious appeals to personal information or information about the arguer's expertise. Our concern now is to understand the ways in which such information can be used to manipulate an audience.

Establishing Common Interests

Suppose you have a difficult decision to make and want to talk things over with someone. If you are like me, you will try to pick a person whom you believe has your best interests at heart. I would hardly feel comfortable consulting someone who couldn't care less about what happens to me. And, to a large extent, our willingness to accept advice is proportional to our confidence that the advisor is going to be sympathetic to our problem. This fact can be used to manipulate the audience for an argument. If I can convince you that we share a common interest, or a common set of values, I can probably secure your trust. My hope is that you will assume the following: *If his values or interests correspond to mine, and if he believes a claim based on these values or interests, then I too should accept that claim and his arguments in its defense.* Thus, my goal in attempting to establish common interests or values is to manipulate you into setting aside any critical reservations you may have even before I make my case for whatever is at issue.

Common interests, values, and the like can be established in subtle ways. A carefully chosen word or two can do the trick:

> You and I both know the value of working for the things we get. It's people who don't take seriously the responsibility to provide for oneself and one's family that can't understand the need for the welfare reform I want to propose.

Although no argument has yet been given, the audience is now primed to accept whatever comes next. Note that the author of this passage does not refer simply to his or her values, but instead makes arguer and audience parties to a shared set of values. Phrases like "you and I"—phrases involving pronouns intended to jointly identify author and audience—are often used to good effect in establishing common interests. Beware of an appeal that begins

> We all realize that . . .

or

> There are not too many of us here who don't believe . . .

The decision to write or speak in the first-person plural when advancing an argument is often a sign that the author is trying to get us to identify with his or her interests.

Common interests can be established, indirectly, by insinuating that one who holds a contrary view to that at issue does not share our interests, values, sensitivities, and so on. During a debate between two candidates for mayor in the city where I live, one of the candidates began with the following:

> I was born in this city and have lived here all my life. I went to City High School, and probably some of you still remember the state championship basketball team on which I played.

This all sounds quite innocent—we generally like to know something about the personal background of candidates. However, in this particular race, the other candidate had moved to the city from another state less than a year before. Against this background, the preceding remarks take on a new significance. Their author is insinuating, if not overtly claiming, his opponent does not have as much in common with the citizenry as does the author. To understand the effect of this sort of appeal, put yourself in the place of the audience and imagine what you might be thinking at this point. *Perhaps the speaker does not reflect all of my values or views. But at least he has the interests of our community at heart. And, at the very least, he is more likely to share my concerns about the local government than his opponent, who knows little about our city.* The author of the remarks now stands a good chance of winning our allegiance even before the debate has begun.

Emotional appeals can be used to establish common interests. Particularly effective are appeals that exploit our vanities and sympathies. A sales pitch for a new magazine about science and technology might begin its salutation with

> Dear Potential Subscriber:
>
> Because you are among the educational elite—you've worked hard to secure a college degree—we think you will be excited to hear what we have to say about our new magazine. Like you, we realize there is something of a media vacuum surrounding science.

This sort of flattery can be difficult to resist. If the new magazine is indeed written by intelligent people, for intelligent people, what do I say about myself if I do not subscribe? This example suggests that snob appeal can be a very effective device by which to establish common interests between author and audience.

Our sympathies for others with whom we share a common plight can be used effectively to reinforce common interests. If I can convince you that I have been the object of scorn or derision because of beliefs, values, or sentiments that you and I hold in common, I can suggest we are bound together by virtue of facing a common opponent. The following is from a magazine article critical of something called "secular humanism":

> In the humanist tradition, our society has defiled man, becoming so impressed with his intellectual capabilities that it finds difficulty accepting the simple ideas. At the risk of being labeled an oversimplistic, anti-intellectual right-

> **CONUNDRUM**
>
> One way of establishing common interests is to write or speak in the first person with ample references to "you," "I," "me," "we," and "us." By now you are quite familiar with the style in which this book is written. Is its author guilty of engaging in rhetorical manipulation?

winger, let me suggest that much of what ails our society and others can be stated simply.

Here, an attempt is made to get us to sympathize with the author who, at once, holds views similar to the audience and yet is roundly criticized as being "oversimplistic," "anti-intellectual," and a "right-winger" to boot.

Establishing Credibility

The audience for your argument is going to be more likely to accept your position if they have reason to believe it is the result of a fair, balanced, objective investigation of the issues. Nothing can do more to win the respect of an audience. Generally, we will not be successful in convincing an audience of our objectivity by publicly patting ourselves on the back. "Trust me, I've looked carefully at all the facts" is too blatant and transparent to do much to establish credibility. A more effective ploy is to suggest objectivity by insinuating that you at one time held a view at odds with whatever you are currently advocating. So, for example, a car salesman might begin his pitch by admitting that he once worked for the competition and so is intimately familiar with its products. He might go on to confide that he decided to change jobs—to go to work for the competition—so convinced was he of the superiority of the line of cars he now represents. Implicit in the salesman's tale is the claim that his preference is the result of an unbiased study of the data pertinent to the two makes of cars.

A kind of intellectual objectivity can be established in much the same way. Imagine we are attending a debate on the existence of God. One of the speakers steps to the podium and begins:

> You know, I've got to admit something to you. I'm a rather late convert to belief in God. Unlike most of you, I grew up in a family that did not attend church and in which religion was never discussed in anything other than the most derisive of terms. In college, it was fashionable to lampoon people who believed all that religious mumbo jumbo, and I must say, I was right in fashion. We regarded religious belief as not much different from the most primitive and naive of superstitions. In my case, belief in God came almost out of the blue. After college, my job required me to spend many nights on the road. One evening, with nothing much to do, I picked up the small Bible from the nightstand in my motel room. I began reading and, for the first time in my life, paid careful attention to what it had to say.

You can fill in the details, and I'm sure you have figured out where this little story goes next. Note how effectively the speaker has established his or her objectivity and credibility. Anyone who is this intimately aware of the attractions of the opposed view must have arrived at his or her current view on the basis of an objective investigation of both sides of the issue. An argument has yet to be mounted, but the audience is already predisposed to accept the views of one of the debaters! Of course, this tactic could just as effectively be employed by an advocate of the opposed point of view. One can easily imagine the rebuttal portion of the debate opening with

> Well, what can I say. First, I must tell you I grew up in a very religious setting. My mother was an ordained minister and prayer was a daily ritual around our house.

Here we go again!

Undercutting the Credibility of an Opponent

Much as the audience for an argument will be ready to accept the view of one whose credibility is established, they will be equally ready to reject the appeals of one whose credibility is in question. The credibility of an opponent can be undermined in several ways. One effective technique is the use of ridicule or humor. If an opponent of his or her position can be characterized in a humorous way, the implication is that the position need not be taken seriously. In the 1984 presidential election debates, President Ronald Reagan made effective use of this strategy. His opponent, Walter Mondale, persisted in making a single point time and again about increases in government spending during Reagan's first term as President. At first, Reagan tried to defend his record. Mondale would repeat substantially the same complaints. Finally, Reagan turned to the camera, smiled, and said, "There he goes again." The audience laughed. After that, every time Mondale would bring the subject up again, Reagan would, with a twinkle in his eyes, repeat the now-famous line: "There he goes again." The effect of this clever little strategy was to leave the impression that Mondale's complaints were so superficial as to deserve nothing more by way of reply than a fatherly chiding.

An opponent's lack of expertise or education can often be cited to undercut his or her credibility:

> My worthy opponent in this debate is going to try to convince you that chiropractic medicine is unscientific. Does she believe that chiropractors are quacks? Yes. But let's ask a few more questions of my opponent. Is she a chiropractor? No. Has she, like me, observed literally thousands of patients improve as the result of a chiropractic manipulation of the spine? No. Has she even read a textbook on basic chiropractic techniques and theory? Probably not.

It is going to be hard to put much credibility in the words of someone who appears to know as little about the topic as our speaker's "worthy opponent."

A particularly insidious way of undercutting the credibility of an opponent is to suggest that he or she cannot be relied on to tell the truth. This way of undercutting credibility is called **poisoning the well.** If an audience can be convinced that a speaker cannot be trusted to tell the truth, then even the speaker's insistence that he or she is telling the truth will be taken as a ruse. The "well" of the speaker's credibility had been effectively poisoned so that even attempts to establish credibility will be assumed to lack credibility. An opponent's veracity might be called into question by the suggestion that he or she has lied in the past:

> Smith lied to her parents when she was caught red handed taking something from the store. So, what makes you think she is telling the truth now when she says . . .

If we are convinced of Smith's propensity to lie, anything she might say to reassure us now that she is telling the truth is bound to be suspect.

Poisoning the well can be accomplished in much more discrete ways. Someone might suggest that a person's commitment to an ideology outweighs his or her commitment to truth:

> I don't think you can take Rush Limbaugh's defense of the candidate for attorney general seriously. The candidate is a conservative Republican, and so we can expect Limbaugh to try to explain away any charges leveled against her in her confirmation hearings.

Here, the not-so-subtle suggestion is that any argument Rush Limbaugh might give in defense of the candidate is motivated by his political beliefs, not by a desire to get at the truth.

Credibility can be undermined by characterizing a person in such a way that the very act of asserting the veracity of what one says is evidence of deception. Suppose that someone is standing trial for child molestation. The prosecuting attorney might caution the jury:

> Ladies and gentlemen, a sad fact in cases like this is that people who molest children often are incapable of admitting, even to themselves, what they have done. Is it any wonder the accused denies having molested the victim in this case?

If we are prepared to accept the claim that child molesters will steadfastly deny what they have done—that this is part of what it is to be a child molester—the accused's protestations to the contrary will do little more than confirm our suspicions that he or she is guilty of child molestation. By a curious twist of logic, the claim

> I am not a child molester

has become evidence that the very thing denied in the claim is so. This strategy can be a quite effective method of poisoning the well.

Finally, credibility can be undermined by establishing that an advocate stands to gain if the view he or she favors is accepted:

> We can disregard Jones's arguments for extending the city's light-rail system. Is it just a coincidence that his sister's company was the contractor on the last big light-rail project the city undertook?

Jones's well has been poisoned by the suggestion that whatever he says in defense of additional light-rail is occasioned by self-interest, not what is in the best interest of the city. If we are convinced Jones stands to make money in the event the city decides to add to its light-rail system, we may suspect the veracity of any claim he cites in defense of his position.

Irrelevant Thesis

We all have had the embarrassing experience of finding ourselves lost in our arguments. In the midst of a heated dispute, it dawns on us that we have completely lost track of our original train of thought. Though we are arguing and perhaps even doing a decent job, we have lost sight of what originally prompted the argument. Or, if we remember, we can't figure out how we got where we are now in the argument nor what we are arguing now has to do with our original topic. When this happens, we are the inadvertent victims, perhaps even the perpetrators, of a common rhetorical ploy—the introduction of an **irrelevant thesis.** To introduce an irrelevant thesis is, simply, to change the topic. Though many irrelevant theses are introduced innocently and unintentionally, they can also be introduced as a means of manipulating the audience for an argument.

Suppose I am bent on defending a claim but find that my arguments are not particularly effective; it may be that my audience is not convinced or that an opponent is succeeding in countering my arguments. One tactic is to change the thesis at issue; I might simply state another claim, but one I will be able to defend effectively. Once I set about arguing for this new claim, there is a good chance my audience and even my opponent will shift his or her attention to my new, improved argument and lose sight of the original issue. With any luck, I will also steer attention away from my earlier difficulties. This tactic can be particularly effective if I can manage to do a credible job of defending my new thesis, for my audience will soon become focused on trying to follow and perhaps counter my new battery of arguments.

Imagine, for example, a debate on the merits of a proposed new tax on cigarettes. Suppose also that one party to the debate has done an effective job of convincing the audience that cigarettes are an addictive drug and so should be regulated by heavier taxation. By levying a heavy tax on tobacco, we can discourage new users. An opponent, frustrated by his or her inability to counter this argument, might respond:

> Don't keep insisting that smoking is an addiction. The decision to smoke cigarettes is one people make of their own free will. I have yet to meet a person who admits to having been forced to start smoking.

This new thesis—that people freely choose to smoke—may be much easier to defend. But it is not the thesis at issue. The question of whether smoking is addictive is independent of the question of whether people freely choose to smoke, for it is easily possible that both claims are true. This example illustrates a further point about effective deployment of an irrelevant thesis: If the audience for an argument is to be manipulated into losing sight of what is at issue, it is important that the new thesis be relevant to the topic at issue. The new thesis must appear to involve an issue whose resolution will be relevant to the debate. An audience would not fall for the "bait and switch" of the following:

> Don't tell me smoking is an addiction. My grandfather smoked for some forty years and never had a sick day in his life.

Although this appeal is, loosely speaking, on the topic, it plainly has nothing to do with the claim at issue. Thus, an effective instance of irrelevant thesis must make use of information that is not plainly irrelevant to the topic at issue.

Criticism can be deflected by judicious insertion of an irrelevant thesis. Although contrived, the following passage typifies the kind of exchange that often occurs in political debate:

> My opponent in this race wants to know how I voted on the balanced-budget amendment when it came before the Senate. But what I want to know is why she is so opposed to spending to keep our military strong.

The strategy here is quite transparent. The candidate has simply ignored the issue of his or her vote on the amendment under discussion and has moved on to something else. Nevertheless, this tactic can be effective, more from persistence than from stealth. If the candidate continues to insist the opponent's record on military spending ought to be the issue, he or she can probably wear down the audience. Once it is clear the candidate is not going to address the issue of the balanced-budget amendment, the opposition may capitulate and go on to another topic.

Effective counterargumentation can often benefit from the introduction of an irrelevant thesis. If an opposed argument seems well defended and invulnerable to effective criticism, the battle is not lost. It may be possible to introduce a thesis guaranteed to entice the opposition into arguing for a more vulnerable claim. Suppose that a powerful and compelling argument has been mounted against clear-cutting (the practice of removing all timber from a tract of land). The argument makes a strong case that this practice is an environmental disaster. You, on the other hand, are in favor of clear-cutting but have found no points of vulnerability in your opponent's position. You might try the following tactic:

> No doubt, clear-cutting will do some environmental damage. But if you think about it, what doesn't? But this must be balanced against the rights of people to do what they will with the property they own. You have no right to tell any landowners what they can do with their land. If they want to remove all the timber or even pave the cleared land with concrete, that's their own business.

It is hard to imagine an opponent of clear-cutting who would not find this last suggestion appalling and who would not lose sight of the original issue in an attempt to contest the newly raised issue. This tactic is sometimes called **red herring,** a name derived from a technique for training dogs to follow a scent. Legend has it that a bag of red herring would be dragged across the trail to distract the dogs from the original scent.

When an arguer proposes a solution to a problem, an effective, though irrelevant, method of response is to counter by pointing out that the solution is less than perfect. Suppose someone proposed stricter controls on auto emissions as a means of combating air pollution. A reply might take this solution to task:

> Stricter emission controls are not going to solve the problem of pollution. Cars and trucks are only one minor contributing factor. Even if we banned the internal combustion engine, we would still have air pollution from a nearly inexhaustible number of sources.

The point of the original argument is not to suggest that the proposal at issue will eradicate pollution, only that it will lessen the overall level of air pollution. Thus, the claim that stricter emissions standards will not eliminate air pollution is irrelevant. This type of irrelevant thesis is called **unattainable perfection.**[2] The fact that a solution is not perfect is usually irrelevant to the question of whether the solution will do what it is designed to do.

LOGICAL SELF-DEFENSE

In dealing with fallacious arguments, the trick is to spot the mistake involved in the argument. The problem we face when confronted with a manipulative appeal is considerably different. As noted earlier, the most insidious feature of a manipulative appeal is that the audience will be influenced without being aware manipulation has taken place. The key, therefore, to responding to a manipulative appeal is, first, to recognize that the appeal involves manipulation, not rational persuasion and, second, to bring this to the attention of the audience. (Keep in mind, you may be the audience!)

The first thing to do is to understand how the appeal manipulates. Is it designed to play on our emotions? If so, which ones? Does it attempt to undercut or establish credibility? Does it introduce a new thesis as a means of distraction? Second, the appeal may need to be exposed for what it is to an audience. If an appeal exploits emotion, it will probably be counterproductive to point out that the appeal is manipulative. This makes it look as though you lack sympathy—that you are not moved by the emotional aspects of the debate. Instead, point out that the appeal is designed to deflect interest from the issue by playing on the sentiments of the audience. Point out, that is, what the author of the appeal is up to! When manipulation is aimed at undercutting or establishing credibility, again draw attention to the strategy being employed. Often it will be possible to point out how easy it would be to "fight fire with fire," by similarly undercutting the credibility of the person doing the manipulating. After all, how credible is someone who is capable of engaging in this sort of manipulation? If your "well" has been effectively poisoned, your best response is to detail how this tactic works and to then acknowledge the impossibility of a credible response if the audience is convinced of your lack of credibility.

If an irrelevant thesis is introduced, the most effective response is to point out how the new thesis differs from that at issue and explain why it is irrelevant. This can be accomplished by stating both theses and showing how arguments for one are not arguments for or against the other. In presenting an argument, the chances of becoming the victim of an irrelevant thesis can be lessened by making sure your audience knows what you are doing when you are doing it. Reiterate the thesis often enough to keep it in the minds of your audience and let them in on your strategy. If, for example, you are going to mount a second argument, let them know what claim you are supporting and how it differs from the main claim at issue. The last bit of

---

[2]This catchy name was coined by Don S. Levi in *Critical Thinking and Logic* (Salem, Wis.: Sheffield, 1991).

advice is the hardest to follow: *Stick to the point.* Try not to get so involved in the give-and-take of the argumentative process that you lose sight of the main issue. Be ever willing to say, if only to yourself, "That is very interesting, but not what is at issue." Judging by my experience, we are not always going to succeed in resisting the tangents and tangles lurking in nearly every interesting debate. We all will, on occasion, stray from the point. But this is no reason not to try to stick to the point. To think otherwise is to fall prey to one of the manipulative devices discussed earlier, the claim that a proposal involves an unattainable perfection!

MEDIA WATCH: ADVERTISING

At the most basic level, the job of the mass media is to deliver an audience to those who pay the bills—advertisers. Whereas media programming is designed to attract an audience, the ads themselves are designed to get the audience to *do* something: to buy a product or service, to contribute to a worthy cause, to refrain from socially and personally destructive behavior, to support a political candidate, idea, or party. As we shall soon see, advertisers frequently traffic in fallacious appeals, particularly those

---

The following facts and figures will give you a sense of just how big a business advertising is. Unless otherwise indicated, all dollar amounts are for spending in the United States alone.

- Total media advertising spending for 1998: $112.4 billion
- Total spending and per capita spending for the top ten global ad markets for 1998:

United States	$112.4 billion	$379.40 per person
Japan	$37.9 billion	$319.00 per person
Germany	$22.3 billion	$257.90 per person
United Kingdom	$18.9 billion	$284.20 per person
France	$10.6 billion	$174.50 per person
Brazil	$10.1 billion	$48.70 per person
Italy	$7.2 billion	$112.10 per person
Spain	$5.2 billion	$122.40 per person
Australia	$5.1 billion	$255.40 per person
Canada	$4.9 billion	$147.40 per person

- Advertising spending by medium for 1998:

Television	$44.73 billion
Newspapers	$40.57 billion
Magazines	$13.6 billion
Radio	$11.58 billion
Outdoor	$1.91 billion

continued

- Advertising spending by the top ten advertisers for 1997:

General Motors	$2.23 billion
Procter & Gamble	$1.70 billion
Philip Morris	$1.32 billion
Chrysler	$1.31 billion
Ford	$973 million
Pepsico	$797 million
Time Warner	$779 million
Walt Disney	$746 million
Johnson & Johnson	$739 million
Sears, Roebuck & Co.	$734 million

- Spending in the top ten ad categories for 1997:

Automotive	$12.87 billion
Retail	$10.86 billion
Business and consumer services	$9.03 billion
Entertainment and amusements	$5.89 billion
Food and food products	$4.19 billion
Drugs and remedies	$3.98 billion
Cosmetics and toiletries	$3.68 billion
Travel, hotels, and resorts	$2.84 billion
Computers, office equipment	$2.33 billion
Direct response companies	$1.88 billion

- The 1997 cost of a full-page ad in *Reader's Digest,* the largest circulation magazine in the United States (circulation: 15.7 million, monthly):

  $179,000—black and white $208,000—color

- The 1997 cost of a full-page ad in the *Wall Street Journal,* the largest circulation newspaper in the United States (circulation: 1.73 million, daily):

  $137,303—black and white $172,283—color

Source: *Advertising Age* magazine.

Do we, the consumers, benefit from advertising? Perhaps. The high-volume production of nationally advertised brands probably leads to lower prices. But, then, somewhere between a quarter and a third of the cost of a nationally advertised product is due to the cost of advertising and merchandising.

discussed under the headings of relevance and distortion. And, as some of the examples in this chapter suggest, advertisers use manipulation to influence our decisions and behavior.

Irrelevance

Many ads depend on claims that provide little or no relevant information about their products. Particularly common are ads that involve an irrelevant appeal to authority. You've seen, heard, and read numerous ads in which a well-known figure from the world of entertainment, sports, or politics urges us to buy a particular product. Michael Jordan wouldn't be seen on a basketball court without his Nikes. Jerry Seinfeld goes nowhere without his American Express Card. Countless television and print ads for various medicinal products feature actors dressed to look like doctors and laboratory scientists. Phrases like *clinically proven* and *laboratory tested* are thrown in to suggest there is evidence for whatever is being claimed.

The fact that a product has been on the market for a long time is often featured in advertising:

> After 65 years, we're still a soft touch—*MD Toilet Paper*

Is there any reason to think that the length of time a manufacturer of toilet paper has been in business is a factor in determining the relative merits of its product? The number of people who use a product will often be emphasized:

> America's #1 caramels—*Farley's*

Assume this claim is true; assume, that is, that we Americans consume more Farley's caramels than any other brand. This doesn't seem to be much of a reason to prefer Farley's over other brands for it suggests neither that Farley's are better tasting or better for us nor even that they are less expensive.

Distortion

Distortion by omission is a common flaw in advertising and is, perhaps, only to be expected. Advertisers are naturally going to emphasize those facts and features of their products that will make us want to purchase and use them. An ad for a long-distance carrier might highlight the fact that its rate per minute is lower than the rates of most of the competition. It might fail to point out, however, that its lowest rates are not in effect at all times. Many ads involving pseudo-differentiation (see Chapter 2) are guilty of a sort of omission as well. Here is one such claim:

> Nothing cures better—*Mycelex-3*

The impression this ad wants to leave is that Mycelex-3 does whatever it does better than any of its competitors. But what does the ad actually say? Not that Mycelex-3 is better than the competition. Instead, it tells us that none of the competition is better than Mycelex-3. What the ad conspicuously leaves out is whether or not the competitors cure *as well as* Mycelex-3.

One form of distortion that is used heavily, particularly in television advertising, is a close relative of the fallacy of the straw man. The products or services of the competition are lampooned. An ad for an airline shows us a traveler on another airline, wedged into the narrowest of seats, eating a meal from a tiny cardboard box. An ad for a muffler shop features an unhappy customer sitting in the waiting room, covered in cobwebs, at a mythical competitor. The resemblance of such ads to the straw man fallacy stems from the fact that their targets are but caricatures of their real competitors.

Manipulation

Ads do not need to provide reasons or even the pretense of reasons why we should buy their products and services in order to influence our consumer choices. Think for a moment of the Budweiser beer ads featuring a cast of charming frogs and not-so-charming lizards. Or of the Chihuahua that has become the spokesperson or, more accurately, spokes-dog for Taco Bell. The point of these highly successful ad campaigns is clearly not to provide us with a reason to buy Bud or to eat at Taco Bell. The ads grab our attention and amuse us, but they don't tell us anything about the products they are pushing. What they attempt to do is to etch in our consciousness a brand name. This technique is as old as advertising itself and is essentially manipulative. Get consumers to think of a particular brand when they think of a product line. When they are shopping for the products, your brand will come to mind and they will likely choose accordingly.

Humor is but one of many techniques by which brand familiarity can be insinuated. Brand familiarity is the name of the game in various tie-ins between products and movies and the placement of commercial products in the movies themselves. McDonald's will give away figurines from the latest Walt Disney feature-length cartoon; all the cars featured in a James Bond film will be made by the same manufacturer. Powerful visual images, jingles, slogans, and product packaging can be equally effective as a means of establishing a brand name. Who can forget the simple melody accompanying "Oh, I'd like to be an ____ ____ wiener, that is what I'd really like to be"? Need we mention the brand name? Effective product slogans will stick with us long after an ad campaign is over.

> You're in good hands with Allstate.
>
> The Marines are looking for a few good men.
>
> Nike . . . just do it

These are a few of the more memorable ad slogans of the past few years. Simple reiteration of a product name can be an effective means of reinforcing brand familiarity. Print ads often mention a brand name dozens of times. A recent quarter-page ad for Wisk laundry detergent in my local newspaper used the name Wisk seventeen times, including eleven pictures of Wisk containers of various sorts. Well-known music can be used to great associative effect. For years, United Airlines ran television ads featuring breathtaking images of jets soaring in the deep blue sky above the clouds, all against the backdrop of George Gershwin's *Rhapsody in Blue.*

Reinforcing brand familiarity is not the only manipulative technique advertisers use. Ads can influence us (particularly television and pictorial print ads) by sketching pictures of the kind of person advertisers think we'd like to be or of the kind of life we'd like to live. A TV ad for a sport utility vehicle might show us the SUV in question challenging the most hazardous mountain terrains. The driver is a virile out-doors person, doing the things many of us can only fantasize about. Never mind the fact that the average SUV owner rarely drives his or her rig beyond the confines of the city. We'd like to live the life portrayed in the commercial, and that's enough to get many of us in the door at the local SUV dealer.

Ads can also manipulate by getting us to identify with the characters and situa-tions in the vignettes they often spin out. Commercials for detergent and other clean-ing products often portray a harried homemaker struggling to restore the luster to water-stained stemware or to bring out the shine underneath that dirty kitchen floor. Beer commercials tell a tale about two male buddies out fishing or a group of guys bonding around the Monday night football game. These ads are designed for and pitched to the groups of people marketing research has shown are most likely to buy the products in question. The strategy is clear: If people in my situation use this product, I should use it as well. Many ads are designed for a specific audience—teenagers, young children, prospective brides, homemakers, people of a particular ethnic background, and so on—and then run in venues that predictably will attract a lot of people from the group the ad is written for. Ads for toys and candy are run on Saturday-morning cartoon shows. SUV and beer ads are a mainstay of football games. Ads for financial services are featured on televised golf matches.

Our sensibilities can be manipulated by getting us to feel good about the com-panies manufacturing the products and services we are being sold. A TV ad for major league baseball might tell us of the local charities in which several players are involved or devote thirty seconds of air time to urging kids to stay in school. The per-son doing the urging, of course, will be a well-known, highly visible player. Com-panies can entice us to buy their wares by portraying themselves as being socially responsible. A paper manufacturer tells us of its efforts to encourage recycling and to reforest the acreage it has "harvested." (Note the euphemism here.)

Recently, Aurora Foods, the makers of Log Cabin Syrup, introduced a new con-tainer—a plastic syrup bottle shaped like a log cabin. Here is the written copy from the newspaper ad announcing this change:

Now There's a New Look for America's Favorite Log Cabins

We've shaped up our bottle—and helped shape up log cabins in our national parks. Now when you buy Log Cabin® in its unique cabin-shaped bottle, you can help shape up America's historic log cabins. Log Cabin has partnered with the National Park Foundation and will donate up to $250,000 in 1998 to edu-cation and the restoration of the original gatekeeper's cabin in Grand Canyon National Park.

Note the little weasel inserted in the ad. Log Cabin will donate *up to* $250,000. To restoration of the gatekeeper's cabin? Well, to restoration *and* education. What do you suppose is meant by the latter? Note also the number of times the words *log* and *cabin* appear in this brief ad. The ad also features a "25 cents off" coupon on which is prominently displayed the touching slogan "In the heart of every home, there's a little log cabin." The syrup bottle pictured in the accompanying ad says on its label, "Log Cabin Original Syrup—A family tradition since 1887."

Boredom, anxiety, rejection, fear, envy, sloth—in TV commercials there are remedies for each of these, and more. The remedies are called Scope, Comet, Toyota, Bufferin, Alka-Seltzer, and Budweiser. They take the place of good works, restraint, piety, awe, humility, and transcendence. On TV commercials, moral deficiencies as we customarily think of them do not really exist. A commercial for Alka-Seltzer, for example, does not teach you to avoid overeating. Gluttony is perfectly acceptable—maybe even desirable. The point of the commercial is that your gluttony is no problem—Alka-Seltzer will handle it. The Seven Deadly Sins, in other words, are problems to be solved through chemistry and technology. On commercials, there are no intimations of the conventional roads to spiritual redemption. But there is Original Sin, and it consists of our having been ignorant of a product that offers happiness. We may achieve a state of grace by attending to the good news about it, which will appear every six or seven minutes. It follows from this that he or she is most devout who know of the largest array of products; they are heretics who willfully ignore what is there to be used.

Source: Neil Postman and Steve Powers, *How to Watch TV News* (New York: Penguin Books, 1992), p. 125.

Undoubtedly the most common form of manipulation employed in the presentation of commercial messages is the simple, blatant appeal to one or more of several powerful emotions. This is probably the most effective form of manipulation as well. Appeals to fear, guilt, pity, and vanity permeate the airwaves and the pages of newspapers and magazines. "Aren't you glad you use Dial [deodorant soap]? Don't you wish everybody did?" "For those who care enough to give the very best—Hallmark." "Grey Poupon—it's not for everyone." Emotionally laden visual images associated with a particular product can be hard to forget. A particularly powerful example is the television ad in which a baby is shown playing and laughing within the protective confines of a heavy-duty Michelin tire.

Political Advertising

Political advertising tries to win our allegiance to a candidate, party, issue, or proposal, the latter often in the form of a ballot measure. Such advertising deserves special mention because it is the one type of commercial message in which we might expect to find some minimal level of rational deliberation about timely issues and ideas. For the most part, however, political advertising utilizes the same tried-and-true techniques that typify other types of advertising. Candidates and ideologies are all neatly packaged and promoted. Caricatures, often humorous, of the opposition are created and criticized. Slogans and jingles abound as do appeals to pity, compassion, fear, and vanity. Whereas the goal of much advertising is to insinuate brand familiarity, the goal of political advertising is often to establish familiarity with a candidate's name, ballot measure number, and so on.

In addition, political ads face a special problem. On the one hand, political-ad writers must find a way of distinguishing the candidate from his or her opponents, of making one position look more attractive than its alternatives. But on the other hand, they must take pains not to offend voters, which requires making the ideological commitments of a candidate or ideological position as palatable as possible to as many people as possible. (All bets are off in characterizing the view of the opposition. The use of the straw man is the rule rather than the exception in the portrayal of the views of the opposition to a candidate, proposal, or party.) The end result is often a commercial message that provides little more than pseudo-differentiation, steeped in visual images rich in values thought attractive to the audience. Candidates will be pictured hard at work on the job or hard at play with the family. Patriotic symbols, like the flag and the national anthem, are a common ingredient.

Here, for example, is the text of a thirty-second television spot from the 1998 reelection campaign of the governor in the state where I live. The name of the state has been deleted to make clear just how generic and superficial is the message this spot contains. The candidate in question is pictured wearing casual outdoor attire. He is standing on the banks of one of the state's more scenic rivers and is holding in one hand a brochure entitled "The ____ Challenge." Here is the complete text of the ad:

> I never forget how lucky I am to live in ____. But we can't take our quality of life or our state for granted. The ____ Challenge is my plan for ____'s future. It focuses on children by improving public schools, and reduces juvenile crime by helping kids succeed and stay out of trouble. And it protects our quality of life and keeps ____ a great place to live. That's the future I want for ____, and we can have it if we'll all work together. So call for a copy of the ____ Challenge, and, together, we'll make our state even better.

What do we learn about the candidate and his or her views in this thirty-second spot? We know the candidate is concerned about the quality of life in the state and has a plan to maintain and even improve it. The candidate even points out some of the specific things he or she will do: focus on children, improve schools, reduce juvenile crime. The phrase *quality of life* is a carefully crafted, euphemistic way of alluding to the candidate's concern for the environment. The candidate has also made it clear that he or she has a lot in common with the rest of us. *We* can't take our state for granted. *We* have a bright future if *we* work together.

Do you suppose the candidate's opponent would disagree with much that is said in this ad? Does, as the ad subtly implies, he or she not have a plan? Does the opponent not want to reduce juvenile crime or improve schools? Would he or she like to see the environment damaged? It is hard to imagine any candidate in any race in any state who would not subscribe to the message contained in this spot. No doubt there may be some substantial differences between, say, how the candidate and his or her opponent would go about improving schools, reducing juvenile crime, or dealing with environmental problems. But the point of a political ad is rarely going to be to air such differences. It is, rather, to keep the name of the candidate, the number of the ballot measure, or whatever, fixed in the mind of potential voters without saying much that will offend them.

CHAPTER SUMMARY

1. Persuasion can be accomplished by rational deliberation, overt coercion, or manipulation. Both rational deliberation—argumentation—and overt coercion are open and direct; we generally know when we are being coerced or when someone is mounting an argument. Manipulation can be much more difficult to detect. It involves subtly steering a person in the direction of a particular decision while leaving the impression that the decision was a product of his or her own rational deliberation.

2. To understand a manipulative appeal, we must analyze it in light of the interplay between author and audience. The goal of such analysis is to discover how the appeal manages to work on its audience.

3. Manipulation is often designed to exploit our emotions, but our rational sensibilities can be manipulated as well.

4. Manipulation is difficult to counter since, if it is successful, it will generally go unnoticed. The way to respond to a manipulative appeal is to expose it by explaining how the appeal has succeeded in manipulating the audience.

5. Advertising often involves fallacious argumentation or manipulation. The most common fallacious appeals involve irrelevance and distortion. Ads manipulate by playing on our emotions, by getting us to identify with products, and by extolling the virtues of their manufacturers. The most common form of manipulation in advertising is the constant repetition of the brand name in an effort to get us to think of the brand when we are making our purchasing decision.

MANIPULATIVE TECHNIQUES

EMOTIONAL MANIPULATION

Appeals to fear
  Example: Go ahead and vote for the Democratic candidate, that is, if you don't care what happens to the economy in the next few years.

Appeals to vanity (snob appeal)
  Example: All vodka. No pretense. —*ad for Smirnoff Vodka*

Appeals to sympathy, pity, or compassion
  Example: Smith would be the best choice for the promotion. Keep in mind that she has an out-of-work husband and five hungry kids to feed.

RHETORICAL MANIPULATION

Establishing common interests   Convincing an audience that the arguer shares interests, values, or goals with the audience or that an opponent has competing interests, values, or goals.
  Example: You, like me, are interested in improving our schools. Otherwise, you would not be at this meeting. So, let's consider my proposal to . . .

Establishing credibility   Convincing an audience that an arguer is objective and unbiased.
  Example: When I first read about the proposal we are going to be debating, I was in favor of it. But then I did some investigating. I looked carefully at the positions of both sides. And I have to tell you, I've gradually come to understand that my original position was mistaken. This proposal is deeply flawed.

Undercutting credibility   Getting an audience to doubt the credibility of a person holding an opposed view. Credibility can be brought into question by the use of ridicule, by questioning an opponent's expertise or education, by suggesting an opponent stands to gain from what he or she argues, or by poisoning the well. **Poisoning the well** occurs when an audience is persuaded that even the claim to be telling the truth by an opponent lacks credibility.

Examples: My opponent in this debate, who unfortunately has not had the time or opportunity to explore the issues thoroughly, wants to suggest that . . .

> Whatever Albert Shanker says about the need for higher pay for teachers needs to be taken with a grain of salt. As the president of the biggest teacher's union in the country, he is bound to distort things in favor of the interests of teachers.

Irrelevant thesis   Changing the subject as a way of deflecting attention from a weakness in one's own appeals or of countering opposed appeals. To establish that a proposed solution is less than perfect is to engage in a variety of irrelevant theses called *unattainable perfection.*

Examples: There is absolutely no point in mandating new safety requirements for automobiles. No matter what we do, there will always be people who are going to drive dangerously and end up harming themselves and others.

> Sure, my opponent wants stricter safety requirements for new cars. But life is full of risks. I suppose my opponent would also be in favor of making motorcycle riders wear safety helmets.

EXERCISES

A. Each of the passages below engages in some sort of manipulation. Some involve arguments or even counterarguments. In addition, many involve fallacious appeals discussed in previous chapters. Your assignment is to figure out how each passage manipulates. Comment on the manipulative techniques employed in each *and* on any fallacies you find. Be on the lookout particularly for fallacies of relevance and distortion. In each case, try to engage in logical self-defense: Describe the strategy you would follow in attempting to respond to the appeal.

(Answers to Exercises 5, 26, and 32 are given on pages 281–282.)

1. Rush Limbaugh claims that the media in this country are dominated by liberals. And this from a guy who claims to have "talent on loan from God." Too bad he couldn't have qualified for a bigger loan.

2. **The sky keeps its true color a secret, and only shares it with those who climb the mountain.**
   Escape. Serenity. Relaxation. The 1999 Toyota 4Runner Limited puts them all well within your reach. With features like a leather-trimmed interior, a CD sound system as well as more than a dozen new refinements, you might actually find the journey as rewarding as the destination. —*Ad for Toyota 4Runner sport utility vehicle*

3. You say you want to reduce the level of violence in television programming for children. Next, I suppose you are going to want to ban ads selling products designed for children.

4. Any competent salesperson is going to tell you exactly what you want to hear in order to sell you on his or her product. So, you can disregard anything the salesperson says about the merits of whatever he or she is trying to sell or the liabilities of the competition's products.

5. We are all intelligent, prudent people here. And I know you are capable of seeing through all the emotional rhetoric that surrounds this issue. I'm confident that when you carefully listen to all the facts, you will agree that we must act, and act now, to impeach our city council member.

6. My opponent's arguments for government-funded health care are not only expensive, they are unrealistic. No matter what legislation we enact, there are always going to be people who will slip through the cracks, so to speak. His proposal will not guarantee decent health care for everyone, but it will certainly empty our pocketbooks.

7. My client is a single parent and the sole support for his five children. If you find him guilty and send him off to serve time in prison, his children will be deprived of the one person—their father—whose love and guidance they desperately need.

8. The bill before Congress calling for interest-free loans for college students must be passed. No one would deny that every child in this country ought to have the chance to get a decent education.

9. Spokesperson for an athletic-shoe manufacturer charged with employing young children in its overseas shoe factories:

    Look. I've got three small children at home. Do you really think I could work for a company that knowingly exploited kids like mine and yours?

10. However, I must point out that further rounds of strike threats and/or delaying tactics will only serve to harden our position as health plan members continue to suffer the effects of this protracted dispute. —*from a letter from a management spokesperson to the chief negotiator of a nursing union*

11. Anyone who's in the magazine business thinks about advertisers when they write about something. And anyone who says they don't is a liar. —*John F. Kennedy Jr., editor and publisher of* George *magazine*

[Note: Exercises 12 and 13 are taken from a pamphlet opposing an Oregon ballot measure, Measure 16, that would allow for physician-assisted suicide.]

12. Measure 16 allows doctors to prescribe life-ending pills to terminally ill patients, but those pills—the 60 to 100 you must keep in your body to induce death—fail in up to 25 percent of the cases. The result can be vomiting, convulsions, brain impairment, kidney damage, comas, and lingering death.

13. Measure 16 does not define "resident of Oregon." It is highly likely that people from other states, like California and Washington, will come to Oregon to commit suicide. And Oregon taxpayers may have to pay for the disposal of the bodies.

14. Social Security is no longer secure. Unless you and I act—and act immediately—our Social Security benefits could be drastically reduced or destroyed. Help us elect Democratic candidates to Congress. *—from a letter soliciting funds for the Democratic Party*

15. *Vacuum cleaner salesperson:* This is the model I would buy if I could afford it.

16. *Carpet salesperson:* We don't sell much of this particular brand of carpet. Most people just worry about appearance and are not willing to spend the sort of money it takes to get this kind of quality.

17. As I understand it, you propose redistributing the wealth by taxing the rich at higher rates than the poor. You seem to think this will counteract the unfair economic advantages that accrue to the wealthy. This proposal makes no sense. Go ahead and redistribute to your heart's content. In no time at all, the hardworking people who had the money in the first place will have it all back again.

18. We're the biggest and most prestigious employee organization of any kind (26,000 members statewide). We got that way the same way you did—by being the best. So, naturally, we're very interested in you and what interests you. *—from a union membership-drive flier*

19. You can't believe what Professor Carey says about the importance of higher salaries for teachers. As a teacher himself, he would naturally be in favor of increasing his pay.

20. When I was seventeen, I had an abortion. At the time it seemed like the only solution. But let me tell you, not a day has gone by since then on which I have not deeply regretted what I did. I only wish that some caring person would have taken the time to help me think about the consequences of my decision. So, when I tell you that I am opposed to abortion, I think I know what I am talking about.

21. Now, don't lend me the money unless you really want to. I can get by without eating much for a few days.

22. Presidential candidate Pat Buchanan on why he did not want to debate a rival candidate, then Vice President Dan Quayle:

    I don't want to be charged with child abuse.

23. To the editor: Here we go again. Last week you published a letter to the effect that if a unilateral ban on assault weapons were in effect, countless lives would be saved. Where does the writer get that idea?

    Prohibition sure didn't prevent people from obtaining liquor. Drug laws are not stopping people from getting drugs. Abortion bans did not stop women from getting abortions. And yet we are expected to believe that a gun ban will, somehow, magically, prevent lawbreakers from obtaining guns.

    Really, now. Just how stupid, or how blindly liberal, do anti-gunners think we are?

24. Caption under a picture of a mink in a small wire cage in a pamphlet published by People for Animal Rights:

    This mink is waiting to be killed for his fur. He has lived his entire life in a small cage, unable to act out any of his basic natural instincts in this barren, artificial environment. He will be killed by primitive electrocution and his skin will be scraped off his back to make a luxury fur garment. This mink is just one of millions of animals who are prisoners of human vanity.

25. Many politicians have come out in favor of a ban on professional boxing. They base their position on a recent AMA report that says professional boxers run a high risk of brain damage. I think, however, we can safely discount this political stance. If you are a politician and you want publicity, take a strong public stand on something that will get you very little criticism. Pick on child abusers or smokers or professional boxing, the brutality of which very few people would be willing to defend. So, every few years we can expect business as usual—some politician trying to increase his or her public visibility will put together a task force and register his or her grave concern with the plight of the poor professional boxer.

26. To the editor: The Speaker of the House suggests that retirees with an annual income of more than $100,000 should buy their own health insurance. In accordance with the recent "Contract with America" and its accountability legislation, Congress must obey the laws it imposes on the public. It seems only right that all federal employees earning more than $100,000 a year should buy their own health insurance.

27. Ownership of a townhouse at the city's superb new KOIN Center may not be for everyone. The ultimate experience in city living awaits the forty-four exclusive few who make their decisions early. Call now for a private tour.
    —*ad for townhouses on the top floors of a new skyscraper*

28. From a letter enclosed with a bill (the accuracy of which was in dispute):
    Dear Mr. Carey:
    Considerate customers like yourself are a pleasure to serve. Thank you, Mr. Carey, for your acceptance of the $107.48 bill which resulted from a nonregistering meter. We at the Gas Company enjoy hearing from our customers and hope that you will call us whenever we can help you.
    Sincerely,

29. *College budgetary officer:* One way we can save money is by reducing the budget for library acquisitions. It is hard to take faculty protests against this measure seriously when 40 percent of the books in the library have never even been checked out.

30. House Speaker Newt Gingrich's spokesperson commenting on allegations of impropriety by Gingrich in the news media:
    It is the ugliest side of American politics and journalism. The same two or three people are always being quoted or referred to: a person who wasn't given a job, another who was fired, an ex-wife after a bitter divorce. It would've been nice to have had it balanced. Most of the press was dismayed by the results of the election. I don't think Newt will ever get fair treatment from the press. The animus is there.

31. To the editor: As a bow hunter who is frequently disgusted with rampant misguided antihunting bias in the media, it was a pleasant surprise to read "Ted Nugent's Wilderness Workout." Hunters and fishermen were at the forefront of the environmental movement long before it became trendy. Those of us who utilize the outdoors for hunting, fishing, or other activities realize that we have the most to lose from the poisoning of our air, water, and soil and from the destruction of natural habitat. And if there were anything environ-

mentally damaging in the proposal to open part of the national forest to increased logging, don't you think we would be the first to protest?

32. To the editor: As a therapist of eighteen years who has witnessed the devastation of lives by sexual perpetration, I am insulted and offended by your Joan Beck column "Dredging Memories the Hottest Therapy" and its blatant disrespect for the pain experienced by the survivors of sexual abuse and trauma.

    Trivializing survivors' pain, and my clinical work, by labeling it "trendy" and "hottest" adds further trauma to those who are courageous and willing to explore the depths of their psychic pain.

    When will we stop blaming those who have been victimized and ridiculing those who seek to empower the disempowered? Your newspaper's encouragement of this stance only serves to perpetuate the gross imbalance of power between adults and children in our culture.

    As for the False Memory Syndrome Association mentioned in the column, it is to be expected that when accused of such grievous crimes, the perpetrators would band together in an attempt to discredit those they have victimized.

    If we are ever to right the injustices we have condoned by our long-standing denial, we must stop blaming those who have suffered the injustice and assist the survivors of childhood sexual abuse to surpass their traumatization by holding their perpetrators and our whole society accountable.

33. To the editor: Your argument for mandatory helmet use by motorcyclists is a fine example of do-gooders doing nothing: Helmet laws do nothing to prevent accidents. Before we can do something about the death rate, we must do something about the accident rate. While it may be a privilege to operate a motor vehicle, the accident rate says it is a privilege easily gained by anyone who can memorize the driver's manual. The most common causes of motorcycle accidents are motorists cutting off motorcyclists, motorists making turns from the wrong lanes into motorcyclists, and motorists failing to yield right-of-way to motorcyclists. Clearly, helmet laws do nothing to prevent this. We would all just be safer if motorists learned to pull out of a driveway legally.

34. *(In response to 33)*

    A privilege easily gained? Anybody who can memorize the entire 120-page driver's manual deserves a license. If the only people on the road are those who have gone through the driver's manual with a fine tooth comb, we don't have to worry about too many accidents. Everybody's going to be at home reading.

35. To the editor: Syndicated columnist Clarence Page complained that preference is given the children of alumni of Yale and Harvard and that this is another form of quota and is thus no more defensible than racial quotas.

    This argument is, at best, fatuous. What Yale or Harvard or, for that matter, any other privately funded school does should be only very peripherally under public control. So long as these schools do not engage in criminal or morally unacceptable actions, they should be left alone to pursue whatever courses their supporters desire.

36. Consider the evolution display in the Museum of Biology in Moscow, which I recently visited. . . . Every standard argument for evolution was there, even though all of them were overstated and one-sided, and several were downright fraudulent. All were designed to indoctrinate a school student "in the party line."

    I truly wept as I thought of generations of Russian children faced with these and other displays without any alternate explanation. How could a child conclude anything other than that he descended from the animals? No wonder the country is shrouded in such darkness, unable to grope its way out, even now that its peoples are trying. The shrine to Darwin, which occupied one full wall of the room, says it all: "There is no God. Natural selection created you from the animals." —*John D. Morris, "Can Scientists Study the Past?"*

37. While testifying before Congress on the construction of the Fermilab particle accelerator, physicist Robert W. Wilson was asked how the accelerator would contribute to military technology. He replied: "It has nothing to do directly with defending our country except to make it worth defending."

38. To the editor: Lately there has been much attention focused on the "Christian Right." The attitude is that the Christian Right imposes its beliefs on everyone else.

    We Christians have opinions and beliefs, just as non-Christians do. Only when non-Christians—and especially liberals—get their way it is democracy, and when Christians say something about morality, it is imposing.

    Maybe we Christians don't like how liberals have imposed a belief system on society that has condemned morality, responsibility, commitment to marriage and family, self-reliance, and, most important of all, Jesus. It is the religion of self, where right and wrong do not exist except as defined by the individual.

    How long will it take before people see this doesn't work? For once I'd like to say, "Please stop imposing your religious chaos on me!"

39. For decades, public and private organizations have waged a massive campaign to discourage cigarette smoking. For most of the time, the target of this effort has been the smoker. Recently, however, the emphasis has undergone a major shift. Today there are scientists who claim that cigarette smoke in the air can actually cause disease in nonsmokers. We hear a great deal about "secondhand smoke" and "passive smoking."

    But is this new approach wholly motivated by concern for the nonsmoker, or is it the same old war on smoking in a new guise?

    These doubts are raised when we recall statements like the following, by a spokesperson for the American Lung Association:

    > Probably the only way we can win a substantial reduction [in smoking] is if we can somehow make it nonacceptable socially. . . . We thought the scare of medical statistics and opinions would produce a major reduction. It really didn't.

    Obviously, one way to make smoking "nonacceptable socially" would be to suggest that secondhand smoke could cause disease. So it is not surprising that we are now seeing a flurry of research seeking scientific support for these suggestions. . . .

Of course, if antismoking advocates want to work for the abolition of smoking, that is their right. We only wish they would come out from behind their secondhand smoke screen. —*from an ad by the R. J. Reynolds Tobacco Company*

40. On September 23, 1952, vice-presidential candidate Richard Nixon went on television to answer charges that he had accepted $18,000 in personal gifts during the campaign. Nixon began by giving a complete accounting of his financial situation: what he owned and what he owed. He then went on to say:

> Well, that's about it. That's what we have and that's what we owe. It isn't very much, but Pat [Nixon's wife] and I have the satisfaction that every dime that we've got is honestly ours. I should say this—that Pat doesn't have a mink coat. But she does have a respectable Republican cloth coat. And I always tell her that she'd look good in anything.
>
> One other thing I probably should tell you, because if I don't they'll probably be saying this about me too, we did get something—a gift—after the election. A man down in Texas heard Pat on the radio mention the fact that our two young daughters would like to have a dog. And, believe it or not, the day before we left on this campaign trip we got a message from Union Station in Baltimore saying they had a package for us. We went down to get it. You know what it was?
>
> It was a little cocker spaniel dog in a crate that he had sent all the way from Texas. Black and white spotted. And our little girl—Trisha, the six-year-old—named it Checkers. And you know the kids love that dog, and I just wanted to say this right now, that regardless of what they say about it, we're gonna keep it.

B. Thumb through a glossy magazine, like *People Magazine* or *Vogue,* or an edition of a national newspaper, such as the *Wall Street Journal.* Pick out five advertisements and discuss the techniques used in the selling of the product, service, candidate, and so on. Look for fallacies of distortion and relevance as well as the use of manipulative techniques.

SOLUTIONS

Exercise A

5. There are two kinds of manipulation going on in this passage. The first is an appeal to vanity. We, the audience, are complimented on our intelligence and critical acumen. The second is an attempt to establish interests (or, in this case, sensibilities) in common with the speaker or writer. Note that it is not *us,* the audience, who are intelligent and prudent. It is *we*—you, I, and the speaker or writer.

26. *Irrelevant thesis.* At issue is whether retirees who have an annual income of over $100,000 ought to pay for their own health insurance. In the name of consistency, the passage argues that federal workers (presumably, including members of Congress) who are earning over $100,000 a year should pay as well. But at issue is the question of whether the government should fund health insurance for a rather small group of retirees, not people still working.

32. *Undercutting credibility by poisoning the well.* Members of the False Memory
    Syndrome Association (the FMSA) are said to "band together" to "discredit
    those they have victimized." Thus, a denial that the accused is guilty of, say,
    child abuse, will lack credibility because this is just what we would expect from
    child abusers. Often such people will be said to be "in denial," another potent
    strategy for undercutting credibility. The passage also attempts to manipulate by
    a pretty blatant appeal to pity: "trivializing" survivors' pain and traumatizing
    "those who are courageous and willing to explore the depths of their psychic
    pain." The passage also comes very close to giving a circular argument by using
    a question-begging epithet (see Chapter 7). Note that members of the FMSA are
    initially described as the "accused" and then later, in the same sentence, as "per-
    petrators." Undoubtedly, many members of the FMSA have been accused of
    some impropriety based on recovered memories. Whether some, most, or all are
    guilty is another matter.

Index/Glossary

Page numbers in **boldface** type denote the primary use of key terms.

hard news, 15–16,
149–156, 158–159
manipulation of, by external sources, 158
newsworthiness, 15–16,
148–156
ownership of, 156–157
science and medicine in,
232–238
sources of, 13, 14,
147–148
See also mass media
newspapers, 14

omitting information,
10–11, 131–136, 159,
269
open-mindedness: A willingness to revise beliefs
in light of new informa-
tion. **17**–18, 20
oversimplification,
132–134, 200

paraphrasing: To give a
reading of an argument
set out in standard form.
9, 85–87
anecdotal evidence and, 89
complex arguments and,
92–93, 95
counterarguments and,
91–92
distortion use in, 143–147
fallacies and, 103–104
independent arguments,
93–94
independent premises,
93–95
point of view and, 87–88
poorly constructed argu-
ments, 89–91
sympathetic reading, 9,
87–88, 103, 205, 207
See also argument
personal attacks, **108**–114,
259, 262–264
personal information
fallacious use of, 108–111,
123–124
manipulation of audience
using, 259–264, 274
nonfallacious use of,
113–114
personalization of news,
153–155

personification: Attributing
human characteristics to
abstractions, inanimate
objects, and nonhuman
animals.
perspective, lack of,
134–136
persuasive definition: An
opinion, prejudice, or
bias masked as a defini-
tion. 48–**49**, 50
pity, appeals to, 257–258,
272, 274
plausibility: A statement is
plausible if it is highly
likely to be true even
though it is possible it
may be false. **59**–61, 78
inferential strength testing
and, 68–71
of premises, 9, 57–58,
59–61
standard form and, 9
weak refutation and, 76
See also claims
point of view: The beliefs
and attitudes on a particular topic that may pro-
vide much of the
motivation for the view
advocated or opposed in
an argument. **87**–88, 95
personal attacks using, 109
See also critical point of
view; world view
poisoning the well,
262–263, 275
political advertising, 117,
272–273
precising definition: A
method of definition in
which the use of a word
or phrase, in a given
context, is specified. **43**
precision
false, as fallacy, 138–139,
159
reasonable levels of, 60
sample size and, 215–216
premise indicators: Words
and phrases, like *since*
and *because of the fact
that,* used in composing
arguments to indicate
that what comes next is a
premise. 82–**83**

premises: In an argument,
the claim or claims
intended to provide sup-
port for the argument's
conclusion. **3**–4, 19
assessing, 59–61
identification of, 82–83
independent vs. depend-
ent, 93–95
inference, strength of. *See*
inferential strength
paraphrasing. *See* para-
phrasing
plausibility of. *See* plausibility
See also argument; claims
presupposition: Claims that
must be assumed to be
true if a given claim or
argument is to have a
point. **183**
primary subject: In an
argument by analogy,
that which the conclu-
sion of the argument is
about. **194**
See also argument by
analogy
probative worth, 113
prospective causal study: A
study in which subjects
are selected for the experimental group who have
already been exposed to
the suspected cause; con-
trol subjects are selected
who have not been
exposed to the suspected
cause. **227**–228, 240
pseudo-claim: Claims, generally found in advertisements, that are so vague
as to assert practically
nothing. **40**–42
pseudo-differentiation:
Claims, generally found
in advertisements, that
are comparatively vague.
42, 269, 273
psychological explanation:
To explain human behav-
ior by reference to some
sort of mental phenom-
ena, like aims, goals,
feelings, wants, and
desires. **180**

qualifiers: Words and phrases, like *probably, possibly,* and *it is almost certain that,* used to express the degree of confidence an arguer has in his or her conclusion. **63,** 66–67, 70
misleading, as fallacy, 139, 159
misleading, as manipulation, 269
recognition of arguments and, 83–84
vagueness and, 38–39
See also argument; weasels
quantifiers: Words and phrases, like *all, most,* and *a few,* used to place limits on general claims.
question-begging epithets: Descriptive terms used in stating the premises of an argument that apply only on the assumption that the conclusion has been established. 182–**183**

radio, 13, 14, 147–148, 157
See also mass media
randomized causal study: A type of study in which subjects are randomly assigned to experimental and control groups and in which the suspected cause is subsequently administered to the experimental group. **226,** 227–228, 239
random sample: A sample in which every member of the population has an equal chance of being selected. **216,** 217–218
rationality vs. emotionality, tension between, 252–253
rational manipulation, 251
red herring: A claim, different from what is at issue in an argument,

introduced to direct attention away from the claim at issue. 265–266
reductionistic explanation: To explain something by reference to its component parts and the ways in which they interact to produce the phenomena being explained. **176**
redundancy, fallacies involving, 178–180
referential ambiguity: Ambiguity brought about by a failure to make clear what a key word or phrase is being used to refer to. 31–32, 49
regression fallacy, **230**
relevance: Having bearing. Claims can be relevant to a topic without being relevant to a particular argument on that topic. 104
advertising and, 269
fallacies of, 106–124
irrelevant thesis, 264–267, 275
probative worth, 113
test for, 105–106
types of, 104–105
See also claims; distortion
reliability of sampling argument, 215–219, **239**
remarks, clarity of, 29, 49
See also claims
representative sample, **218**
retrospective causal study: A type of study in which a group of subjects is selected, all of whom have the effect being studied. These subjects are compared to another group, none of whom have the effect, in an attempt to discover possible causal factors. **227,** 228, 240
rhetoric: The study of effective methods of persuasion with particular emphasis on style and

techniques for effective presentation. **258**
rhetorical manipulation, **258**–266, 274–275

sample: A group of things selected from a larger population. **214**
experimental vs. control group in, 224–225
margin of error and, 216, 225–226
random, 216, 217–218
as representative, 218
size of, 215–218, 225–226
unbiased questioning of, 219
sampling argument: An argument in which a conclusion about a population is drawn based on information derived from a sample of that population. 138, **214**–215, 239
fallacies involving, 220
requirements for reliability of, 215–219, **239**
sarcasm, **84**–85
science
news media and, 232–238
as term, 233
scientific method, 223
self-reflective: In critical thinking, the willingness to consider the ways in which our expectations, beliefs, preconceptions and biases can influence our evaluation of the thinking and reasoning of others. **17**–19, 20
semantic ambiguity: Ambiguity brought about by a failure to specify what sense of a word or phrase is intended. **31,** 49
sensationalism, news media and, 155
significance, level of, 217
significance, statistical. *See* statistical significance
skepticism: Unwillingness to accept things at face value and readiness to question that for which

weaknesses. *See* inferential strength

weak refutation: Argument criticism in which the goal is to get at the weaknesses in an argument that is not altogether mistaken. **76,** 78

weasels: Statements that appear to make an unequivocal claim but, through the subtle use of exclusionary and qualifying phrases, considerably weaken that which they appear to be asserting. **38**–39, 41–42, 60, 63, 271
See also qualifiers

world view, **13**–14, 19
See also critical point of view; point of view